D0189101

From Covenant to Community

JUDAISM, CHRISTIANITY, AND ISLAM

The Classical Texts
and Their Interpretation

VOLUME 1

From Covenant to Community

F. E. PETERS

Princeton University Press

Princeton, New Jersey

Copyright © 1990 by Princeton University Press

Published by Princeton University Press, 41 William Street,
Princeton, New Jersey 08540
In the United Kingdom: Princeton University Press, Oxford

All Rights Reserved

Library of Congress Cataloging-in-Publication Data

Peters, F. E. (Francis E.)
Judaism, Christianity, and Islam : the classical texts
and their interpretation / F.E. Peters.
p.   cm.
Also published in a single volume.
Includes index.
Contents: v. 1. From covenant to community — v. 2. The word
and the law and the people of God — v. 3. The works
of the spirit.
ISBN 0-691-02044-2 (v. 1 : acid-free paper)
ISBN 0-691-02054-X (v. 2 : acid-free paper)
ISBN 0-691-02055-8 (v. 3 : acid-free paper)
1. Judaism. 2. Christianity. 3. Islam. I. Title.
BL80.2.P455   1990b
291—dc20   90-36670

This book has been composed in Linotron Perpetua type

Princeton University Press books are printed on acid-free
paper, and meet the guidelines for permanence and durability
of the Committee on Production Guidelines for Book
Longevity of the Council on Library Resources

Printed in the United States of America by Princeton
University Press, Princeton, New Jersey

(Pbk.)   3   5   7   9   10   8   6   4   2

For

Barakat Ahmad

in whose true spirit this work was conceived,
and to whose joyfully recollected memory
it is now gratefully dedicated

Contents

CHAPTER 3

The Good News of Jesus Christ 115

Preface

"Hear, O Israel," the Lord said to His Chosen People near the beginning of their extraordinary relationship. And that is the matter of this book: what His people heard from the Lord and how they understood it. Not merely the original Israelites, but His other peoples, the Christians and Muslims: they too chosen, as they say; they too, as they claim, authentic "sons of Abraham."

What they heard when God spoke to them is not difficult to discover. Jews, Christians, and Muslims alike felt strongly and thought carefully enough about it to preserve the words of God inside the covers of a Book, or rather, three books—the Bible, the New Testament, and the Quran—which they eye somewhat uneasily in each other's hands. So it is in the first instance God's words that have been reproduced here, not in their entirety—the integral texts are readily enough available—but in extracts and, more importantly, in a manner that will make it somewhat simpler to comprehend the other element of what is undertaken in this work: How did the Jews, Christians, and Muslims understand what they had heard?

The words of God to Abraham and later to Moses on Sinai, they had all heard. The Bible is Scripture for all three religious communities, and indeed it is the basis of each's claim to be God's own people. But each group understood those words differently, whether as a basis of belief or as a directive to action. And even in each group's own, more particular and privileged communication with or from God—the Jews' Mishna, for example, or the letters of Paul, or the traditions from the Prophet Muhammad—there is little enough agreement within the community itself on what exactly God meant or what precisely was the good to be done or the evil to be avoided.

What I have attempted is to lay out the kinds of issues these three intimately related groups chiefly thought about, the questions that most interested them, and particularly such matters as might encourage comparison among the three; I have then selected standard or well-known or important texts to illustrate those matters. Jews, Christians, and Muslims all thought about the Law of God, for example, and how God ought to be worshiped, about authority and the authorities, about angels and heaven and hell; each group attempted on occasion to state what it believed and to make its members somehow conform to it; and most consequential of all perhaps, the three religious communities shared an invincible conviction that God's revelation to them was not confined to that revered and well-guarded Book we call Scripture.

This is obviously not a history of Judaism, Christianity, and Islam, and even less of the three communities of believers. The historically minded will doubtless be puzzled, and perhaps dismayed, at the sometimes odd juxtaposition of authorities or events. I have no remedy for either the puzzlement or the dismay except to refer them to histories of the faiths or the communities, of which there is certainly no lack. Here the objective is to keep the three communities of believers in one line of sight and to focus on each through a single topic that interested them all. Thus, after the first four chapters, which follow a rough time line, the presentation moves to a topical arrangement that violates the chronological order at almost every turn but has the advantage, I hope, of hearing each group out on subjects of parallel or mutual or polemical concern.

It is, in any event, the same way the sources themselves deal with the matter. Though Scripture is often cast in the form of history, not many of those who came after viewed the sacred books through the eyes of the historian. There is the Jew Josephus, yes, and the Christian Eusebius, and Muhammad's biographer Ibn Ishaq. But for the rest, the authors represented in these pages are chiefly lawyers, theologians, priests, and visionaries—Jewish, Christian, and Muslim believers who were disinterested in the past as past, since for them the past was, like the Torah in the Talmud and like the Bible in both the Gospels and the Quran, eternally present. In reading the third-century rabbis, for example, one cannot really tell that there was no longer a Temple in Jerusalem and that no priests had made sacrifice there for more than a century, much less when that catastrophic destruction took place or what merely human acts contributed to it.

Nor were those same authorities much interested in the present as present. We catch contemporary reflections, of course, but their primary concern was not to bring us up to date on the present state of the People of God, on how well or poorly the Law of God was being observed. Our authors tell us, for example, that there were rules governing the conduct of Christians and Jews living under Islam; but they do not tell us, as other kinds of sources do, which regulations were actually in force and for whom, or which were simply on the books. Since the "books" in question are likely to have been holy books or equally holy traditions, to be on them or in them was what really mattered and not how many "commoners of the land" were actually fornicating, killing their neighbors, or violating the Sabbath. We have ways of discovering, or guessing about, the latter, but not from our lawyers and divines, who had more important things to concern them.

In reproducing rather than retelling Scripture, I have allowed God speak for Himself, and I have extended the courtesy to the Jews, Christians, and Muslims as well. And those children of a voluble God have spoken, sometimes clearly and eloquently; at times obscurely, perhaps because they did not understand or perhaps because they chose not to say; sometimes gently and sometimes rudely, especially when they are speaking of each other. I have kept my own explanations to a minimum on the simple principle that all these "Peoples of the Book" are capable of and should be permitted to speak for themselves. I have supplied some factual data, provided contexts where such seemed required, and attempted some explanatory transitions across what is a somewhat discontinuous terrain. Much is missing, to be sure: saints are often more interesting than their writings and religious art more striking than tracts on iconoclasm. God's own preference for history over theology is well known.

I have made here almost no judgments about authenticity: these are the received texts, scriptural and otherwise, of each community. And I have tried, despite strong professional and personal inclinations to the contrary, not to seduce the reader into the enormous historical and textual problems that almost every one of these texts—and often every line and every single word of them—has raised over the centuries among believers and nonbelievers alike. Thus there are no traces here of the revelations of Julius Wellhausen or Ignaz Goldziher, no echoes of the prophetic voices of Rudolf Bultmann or Joseph Schacht, of Jacob Neusner or Patricia Crone, no sign of "P" or "E" or "J" or the even more celebrated "Q". And finally, I have attempted to reduce technical vocabulary, particularly of the transliterated variety, to an absolute minimum: lovers of *halakha* and *hadith* will have to be served elsewhere.

This work was originally composed as a companion for my *Children of Abraham: Judaism, Christianity, Islam*. It is in a sense the flesh to the latter's bone, and, in the ineluctable manner of flesh, has put on quite a bit of weight in the process. Nor is the order exactly the same as in that earlier work. Here the matter is divided into three parts: From Covenant to

Community; The Word and the Law and the People of God; The Works of the Spirit. But even though the arrangement is different, the same general topics are covered. More important, the time parameters of the earlier work are this one's as well: we begin here literally at the beginning, but break off while each religious complex is still in its "classical" or, perhaps less provocatively, its "scholastic" period. To put it another way, this collection ends before the great movements of modernism and reform touched—at different moments and in differing degrees—Judaism, Christianity, and Islam and rendered them different. Not everyone will be happy with such a peremptory leave-taking, particularly those who prefer the reformed to the traditional versions of these communities. No matter. Given the limitations of the guide, it cannot be otherwise.

The only abbreviations requiring explanation are: B.C.E. = Before the Common Era, and C.E. = the Common Era. The M prefix before a title means Mishna; BT = Babylonian Talmud and JT = Jerusalem or Palestinian Talmud.

The texts used for this work have all been published in one place or another, often in many places since, as I have said, my objective throughout is to place before the reader the "classical texts" of the three religious communities. They are not only published; most of them are very well known to the members of the community whose heritage they are. Thus they have also been translated out of their original Hebrew and Aramaic, Greek and Latin, Arabic and Persian into a variety of other languages, including English. The question is not where to find the texts but which to choose and whose version to prefer.

Of the translations used in compiling this dossier, some are mine and some, as noted in the Acknowledgments, are from other hands. Where I have used others' versions, I have generally modified them only to the extent of standardizing names—the English word "God" has replaced the translators' untranslated "Allah" throughout, for example—and of reducing all dates to those of the Common Era.

Stockport, New York

Acknowledgments

Translations of the Hebrew Bible are derived from *A New Translation of the Holy Scriptures according to the Massoretic Text*, second edition, Philadelphia: Jewish Publication Society of America, 1982.

Translations of the biblical apocrypha are derived from *The Apocryphal Old Testament*, edited by H.D.F. Sparks, Oxford: Clarendon Press, 1984.

Translations of the deutero-canonical books and the New Testament are derived from *The New English Bible with the Apocrypha*, corrected impression of the second edition, New York: Oxford University Press, 1972. Translations of the New Testament apocrypha are derived from Edgar Hennecke and Wilhelm Schneemelcher (eds.), *New Testament Apocrypha*, 2 vols., translated by R. McLean Wilson et al., Philadelphia: Westminster Press, 1963–1965.

Translations of the Quran are derived from Ahmed Ali, *Al-Qur'an*, Princeton: Princeton University Press, 1988.

A Brief Chronology

B.C.E. is an abbreviation of "Before the Common Era" and C.E. of the "Common Era." The Common Era is that of the Gregorian calendar, where time is measured before or after what was thought to be the birth year of Jesus: in Latin, *Anno Domini*, the "Year of the Lord," abbreviated A.D. In fact, Jesus' date of birth is now placed in or about 4 B.C.E.

Muslims also use a "before" and "after" system. In their case the watershed date is that of the *Hijrah* or Emigration of Muhammad from Mecca to Medina in 622 C.E., called in the West A.H., or *Anno Hegirae*.

Jewish time reckoning is only "after," that is, from the Creation of the World, normally understood to be about 4000 years B.C.E.

B.C.E.

ca. 1700	God's Covenant with Abraham
ca. 1200	The exodus from Egypt; the giving of the Torah to Moses on Mount Sinai
ca. 1000	David, king of the Israelites, captures Jerusalem and makes it his capital
ca. 970	Solomon builds the First Temple in Jerusalem
621	Josiah centralizes all Jewish worship in the Temple in Jerusalem
587	Babylonians under Nebuchadnezzar carry Israelites into exile in Babylon; the destruction of Solomon's Temple
538	Exiles return to Judea; Ezra; Nehemiah; rebuilding of Jerusalem Temple
332	Alexander the Great in the Near East; Greek dynasties rule Palestine
ca. 280	Translation of Bible in Greek: the "Septuagint"
200	The Seleucid dynasty of Syria replaces the Ptolemies as rulers of Palestine
175–164	Antiochus IV Epiphanes; profanation of the Temple
164	Maccabean revolt; Jewish independence
164–37	The Hasmonean dynasty rules Palestine

37–4 Herod the Great, king of Judea
ca. 25–45 C.E. Philo in Alexandria
20 Herod begins restoration of the Temple
ca. 4 Birth of Jesus in Bethlehem

C.E.

6 Romans take over direct rule of Judea
26–36 Pontius Pilate, Roman prefect of Judea
ca. 30 Execution of Jesus in Jerusalem
the 50s Letters of Paul
ca. 60–70 Composition of Mark, earliest of the Gospels
ca. 62 Death of James in Jerusalem and Peter and Paul in Rome
66 Jewish insurrection in Palestine; flight of Yohanan ben Zakkai to Jabneh (Jamnia) and of Jewish Christians to the Transjordan
70 Romans under Titus destroy Herod's Temple
ca. 80–100 Remaining three canonical Gospels written
ca. 100 Death of the Jewish historian Josephus
135 Second Jewish revolt in Palestine; Jerusalem leveled and Jews forbidden to live there
ca. 200 Widespread persecutions of Christians in the Roman Empire; redaction of the Mishna by Judah "the Prince"
ca. 250 Antony, the first hermit, withdraws to the desert of Egypt
303 Last violent persecution of Christians by Diocletian
313 Constantine, the first Christian emperor, suspends persecution of Christians
318 Pachomius founds the first monastery, or community of ascetics, in Egypt
325 First ecumenical council of the Christian Church at Nicea
330 Constantine and his mother Helena begin the conversion of Jerusalem into a Christian holy city
340 First Christian monasteries founded in the West
381 Decree establishing Christianity as the official religion of the Roman Empire
399 Death of the Christian mystic Evagrius of Pontus
410 Visigoths sack Rome
425 Office of Nasi, or Patriarch, abolished in the Roman Empire
430 Death of Augustine, Latin theologian of Hippo in North Africa
451 Ecumenical council of Chalcedon
ca. 500 Completion of the *gemaras* at Tiberias and (ca. 600) in Iraq: thus the final versions of the "Jerusalem" and "Babylonian" Talmuds
ca. 535 Benedict founds his monastery at Monte Cassino
ca. 570 Birth of Muhammad at Mecca

Introduction

The Bible begins at the creation of the world, and there is surely a lesson in that. But the Jews—to use our word rather than theirs at this point— begin their own proper history not where the Bible begins, nor where the modern historian might seek them out—when the "Hebrews" emerge as a distinct racial, ethnic, cultural, or linguistic group—but at quite another moment that stands recorded and underlined in the biblical book called Genesis. The account falls in the twelfth chapter of that work, when God speaks to, and in the end concludes a covenant with, a man thereafter called Abraham. In Genesis the covenant is still only a promise, with no immediate boon save an heir, though Abraham is called upon to perform the simple but painful condition laid down by the Lord: the circumcision of himself and all the males, slave and free, of his household. But the promise of future reward is quite specific: Abraham and his descendants would have an ongoing, expanding, and even glorious tribal identity and, more, a land of their own, surely a heady vision for what must have been a marginal clan of nomads wandering the byways of the Middle East: a Chosen People and a Promised Land, a twin identity that forever there- after both explained the past and underwrote the future for the Jews.

If we listen to the Christians and the Muslims, their history too began in that same moment of promise to Abraham. They too are the offspring of that selfsame promise, siblings, perhaps, of the Jews, but only as Isaac was to Ishmael or Jacob to Esau: the replacement issue of the first-born son. Christians and Muslims are constrained by the immutable givens of history, their history, to yield to the Jews the title of the first- born of Abraham; they themselves are instead, they would insist, his *rightful* heirs.

The Bible is the record of that famous covenant, *the* Covenant as it concerns these three communities, the story of God's offer and its accep- tance and of the glories and the pains of that pioneer people called, in clan fashion, the Children of Israel, as they struggled under its charge from tribe to people to nation. And it is more: the Bible is the charter docu- ment of the three faiths, viewed directly and studied carefully by Jews and

Christians alike for its lessons on the past and its presentiments of the future, and regarded by Muslims through its reissue in the Quran. The claims of the three stand or fall on its understanding. It is also the past of all of them, something that must be made to yield sense no less than satisfaction.

Then it ends. Beyond the return from Exile and beyond Daniel there is no Bible, no sacred text to carry the Covenant forward. There is history, surely, some of it holy if not sacred, like the books of Maccabees; much of it religious, like the abundant, though noncanonical, "apocrypha" produced by the rapidly and radically changing times from the arrival of Alexander to the birth of Jesus. Both Jews and Christians pick their way through the historical debris of those days: the Jews curiously, looking beyond to the Mishna and Talmud, the five-centuries-distant documents of a renewed Covenant; the Christians anxiously, for there if anywhere, in those centuries from the Exile to the Romans, lies the embryonic tissue that shaped and sustained the birth of the Christian movement in the first century C.E. If the Christians are the newborn of the Covenant, they are also children of the age of the Apocrypha and carry its sectarian and apocalyptic sensibilities full upon them. The Muslims, finally, have looked away. Their perception of the career of the Chosen Peoples takes leave of mere history after the Exile. Muslim sacred history knows and cares nothing of the age of the Apocrypha, the doings, religious or otherwise, of the Greeks and the Romans. It looks briefly at Jesus and then passes on, oblivious of Church and Synagogue, to the sixth-century call of the Last Messenger of the Covenant.

We shall not look away here. We shall follow God's Chosen People across the difficult passage that leads from Daniel to Jesus, from "Israelite," with its antique ring, to "Jew," with its modern one. It is a troubled time, when Israel takes on new and powerful political foes: the Hellenistic monarchies and finally the Romans (the last, one is tempted to say, secular sovereigns that Jews will know until modern times, though the truth is that Rome was not so much secular as pagan, a condition that by hindsight seemed almost benign). It was also the era when the Children of Abraham met not so much a religious foe, which the old paganism was, as a genuine rival, Hellenism, which showed forth even at that time and that place all the dangerously attractive traits that were later described as "rationalism," or "modernism," or "humanism." It was in fact all those things, and it presented itself to the Jews to challenge and beguile them, as it later would to both Christianity and Islam in turn.

The "lives" of Jesus and Muhammad are then set out as their followers read and understand them. Although there are formal, biographical
similarities, the accounts are fundamentally discontinuous. Both derive
from literary works, but the first, the Gospels, are part of the Christians'
Scripture, and rightly so, since they present what were judged to be sacral
events. Muhammad's life emerges from a traditional biography—Muslim
Scripture, the Quran, is quite otherwise—where the miraculous elements
are intrusive. The Christian cannot but study the "Good News of Jesus
Christ," since the sacred work of Jesus is revealed therein; the Muslim
reads the "Life of the Prophet of God" simply as an act of piety: revelation lies elsewhere.

At that point, the death of Muhammad in 632 C.E., the primary data
are complete, the covenantal evidence is in. And the argument begins. Or
rather, continues, since the debate over the Covenant and its heirs had
begun deep within Jewish history, before there were Muslims or even
Christians. The Israelites had early fashioned a dream of a "kingdom of
priests," a dream that found only fitful fulfillment as long as there was a
"kingdom of kings." But the Israelite monarchy disappeared forever in
the debris of Herod's successors, and that longed-for priesthood of all
believers found a second life in the program of the Pharisees. The Pharisaic ideal prevailed under the rabbis, revitalized perhaps by its very sur-
vival. At the outset the Christians had appeared to share that same dream,
for polemical and competitive reasons if for no other. Once separated
from the main body of the Jews, however, the course of the Christian
community took a quite different turn. It became what the Israelites had
once been: a community of priests. Christianity was born, just barely, in
the age of Temple Judaism and remained faithful to that model, which
may have been, not entirely by coincidence, far more congenial than the
purified and separatist Torah Judaism of the rabbis to the Gentiles entering the Church in increasing numbers in the second and third centuries
of the new era.

By 200 C.E. Jews and Christians stood as communities apart, the first
deeply transformed from the remote days of the monarchy by the experience of the Exile, its encounter with Hellenism, its apocalyptic moment
in the face of Roman imperial might, and, in the end, its argument with
its own Christians, sectarians at first, then schismatics, and finally apostates from what was understood as normative Judaism in the second
century C.E. Jews had embarked upon their long Second Exile, a life of
near invisibility in the city and countryside, pacifist and parochial, medi-

tative and self-contemplative, aliens in lands of their masters, eventually their Christian and Muslim masters. The Christians, on the other hand, stood poised on the brink of explosive growth in numbers, in public and private power, and in architectural, liturgical, and theological grandeur—a growth unchecked in the East until the rise of Islam.

The separation of Jews and Christians was a painful process and left a continuing legacy of hostility between the two groups. But it had another, rather odd effect. If the Jews were not an entirely admired minority in the Roman Empire—two major Jewish insurrections made their political loyalty more than a little suspect in Roman eyes—they were a protected one, the beneficiaries of various exemptions, many of them going back to Greek days, from the empire's laws and customs. It took some time, but once the Christians were finally identified as a separate religious community from the Jews, they escaped some of the odium and all of the protections that had been the Jewish lot. The Christians, as it turned out, were as stiff-necked as the Jews on the matter of monotheism, and they had to pay the price: there were Roman religious persecutions of the Christians of varying scope and duration throughout the third century C.E. The Christians weathered them and in the end converted their persecutors, something the Jews had been unable or had forsworn to do. The consequence was enormous and longstanding: after the conversion of Constantine, many Christians lived out more than a millennium as subjects of a Christian Roman Empire, full-fledged citizens and rather comfortably at home in both the City of God and the City of Man.

The Christians' dual estate, the catholic Christian church and the catholic Christian empire, grew increasingly alike in the fourth, fifth, and sixth centuries. Roman law held its ground against the growing body of Church law; but the administrative style of the empire, with its centralized governance and its hierarchization of authority, was echoed in the Church. Bishops and provincial governors, patriarchs and prefects—the jurisdiction was almost identical. There lacked only a counterpart of the emperor himself, or perhaps two, since there was often a twin *imperium* in Rome and Constantinople. Predictably, that lack too was filled, and the long and destructive controversy, and the subsequent schism, over the issue of an "imperial bishop," an absolute primate in Rome—or perhaps in Constantinople—shook the Christian Church for centuries to come.

In its growth to community maturity, Islam faced the same problem of identity and authority. What was easy for the Prophet and his generation was not so for their successors. The political and social organism that constituted Islam as surely as the body of believers grew with spectacular speed and dimension. The growth to political maturity, which had taken many centuries for Israel amid peoples who were enemies but not rivals and which had occurred in Christianity only after a breathing space of nearly three centuries, was a lightening-like process in Islam: empire descended like a crown upon Muslim heads within decades of the Prophet's death, an empire that thrust the new community into the company of a powerful, confident, and nearly fully grown Christendom. Even within the lifetime of Muhammad, the Islamic community had had Christian and Jewish subjects; shortly those same subjects outnumbered their masters in a newly expanded "Abode of Islam" that reached from Spain around the southern Mediterranean basin eastward to the Indus.

But who should rule such a creation? A prophet or a king? A political Caliph or a charismatic Imam? The issue flamed early and persisted late. There was scarcely time to think, so rapid was the progress of Islam's political fortunes; but there were some who from the outset stood against the secularizing flood of event for a spiritual Islam governed not by the strongest but by the spiritual best, the very men, it was maintained, who had been signaled by the Prophet himself: his cousin and son-in-law Ali and after him his heirs. This was the position of the "Party of Ali," the Shi'at Ali or Shi'ites, and they maintained it staunchly in the face of centuries of actual rule by the titled, the rich, and the powerful, namely the consensually agreed-upon Caliphs of Sunni Islam.

Judaism,
Christianity,
and Islam

1. The Covenant and the History of the Chosen People

1. "In the Beginning"

The Bible is the foundation of men's belief in the One True God, the one and the same deity that is called Yahweh by the Jews, Our Father who is in heaven by the Christians, and Allah by the Muslims. And whether memorized, ignored, transcended, or superseded, it was and remained the charter and testament of all the children of Abraham.

Abraham does not appear at the outset, however; the Bible begins absolutely, "in the beginning," truly the very beginning, before the world was. Abraham still lay many generations in the future.

When God began to create the heaven and the earth—the earth being unformed and void, with darkness over the surface of the deep and a wind from God sweeping over the water—God said, "Let there be light"; and there was light. God saw that the light was good, and God separated the light from the darkness. God called the light Day, and the darkness He called Night. And there was evening and there was morning, a first day. (Genesis 1:1–5)

So the Bible starts bereshit, "in the beginning," not of history but of the world, whence the book called Genesis proceeds, day by day, through God's creation of the earth, the heavens and their bodies, all living creatures beneath the waters and in the air above.

God said, "Let the earth bring forth every kind of living creature: cattle, creeping things, and wild beasts of every kind." And it was so. God made wild beasts of every kind and cattle of every kind, and all kinds of creeping things of the earth. And God saw that this was good. And God said, "Let us make man in our image, after our likeness. They shall rule the fish of the sea, the birds of the sky, the cattle, the whole earth, and all the creeping things that creep on earth." And God created man in His image, in the image of God He created him; male and female He created them. God blessed them and God said to them, "Be fertile and increase, fill the earth and master it; and rule the fish of the sea, the birds of the sky, and all the living things that creep on earth. . . ."

God said, "See, I give you every seed-bearing plant that is upon all the earth, and every tree that has seed-bearing fruit; they shall be yours for food. And to all the animals on land, to all the birds of the sky, and to everything that creeps on earth, in which there is the breath of life, [I give] all the green plants for food." And it was so. And God saw all that He had made, and found it very good. And there was evening and there was morning, the sixth day. . . .

Such is the story of heaven and earth when they were created. (Genesis 1:24–2:4)

It was by no means the whole story. This account of the making of the world and its denizens offered by Genesis, though it is quite detailed in its own way, was endlessly explained in the sequel; details were added; its silences filled; its unposed questions answered out of men's ever deepening understanding of how God worked and how the world worked.

Part of that understanding came from other sources that had little to do with the Bible, other peoples' stories about how the world began—the Babylonians' and Egyptians', for example—and, more consequentially in the long run, other peoples' demonstrations about how the world must have come into being. The Greeks, with whom all the children of Abraham would eventually come into contact, had a number of such demonstrations, scientific in both their intent and their effect, and Jews, Christians, and Muslims have devoted, and still devote, a substantial degree of their attention and energies to refuting or reconciling them.

2. The Quran on Creation

The Christians accepted Genesis as Scripture—that is, God's true word—and so their account of Creation is identical with that of the Jews, though it was read, of course, in a Greek or later a Latin translation, and often commented upon in a very different way. For the Muslims, on the other hand, the scripture called the Quran superseded the Book of Genesis; and though its source is the same as that in Genesis, God Himself, there are obvious differences in detail in its view of Creation.

It was God who raised the skies without support, as you can see, and assumed His throne, and enthralled the sun and the moon (so that) each runs to a predetermined course. He disposes all affairs, distinctly explaining every sign that you may be certain of the meeting with your Lord.

And it was He who stretched the earth and placed upon it stabilisers and rivers; and made two of a pair of every fruit; (and) He covers up the day with the night. In these are signs for those who reflect.

On the earth are tracts adjoining one another, and vineyards, fields of corn and date-palm trees, some forked and some with single trunks, yet all irrigated with the selfsame water, though We make some more excellent than others in fruit. There are surely signs in them for those who understand. (Quran 13:2–4)

Much of the "biblical" material in the Quran, or perhaps better, the Torah material in the Quran—the Quran is in its entirety "Bible" to the Muslim—is not presented in a continuous narrative line in the manner of Genesis but often simply alluded to, frequently to support or illustrate another point. Hence the subject of Creation comes up in different places, as here again in Quran 32, where the moral conse-quences to Creation are homiletically drawn at the beginning and the end.

It is God who created the heavens and the earth and all that lies between them, in six spans, then assumed all authority. You have no protector other than Him, nor any intercessor. Will you not be warned even then? He regulates all affairs from high to low, then they rise to perfection step by step in a (heavenly) day whose measure is a thousand years in your reckoning. Such is He, the knower of the unknown and the known, the mighty and the merciful, who made all things He created excellent; and first fashioned man from clay, then made his offspring from the extract of base fluid, then proportioned and breathed into him His spirit, and gave you the senses of hearing, sight and feeling, and yet how little are the thanks you offer. (Quran 32:4–9)

It is already apparent that, among other differences between Genesis and the Quran, there is the matter of chronology, as the Muslims themselves were well aware.

The people of the Torah [that is, the Jews] say that God began the work of Creation on Sunday and finished on Saturday, when He took His seat upon the Throne, and so they take that as their holy day. The Chris-tians say the beginning (of Creation) fell on a Monday and the ending on Sunday, when He took His seat on the Throne, so they take that as their holy day. Ibn Abbas [a companion of Muhammad and an active transmit-ter of traditions from the Prophet] said that the beginning was on a Saturday and the ending on a Friday, so that the taking of His seat was also on a Friday, and for that reason we keep it as a holy day. It was said by the Prophet, may God bless him and give him peace, "Friday is the mistress among the days. It is more excellent in God's sight than either the Breaking of the Fast (at the end of Ramadan) or the Feast of Sacrifice (in connection with the Pilgrimage liturgy). On it occurred five special things, to wit: Adam was created, on it his spirit was breathed into him, he was wedded, he died, and on it will come the Final Hour. No human ever asks his Lord for anything on Friday but that God gives him what he asks." Another version of this Prophetic tradition reads: ". . . ask, so long as it is not something forbidden." (Al-Kisaʾi, *Stories of the Prophets*) [JEFFERY 1962: 171–172]

3. Adam and Eve

We return to the second chapter of the Book of Genesis, to the account of the creation of Adam and Eve.

When the Lord God made earth and heaven—when no shrub of the field was yet on earth and no grasses of the field had yet sprouted, because the Lord God had not sent rain upon the earth and there was no man to till the soil, but a flow would well up from the ground and water the whole surface of the earth—the Lord God formed man [in Hebrew *adam*] from the dust of the earth. He blew into his nostrils the breath of life, and man became a living being.

The Lord God planted a garden in Eden, in the east, and placed there the man whom He had formed. And from the ground the Lord God caused to grow every tree that was pleasing to the sight and good for food, with the tree of life in the middle of the garden, and the tree of knowledge of good and bad. . . .

The Lord God took the man and placed him in the garden of Eden, to till it and tend it. And the Lord God commanded the man, saying, "Of every tree of the garden you are free to eat; but as for the tree of knowledge of good and bad, you must not eat of it; for as soon as you eat of it, you shall die."

The Lord God said, "It is not good for man to be alone. I will make a fitting helper for him." And the Lord God formed out of the earth all the wild beasts and all the birds of the sky. He brought them to the man to see what he would call them, and whatever the man called each living creature, that would be its name. And the man gave names to all cattle and to the birds of the sky and to all the wild beasts; but for Adam no fitting helper was found. So the Lord God cast a deep sleep upon the man;

and while he slept, He took one of his ribs and closed up the flesh at that spot. And the Lord God fashioned the rib that He had taken from the man into a woman; and He brought her to the man. Then the man said: "This one at last is bone of my bones, and flesh of my flesh. This one shall be called Woman [in Hebrew *ishshah*], for from man [*ish*] was she taken." Hence a man leaves his father and mother and clings to his wife, so that they become one flesh. Now they were both naked, the man and his wife, yet they felt no shame. (Genesis 2:5–25)

4. The Christians Regard Eve

From the very outset of their tradition, beginning with Paul, the Christians showed considerable interest in the text of Genesis. Adam in particular, the prototype of Christ, and, to a somewhat lesser extent, his mate Eve served a number of purposes for Christians. Paul, for example, in his first Letter to the Corinthians, works the changes on the meaning of the word "head," all woven around Genesis 2:5–25, to illustrate the role of women in the Church and in the world.

I wish you to understand that, while every man has Christ for his Head, woman's head is man, as Christ's Head is God. A man who keeps his head covered when he prays or prophesies brings shame on his head; a woman, on the contrary, brings shame on her head if she prays or prophesies bareheaded. . . . A man has no need to cover his head, because man is the image of God and the mirror of His glory, whereas woman reflects the glory of man. For man did not originally spring from woman, but woman was made out of man; and man was not created for woman's sake, but woman for the sake of man; and therefore it is woman's duty to have a sign of authority on her head, out of regard for the angels. And yet, in Christ's fellowship woman is as essential to man as man to woman. If woman was made out of man, it is through woman that man now comes to be; and God is the source of all. (Paul, *To the Corinthians* 1.11: 3–12)

The Christian bishop Augustine (d. 430 C.E.) also contemplated this scene of Creation, but from a far wider theological perspective.

From the words (of Paul) "Till we come to a perfect man, to the measure of the fullness of Christ" (Eph. 4:13), and from his words "Conformed to the image of the Son of God" (Rom. 8:29), some conclude that women shall not rise as women (at the final resurrection), but that all shall be men, because God made man only of earth and woman of the man. For my part, they seem to be wiser who make no doubt that both sexes shall rise. For there shall be no lust, which is now the cause of confusion. For before they sinned, the man and woman were naked and were not ashamed. From those bodies, then, vice shall be withdrawn, while nature shall be preserved. And the sex of woman is not a vice, but nature. It shall then indeed be superior to carnal intercourse and child-bearing; nevertheless, the female members shall remain adapted not to the old uses but to a new beauty which, so far from provoking lust, now extinct, shall excite praise to the wisdom and clemency of God, who both made what was not and delivered from corruption what He made.

For at the beginning of the human race the woman was made of a rib taken from the side of the man while he slept; for it seemed fit that even then Christ and his Church should be foreshadowed in this event. For that sleep of the man was the death of Christ, whose side, as he hung lifeless upon the cross, was pierced with a spear, and there flowed from it blood and water, and these we know to be the sacraments from which the Church is "built up." For the Scripture used this very word, not saying "He formed" or "He framed," but "built her up into a woman" (Gen. 2:22); whence also the Apostle (Paul) speaks of the "building up" of the body of Christ (Eph. 4:12), which is the Church.

The woman therefore, is the creature of God even as the man, and by her creation from man is unity commended; and the manner of her creation prefigured, as has been said, Christ and the Church. He, then, who created both sexes, will restore both. (Augustine, *City of God* 22.17) [AUGUSTINE 1948: 2.636–637]

5. The Original Sin and Its Transmission

The chief interest of this chapter of Genesis, at least for Jews and Christians—the Muslims, as we shall soon see, were far more interested in the fall of the angels—was its description of the "original sin" and what followed from it.

Now the serpent was the shrewdest of all the wild beasts that the Lord God had made. He said to the woman, "Did God really say: You shall not eat of any tree of the garden?" The woman replied to the serpent, "We may eat of the fruit of the other trees of the garden. It is only about the fruit of the tree in the middle of the garden that God said: You shall not eat of it or touch it, lest you die." And the serpent said to the woman, "You are not going to die, but God knows that as soon as you eat of it your eyes will be opened and you will be like divine beings who know good and bad." When the woman saw that the tree was good for eating and a delight to the eyes, and that the tree was desirable as a source of wisdom, she took of the its fruit and ate. She also gave some to her husband, and he ate. Then the eyes of both of them were opened and they perceived that they were naked; and they sewed together fig leaves and made themselves loincloths. (Genesis 3:1–7)

We stand here before a base text of the Jewish understanding of sin, for it was from this act of Adam that sin entered the world and forever altered human nature.

Once he [that is, Adam] had transgressed, death raged beyond his time, mourning acquired its name, sorrow was prepared, suffering was created, toil received its full measure. Pride began to take up its residence. Sheol demanded to revitalize itself with blood and seized children. The desire of parents was created; the greatness of humanity was diminished and goodness grew faint. (2 Baruch 56:6)

If Adam was the first to sin and brought death upon all those who did not yet exist in his time, nevertheless, each of those born of him has prepared for himself the punishment to come or prepared glory for himself. . . . We are all our own Adams. (2 Baruch 44:15–19)

Both texts, which confirm the reality of "original sin" and at the same time vindicate human freedom, are from the "Apocalypse of Baruch," a Jewish work of the era just after 70 C.E. and so almost contemporary with the similar but profoundly different meditation of the former Pharisee Paul on Adam's sin.

It was through one man that sin entered the world, and through sin death, and thus death pervaded the whole human race inasmuch as all men have sinned. (Paul, *To the Romans* 5:12)

This is the terse summary of Paul, who is hurrying on to other things, to Jesus, the second Adam, who freed mankind of this universal grip of sin (see Chapter 3 below). For a more elaborate Christian explanation of the consequences of Adam's sin we must turn back to Augustine.

The first men would not have suffered death if they had not sinned. . . . But having become sinners, they were so punished with death that whatever sprang from their stock should also be punished with the same death. For nothing could be born of them other than what they themselves had been. The condemnation changed their nature for the worse in proportion to the greatness of their sin, so that what was previously a punishment in the man who had first sinned, became part of the nature in others who were born. . . . In the first man, then, the whole human nature was to be transmitted by the woman to posterity when that conjugal union received the divine sentence of its own condemnation, and what man became, not when he was created but when he sinned and was punished, this he propagated, so far as the origin of sin and death are concerned.

For God, the author of all natures, not of vices, created man upright; but man, being by his own will corrupted and justly condemned, begot corrupted and condemned children. For we were all in that one man when we were all that one man, who fell into sin by the woman who had been made from him before the sin. For not yet was the particular form created and distributed to us, in which we as individuals were to live; but already the seminal nature was there from which we were to be propagated; and when this was vitiated by sin and bound by the chain of death and justly condemned, man could not be born of man in any other state. And thus from the bad use of free will there originated a whole series of evils, which with its train of miseries conducts the human race from its depraved origin, as from a corrupt root, on to the destruction of the second death, which has no end, those alone excepted who are freed by the grace of God. (Augustine, *City of God* 13.13–14)
[AUGUSTINE 1948: 2:255–256]

The bodily or genetic transmission of the original sin, which was variously defined by medieval authorities as "a langor of nature" or "an inordinate disposition arising from the destruction of the harmony which was essential to original justice," was obviously a troublesome matter, as Thomas Aquinas's (d. 1277 C.E.) address to the question indicates.

In endeavoring to explain how the sin of our first parent could be transmitted by way of origin to his descendants, various writers have gone about it in various ways. For some, considering that the subject of sin is in the rational soul, maintained that the rational soul is transmitted with the semen, so that an infected soul would seem to produce other infected souls. Others, rejecting this as erroneous, endeavored to show how the guilt of the parents' souls can be transmitted to the children, even though the soul itself is not transmitted, from the fact that defects of the body are transmitted from parent to child. . . . Now since the body is proportioned to the soul, and since the soul's defects are experienced in the body, and vice versa, in like manner, they say, a culpable defect of the soul is passed on to the child through the transmission of semen, although the semen itself is not the subject of guilt.

But all these explanations are insufficient. For granted that some bodily defects are transmitted by way of origin from parent to child, and granted that even some defects of the soul are transmitted, in consequence, because of a defect in a bodily disposition, as in the case of idiots begetting idiots, nevertheless, the fact of having an inherited defect seems to exclude the notion of guilt, which is essentially something voluntary. Therefore, even granted that the rational soul were transmitted (genetically), from the very fact that the stain on the child's soul is not in its will, it would cease to be a guilty stain implicating its subject in punishment; for as Aristotle says (*Ethics* 3, 5), "no one blames a man born blind; one rather takes pity on him."

The path around the difficulty of explaining the genetic inheritance of a spiritual disposition passes through one of the theologians' most familiar and friendly territories, the argument from analogy. Thomas continues:

Therefore we must explain this matter otherwise, by saying that all men born of Adam may be considered one man inasmuch as they have one common nature, which they receive from their first parents. Even as in political matters all who are members of one community are reputed as one body, and the whole community as one man. . . . Accordingly, the multitude of men born of Adam are so many members of one body. Now the action of one member of the body, of the hand, for instance, is voluntary, not by the will of the hand but by the will of the soul, the first mover of the body's members. Therefore, a murder which the hand commits would not be imputed as a sin to the hand considered by itself apart from the body, but it is imputed to it as something belonging to man and moved by man's first moving principle. In this way, then, the disorder which is in this man born of Adam is voluntary, not by his will, but by the will of his first parent, who, by the movement of generation, moves all who originate from him, even as the soul's will moves all the body's members to their actions.

Hence the sin which is thus transmitted by the first parent to his descendants is called *original*, just as the sin that flows from the soul into the bodily members is called *actual*. And just as the actual sin that is committed by a member of the body is not the sin of that member, except insomuch as that member is a part of the man, . . . so original sin is not the sin of this person, except insomuch as this person receives his nature from his first parent. (Thomas Aquinas, *Summa Theologica* I/2, ques. 81, art. 1) [AQUINAS 1945: 2:665–666]

But the contemporary biology did at least exonerate Eve.

It would seem that if Eve and not Adam had sinned, their children would still have contracted original sin. For we contract original sin from our parents, insofar as we were once in them. . . . Now a man pre-exists in his mother as well as in his father. Therefore a man would have contracted original sin from his mother's sin as well as from his father's.

Not so, says Thomas in answer to his own objection.

Original sin is transmitted by the first parent insofar as he is the mover in the begetting of his children. And so it has been said that if anyone were begotten only materially of human flesh, he would not contract original sin, Now it is evident that, in the opinion of the experts, the active principle of generation is from the father; so that if Eve and not Adam had sinned, their children would not have contracted original sin. . . . The child pre-exists in its father as in its active principle, and in its mother as in its material and passive principle. (Thomas Aquinas, *Summa Theologica* I/2 ques. 81, art. 5) [AQUINAS 1945: 2:671–672]

6. Paradise Lost

They [that is, Adam and his wife] heard the sound of the Lord God moving about in the garden at the breezy time of day; and the man and his wife hid from the Lord God among the trees of the garden. The Lord God called out to the man and said to him, "Where are you?" He replied, "I heard the sound of You in the garden, and I was afraid because I was naked, so I hid." Then He asked, "Who told you that you were naked? Did you eat of the tree from which I had forbidden you to eat?" The man said, "The woman You put at my side—she gave me of the tree, and I ate." And the Lord God said to the woman, "What is this you have done!" The woman replied, "The serpent duped me, and I ate." Then the Lord God said to the serpent,

> "Because you did this,
> More cursed shall you be
> Than all cattle
> And all the wild beasts:
> On your belly shall you crawl
> And dirt shall you eat
> All the days of your life.
> I will put enmity
> Between you and the woman,
> And between your offspring and hers;
> They shall strike at your head,
> And you shall strike at their heel."

And to the woman He said,

> "I will make most severe
> Your pangs in childbearing;
> In pain shall you bear children.
> Yet your urge shall be for your husband,
> And he shall rule over you."

To Adam He said, "Because you did as your wife said and ate of the tree about which I commanded you, 'You shall not eat of it,'

> Cursed be the ground because of you;
> By toil shall you eat of it
> All the days of your life
> Thorns and thistles shall it sprout for you.
> but your food shall be the grasses of the field;
> By the sweat of your brow
> Shall you get bread to eat,
> Until you return to the ground—
> For from it you were taken.
> For dust you are,
> And to dust you shall return."

The man named his wife Eve, because she was the mother of all the living. And the Lord God made garments of skins for Adam and his wife, and clothed them.

And the Lord God said, "Now that the man has become like one of us, knowing good and bad, what if he should stretch out his hand and take also from the tree of life and eat, and live forever!" So the Lord God banished him from the garden of Eden, to till the soil from which he was taken. He drove the man out, and stationed east of the garden of Eden the cherubim and the fiery ever-turning sword, to guard the way to the tree of life. (Genesis 3:8–24)

And their descendants will inherit the same moral consequences, Augustine assures us.

Justly is shame very specially connected with this lust; justly too these (sexual) members themselves, being moved and restrained not (any longer) at our will, but by a certain independent autocracy, so to speak, are called *pudenda* or "shameful." For as it is written, "They were naked and were not ashamed" (Gen. 2:25)—not that their nakedness was unknown to them, but because nakedness was not yet shameful, because not yet did lust move those members without the will's consent; nor yet did the flesh by its disobedience testify against the disobedience of man. For they were not created blind, as the unenlightened vulgar fancy; for Adam saw the animals and gave them names, and of Eve we read, "The woman saw that the tree was good for food and it was pleasant to the eyes" (Gen. 3:6). Their eyes, therefore, were open, but were not open to this, that is to say, were not observant so as to recognize what was conferred on them by the garment of grace, for they had no consciousness of their members warring against their will.

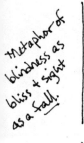

But when they were stripped of this grace, that their disobedience might be punished by fit retribution, there began in the movement of their bodily members a shameless novelty which made their nakedness indecent: it at once made them observant and made them ashamed. And therefore, after they violated God's command by open transgression, it is written: "And the eyes of both of them were opened and they discovered that they were naked; so they stitched fig leaves together and made themselves loincloths."

"The eyes of both of them were opened," not to see, for they already saw, but to discern between the good they had lost and the evil into which they had fallen. And therefore also the tree itself which they were forbidden to touch was called the tree of the knowledge of good and evil from this circumstance, that if they ate of it, it would impart to them this knowledge. For the discomfort of sickness reveals the pleasure of health. "They knew," there, "that they were naked," naked of that grace that prevented them from being ashamed of bodily nakedness, while the law of sin offered no resistance to their mind. And thus they obtained a knowledge of which they would have lived in blissful ignorance had they, in trustful obedience to God, declined to commit that offense which involved them in the hurtful effects of unfaithfulness and disobedience. And therefore, being ashamed of the disobedience of their own flesh, which bore witness to their disobedience even as it punished it, "they stitched fig leaves together and made themselves loincloths," that is, cinctures for their privy parts. . . . Shame modestly covered that which lust disobediently moved in opposition to the will, which was thus punished for its own disobedience. Consequently all nations, being propagated from one stock, have so strong an instinct to cover the shameful parts that some barbarians do not uncover them even in the bath but wash with their drawers on. (Augustine, *City of God* 14.17)

[AUGUSTINE 1948: 2.262–263]

What was there, Augustine asks, that was so terrible about this particular offense that it should have such long-reaching consequences?

If one finds a difficulty in understanding why other sins do not alter human nature as it was altered by the transgression of those first human beings, so that on account of it this nature is subject to the great corruption we feel and see, and to death, and is distracted and tossed with so many furious and contending emotions, and is certainly far different from what it was before sin, even though it was (even) then lodged in an animal body—if, I say, anyone is moved by this, he ought not to think that this sin was a small and light one because it was committed about food, and neither bad nor noxious except because it was forbidden; for in that spot of singular felicity God could not have created or planted any evil thing. But by the precept He gave, God commended obedience, which is, in a way, the mother and guardian of all the virtues in the reasonable creature, which was so created that submission is advantageous to it, while the fulfillment of its own will in preference to the Creator's is destruction. And as this commandment enjoined abstinence from one kind of food in the midst of great abundance of other kinds was so easy to keep—so light a burden to the memory—and, above all, found no resistance to its observance in lust, which only afterwards sprung up as the penal consequence of sin, the iniquity of violating it was all the greater in proportion to the ease with which it might have been kept.

Our first parents fell into open disobedience because already they were secretly corrupted; for the evil act had never been done had not an evil will preceded it. And what is the origin of that evil will but pride? . . . And what is pride but the craving for undue exaltation? And this is undue exaltation, when the soul abandons Him to whom it ought to cleave as its end and becomes an end to itself. This happens when it becomes its own satisfaction. And it does so when it falls away from that unchangeable good which ought to satisfy it more than itself. This falling away is spontaneous; for if the will had remained steadfast in the love of that higher and changeless good by which it was illumined to intelligence and kindled into love, it would not have turned away to find satisfaction in itself, and so become frigid and benighted; the woman would not have believed that the serpent spoke the truth, nor would the man have preferred the request of his wife to the command of God, nor would he have supposed that it was a venial transgression to cling to the partner of his life even in a partnership of sin. (Augustine, *City of God* 14.12–13)

[AUGUSTINE 1948: 2:257–258]

7. Adam and the Fall of the Angels
in the Quran

Christians found the chief moral implications of Genesis in the story of Adam's fall and banishment. Muslims too read the Creation story in a moral manner, chiefly because the Quran presented it from precisely that perspective. Here, however, the emphasis is not on the fall of Adam but on the sin of the angels.

He made for you all that lies within the earth, then turning to the firmament He proportioned several skies: He has a knowledge of everything.

And when the work of Creation was completed, there followed this dialogue in heaven.

Remember when the Lord said to the angels, "I have to place a trustee [Arabic *khalifa*, Caliph] on the earth," they said, "Will You place one there who would create disorder and shed blood, while we intone Your litanies and sanctify Your name?" And God said, "I know what you do not know." Then He gave Adam the knowledge of the nature and reality of all things and everything, and set them before the angels and said, "Tell me the names of these if you are truthful." And they said, "Glory to You, (O Lord), knowledge we have none save what You have given us, for You are all-knowing and all-wise."

Then He said to Adam, "Convey to them their names." And when he had told them, God said, "Did I not I tell you that I know the unknown of the heavens and the earth, and I know what you disclose and know what you hide."

Remember, when We asked the angels to bow in homage to Adam, they all bowed but Iblis, who disdained and turned insolent, and so became a disbeliever.

And We said to Adam, "Both you and your spouse will live in the Garden, eat freely to your fill wherever you like, but approach not this tree or you will become transgressors."

But Satan tempted them and had them banished from the (happy) state they were in. And We said, "Go, one the enemy of the other, and live on the the earth the time ordained, and fend for yourselves."

Then his Lord sent commands to Adam and turned toward him: Indeed He is compassionate and kind. (Quran 2:29–37)

8. The Summons of Abraham

The Book of Genesis leaves Adam and pursues its narrative through the story of Cain and Abel. It then traces the line of Adam through Seth, then Enoch (of whom we shall hear again), down to Noah and the generation of the Flood. The history of Noah's sons Shem, Ham, and Japheth is told; and finally, after the story of the Tower of Babel, the biblical account reaches the immediate ancestors of Abraham.

Now this is the line of Terah: Terah begot Abram, Nahor, and Haran; and Haran begot Lot. Haran died in the lifetime of his father Terah, in his native land, Ur of the Chaldeans. Abram and Nahor took to themselves wives, the name of Abram's wife being Sarai and that of Nahor's wife Milcah, the daughter of Haran, the father of Milcah and Iscah. Now Sarai was barren, she had no child.

Terah took his son Abram, his grandson Lot the son of Haran, and his daughter-in-law Sarai, the wife of his son Abram, and they set out together from Ur of the Chaldeans for the land Canaan; but when they had come as far as Haran, they settled there. The days of Terah came to 205 years; and Terah died in Haran.

The Lord said to Abram, "Go forth from your native land and from your father's house to the land that I will show you.

> I will make of you a great nation,
> And I will bless you;
> I will make your name great,
> And you shall be a blessing.
> I will bless those who bless you
> And curse him that curses you;
> And all the families of the earth
> Shall bless themselves by you."

Abram went forth as the Lord had commanded him, and Lot went with him. Abram was seventy-five years old when he left Haran. Abram took his wife Sarai and his brother's son Lot, and all the wealth that they had amassed, and the persons that they acquired in Haran; and they set out for the land of Canaan.

So Abram ends his long migration from his Iraqi homeland at "Ur of the Chaldeans" to Canaan, the future Land of the Promise.

Abram passed through the land as far as the site of Shechem, at the terebinth of Moreh. The Canaanites were then in the land. When they arrived in the land of Canaan, the Lord appeared to Abram and said, "I will give this land to your offspring." And he built an altar there to the Lord who had appeared to him. From there he moved on to the hill country east of Bethel and pitched his tent, with Bethel on the west and Ai on the east; and he built there an altar to the Lord and invoked the Lord by name. Then Abram journeyed by stages toward the Negeb. (Genesis 11:27–12:9)

9. Melchizedek, High Priest of Salem

After a spell in Egypt, Abraham and his family returned to the land of the Canaanites and made his home at the terebinths of Mamre, in a place called Hebron, where he was immediately caught up in the wars of the local princes and rulers. It was during his return home from one of those campaigns near Damascus that the following incident took place.

When he [that is, Abram] returned from defeating Cherdorlaomer and the kings with him, the king of Sodom came out to meet him in the Valley of Shaveh, which is the Valley of the King. And Melchizedek, king of Salem, brought out bread and wine; he was a priest of God Most High. He blessed him, saying,

> "Blessed be Abram of God Most High,
> Creator of heaven and earth.
> And blessed be God Most High,
> Who has delivered your foes into your hand."

And [Abram] gave him a tenth of everything. (Genesis 14:17–20)

10. A Christian Appreciation of Melchizedek

With those few words the mysterious Melchizedek, "priest of God Most High," disappears from the historical narrative of Genesis as abruptly as he had entered it, though assuredly not from the thoughts of the Jews, who quickly identified him with Shem, the son of Noah, and understood that he was king of Jerusalem. But even more consequentially, Melchizedek reappears in a Messianic context in Psalm 110:4.

The Lord has sworn and will not change His purpose: You [that is, the Messiah, since it is he who is being addressed] are a priest forever, in the succession of Melchizedek.

*There the Christians found Melchizedek and used him for their own purposes. This
is how the author of the New Testament's Letter to the Hebrews understood him.*

This Melchizedek, king of Salem, priest of God Most High, met
Abraham returning from the rout of the kings and blessed him; and
Abraham gave him a tithe of everything as his portion. His name, in the
first place, means "king of righteousness"; next he is king of Salem, that
is, "king of peace." He has no father, no mother, no lineage; his years have
no beginning, his life no end. He is like the Son of God: he remains a
priest for all time.

Consider how great he must be for Abraham the patriarch to give
him a tithe of the finest of the spoil. The descendants of Levi who take
the priestly office are commanded by the Law to receive tithes from the
people, that is, from their kinsmen, although they too are descendants of
Abraham. But Melchizedek, though he does not trace his descent from
them, has received tithes from Abraham himself, and given his blessing to
the man who received the promises; and beyond all dispute the lesser is
always blessed by the greater. (Hebrews 7:1–7)

11. The Covenant and the Promised Land

*Melchizedek was assuredly neither the center nor the point of these chapters of
Genesis. The narrative is heading toward quite another climax, and it has to do with
Abram, as he was still being called.*

Some time later, the word of the Lord came to Abram in a vision,
saying,

> "Fear not, Abram,
> I am a shield to you;
> Your reward shall be very great."

But Abram said, "O Lord God, what can You give me, seeing that
I shall die childless, and the one in charge of my household is Dammesek
Eliezer!" Abram said further, "Since You have granted me no offspring,
my steward shall be my heir." The word of the Lord came to him in reply,
"That one shall not be your heir; none but your very own issue shall be
your heir." He took him outside and said, "Look toward heaven and
count the stars, if you are able to count them." And He added, "So shall
your offspring be." And because he put his trust in the Lord, He reckoned
it to his merit. (Genesis 15:1–6)

On that day the Lord made a covenant with Abram, saying, "To
your offspring I give this land, from the river of Egypt to the great river,

the river Euphrates: the Kenites, the Kenizzites, the Kadmonites, the Hittites, the Perizzites, the Rephaim, the Amorites, the Canaanites, the Girgashites, and the Jebusites." (Genesis 15:17–21)

12. The Birth of Ishmael

The rest of the Bible, and the New Testament and Quran as well, has to do with the fulfillment of this promise made to the descendants of Abraham. Jews, Christians, and Muslims would all one day claim to be the true progeny and heir to Abraham. But that same question of birthright arose in the patriarch's own lifetime.

Sarai, Abram's wife, had borne him no children. She had an Egyptian maid servant whose name was Hagar. And Sarai said to Abram, "Look, the Lord has kept me from bearing. Consort with my maid; perhaps I shall have a son through her." And Abram heeded Sarai's request. So Sarai, Abram's wife, took her maid, Hagar the Egyptian— after Abram had dwelt in the land of Canaan ten years—and gave her to her husband Abram as concubine. He cohabited with Hagar and she conceived; and when she saw that she had conceived, her mistress was lowered in her esteem. And Sarai said to Abram, "The wrong done me is your fault! I myself put my maid in your bosom; now that she sees that she is pregnant, I am lowered in her esteem. The Lord decide between you and me!" Abram said to Sarai, "Your maid is in your hands. Deal with her as you think right." Then Sarai treated her harshly, and she ran away from her.

An angel of the Lord found her by a spring of water in the wilderness, the spring on the road to Shur, and said, "Hagar, slave of Sarai, where have you come from, and where are you going?" And she said, "I am running away from my mistress Sarai."

And the angel of the Lord said to her, "Go back to your mistress, and submit to her harsh treatment." And the angel of the Lord said to her.

> "I will greatly increase your offspring
> And they shall be too many to count."

The angel of the Lord said to her further,

> "Behold, you are with child
> And shall bear a son;
> You shall call him Ishmael,
> For the Lord has paid heed to your suffering.

He shall be a wild ass of a man;
His hand against everyone,
And everyone's hand against him;
He shall dwell alongside of all his kinsmen."

Hagar bore a son to Abram, and Abram gave the son that Hagar bore him the name Ishmael. Abram was eighty-six years old when Hagar bore Ishmael to Abram. (Genesis 16:1–16)

13. The Covenant

This was all prelude. The Promise came to Abraham thirteen years later, and it concerned not Ishmael but another, yet unborn child of the elderly Abraham.

When Abram was ninety-nine years old, the Lord appeared to Abram and said to him, "I am El Shaddai. Walk in My ways and be blameless. I will establish My covenant between Me and you, and I will make you exceedingly numerous."

Abram threw himself on his face; and God spoke to him further, "As for Me, this is My covenant with you: You shall be the father of a multitude of nations. And you shall no longer be called Abram, but your name shall be Abraham, for I make you the father of a multitude of nations. I will make you exceedingly fertile, and make nations of you; and kings shall come forth from you. I will maintain My covenant between Me and you, and your offspring to come, as an everlasting covenant throughout the ages, to be God to you and your offspring to come. I give the land you sojourn in to you and your offspring to come, all the land of Canaan, as an everlasting possession. I will be their God." (Genesis 17:1–8)

God further said to Abraham, "As for you, you and your offspring to come throughout the ages shall keep My covenant. Such shall be the covenant between Me and you and your offspring to follow which you shall keep: every male among you shall be circumcised. You shall circumcise the flesh of your foreskin, and that shall be the sign of the covenant between Me and you. And throughout the generations, every male among you shall be circumcised at the age of eight days. As for the homeborn slave and the one bought from an outsider who is not of your offspring, they must be circumcised, homeborn and purchased alike. Thus shall My covenant be marked in your flesh as an everlasting pact. And if any male who is uncircumcised fails to circumcise the flesh of his foreskin, that person shall be cut off from his kin; he has broken My covenant." (Genesis 17:9–14)

Thus the Covenant was sealed by circumcision. There remained, however, the question of the heir.

And God said to Abraham, "As for your wife Sarai, you shall not call her Sarai, but her name shall be Sarah. I will bless her; indeed, I will give you a son by her. I will bless her so that we shall give rise to nations; rulers of peoples shall issue from her." Abraham threw himself on his face and laughed, as he said to himself, "Can a child be born to a man a hundred years old, or can Sarah bear a child at ninety?" And Abraham said to God, "Oh that Ishmael might live by Your favor!" God said, "Nevertheless, Sarah your wife shall bear you a son, and you shall name him Isaac; and I will maintain My covenant with him as an everlasting covenant for his offspring to come. As for Ishmael, I have heeded you. I hereby bless him. I will make him fertile and exceedingly numerous. He shall be the father of twelve chieftains, and I will make of him a great nation. But My covenant I will maintain with Isaac, whom Sarah shall bear to you at this season next year." And when He was done speaking with him, God was gone from Abraham.

Then Abraham took his son Ishmael, and all his homeborn slaves and all those he had bought, every male in Abraham's household, and he circumcised the flesh of their foreskins on that very day, as God had spoken to him. Abraham wa. ninety-nine years old when he circumcised the flesh of his foreskin, and his son Ishmael was thirteen years old when he was circumcised in the flesh of his foreskin. (Genesis 17:15–25)

14. Ishmael and the Ishmaelites

The Lord took note of Sarah as He had promised, and the Lord did for Sarah as He had spoken. Sarah conceived and bore a son to Abraham in his old age, at the set time of which God had spoken. Abraham gave his newborn son, whom Sarah had borne him, the name of Isaac. And when his son Isaac was eight days old, Abraham circumcised him, as God had commanded him. Now Abraham was a hundred years old when his son Isaac was born to him. Sarah said, "God has brought me laughter; everyone who hears will laugh at me." And she added,

> "Who would have said to Abraham
> that Sarah would suckle children!
> Yet I have borne a son in his old age."

The child grew up and was weaned, and Abraham held a great feast on the day that Isaac was weaned.

Sarah saw the son whom Hagar the Egyptian had borne to Abraham playing. She said to Abraham, "Cast out that slave woman and her son, for the son of that slave shall not share in the inheritance with my son Isaac." The matter distressed Abraham greatly, for it concerned a son of his. But God said to Abraham, "Do not be distressed over the boy or your slave; whatever Sarah tells you, do as she says, for it is through Isaac that offspring shall be continued for you. As for the son of the slave woman, I will make a nation of him, too, for he is your seed."

Ishmael, then, is to be neither glorified nor entirely rejected.

Early the next morning Abraham took some bread and a skin of water, and gave them to Hagar. He placed them on her shoulder, together with the child, and sent her away. And she wandered about in the wilderness of Beer-sheba. When the water was gone from the skin, she left the child under one of the bushes, and went and sat down at a distance, a bowshot away; for she thought, "Let me not look on as the child dies." And sitting thus afar, she burst into tears.

God heard the cry of the boy, and an angel of God called to Hagar from heaven and said to her, "What troubles you, Hagar? Fear not, for God has heeded the cry of the boy where he is. Come, lift up the boy and hold him by the hand, for I will make a great nation of him." Then God opened her eyes and she saw a well of water. She went and filled the skin with water, and let the boy drink. God was with the boy and he grew up; he dwelt in the wilderness and became a bowman. He lived in the wilderness of Paran [that is, in Sinai]; and his mother got a wife for him from the land of Egypt. (Genesis 21:1–21)

Genesis returns to the subject of Ishmael one final time in Chapter 25.

This is the line of Ishmael, Abraham's son, whom Hagar the Egyptian, Sarah's slave, bore to Abraham. These are the names of the sons of Ishmael, by their names, in the order of their birth: Nebaioth, the first-born of Ishmael, Kedar, Abdeel, Mibsam, Mishma, Dumah, Massa, Hadad, Tema, Jetur, Naphish, and Kedmah. These are the sons of Ishmael and these are their names by their villages and by their encampments: twelve chieftains of as many tribes. These were the years of the life of Ishmael: one hundred and thirty-seven years; then he breathed his last and died, and was gathered to his kin. They dwelt from Havilah, by Shur, which is close to Egypt, all the way to Asshur; they camped alongside all their kinsman. (Genesis 25:12–18)

15. The Arabs as Ishmaelites

This is the end of the story in the canonical Scripture. But when the anonymous Pharisee sat down sometime between 135 and 105 B.C.E. to retell the story of Abraham, Isaac, and Jacob under the name of "The Book of Jubilees," he knew somewhat more than what Genesis revealed about the descendants of Ishmael. First, Abraham summoned Ishmael and his twelve sons, Isaac and his two, and the sons of another of his women, Keturah, and bade them to continue to observe circumcision, to avoid all fornication, uncleanness, and intermarriage with the Canaanite population of the land. The passage then concludes.

And he [that is, Abraham] gave gifts to Ishmael and his sons, and to the sons of Keturah, and he sent them away from his son Isaac, and he gave his son Isaac everything. And Ishmael and his sons, and the sons of Keturah and their sons, went together and settled between Paran to the borders of Babylon, in all the land that is toward the East, facing the desert. And these mingled with each other, and they were called Arabs and Ishmaelites. (Jubilees 20:11–13)

Four or five centuries later, the Babylonian rabbis were imagining a series of lawsuits that would have taken place before Alexander the Great when that conqueror entered Palestine in the 330s B.C.E. Three peoples laid claim against the Jews to the land of Israel: the Phoenicians, who claimed descent from the original Canaanites; the Egyptians, who claimed they had been robbed by the children of Israel at the time of the Exodus; and finally "the Ishmaelites and the Ketureans," who had an obvious, if partial, claim on the land as the other heirs of Abraham. A rabbi named Gebiha ben Pesiha requests permission to go and plead the Jews' case before Alexander, so that if it is lost people might say, "You have defeated one of our ignorant men," while, if he prevails, it will be said that "the Law of Moses our Teacher has defeated them."

So they gave him permission and he went and pleaded against them. "Whence do you adduce your proof?" he asked them [that is, the Ishmaelites and Ketureans]. "From the Torah," they replied. "Then I too," he said, "will bring proof only from the Torah, for it is written, 'And Abraham gave all that he had to Isaac. But to the sons of the concubines which Abraham had, Abraham gave gifts' (Gen. 25: 1–4); if a father made a bequest to the children in his lifetime and sent them away from each other, has one any claim on the other?"

What gifts? Rabbi Jeremiah ben Abba said: This teaches that he imparted to them the (secrets of the) unholy arts [that is, of sorcery and demonology]. (BT.Sanhedrin 91a)

It may be doubted that any such case actually occurred. What is certain, however, is that the genealogy of the Arabs as descendants of Ishmael was well established, and widely disseminated, long before the coming of Islam. Josephus says that the Arabs were circumcised at the age of thirteen "because Ishmael, the founder of their race, born to Abraham's concubine, was circumcised at that age" (Antiquities 1.12.2), and that the sons of Ishmael "occupied the whole country extending from the Euphrates to the Red Sea and called it Nabatene, and it is these who conferred their name on the Arab nation and its tribes in honor of both their own prowess and the fame of Abraham" (Antiquities 1.12.4). And finally, this is how the story of the Ishmaelites is presented in the Church History *of Sozomen about 440 C.E. The author had just been discussing "Saracens," a common name for Arabs before and after Islam.*

This tribe (of Saracens) takes its origins from Ishmael the son of Abraham and had that appellation as well: the ancients called them Ishmaelites from their ancestry. And to avoid the charge of bastardy and the low birth of the mother of Ishmael, they called themselves "Sara-cens" as if descended from Abraham's wife Sarah. Possessing this kind of descent, all of them are circumcised like the Hebrews and abstain from the flesh of swine and observe among themselves many of the latter's customs. Nor should one think that they have always lived in the same manner, whether by reason of the passage of time or by their intercourse with the surrounding peoples. For it was long after them that Moses legislated, and then only for those who went out of Egypt. Those who lived near the Ishmaelites, being demon worshipers, likely destroyed the Ishmaelites' ancestral way of life, the only norm by which the ancient Hebrews lived before the Mosaic legislation, relying on unwritten customs. Those same demons the Ishmaelites too doubtless reverenced, and they especially honored them and called upon them in the manner of the cult practices of their neighbors and so demonstrated the reason why they neglected their ancestral laws. The passage of a long time caused them to forget some and allow others to grow antiquated. Afterwards some of them became acquainted with the Jews and learned whence they had come. They reverted back to their ancestry and took up the Hebrew customs and laws. From that time many among them still live in the Jewish fashion. (Sozomen, *Church History* 6.38.1–13)

That same descent was re-established in the Quran, which puts not only Ishmael but also his father Abraham at Mecca in the patriarchal era. And if the identification of Ishmael as the father of the Arabs was useful for Muhammad, it served equally well for Jewish exegetes living under Islam, as is graphically illustrated by the meditations of this anonymous tenth-century rabbi on Genesis, which are rather more direct than is usual in this genre.

It says: "And he [that is, Ishmael] shall be a man like the wild ass." (Gen. 16:12), that is to say, like an animal that dwells in the desert, so your son Ishmael will find shelter in the desert. And with this, she [Hagar] realized that Ishmael her son would have no portion in the land of Canaan, short of a foothold. With this statement he [God?] disabused her of her view and so obliged her to return and submit to Sarah because the promises (made to Abraham) would not be fulfilled in her son.

And when Abraham and Sarah heard this statement from her, they rejoiced, understanding that he would still be blessed by other seed, from her or from another woman, because Sarah was an old woman, and that the promise would be fulfilled. Sarah too was astonished to hear Hagar, imagining that Abraham would have a child from her or from another woman.

Then the announcement was made that Abraham would have another son, and he was Isaac and it was he of whom the promises had been spoken.

And it says: "His hand shall be against every man" (ibid.), meaning that at the end of his lifetime Ishmael will enter a settled area and will dwell in settlements, and will reign over settlements and rule nations. Of this it is written in Daniel (11:24), "In time of peace he will overrun the richest districts of the province and succeed in doing what his fathers and forefathers failed to do, distributing spoil, booty, and property to his followers, etc." At first he will come forth with only a few people and he will manipulate with plots and cunning, as it says, "he will enter into fraudulent alliances, and although the people behind him are but few, he will rise to power" (Dan. 11:23). And he will stretch his arm upon the nations, as it says: "His hand shall be against every man." This is what Zechariah has said (6:4), "(The chariot) with the roan horse went forth (to the east), and they were eager to go and range over the whole earth." So he said, "Go and range over the earth," and they did so.

The roan horses are the Ishmaelites from whom some Arab tribes emerged with the "Defective." They took the kingship from the Midianites, from (the Shah) Yazdgard [635–651 C.E.], of whom it is written (Dan. 11:21), "A contemptible creature will succeed," and he is called (ibid. 7:8) "the Little Horn," of which it is said, "and three of the first horns were uprooted to make way for it" (ibid.).

And there was no nation in the world that had happen to it what happened to Ishmael. No one spoke like it, as it was written (ibid.), "And a mouth speaking great things." Of its leaders it is said (Dan. 8:23), "a king shall appear, harsh and grim, a master of stratagem." At first the Ishmaelite nation lived in the desert and did not have the "yoke of kingship," as it is written, "a wild ass used to the wilderness snuffing the wind in her lust." And when this nation grew up it entered the settled areas and imposed its yoke on kingdoms and on deserts. And they did not leave these places and they are in their hands up to this day, a period of 372 years [from the Hijra, that is, 982 C.E.]. . . . And just as the saying "His hand shall be against every man" was fulfilled, so shall the saying "and every man's hand shall be against him" will (also) be fulfilled, as it is written in Habakkuk (2:8), "Because you have plundered many mighty nations, all the rest of the world will plunder you." (MS Adler 7320)

[SOKOLOW 1981: 313–316]

16. The Binding of Isaac

We return to the narrative in Genesis:

Sometime afterward, God put Abraham to the test. He said to him, "Abraham," and he answered, "Here I am." And He said, "Take your son, your favored one, Isaac, whom you love, and go to the land of Moriah, and offer him there as a burnt offering on one of the heights which I will point out to you." So early next morning, Abraham saddled his ass and took with him two of his servants and his son Isaac. He split wood for the burnt offering, and he set out for the place of which God had told him. On the third day Abraham looked up and saw the place from afar. Then Abraham said to his servants, "You stay here with the ass. The boy and I will go up there; we will worship and we will return to you."

Abraham took the wood for the burnt offering and put it on his son Isaac. He himself took the firestone and the knife; and the two walked off together. Then Isaac said to his father Abraham, "Father!" And he answered, "Yes, my son." And he said, "Here are the firestone and the wood; but where is the sheep for the burnt offering?" And Abraham said, "God will see to the sheep for His burnt offering, my son." And the two of them walked on together.

They arrived at the place of which God had told him. Abraham built an altar there; he laid out the wood; he bound his son Isaac; he laid him on the altar, on top of the wood. And Abraham picked up the knife to slay his son. Then an angel of the Lord called to him from heaven. "Abraham! Abraham!" And he answered, "Here I am." And he said, "Do not raise your hand against the boy, or do anything to him. For now I know that you fear God, since you have not withheld your son, your favored one, from Me." When Abraham looked up, his eye fell upon a ram, caught in the thicket by its horns. So Abraham went and took the ram and offered it up as a burnt offering in place of his son. And Abraham named that site Adonai Jireh, hence the present saying, "On the mount of the Lord there is vision."

To this point the account appears to describe a somewhat arbitrary test to which the Lord had put Abraham's conviction. In the immediate sequel it becomes clear that the test of the "binding of Isaac" was the act whereby Abraham and his descendants "merited" the Promise that God had made to them, which is now renewed:

The angel of the Lord called to Abraham a second time from heaven and said, "By Myself I swear, the Lord declares: because you have done this and have not withheld your son, your favored one, I will bestow My blessing upon you and make your descendants as numerous as the stars of heaven and the sands on the seashore; and your descendants shall seize the gates of their foes. All the nations of the earth shall bless themselves by your descendants, because you have obeyed My command. . . ."

Then the angel of the Lord called from heaven a second time to Abraham: "This is the word of the Lord: By My Own Self I swear: inasmuch as you have done this and have not withheld your son, your only son, I will bless you abundantly and greatly multiply your descendants until they are as numerous as the stars in the sky and the grains of sand on the seashore. Your descendants shall possess the cities of their enemies. All nations on earth shall pray to be blessed as your descendants are blessed, and this because you have obeyed Me." (Genesis 22:1–18)

17. The Christian as the Offspring of Abraham

Abraham is, of course, the crucial figure in the entire history of the Covenant, as we shall see again and again. The Jews, founding themselves on the simple sense of Genesis, regarded themselves as natural heirs of both Abraham and the Covenant. For the Christian and Muslim contestants, however, the point had to be argued, and strenuously. This is the classic Christian argument, perhaps taken from the preaching of John the Baptist, who had admonished his fellow Jews: "Do not presume to

say to yourselves, 'We have Abraham as a father.' I tell you, God can make children
of Abraham out of these stones here" (Matt. 3:9). Here Paul explains.

What, then, are we to say about Abraham, our ancestor in the
natural line? If Abraham was justified by anything he had done, then he
had ground for pride. But he had no such ground before God; for what
does Scripture say? "Abraham put his faith in God, and that faith was
counted to him as righteousness." Now if a man does a piece of work, his
wages are not "counted" to him as a favor; they are paid as a debt. But
if without any work to his credit he simply puts his faith in him who
acquits the guilty, then his faith is indeed "counted as righteousness"
(Gen. 15:6).

Paul connects the Promise directly with Abraham's monotheistic faith and not, as
the passage in Genesis 22:16–18 suggests, on his perfect obedience in the matter
of the "binding of Isaac."

Consider, we say "Abraham's faith was counted as righteousness";
in what circumstances was it so counted? Was he circumcised at the time
or not? He was not yet circumcised but uncircumcised; and he later
received the symbolic rite of circumcision as a hallmark of the righteousness which faith had given him when he was still uncircumcised. Consequently, he is the father of all who have faith when uncircumcised, so that
righteousness is "counted" to them; and at the same time he is the father
of such of the circumcised as do not rely on their circumcision alone but
also walk in the footsteps of the faith which our father Abraham had
while he was yet uncircumcised.

For it was not through law that Abraham, or his posterity, was given
the promise that the world would be their inheritance, but through the
righteousness that came from faith. For if those who hold by the law, and
they alone, are heirs, then faith is empty and the promise goes for nothing, because law can bring only retribution. But where there is no law,
there can be no breach of law. The promise was made on the ground of
faith, in order that it might be a matter of sheer grace, and that it might
be valid for all Abraham's posterity, not only for those who hold by the
law, but for those also who have the faith of Abraham. For he is the father
of us all, as Scripture says, "I have appointed you to be the father of many
nations." This promise, then, was valid before God, the God in whom he
put his faith, the God who makes the dead live and summons things that
are not yet in existence as if they already were. . . . Without any weaken-
ing of his faith he contemplated his own body, as good as dead (for he was
about a hundred years old) and the deadness of Sarah's womb, and never

doubted God's promise in unbelief, but, strong in faith, gave honor to God, in the firm conviction of his power to do what he had promised. And that is why Abraham's faith was "counted to him as righteousness."

Those words were written not for Abraham's sake alone, but for our sake too: it is to be "counted" in the same way to us who have faith in the God who raised Jesus our Lord from the dead; for he was given up to death for our misdeeds, and raised to life to justify us. (Paul, *To the Romans* 4:1–25)

That the circumcision of Abraham was simply a sign—a "symbolic rite," as Paul called it—and did not constitute his justification was argued from a different point of view by the Christian Justin in his debate with the rabbi Trypho or Tarphon sometime about 150 C.E.

If circumcision had been necessary as you [that is, Trypho and the Jews] suppose, God would not have created Adam uncircumcised, nor would He have looked with favor upon the sacrifice of Abel which he offered in uncircumcision, nor would Enoch have been pleasing to God in uncircumcision. . . . Lot, uncircumcised, was delivered out of Sodom. . . . Noah is the father of the human race; but with his children, while he was uncircumcised, he entered into the ark. Melchizedek, the priest of the Most High, was uncircumcised, to whom Abraham, the first to receive circumcision after the flesh, gave tithes, and Melchizedek blessed him. It was according to his succession [that is, Melchizedek] that God declared through David that he would make him a priest forever. . . .

We are constrained to concede that Abraham accepted circumcision as a sign and not as righteousness by both Scripture and the events themselves. It was rightly said of his people that whoever was not circumcised by the eighth day would be cut off from his tribe. But the fact that the female gender cannot receive circumcision is an argument that it was given as a sign and not as the work of justice, for God so made women that as far as regards justice and virtue, they likewise are capable of full observance. (Justin, *Dialogue with Trypho* 19, 23)

18. The New Covenant and the Old: The Christian View

The Christians were hardly in a position to deny, even if they had been so inclined, that a Covenant had been sealed between God and Abraham and his descendants and that those latter were, in some sense, the Jews. What they could and did do was take their point of departure from a well-known text of Jeremiah (Jer. 31:31–34, cited in Chapter 2 below) and argue that there would be a second or New Covenant to supersede the first.

Had that first Covenant been faultless, there would have been no need to look for a second in its place. But God, finding fault with them, says, "The days are coming, says the Lord, when I will conclude a new Covenant with the House of Israel and the House of Judah. It will not be like the Covenant I made with their forefathers when I took them by the hand to lead them out of Egypt; because they did not abide by the terms of that Covenant, and I abandoned them, says the Lord. For the Covenant I will make with the house of Israel after these those days, says the Lord, is this: I will set my laws in their understanding and write them on their hearts; and I will be their God and they will be my people . . . " (Jer. 31:31–34). By speaking of a new Covenant, He has pronounced the first one old; and anything that is growing old and aging will shortly disappear. (Hebrews 8:7–13)

19. The Rabbinic Response: There Will Be No New Covenant

The Jews were not much inclined to argue this or any other point with the Christians, though perhaps the Christian claim to a New Testament lies somewhere behind this kind of text.

It is written, "For this commandment is not in heaven" (Deut. 30:11–12). Moses said to the Israelites, "Lest you should say, Another Moses is to arise and to bring us another Law from heaven; therefore I make it known to you now that it is not in heaven." Rabbi Hanina said: The Law and all the implements by which it has been carried out have been given, namely, modesty, beneficence, uprightness and reward. (*Deuteronomy Rabbah* 8.6)

20. The Quran's Account of the Covenant

The Muslim for his part was not constrained to argue the case of his spiritual descent from Genesis; he had his own account of the Covenant in the Quran. It begins with Abraham in a state of idolatry, of "associating," as the Quran puts it, other gods with the One True God.

Remember when Abraham said to Azar, his father: "Why do you take idols for gods? I certainly find you and your people in error." Thus We showed to Abraham the visible and invisible world of the heavens and the earth, that he could be among those who believe. When the night came with her covering of darkness, he saw a star, and (Azar, his father) said, "This is my Lord." But when the star set, (Abraham) said, "I love not those that wane." When (Azar) saw the moon rise all aglow, he said, "This is my Lord." But even as the moon set, (Abraham) said; "If my Lord had not shown me the way, I would surely have gone astray." When (Azar) saw the sun rise all resplendent, he said, "My Lord is surely this, and the greatest of them all." But the sun also set, and (Abraham) said, "O my people, I am through with those you associate with God. I have truly turned my face toward Him who created the heavens and the earth: I have chosen one way and I am not a idolater."

His people argued and he said, "Do you argue with me about God? He has guided me already, and I fear not what you associate with Him, unless my Lord wills, for held within the knowledge of my Lord is everything. Will you not reflect? And why should I fear those you associate with Him when you fear not associating others with God for which He has sent down no sanction? Tell me whose way is the way of peace, if you have the knowledge. They alone have peace who believe, and do not intermix belief with denial, and are guided on the right path.

This is the argument We gave to Abraham against his people. We exalt whosoever We please in rank by degrees. Your Lord is wise and all-knowing. And We gave him Isaac and Jacob and guided them, as We had guided Noah before them, and of his descendants, David and Solomon and Job and Joseph and Moses and Aaron. Thus do We reward those who are upright and do good. Zachariah and John We guided, and guided Jesus and Elias who were all among the upright. And we gave guidance to Ishmael, Elisha and Jonah and Lot; and We favored them over all the other people of the world, as We did some of their fathers and progeny and brethren, and chose them, and showed them the right path.

This is God's guidance: He guides among His creatures whom He will. If they had associated others with Him, surely vain would have been all they did. Those are the people to whom We gave the Book and the Law and the Prophethood. But if they reject these things We shall entrust them to a people who will not deny. (Quran 6:74–89)

21. Abraham as the First Muslim

Abraham . . . prayed: "Accept this from us, O Lord, for You hear and know everything; and make us submitters (*muslimin*) to your will and make our progeny a people submissive to You (*ummah muslimah*). Teach us the way of worship and forgive our trespasses, for You are compassionate and merciful; and send, O Lord, an apostle from among them to impart Your message to them, to teach them the Book and the wisdom, and correct them in every way; for indeed You are mighty and wise."

And who will turn away from the religion of Abraham but one dull of soul? We made him the chosen one here in the world, and one of the best in the world to come, (for) when his Lord said to him, "Submit" (*aslim*)," he replied: "I submit (*aslamtu*) to the Lord of all the worlds." And Abraham left this legacy to his sons, and to Jacob, and said, "O my sons, God has chosen this as the faith for you. Do not die but as those who have submitted to God (*muslimuna*)."

Were you present at the hour of Jacob's death? "What will you worship after me?" he asked his sons, and they answered, "We shall worship your God and the God of your fathers, of Abraham and Ishmael and Isaac, the one and only God, and to Him we are submitters (*muslimuna*)."

Those were the people, and they have passed away. Theirs is the reward for what they did, and yours will be for what you do. You will not be questioned about their deeds.

And they say, "Become Jews or become Christians, and find the right way." Say: "No, we follow the religion of Abraham, the upright, who was not an idolater." (Quran 2:127–135)

According to the Life of the Apostle of God, *this is how Muhammad himself urged the matter in respect to both the Jewish and the Christian claims to be the sons of Abraham, and so of the Covenant.*

The Jewish rabbis and the Christians of Najran, when they were before the Apostle (in Medina), broke into disputing. The Jews said that Abraham was nothing but a Jew. The Christians said that he was nothing but a Christian. So God revealed concerning them (Quran 3:55–58): "O People of the Scripture, why will you argue about Abraham, when the Torah and the Gospel were not revealed until after him. Have you then no sense? . . ."

Abraham was not a Jew nor not yet a Christian, but he was an upright man who surrendered to God, and he was not of the idolaters. Lo! those of mankind who have the best claim to Abraham are those who followed him, and this Prophet and those who believe (with him); and God is the Protecting Friend of the believers. (*Life* 383–384)

[IBN ISHAQ 1955:260]

22. Jacob's Dream

To return once again to the account in Genesis of Isaac's two sons, Esau and Jacob, it was through the latter that the Covenant would be fulfilled. But Isaac's wife, Rebecca, feared that the young man would marry one of the local Hittite women, and so Jacob was sent away eastward, back along the route traced by his grandfather Abraham.

So Isaac sent for Jacob and blessed him. He instructed him, saying, "You shall not take a wife from among the Canaanite women. Up, go to Paddan-aram, to the house of Bethuel, your mother's father, and take a wife from among the daughters of Laban, your mother's brother. May El Shaddai bless you, make you fertile and numerous, so that you become an assembly of peoples. May He grant the blessing of Abraham to you and your offspring that you may possess the land where you are sojourning, which God gave to Abraham. . . ."

Jacob left Beer-sheba, and set out for Haran. He came upon a certain place and stopped there for the night, for the sun had set. Taking one of the stones of that place, he put it under his head and lay down in that place. He had a dream; a stairway was set on the ground and its top reached to the sky, and angels of God were going up and down on it. And the Lord was standing beside him and He said, "I am the Lord, the God of your father Abraham and the God of Isaac: the ground on which you are lying I will give to you and to your offspring. Your descendants shall be as the dust of the earth; you shall spread out to the west and to the east, to the north and to the south. All the families of the earth shall bless themselves by you and your descendants. Remember, I am with you: I will protect you wherever you go and will bring you back to this land. I will not leave you until I have done what I have promised you."

Jacob awoke from his sleep and said, "Surely the Lord is present in this place, and I did not know it!" Shaken, he said, "How awesome is this place! This is none other than the abode of God, and that is the gateway to heaven." Early in the morning, Jacob took the stone that he had put under his head and set it up as a pillar and poured oil on the top of it. He named the site Bethel; but previously the name of the city had been Luz.

Jacob made a vow, saying, "If God remains with me, if He protects me on this journey that I am making, and gives me bread to eat and clothing to wear, and if I return safe to my father's house—the Lord shall be my God. And this stone, which I have set up as a pillar, shall be God's

abode; and of all that You give me, I will set aside a tithe for You."
(Genesis 28:1–23)

This was by no means the only stone marking the presence of God in the Middle East. We shall observe another at Mecca: the black stone embedded in the Arabs' Beth-El, the House of God called the Ka'ba.

23. Jacob Becomes Israel

Jacob finds not one wife but two among Laban's daughters in Paddan-aram, and eventually he and Rachel and Leah and their children return to the lands of Abraham and Isaac in Canaan. On the way, Jacob has another encounter with the divine.

That same night he arose, and taking his two wives, his two maid servants, and his eleven children, he crossed the ford of the Jabbok. After taking them across the stream, he sent across all his possessions. Jacob was left alone. And a man wrestled with him until the break of dawn. When he saw that he had not prevailed against him, he wrenched Jacob's hip at its socket, so that the socket of his hip was strained as he wrestled with him.

Then he said, "Let me go, for dawn is breaking." But he answered, "I will not let you go, unless you bless me." Said the other, "What is your name?" He replied, "Jacob." Said he, "Your name shall no longer be Jacob, but Israel, for you have striven with beings divine and human, and have prevailed." Jacob asked, "Pray tell me your name." But he said, "You must not ask my name!" And he took leave of him there. So Jacob named the place Peniel, meaning, "I have seen a divine being face to face, yet my life has been preserved." The sun rose upon him as he passed Penuel, limping on his hip.

The anonymous narrator or later editor then adds his own legal gloss to the text of Genesis.

That is why the children of Israel to this day do not eat the thigh muscle that is on the socket of the hip, since Jacob's hip socket was wrenched at the thigh muscle. (Genesis 32:22–32)

24. The Descendants of Jacob

Now the sons of Jacob were twelve in number. The sons of Leah: Reuben—Jacob's firstborn—Simeon, Levi, Judah, Issachar, and Zebulun. The sons of Rachel: Joseph and Benjamin. The sons of Bilhah, Rachel's maid: Dan and Naphtali. And the sons of Zilpah, Leah's maid: Gad and Asher. These are the sons of Jacob who were born to him in Paddan-aram.

And Jacob came to his father Isaac at Mamre, at Kiriath-arba, now Hebron, where Abraham and Isaac had sojourned. Isaac was a hundred and eighty years old when he breathed his last and died. He was gathered to his kin in ripe old age, and he was buried by his sons his sons Esau and Jacob. (Genesis 35:23–29)

In the years that follow, Jacob and his offspring, the "Children of Israel," migrate into Egypt, where they serve the Pharaoh and where Joseph rises to high position at the royal court.

Thus Israel settled in the country of Egypt, in the region of Goshen; they acquired holdings in it, and were fertile and increased greatly.

Jacob lived seventeen years in the land of Egypt, so that the span of Jacob's life came to one hundred and forty-seven years. And when the time approached for Israel to die, he summoned his son Joseph to him, "Do me this favor, place your hand under my thigh as a pledge of your steadfast loyalty: please do not bury me in Egypt. When I lie down with my fathers, take me up from Egypt and bury me in their burial place." He replied, "I will do as you have spoken." And he said, "Swear to me." And he swore to him. Then Israel bowed at the head of the bed. (Genesis 47:27–31)

So it was done. Jacob was embalmed in the Egyptian manner and then taken for burial.

"In the cave which is in the field of Ephron the Hittite, the cave which is in the field of Machpelah, facing Mamre, in the land of Canaan, the field that Abraham bought from Ephron the Hittite for a burial site— there Abraham and his wife Sarah were buried; there Isaac and his wife Rebekah were buried; and there I buried Leah." (Genesis 49:29–31)

The blissful period of the vizirate of Joseph in Egypt did not last, however.

Joseph died, and all his brothers, and all that generation. But the Israelites were fertile and prolific; they multiplied and increased very greatly, so that the land was filled with them.

A new king arose over Egypt, who did not know Joseph. And he said to his people, "Look, the Israelite people are much too numerous for us. Let us deal shrewdly with them, so that they may not increase; otherwise in the event of war they may join our enemies in fighting against us and rise from the ground." So they set taskmasters over them to oppress them with forced labor; and they built garrison cities for Pharaoh: Pithom and

Raamses. But the more they were oppressed, the more they increased and spread out, so that the [Egyptians] came to dread the Israelites.

The Egyptians ruthlessly imposed upon the Israelites the various labors that they made them perform. Ruthlessly they made life bitter for them with harsh labor at mortar and bricks and with all sorts of tasks in the field. (Exodus 1:6–14)

25. Moses in Egypt

A long time after that, the king of Egypt died. The Israelites were groaning under the bondage and cried out; and their cry for help from the bondage rose up to God. God heard their moaning, and God remembered His covenant with Abraham and Isaac and Jacob. God looked upon the Israelites, and God took notice of them. (Exodus 2:23–25)

God's chosen instrument for the liberation of Israel from Egypt was Moses, a descendant of Levi who had been adopted and raised at the Pharaoh's court.

Now Moses, tending the flock of his father-in-law Jethro, the priest of Midian, drove the flock into the wilderness, and came to Horeb, the mountain of God. An angel of the Lord appeared to him in a blazing fire out of a bush. He gazed, and there was a bush all aflame, yet the bush was not consumed. When the Lord saw that he had turned aside to look, God called to him out of the bush: "Moses! Moses!" He answered, "Here I am." And He said, "Do not come closer. Remove your sandals from your feet, for the place on which you stand is holy ground. I am," He said, "the God of your father, the God of Abraham, the God of Isaac, and the God of Jacob." And Moses hid his face, for he was afraid to look at God.

And the Lord continued, "I have marked well the plight of My people in Egypt and have heeded their outcry because of their taskmasters; yes, I am mindful of their sufferings. I have come down to rescue them from the Egyptians and to bring them out of that land to a good and spacious land, a land flowing with milk and honey, the home of the Canaanites, the Hittites, the Amorites, the Perizzites, the Hivites, and the Jebusites. Now the cry of the Israelites has reached Me; moreover, I have seen how the Egyptians oppress them. Come, therefore, I will send you to the Pharaoh, and you shall free My people, the Israelites, from Egypt."

Moses said to God, "When I come to the Israelites and say to them 'The God of your fathers has sent me to you,' and they ask me, 'What is His name?' what shall I say to them?" And God said to Moses, "Ehyeh-Asher-Ehyeh" [possibly, "I Am That I Am"]. He continued, "Thus shall you say to the Israelites, 'Ehyeh sent me to you.' " And God said further to Moses, "Thus shall you speak to the Israelites: The Lord, the God of your fathers, the God of Abraham, the God of Isaac, and the God of Jacob, has sent me to you:

> This shall be My name forever,
> This My appellation for all eternity.

Go and assemble the elders of Israel and say to them: the Lord, the God of your fathers, the God of Abraham, Isaac, and Jacob, has appeared to me and said, 'I have taken note of you and of what is being done to you in Egypt, and I have declared: I will take you out of the misery of Egypt.' " (Exodus 3:1–35)

Moses has little success with his fellow Israelites, and even less with the Pharaoh.

Afterward Moses and Aaron went and said to Pharaoh, "Thus says the Lord, the God of Israel: Let My people go that they may celebrate a festival for Me in the wilderness." But Pharaoh said, "Who is the Lord that I should heed Him and let Israel go?" (Exodus 5:1–2)

The Lord said to Moses and Aaron, "When Pharaoh speaks to you and says, 'Produce your marvel,' you shall say to Aaron, 'Take your rod and cast it down before Pharaoh.' It shall turn into a serpent." So Moses and Aaron came before Pharaoh and did just as the Lord had commanded: Aaron cast down his rod in the presence of Pharaoh and his courtiers, and it turned into a serpent. Then Pharaoh, for his part, summoned the wise men and the sorcerers; and the Egyptian magicians, in turn, did the same with their spells: each cast down his rod, and they turned into serpents. But Aaron's rod swallowed their rods. Yet Pharaoh's heart stiffened and he did not heed them, as the Lord had said. (Exodus 7:8–13)

The Pharaoh must be persuaded, and so the Lord sends a series of plagues and portents upon the Land of Egypt (Exod. 7:14–10:29). The Pharaoh is frightened but unmoved. Then comes the final, crushing punishment.

Moses said, "Thus says the Lord: Toward midnight I will go forth among the Egyptians, and every first-born in the land of Egypt shall die, from the first-born of Pharaoh who sits on his throne to the first-born of the slave girl who is behind the millstones; and all the first-born of the cattle. And there shall be a loud cry in all the land of Egypt, such as had never been or will ever be again; but not a dog shall snarl at any of the Israelites, at man or beast—in order that you may know that the Lord makes a distinction between Egypt and Israel." (Exodus 11:4–7)

The Israelites, forewarned, ate a hasty late-night meal, the prototype of the later Passover (Exod. 12:1–27), and fled the land of Egypt. Four hundred and thirty years of slavery were over.

26. Moses and the Pharaoh in the Quran

The story of Moses' confrontation with the Pharaoh in Egypt is one of the most often repeated biblical tales in the Quran. It was a marvelous story, surely, filled with wonders, but it also emphasized a point on which Muhammad felt strongly: the punishment reserved for those who disbelieve and mistreat God's prophets. This is one of the later Quranic versions of the story.

(After these apostles) . . . We sent Moses with Our miracles to Pharaoh and his nobles, who acted unjustly in their regard. See then the end of the authors of evil. And Moses said, "O Pharaoh, I have been sent by the Lord of all the worlds; I am duty bound to speak nothing of God but the truth. I have brought from your Lord a clear sign; so let the people of Israel depart with me." He said, "If you brought a sign, then display it, if what you say is true."

At this Moses threw down his staff and lo, it became a live serpent. And he drew forth his hand, and behold, it looked white to those who beheld it. The nobles of the Pharaoh said: "He surely is a clever magician. He wishes to drive you away from your land." "So what do you advise?" They said: "Put him and his brother off awhile, and send out heralds to the cities to bring all the wise magicians to you."

The magicians came to Pharaoh. They said, "Is there a reward for us if we succeed?" "Yes," he said, "you will be among the honored." So they said. "O Moses, you may cast your spell first, or we shall cast ours." "You cast it first," answered Moses. When they cast their spell, they bewitched the eyes of the people and petrified them by conjuring up a great charm.

We said to Moses, "Throw down your staff," and it swallowed up their conjurations in no time. Thus the truth was upheld and the falsehood that they practiced was exposed. Thus there and then they were vanquished and overthrown, humiliated. The sorcerers fell to the ground in homage and said; "We have come to believe in the Lord of the worlds, the Lord of Moses and Aaron. . . ."

Then the leaders of Pharaoh's people said to him: "Will you allow Moses and his people to create disorder in the land and discard you and your gods?" He said, "We shall now slay their sons and spare their women, and subdue them." Moses said to his people: "Invoke the help of

God and be firm. The earth belongs to God, He can make whom He wills among His creatures inherit it. The future is theirs who take heed for themselves." "We were oppressed," they said, "before you came to us and since you have come to us." He answered: "It may be well that God will soon destroy your enemy and make you inherit the land, and then see how you behave."

Already We afflicted the people of Pharaoh with famine and the dearth of everything that they might take heed. Yet, when good came their way, they said, "It is our due," but when misfortune befell them, they put the omen down to Moses and those who were with him. But surely the omen was with God, yet most of them did not understand. They said: "Whatsoever the sign you have brought us, we shall not believe in you."

So We let loose on them floods and locusts, and vermin and frogs and blood—how many different signs. But they still remained arrogant, for they were a people full of sin.

Yet when punishment overtook them, they said, "O Moses, invoke your God for us as you have been enjoined. If the torment is removed, we shall certainly believe in you and let the People of Israel go with you." But no sooner was the punishment withdrawn for a time to enable them to make good their promise than they broke it. So we took vengeance on them and drowned them in the sea for rejecting Our signs and not heeding them. (Quran 7:103–136)

27. Paul Interprets the Exodus

After escaping across the parted waters of the Red Sea, which engulfed the pursuing Egyptians, the Israelites wandered for forty years in the wilderness of Sinai, now saved from starvation by the Lord, now chastised for their lapses into idolatry and infidelity to the Covenant. This is how the Christian Paul read the major events— and the lessons—of the Exodus.

You should understand, my brothers, that our ancestors were all under the pillar of cloud, and all of them passed through the Red Sea; and so they all received baptism into the fellowship of Moses in cloud and sea. They all ate the same supernatural food [that is, the manna in the desert], and all drank the same supernatural drink; I mean, they all drank from the supernatural rock that accompanied their travels [cf. Exod. 17:6]—and that rock was Christ. And yet most of them were not accepted by God, for the desert was strewn with their corpses.

These events happened as symbols to warn us not to set our desires on evil things, as they did. Do not be idolaters, like some of them; as Scripture has it, "the people sat down to feast and rose up to revel." Let us not commit fornication, as some of them did—and twenty-three thousand died on one day [Num. 25:9]. Let us not put the power of the Lord to the test, as some of them did—and were destroyed by serpents [cf. Num. 21:6]. Do not grumble against God, as some of them did—and were destroyed by the Destroyer [cf. Num. 16:49]. All these things that happened to them were symbolic and were recorded for our benefit as a warning. For upon us the fulfillment of the ages has come. (Paul, *To the Corinthians* 1.10:1–11)

28. Biblical Miracles

The miraculous feeding of the Israelites with manna and the supply of water from a rock struck by Moses' staff, Paul read typologically as Christ—perhaps by implication as a foreshadowing of the Eucharist (cf. John 6:30). His Alexandrian contemporary Philo, another Hellenized Jew of the Diaspora, used the same events as an occasion to give his views on miracles.

Though this supply of food never failed and continued to be enjoyed in abundance, a serious scarcity of water again occurred. Sore-pressed by this, their mood turned to desperation, whereupon Moses, taking the sacred staff with which he accomplished the signs in Egypt, under inspiration smote the steep rock with it. It may be the rock contained originally a spring and now had its artery clean severed, or perhaps then for the first time a body of water collected in it through hidden channels was forced out by the impact. Whichever is the case, it opened under the violence of the stream and spouted out its contents.

Philo was aware, then, that apparent miracles were subject to rationalization. That was not the interpretation he chose however.

If anyone disbelieves these things, he neither knows God nor has ever sought to know Him; for if he did, he would at once have perceived, yes, perceived with a firm apprehension, that these extraordinary and seemingly incredible events are but child's play to God. He has but to turn his eyes to things which are really great and worthy of his earnest contemplation: the creation of heaven and the rhythmic movements of the planets and the fixed stars; the light that shines upon us from the sun by day and from the moon by night ... the yearly seasons with their well-marked diversities and other beauties innumerable. He who should wish to describe the several parts, or rather any one of the cardinal parts of the universe, would find life too short, even if his years were prolonged beyond those of all other men. But these things, though truly marvelous, are held in little account because they are familiar. Not so with the unfamiliar; though they be but small matters, we give way before what seems so strange and, drawn by their novelty, regard them with amazement. (Philo, *Life of Moses* 1.210–213)

29. The Death of Moses

For all the services he rendered to the Lord and for all the privileges granted to him, including the reception of the tablets of the Law on Sinai and an extraordinary vision of God, Moses was not destined to enter the Land of the Promise to which he had led his and God's people.

Moses went up from the steppes of Moab to Mount Nebo, to the summit of Pisgah, opposite Jericho, and the Lord showed him the whole land: Gilead as far as Dan; all Naphtali; the land of Ephraim and Manasseh; the whole land of Judah as far as the Western Sea; the Negeb; and the Plain—the Valley of Jericho, the city of palm trees—as far as Zoar. And the Lord said to him, "This is the land of which I swore to Abraham, Isaac, and Jacob, 'I will give it to your offspring.' I have let you see it with your own eyes, but you shall not cross there."

And then his death, or his presumed death.

So Moses the servant of the Lord died there, in the land of Moab, at the command of the Lord. He buried him in the valley in the land of Moab, near Beth-peor; and no one knows his burial place to this day. Moses was a hundred and twenty years old when he died; his eyes were undimmed and his vigor unabated. And the Israelites bewailed Moses in the steppes of Moab for thirty days.

The period of wailing and mourning for Moses came to an end. Now Joshua son of Nun was filled with the spirit of wisdom because Moses had laid his hands upon him; and the Israelites heeded him, doing as the Lord had commanded Moses.

Never again did there arise in Israel a prophet like Moses whom the Lord singled out, face to face, for the various signs and portents that the Lord sent to him to display in the land of Egypt, against Pharaoh and all his courtiers and his whole country, and for all the great might and awesome power that Moses displayed before all Israel. (Deuteronomy 34:1–12)

30. The Promised Land:
The Covenant Recalled and Renewed

We resume the narrative at a point late in the life of Moses' successor, Joshua, the son of Nun, when the Israelites were already in possession of substantial parts of the land that had been promised to them.

Much later, after the Lord had given Israel rest from all the enemies around them, and when Joshua was old and well advanced in years, Joshua summoned all Israel, their elders and commanders, their magistrates and officials, and said to them: "I have grown old and am advanced in years. You have seen all that the Lord your God has done to all those nations on your account, for it was the Lord your God who fought for you. See, I have allotted to you, by your tribes, (the territory of) these nations that still remain, and that of all the nations that I have destroyed, from the Jordan to the Mediterranean Sea in the west. The Lord your God Himself will thrust them out on your account and drive them out to make way for you, and you shall occupy their land as the Lord your God promised you."

That was the Lord's part of the Covenant. The Israelites are then instructed on their responsibilities.

But be most resolute to observe faithfully all that is written in the book of the Teaching of Moses, without ever deviating from it to the right or to the left, and without intermingling with these nations which are left among you. Do not utter the names of their gods or swear by them; do not serve them or bow down to them. But hold fast to the Lord your God as you have done to this day.

The Lord has driven out great, powerful nations on your account, and not a man has withstood you to this day. A single man of you would put a thousand to flight, for the Lord your God Himself has been fighting for you, as He promised you. For your own sakes, therefore, be most mindful to love the Lord your God. For should you turn away and attach yourselves to the remnant of those nations—to those that are left among you—and intermarry with them, you joining them and they joining you, know for certain that the Lord your God will not continue to drive these nations out before you. (Joshua 23:1–13)

In the wake of this pointed reminder from the Lord, Joshua assembled at Shechem all the tribes of Israel and their leaders for a formal ceremony of renewal. After recalling all the events that had befallen them from the days of Abraham to the present, Joshua continues.

Now, therefore, revere the Lord and serve Him with undivided loyalty; put away the gods that your forefathers served beyond the Euphrates and in Egypt, and serve the Lord. Or, if you are loath to serve the Lord, choose this day which ones you are going to serve—the gods that your forefathers served beyond the Euphrates, or those of the Amorites in whose land you are settled; but I and my household will serve the Lord."

In reply, the people declared, "Far be it from us to forsake the Lord and serve other gods! For it was the Lord our God who brought us and our fathers up from the land of Egypt, the house of bondage, and who wrought those wondrous signs before our very eyes, and guarded us all along the way that we traveled and among all the peoples through whose midst we passed. And then the Lord drove out before us all the peoples—the Amorites—that inhabited the country. We too will serve the Lord, for He is our God."

Joshua, however, said to the people, "You will not be able to serve the Lord, for He is a holy God. He is a jealous God; He will not forgive your transgressions and your sins. If you forsake the Lord and serve alien gods, He will turn and deal harshly with you and make an end of you, after having been gracious to you." But the people replied to Joshua, "No we will serve the Lord!' Thereupon Joshua said to the people, "You are witnesses against yourselves that you have by your own act chosen to serve the Lord." "Yes, we are!" they responded. "Then put away the alien gods that you have among you and direct your hearts to the Lord, the God of Israel." And the people declared to Joshua, "We will serve none but the Lord our God and we will obey none but Him."

On that day at Shechem, Joshua made a covenant for the people and he made a fixed rule for them. Joshua recorded all this in a book of divine instruction. He took a great stone and set it up at the foot of the oak in the sacred precinct of the Lord; and Joshua said to all the people, "See, this very stone shall be a witness against us, for it heard all the words that the Lord spoke to us; it shall be a witness against you, lest you break faith with your God." Joshua then dismissed the people to their allotted portions. (Joshua 24:14–28)

31. Saul: A King for Israel

The Israelites conquered the Land of the Promise as a tribal confederation and for many generations continued to live under that form of loose confederacy, with occasional leaders called "Judges" arising as opportunity presented or crisis de-

manded. In this settled land of settled peoples other models of government presented
themselves, and eventually the people demanded a king. According to the biblical
account, the request was granted only reluctantly by the Lord, whose choice fell
upon Saul, "a young man in his prime; there was no better man among the Israelites
than he. He was a head taller than any of his fellows" (1 Sam. 9:2). The Lord
communicated His will to Samuel.

Now the day before Saul came, the Lord had revealed the following
to Samuel: "At this time tomorrow, I will send a man to you from the
territory of Benjamin, and you shall anoint him ruler of My people Israel.
He will deliver My people from the hands of the Philistines; for I have
taken note of My people, their outcry has come to Me." (1 Samuel 9:
15–17)

Samuel took a flask of oil and poured some on Saul's head and kissed
him, and said, "The Lord herewith anoints you ruler over His own people." (1 Samuel 10:1)

And Samuel said to the people, "Do you see the one whom the Lord
had chosen? There is none like him among all the people." And all the
people acclaimed him, shouting, "Long live the king!"

Samuel expounded to the people the rules of the monarchy and
recorded them in a document which he deposited before the Lord.
Samuel then sent the people back to their homes. (1 Samuel 10:24–25)

32. "Obedience Is Better Than Sacrifice"

Saul ruled as king over Israel for twenty-two years, but he did not enjoy divine favor
to the end. The Lord had commanded him to destroy the neighboring Amelekites
utterly, "men and women, children and babes in arms, herds and flocks, camels and
asses" (1 Sam. 15:3). The people were not spared, as commanded, but Saul kept
the flocks and herds. God's reaction followed swiftly.

The word of the Lord then came to Samuel: "I regret that I made
Saul king, for he has turned away from Me and has not carried out My
commands." Samuel was distressed and he entreated the Lord all night
long. Early in the morning Samuel went to meet Saul. Samuel was told,
"Saul went to Carmel, where he erected a monument for himself; then
he left and went on down to Gilgal."

When Samuel came to Saul, Saul said to him, "Blessed are you of the
Lord! I have fulfilled the Lord's command." "Then what," demanded
Samuel, "is this bleating of sheep in my ears, and the lowing of oxen that
I hear?" Saul answered, "They were brought from the Amelekites, for the

troops spared the choicest of the sheep and oxen for sacrificing to the Lord your God. And we proscribed the rest." Samuel said to Saul, "Stop! Let me tell you what the Lord said to me last night!" "Speak!" he replied. And Samuel said, "You may look small to yourself, but you are the head of the tribes of Israel. The Lord anointed you king over Israel, and the Lord sent you on a mission, saying, 'Go and proscribe the sinful Amelekites; make war on them until you have exterminated them.' Why did you disobey the Lord and swoop down on the spoil in defiance of the Lord's will?" Saul said to Samuel, "But I did obey the Lord! I performed the mission on which the Lord sent me: I captured King Agag of Amalek, and I proscribed Amalek, and the troops took from the spoil some sheep and oxen—the best of what had been proscribed—to sacrifice to the Lord your God at Gilgal." But Samuel said:

> "Does the Lord delight in burnt offerings and sacrifices
> As much as in obedience to the Lord's command?
> Surely, obedience is better than sacrifice,
> Compliance than the fat of rams.
> For rebellion is like the sin of divination,
> Defiance, like the iniquity of teraphim.
> Because you rejected the Lord's command,
> He has rejected you as king."

. . . But Samuel said to him, "The Lord has this day torn the kingship over Israel away from you and has given it to another who is worthier than you." (1 Samuel 15:10–28)

33. David, King of Israel

The better man was David, a young shepherd of the family of Jesse in Bethlehem. He was anointed by Samuel at God's own command in a private ceremony (1 Sam. 16:12–13) and thereafter began a spectacular rise as a warrior for Israel against the Philistines. Saul soon took notice and attempted to kill the man he had already identified as his rival. David fled, and even after Saul and his three sons were slain by the Philistines at Mount Gilboa, David still had to contend with Abner, Saul's chief commander, and other supporters of the house of Saul. There was a civil war, and only when Abner and his forces were defeated was David, then ruling at Hebron, acknowledged as king by all the Israelites.

All the tribes of Israel come to David at Hebron and said, "We are your own flesh and blood. Long before now, when Saul was king over us, it was you who led Israel in war; and the Lord said to you: You shall shepherd My people Israel; you shall be ruler of Israel." All the elders of Israel came to the king at Hebron, and King David made a pact with them in Hebron before the Lord. And they anointed David king over Israel.

David was thirty years old when he became king, and he reigned forty years. In Hebron he reigned over all Israel and Judah thirty-three years. (2 Samuel 5:1–5)

34. The Ark Installed in Jerusalem

After his consecration as king over all the Israelites, David captured the Jebusite city of Jerusalem not far from Hebron, an event noted almost casually in the second book of Samuel.

. . . David captured the stronghold and renamed it the City of David; David also fortified the surrounding area, from the Millo inward. David kept growing stronger, for the Lord, the God of Hosts, was with him. (2 Samuel 5:7–10)

In the biblical narrative far more attention is given to another, more pregnant event in the history of David and Jerusalem: the transfer of the Ark of the Covenant to the king's new capital. The first attempt to move it there was stymied by an accident, and the arrival of the Ark was delayed for three months. The Ark meanwhile rested in the house of Obed-edom, a man of Gath in Philistia.

It was reported to King David: "The Lord has blessed Obed-edom's house and all that belongs to him because of the Ark of God." Thereupon David went and brought up the Ark of God from the house of Obed-edom to the City of David, amid rejoicing. When the bearers of the Ark of the Lord had moved forward six paces, he sacrificed an ox and a fatling. David whirled with all his might before the Lord; David was girt with a linen ephod. Thus David and all the House of Israel brought up the Ark of the Lord with shouts and with blasts of the horn.

As the Ark of the Lord entered the City of David, Michal daughter of Saul looked out of the window and saw King David leaping and whirling before the Lord; and she despised him for it.

They brought in the Ark of the Lord and set it up in its place inside the tent which David had pitched for it, and David sacrificed burnt offerings and offerings of well-being before the Lord. When David finished sacrificing the burnt offerings of well-being, he blessed the people in the name of the Lord of Hosts. And he distributed among all the people—the entire multitude of Israel, man and woman alike—a loaf of bread, a cake made in a pan, and a raisin cake. (2 Samuel 6:12–19)

35. The Establishment of the House of David

When the king was settled in his palace and the Lord had granted him safety from all the enemies around him, the king said to the prophet Nathan: "Here I am dwelling in a house of cedar, while the Ark of the Lord abides in a tent!" Nathan said to the king, "Go and do whatever you have in mind, for the Lord is with you."

But that same night the word of the Lord came to Nathan: "Go and say to my servant David: Thus said the Lord: Are you the one to build a house for Me to dwell in? From the day that I brought the People of Israel out of Egypt to this day I have not dwelt in a house, but have moved about in Tent and Tabernacle. As I moved about wherever the Israelites went, did I ever reproach any of the tribal leaders whom I appointed to care for My people of Israel: Why have you not built Me a house of cedar?"

. . . "When your days are done and you lie with your fathers, I will raise up your offspring after you, one of your own issue, and I will establish his kingship. He shall build a house for My name, and I will establish his royal throne forever." (2 Samuel 7:1–13)

36. The Threshing Floor on Mount Moriah

David, now filled with assurance, determines to take a census of his people, this despite God's warning that he should not do so.

But afterward David reproached himself for having numbered the people. And David said to the Lord, "I have sinned grievously in what I have done. Please, O Lord, remit the guilt of your servant, for I have acted foolishly."

The Lord sends a pestilence upon Israel as a punishment for David's folly. Seventy thousand people die.

But when the angel extended his hand against Jerusalem to destroy it, the Lord renounced further punishment and said to the angel who was destroying the people, "Enough! Stay your hand!" The angel of the Lord was then by the threshing floor of Araunah the Jebusite.

When David saw the angel who was striking down the people, he said to the Lord, "I alone am guilty, I alone have done wrong; but these poor sheep, what have they done? Let your hand fall upon me and my father's house!"

Gad [the seer of David] came to David the same day and said to him,
"Go and set up an altar to the Lord on the threshing floor of Araunah the
Jebusite." David went up, following Gad's instructions, as the Lord had
commanded. Araunah looked out and saw the king and his courtiers
approaching him. So Araunah went out and bowed low to the king, with
his face to the ground. And Araunah asked, "Why has my lord the king
come to his servant?" David replied, "To buy the threshing floor from
you, that I may build an altar to the Lord and that the plague against my
people may be checked." And Araunah said to David, "Let my lord the
king take it and offer up whatever he sees fit. Here are oxen for a burnt
offering, and the threshing boards and the gear of the oxen for wood. All
this, O king, Araunah gives to Your Majesty. And may the Lord your
God," Araunah added, "respond to you with favor!" But the king replied
to Araunah, "No, I will buy them from you at a price. I cannot sacrifice
to the Lord my God burnt offerings that have cost me nothing." So David
bought the threshing floor and the oxen for fifty shekels of silver. And
David built there an altar to the Lord and sacrificed burnt offerings and
offerings of well-being. The Lord responded to the plea for the land, and
the plague against Israel was checked. (2 Samuel 24:10–25)

*There is nothing in this account to suggest that we have to do here with anything
more than a simple threshing ground that was rendered holy by a secondary act of
divine providence that had occurred there—secondary in the sense that God had not
manifested Himself but rather that the sword of His avenging angel was stayed in
that place. David built an altar there, and as we shall see, that otherwise unnote-
worthy Jebusite threshing floor at the highest point of Mount Moriah became the
site and center of the principal and then the unique Jewish sanctuary in the land
of Israel.*

37. Solomon and the Temple

*Apparently David had more royal and elaborate plans for that place atop Mount
Moriah in Jerusalem than the erection of a mere altar. The narrative in 2 Samuel
suggests a Davidic temple and then turns aside to other matters. The parallel
account in the books called Chronicles, where Araunah is called Ornan, is both
specific and detailed.*

At that time, when David saw that the Lord had answered him at the
threshing floor of Ornan the Jebusite, then he sacrificed there—for the
tabernacle of the Lord, which Moses had made in the wilderness, and the
altar of burnt offerings, were at that time in the shrine at Gibeon, and

David was unable to go to it to worship the Lord because he was terrified by the sword of the angel of the Lord. David said, "Here will be the House of the Lord and here the altar of burnt offerings for Israel."

David gave orders to assemble the aliens living in the land of Israel, and assigned them to be hewers, to quarry and dress stones for building the house of God. Much iron for nails for the doors of the gates and for clasps did David lay aside, and so much copper it could not be weighed, and cedar logs without number—for the Sidonian and the Tyrians brought many cedar logs to David.

For David thought, "My son Solomon is an untried youth, and the House to be built for the Lord is to be made exceedingly great to win fame and glory throughout all the lands; let me then lay aside material for him." So David laid aside much material before he died. (1 Chronicles 21:28–22:5)

David gave his son Solomon the plan of the porch and its houses, its storerooms and its upper chambers and inner chambers; and of the place of the Ark-cover; and the plan of all that he had by the spirit: of the courts of the House of the Lord and all its surrounding chambers. . . . "All this that the Lord made me understand by His hand on me, I give to you in writing—the plan of all the works." (1 Chronicles 28:11–19)

By this account, then, it was David himself who, under the guidance of the Lord, drew up the plans for the Temple that was to rise on the summit of the eastern hill of Jerusalem. But like Moses detained from entering the Land of Promise, it was reserved for another to build the House of the Lord, David's son Solomon.

38. The Wisdom of Solomon

Solomon was noted for far more than the construction of the Temple in the later traditions of the Jews, Christians, and Muslims. He personified wisdom and mastery of the practical arts, some of them indeed beyond ordinary human competence. This is how the king appeared in the eyes of the medieval Jewish scholar Nachmanides (d. ca. 1270 C.E.).

King Solomon, peace be upon him, whom the Lord had given wisdom and knowledge, derived it all from the Torah, and from it he studied until he knew the secret of all things created, even of the forces and characteristics of plants, so that he wrote even a Book of Medicine, as it is written, "And he spoke of trees, from the cedar that is in Lebanon to the hyssop that springs out of the wall" (1 Kings 5:13).

The Jewish tradition did in fact credit a number of works to Solomon, including the canonical Book of Proverbs and a noncanonical "Wisdom of Solomon," which Nach-manides refers to next.

Now I have seen the Aramaic translation of the book called "The Great Wisdom of Solomon," and in it is written: ". . . It is the Lord alone who gives knowledge that contains no falsehood, (enabling one) to know how the world arose, the composition of the constellations, the begin-ning, the end and the middle of times, the angles at the ends of the constellations, and how the seasons are produced by the movement of the heavens and the fixed positions of the stars, the benign nature of cattle and the fierceness of wild beasts, the power of the wind and the thoughts of man, the relationship of trees and the powers of roots; everything hidden and everything revealed I know."

All this Solomon knew from the Torah, and he found everything in it—in its simple meanings, in the subtleties of its expressions and its letters and strokes. . . .

Scripture likewise relates concerning him, "And Solomon's wisdom excelled the wisdom of all the children of the East and all the wisdom of Egypt" (1 Kings 5:10). That is to say, he was better versed than they in divination and enchanting, for this was their wisdom, as it is said, "For they are replenished from the East, and with soothsayers like the Philis-tines" (Isa. 2:6). What was the wisdom of the children of the East? They knew and were crafty in the divination of birds. "And all the wisdom of Egypt" means that Solomon was better versed in sorcery, which is the wisdom of Egypt and the nature of growing things. As is known from the Book of Egyptian Agriculture, the Egyptians were very well versed in the matter of planting and grafting different species. Thus the Sages have said: "Solomon even planted peppers in the Land of Israel. How was he able to plant them? Solomon was a wise man, and he knew the essence of the foundation of the world. Why was this? It is written, 'Out of Sion, the perfected of beauty, the Lord has shone forth' (Ps. 50:2). Out of Sion the whole world was perfected. How is this known? Why (else) was it called 'the Stone of Foundation'? Because the world was founded from it. Now Solomon knew which of its arteries extended to Ethiopia, and upon it he planted peppers, and immediately it produced fruits, for so he says, 'And I planted trees in them of all kinds of fruits' (Eccles. 2:5)." (Nachmanides, *Commentary on Genesis*) [NACHMANIDES 1971:12–13]

Solomon is mentioned more than once in the Quran, including a long passage (Quran 27:15–44) describing an encounter between the Israelite king and the queen of Saba or Sheba in the Yemen. Invariably in the Muslim sources, as in the Jewish ones, Solomon is depicted as possessing extraordinary power, though with a somewhat different implication regarding its source, since for the Muslims his power included control over the jinn, those preternaturally gifted spirits who stand just below the angels in God's creation and are often associated with the magical arts, as was Solomon himself. It was the jinn, for example, who assisted Solomon in building the Temple in Jerusalem, as these verses of the Quran appear to reflect.

We (subjugated) the wind to Solomon. Its morning journey took one month, and its evening one month. We made a spring of molten brass to flow for him; and many *jinns* labored for him by the will of his Lord. Any one of them who turned from Our command was made to taste the torment of blazing fire. They made for him whatever he wished, synagogues and statues, dishes large as water troughs, and cauldrons firmly fixed (on ovens); and We said: "O house of David, act and give thanks. But few among My creatures are thankful." (Quran 34:12–13)

With this provocative Quranic portrait before them, the later Muslim commentators supplied many additional details, like these on the seal and ring of Solomon.

Ibn Ishaq says that when Solomon died the satans wrote different kinds of magic in a book, which they then sealed with a seal similar Solomon's. On the cover they wrote, "This is what Asaf ibn Barkhiya the prophet wrote for King Solomon." The book was then buried under Solomon's throne, and when the Jews later discovered it, they claimed that Solomon was a magician. Another tradition handed down on the authority of Ibn Ishaq asserts that God deprived Solomon of his kingship and immediately groups of both men and *jinn* apostatized. When, however, God returned the kingship to him, they returned once again to the true faith. Then Solomon collected all the books of magic and buried them under his throne. Satan later brought them out, and it was thought that these books had been sent down by God to Solomon. Thus they followed these books, claiming that they were Scripture. (Tabari, *Commentary* on Quran 2:102)

Solomon was the focus of many legendary stories in Islam, which, as one Quranic expert said, "God alone knows best whether they are true." True or not, they were popular. In this one, for example, Solomon kills the king of Sidon and then takes his daughter, named Jarada, to wife. Jarada professed her belief in the One True God, "and Solomon loved her." His new wife declined, however, into inconsolable grief for her dead father.

So Solomon ordered the satans to fashion an image of her father and dress it in his clothes. Jarada and her servants went and worshiped this

image every morning and evening, as was customary in her father's kingdom. When (his vizier) Asaf reported this to Solomon, the king ordered
the idol destroyed and he punished the woman. Then he went out to a
deserted place to be alone. Ashes were scattered before him and he sat
himself down on them, humiliating himself in penance before God.

On another occasion Solomon had a slave girl named Amina who
became a mother by him. Once, when he went out to purify himself or
to sleep with one of his wives, he entrusted Amina with the signet ring
in which his power lay. She had it for a whole day and then the satan who
lives in the sea came to her. This *jinn*, whose name was Sakhr, and who
had proved useful to Solomon in the building of the Temple, came to her
in the form of Solomon himself and said to her, "Amina, give me my
signet ring!" Then he put the ring on his finger and sat down on Solomon's throne. This ring placed under his command the birds, the *jinn* and
men. Also he changed the outward appearance of (the genuine) Solomon
so that when the latter came to Amina to get back his ring, she mistook
him for a stranger and drove him off.

Solomon . . . wandered among the houses as a beggar. Whenever he
said, "I am Solomon," people responded by throwing dirt at him and
reviling him. Then he went to the fishermen, who employed him to assist
them in the hauling in of fish; for this he was paid two fish a day. Solomon
remained in this condition for forty days, that is, for as long as idolatry
continued to be practiced in his house.

Asaf and the notables of Israel did not acknowledge the sovereignty
of the *jinn* [who had usurped Solomon's throne], but when Asaf questioned the wives of Solomon about (the impostor), they answered: "He
excuses none of us from sex when she is menstruating, nor does he purify
himself afterwards."

*The impostor is thus unmasked by his violation of the code of ritual purity. He
throws the signet ring of Solomon into the sea, where it is swallowed by a fish. The
fish comes into the hands of Solomon, the fishmongers' apprentice, who discovers
the ring and so regains his powers. The commentator concludes:*

Religious scholars reject such interpretations and claim that they
belong to the lying stories of the Jews. The *jinns* are incapable of such acts:
it is a thoroughly detestable notion that God should give the *jinn* such
power over His servants so that they could change the laws (for the
community), or that He should give them such power over the wives of
the Prophets so that they would commit adultery with them. It is true
that there might have been a different law for statues, since God did say

in the Quran, "The *jinn* made for Solomon whatever he wished—palaces, statues . . ." (Quran 34:13), but it is impossible to believe that God would permit his prophet to bow down before an idol. Should something take place (in Solomon's kingdom of which he is) unaware, then certainly he was not held responsible. (Zamakhshari, *Commentary* on Quran 38:34)

39. The House Divided: Judah and Israel

Immediately upon the death of Solomon, his splendid kingdom began to disintegrate. Solomon's foolish son Rehoboam managed to cling to the Judean patrimony, but the northern territories, called "Israel," fell into the hands of one who had already run afoul of Solomon: Jeroboam son of Nebat.

Rehoboam went to Shechem, for all Israel had come to Shechem to acclaim him as king. Jeroboam son of Nebat learned of it while he was still in Egypt; for Jeroboam had fled from King Solomon, and had settled in Egypt. They sent for him; and Jeroboam and all the assembly of Israel came and spoke to Rehoboam as follows: "Your father made our yoke heavy. Now lighten the harsh labor and the heavy yoke which your father laid on us, and we will serve you." (1 Kings 12:1–4)

When they returned, Rehoboam had his answer ready.

"My father made your yoke heavy, but I will add to your yoke; my father flogged you with whips, but I will flog you with scorpions. . . ."

When all Israel saw that the king had not listened to them, the people answered the king:

> "We have no portion in David,
> No share in Jesse's son!
> To your tents, O Israel!
> Now look to your own House, O David."

So the Israelites returned to their homes. But Rehoboam continued to reign over the Israelites who lived in the towns of Judah.

King Rehoboam sent Adoram, who was in charge of the forced labor, but all Israel pelted him to death with stones. Thereupon King Rehoboam hurriedly mounted his chariot and fled to Jerusalem. Thus Israel revolted against the House of David, as is still the case.

When all Israel heard that Jeroboam had returned, they sent messengers and summoned him to the assembly and made him king over all Israel. Only the tribe of Judah remained loyal to the House of David. (1 Kings 12:14–20)

Thus a political schism occurred in the body of Israel. It was compounded by an overt abrogation of the Covenant, what the author of Kings calls "a sin in Israel."

Jeroboam fortified Shechem in the hill country of Ephraim and resided there; he moved out from there and fortified Penuel. Jeroboam said to himself, "Now the kingdom may well return to the House of David. If these people still go up to offer sacrifices at the House of the Lord in Jerusalem, the hearts of these people will turn back to their master, King Rehoboam of Judah; they will kill me and go back to King Rehoboam of Judah." So the king took counsel and made two golden calves. He said to the people, "You have been going up to Jerusalem long enough. This is your god, O Israel, who brought you up from the land of Egypt!" He set up one in Bethel and placed the other in Dan. That proved to be a cause of guilt. . . .

He stationed at Bethel the priests of the shrines that he had appointed to sacrifice to the calves which he had made. And Jeroboam established a festival on the fifteenth day of the eighth month; in imitation of the festival in Judah, he established one at Bethel, and he ascended the altar (there). On the fifteenth day of the eighth month—the month in which he had contrived of his own mind to establish a festival for the Israelites—Jeroboam ascended the altar which he had made in Bethel.

As he ascended the altar to present an offering, a man of God arrived at Bethel from Judah at the command of the Lord. While Jeroboam was standing on the altar to present the offering, the man of God, at the command of the Lord, cried out against the altar: "O altar, altar! Thus said the Lord: A son shall be born to the House of David, Josiah by name; and he shall slaughter upon you the priests of the shrines who bring offerings upon you. And human bones shall be burned upon you."

And the priestly authors of the books of the Kings do not hesitate to attach the moral:

Even after this incident, Jeroboam did not turn back from his evil way, but kept on appointing priests for the shrines from the ranks of the people. He ordained as priests of the shrines anyone who so desired. Thereby the House of Jeroboam incurred guilt—to their utter annihilation from the face of the earth. (1 Kings 12:25–13:34)

Nor was it in northern Israel alone that a breach of the Covenant occurred.

Meanwhile, Rehoboam son of Solomon had become king in Judah. Rehoboam was forty-one years old when he became king, and he reigned seventeen years in Jerusalem—the city the Lord had chosen out of all the tribes of Israel to establish His name there. His mother's name was Naa-mah the Ammonitess. Judah did what was displeasing to the Lord, and angered Him more than their fathers had done by the sins that they committed. They too built for themselves shrines, pillars, and sacred posts on every high hill and under every leafy tree; there were also male prostitutes in the land. (Judah) imitated all the abhorrent practices of the nations which the Lord had dispossessed before the Israelites.

In the fifth year of King Rehoboam, King Shishak of Egypt marched against Jerusalem and carried off the treasure of the House of the Lord and the treasures of the royal palace. He carried off everything; he even carried off all the golden shields that Solomon had made. (1 Kings 14: 21–26)

40. Years of Infidelity, Disaster, Waiting

The theodicy of the Israelite chroniclers is a straightforward one: if Israel sins through infidelity to the Covenant, Israel will be punished. Since the days of Jeroboam, the northern kingdom of Israel was a breeding ground for such infidelity. When God's punishment finally came, it came in the form of the Assyrians.

In the twelfth year of King Ahaz of Judah, Hoshea son of Elah became king over Israel in Samaria—for nine years. He did what was displeasing to the Lord, though not as much as the kings of Israel who preceded him. King Shalmaneser marched against him, and Hoshea be-came his vassal and paid him tribute. But the king of Assyria caught Hoshea in an act of treachery: he had sent envoys to King So of Egypt, and he had not paid the tribute of the king of Assyria, as in previous years. And the king of Assyria arrested him and put him in prison. Then the king of Assyria marched against the whole land; he came to Samaria and be-sieged it for three years. In the ninth year of Hoshea, the king of Assyria captured Samaria [721 B.C.E.]. He deported the Israelites to Assyria and settled them in Halah, at the (River) Habor, at the River Gozen, and in the towns of Media.

Viewed in the sight of the Lord, the southern kingdom of Judah was little better in its observance of the terms of the Covenant. Yet the Lord postponed His judgment on Judah, perhaps because a just king had at last come to the throne in Jerusalem.

In the third year of King Hoshea son of Elah of Israel, Hezekiah son of King Ahaz of Judah became king (in Judah). He was twenty-five years old when he became king, and he reigned in Jerusalem twenty-nine years.

. . . He did what was pleasing to the Lord, just as his father David had done. He abolished the shrines and smashed the pillars and cut down the sacred post. He also broke into pieces the bronze serpent which Moses had made [cf. Num. 21:4–9], for until that time the Israelites had been offering sacrifices to it; it was called Nehushtan. He trusted only in the Lord the God of Israel; there was none like him among all the kings of Judah after him, nor among those before him. (2 Kings 18:1–5)

Such was the reputation of Hezekiah that a millennium afterwards rabbis in Babylonia were discussing the question of whether in fact he had been the Messiah (see Chapter 2 below). According to 2 Kings, "the Lord was with him and he prospered in all that he undertook." What he undertook was to throw off the sovereignty of the king of Assyria, an act of defiance that brought the Assyrians not once but twice to the threshold of Jerusalem. On the first occasion Hezekiah submitted and averted calamity by the payment of large penalties. But the next time, in 701 B.C.E, the Lord had to intervene directly—it is one of the last times in the long history of the Israelites that such intervention occurs—against the Assyrians camped outside the walls of Jerusalem.

That night an angel of the Lord went out and struck down one hundred and eighty-five thousand in the Assyrian camp, and the following morning they were all dead corpses.

So King Sennacherib of Assyria broke camp and retreated, and stayed in Nineveh. (2 Kings 19:35–36)

The saintly Hezekiah was succeeded by his sin-laden son Manasseh, who possesses the blackest reputation in the entire annals of the kings of Israel.

Manasseh was twelve years old when he became king, and he reigned fifty-five years in Jerusalem. . . . He did what was displeasing to the Lord, following the abhorrent practices of the nations which the Lord had dispossessed before the Israelites. He rebuilt shrines which his father Hezekiah had destroyed; he erected altars for Baal and made a sacred post, as King Ahab of Israel had done. He bowed down to all the host of heaven and worshiped them, and he built altars for them in the House of the Lord, of which the Lord had said, "I will establish My name in Jerusalem." He built altars for all the hosts of heaven in the two courts of the House of the Lord. . . . The sculptured image of Asherah which he made, he placed in the House concerning which the Lord had said to David and to his son Solomon, "In this House and in Jerusalem, which I chose out of all the tribes of Israel, I will establish My name forever." (2 Kings 21:1–7)

41. The Reforms of Josiah

Now, if ever, the Lord's judgment should have come. But the theologically satisfying denouement of the destruction of Jerusalem that should have occurred during the fifty-five years of Manasseh's defilement of the city and the land was postponed once again, perhaps because of the presence of a just king, in this case Josiah (640–609 B.C.E.), the grandson of Manasseh, who "did right in the eyes of the Lord; he followed closely in the footsteps of his forefather David, swerving neither right nor left" (2 Kings 22:1–2). Well established in the eighteenth year of his rule, in 622 B.C.E. the king put his hand to the task and in the sequel brought about one of the momentous turning points in the history of Jewish cult practice.

Then the high priest Hilikiah said to the scribe Shaphan, "I have found a scroll of the Teaching in the House of the Lord." And Hilikiah gave the scroll to Shaphan, who read it. . . . The scribe Shaphan also told the king, "The high priest Hilikiah has given me a scroll"; and Shaphan read it to the king.

When the king heard the contents of the scroll of the Teaching, he rent his clothes. And the king gave orders to the priest Hilikiah, and to Ahikam son of Shaphan, Achbor son of Michaiah, the scribe Shaphan, and Saiah the king's minister: "Go, inquire of the Lord on my behalf, and on behalf of the people, and on behalf of all Judah, concerning the words of this scroll that has been found. For great indeed must be the wrath of the Lord that has been kindled against us, because our fathers did not obey the words of this scroll to do all that had been prescribed for us." (2 Kings 22:8–13)

The "book of the law" may have been the core of the one included in the Bible under the name of Deuteronomy, or "The Second Book of Law." The discovery was read as a divine signal for reform, a conclusion confirmed when king and minister consulted Huldah the prophetess "at her home in the Mishneh quarter of Jerusalem" (2 Kings 22:14). They were admonished that unless the terms of the Covenant are restored, God's wrath will descend upon the nation.

At the king's summons, all the elders of Judah and Jerusalem assembled before him. The king went up to the House of the Lord, together with all the men of Judah and all the inhabitants of Jerusalem, and the priests and prophets—all the people, young and old. And he read to them the entire text of the covenant scroll which had been found in the House of the Lord. The king stood by the pillar and solemnized the covenant before the Lord: that they would follow the Lord and observe His commandments, His injunctions, and His laws with all their heart and soul;

that they should fulfill all the terms of this covenant as inscribed upon the scroll. And all the people entered into the covenant.

Then the king ordered the high priest Hilikiah, the priests of the second rank, and the guards of the threshold to bring out of the Temple of the Lord all the objects made for Baal and Asherah and all the host of heaven. He burned them outside Jerusalem in the fields of Kidron, and he removed the ashes to Bethel. He suppressed the idolatrous priests whom the kings of Judah had appointed to make offerings at the shrines in the towns of Judah and in the environs of Jerusalem, and those who made offerings to Baal, to the sun and moon and constellations—all the host of heaven. He brought out the (image of Asherah) from the House of the Lord to the Kidron Valley outside Jerusalem, and burned it in the Kidron Valley; he beat it to dust and scattered its dust over the burial ground of the common people. He tore down the cubicles of the male prostitutes in the House of the Lord, at the place where the women wore coverings for Asherah. (2 Kings 23:1–7)

And then, as a final step in a process of cultic centralization that had begun with David's choice of Jerusalem as his capital and his placing of the Ark on Mount Moriah, Josiah decreed that the Temple of Jerusalem should be the sole place where the Israelites might offer sacrifice to their God.

He brought all the priests from the towns of Judah [to Jerusalem] and defiled the shrines where the priests had been making offerings— from Geba to Beer-sheba. He also demolished the shrines of the gates, which were at the entrance of the gate of Joshua, the city prefect, which were on a person's left (as he entered) the city gate. The priests of the shrines, however, did not ascend the altar of the Lord in Jerusalem, but they ate unleavened bread along with their kinsmen.

The king commanded all the people, "Offer the Passover sacrifice to the Lord your God as prescribed in this scroll of the Covenant." Now the Passover sacrifice had not been offered in that manner in the days of the chieftains who ruled Israel, or during the days of the kings of Israel and the kings of Judah. Only in the eighteenth year of King Josiah (622 B.C.E.) was such a Passover sacrifice offered in that manner to the Lord in Jerusalem. (2 Kings 23:8–9, 21–23)

42. "The End, The End, It Comes, It Comes"

The cult of the Lord was saved for the moment, but there could be no political salvation for Israel. Shishak and the Egyptians had already shown the Israelite monarchies for the fragile things they were. As we have seen, Samaria and the heart of the northern kingdom finally fell to the Assyrians in 721 B.C.E. Later, in 701 B.C.E., when Hezekiah was king in Judah, Jerusalem narrowly escaped destruction when the Assyrians held it under siege. The great powers in turn swirled through Palestine: Assyria, Egypt, and finally Babylonia.

The Israelite kings did what they could, now strengthening the defenses of the city, now attempting to buy off the attackers. They may have had some hope of weathering the storm, but there were others who saw the approaching disaster in different terms and knew with the certainty of inspiration that there was no way of averting the Lord's judgment on Israel.

Then the hand of the Lord came upon me there, and He said to me, "Arise, go out to the valley, and there I will speak with you." I arose and went out to the valley, and there stood the Presence of the Lord, like the Presence that I had seen at the Chebar Canal; and I flung myself down on my face. And a spirit entered into me and set me upon my feet. And He spoke to me, and said to me, "Go, shut yourself up in your house. As for you, O mortal, cords have been placed upon you, and you have been bound with them, and you shall not go out among them. And I will make your tongue cleave to your palate, and you shall be dumb; you shall not be a reprover to them, for they are a rebellious breed. But when I speak with you, I will open your mouth and you shall say to them, 'Thus says the Lord God!' He who listens will listen, and he who does not will not—for they are a rebellious breed." (Ezekiel 3:22–27)

The man taken "captive" by God on the bank of the Chebar Canal in Babylonia was Ezekiel, and the year may have been about 593 B.C.E. The Babylonians had already attacked Jerusalem once; the future, the Lord warned His prophet, would be even worse.

Thus said the Lord God: I set this Jerusalem in the midst of nations, with countries round her. But she rebelled against My rules and My laws, acting more wickedly than the nations and the countries round her; she rejected My rules and disobeyed My laws . . . thus said the Lord God: I, in turn, am going to deal with you, and I will execute judgments in your midst in the sight of the nations. On account of all your abominations, I will do among you what I have never done, and the like of which I will never do again.

Assuredly, parents shall eat their children in your midst, and children shall eat their parents. I will execute judgments against you, and I will scatter all your survivors in every direction.

Assuredly, as I live—said the Lord God—because you defiled My Sanctuary with all your detestable things and all your abominations, I in turn will shear (you) away and show no pity. I in turn will show no compassion. (Ezekiel 5:5–11)

The word of the Lord came to me: You, O mortal, [say:] Thus said the Lord God to the land of Israel: Doom! Doom is coming upon the four corners of the land. Now doom is upon you! I will let loose My anger against you and judge you according to your ways; I will requite you for all your abominations. I will show you no pity and no compassion; but I will requite you for your ways and for the abominations in your midst. And you shall know that I am the Lord.

Thus said the Lord God: A singular disaster; a disaster is coming. Doom is coming! The hour of doom is coming! It stirs against you; the end, the end, it comes, it comes. (Ezekiel 7:1–6)

2. From Israelite to Jew: The Post-Exilic Reconstruction

1. Ruin and Exile

He [that is, Nebuchadnezzar, king of Babylon] exiled all of Jerusalem: all the commanders and all the warriors—ten thousand exiles—as well as all the craftsmen and smiths; only the poorest people in the land were left. He deported Jehoiachin to Babylon; and the king's wives and officers and the notables of the land were brought as exiles from Jerusalem to Babylon. . . .

And the king of Babylon appointed Mattaniah, Jehoiachin's uncle, king in his place, changing his name to Zedekiah. (2 Kings 24:14–17)

This was in 597 B.C.E., and the Judean vassal Zedekiah was intended to serve his Babylonian master on the latter's own terms. Such must not have been the case, however, since ten years later we once again find Nebuchadnezzar standing before the walls of Jerusalem. There was resistance on the part of the decimated Israelites. But the city fell, as inevitably it had to, and on this occasion the punishment was not looting or the exaction of tribute but the wholesale destruction of the city and another draft of exiles for Babylon.

And in the ninth year of his reign, on the tenth day of the tenth month, Nebuchadnezzar moved against Jerusalem with his whole army. He besieged it; and they built towers against it all around. The city continued in a state of siege until the eleventh year of King Zedekiah. By the ninth day [of the fourth month; 587 B.C.E.] the famine had become acute in the city; there was no food left for the common people. Then the wall of the city was breached. All the soldiers (left the city) by night through the gate between the double walls which is near the king's garden. . . .

Zedekiah was captured near Jericho, brought back to Jerusalem, and blinded.

In the fifth month, on the seventh day of the month, in the nineteenth year of Nebuchadnezzar king of Babylon, Nebuzaradan, captain of the king's bodyguard, came to Jerusalem and set fire to the House of the Lord and the royal palace; all the houses in the city, including the mansion of Gedaliah, were burnt down. The Chaldean forces of the captain of the guard pulled down the walls all around Jerusalem. Nebuzaradan, captain of the guard, deported the rest of the people left in the city, those who had deserted to the king of Babylon and any remaining artisans. He left only the weakest class of people to be vinedressers and laborers. (2 Kings 25:1–12)

2. The Quran Reflects on the Destruction of the Temple

The Quran knew that the Temple in Jerusalem was twice destroyed; and although the text is somewhat opaque in its allusion, most of the commentators took the two events to refer to the Babylonian and probably to the earlier Assyrian assault on the city rather than to the Roman assault in 70 C.E.

We [that is, as always, God] announced to the Children of Israel in the Book: "You will surely create disorder twice in the land, and become exceedingly arrogant." So when the time of the first prediction came, We sent against you Our creatures full of martial might, who ransacked your cities; and the prediction was fulfilled. Then We gave you a chance against them, and strengthened you with wealth and children and increased your numbers, and said: "If you do good, you do so for your own good; if you do ill, you will do it for your own loss." So, when the time of the second prediction comes, (We shall rouse another people) to shame you, and enter the Temple as they had the first time, and to destroy what they conquered utterly. (Quran 17:4–7)

3. Life and the Glory of God Returns to Israel

If Ezekiel had foreseen the blackest days of the end, he also saw, in another visionary transport, a new beginning and, in an extraordinary image, literally a new life.

When I have cleansed you of all your iniquities, I will people your settlements, and the ruined places shall be rebuilt; and the desolate land, after lying waste in the sight of every passerby, shall again be tilled. And men shall say, "That land, once ruined, desolate, and ravaged, is now populated and fortified." . . .

Thus said the Lord God: Moreover, in this I will respond to the House of Israel and act for their sake: I will multiply their people like sheep. As Jerusalem is filled with sacrificial sheep during her festivals, so shall the ruined cities be filled with flocks of people. And they shall know that I am the Lord.

The hand of the Lord came upon me. He took me out by the spirit of the Lord and set me down in the valley. It was full of bones. He led me all around them; they were very many of them spread over the valley, and they were very dry. He said to me, "O mortal, can these bones live again?" I replied, "O Lord God, only You know." And He said to me, "Prophesy over these bones and say to them, O dry bones, hear the word of the Lord!" Thus said the Lord God to these bones: I will cause breath to enter you and you shall live again. I will lay sinews upon you and cover you with flesh, and form skin over you. And I will put breath into you, and you shall live again. And you shall know that I am the Lord.

I prophesied as I had been commanded. And while I was prophesying, suddenly there was a sound of rattling, and the bones came together, bone to matching bone. I looked, and there were sinews on them, and flesh had grown, and skin had formed over them; but there was no breath in them. Then He said to me, "Prophesy to the breath, prophesy, O mortal! Say to the breath; Thus said the Lord God: Come, O breath, from the four winds, and breathe into these slain, that they may live again." I prophesied as He commanded me. The breath entered them, and they came to life and stood up on their feet, a vast multitude. (Ezekiel 36:33–37:11)

Nor was that the end of the wonder. The Lord Himself, Ezekiel was shown, would return to the seat of His former glory in Jerusalem, to a new, purified Jerusalem and to a new Temple, whose very plan is given by the Lord to His prophet.

Then he led me to a gate, the gate that faced east. And there, coming from the east with a roar like the roar of mighty waters, was the Presence of the God of Israel, and the earth was lit up by His Presence. The vision was like the vision I had seen when I came to destroy the city, the very same vision that I had seen by the Chebar Canal. Forthwith, I fell on my face.

The Presence of the Lord entered the Temple by the gate that faced eastward. A spirit carried me into the inner court, and lo, the Presence of the Lord filled the Temple; and I heard speech addressed to me from the Temple, though (the) man was standing beside me. It said to me:

O mortal, this is the place of My throne and the place for the soles of My feet, where I will dwell in the midst of the people Israel forever. The House of Israel and their kings must not again defile My holy name by their apostasy and by the corpses of their kings at their death. . . .

(Now) you, O mortal, describe the Temple to the House of Israel, and let them measure its design. But let them be ashamed of their iniquities: When they are ashamed of all they have done, make known to them the plan of the Temple and its layout, its exits and entrances—its entire plan, and all the laws and instructions pertaining to its entire plan. Write it down before their eyes, that they may faithfully follow its entire plan and all its laws. Such are the instructions for the Temple on top of the mountain: the entire area of its enclosure shall be most holy. Thus far the instructions for the Temple. (Ezekiel 43:1–12)

4. Israel: A New Covenant

Ezekiel was a true visionary, and in his apocalyptic sight the restoration of both Israel and Jerusalem appears to be God's work alone. But the destruction of the Holy City and its Temple and the carrying off of large numbers of Israelites into exile in Babylon were events of such obvious magnitude for a people who had always regarded themselves under God's special dispensation that they provoked changes that ran deeper into the life of the community than Ezekiel's transcendent vision could have stooped to encompass. Adjustments had to be made in cult and institution. New reflections and new tones, some despairing and some expectant, were heard among the religious leaders of the people. These leaders were themselves new figures: not, as often before, warriors, kings, and priests, but, like Ezekiel, prophets of the Almighty Himself. And what they were saying was at once disturbing and hopeful.

Thus said the Lord:

> "Restrain your voice from weeping,
> Your eyes from shedding tears;
> For there is a reward for your labor . . .
> They shall return from the enemy's land.
> And there is hope for your future . . .
> Your children shall return to their country."
> (Jeremiah 31:16–17)

Christians, as we have already seen, took those words to refer not to a renewal after the Exile but to a far more profound redrawing of the Covenant in their own day.

See, a time is coming—declares the Lord—when I will make a new covenant with the House of Israel and the House of Judah. It will not be like the covenant I made with their fathers, when I took them by the hand to lead them out of the land of Egypt, a covenant which they broke, so that I rejected them—declares the Lord. But such is the covenant I will make with the House of Israel after these days—declares the Lord: I will put My Teaching into their innermost being and inscribe it upon their hearts. Then I will be their God, and they shall be My people. No longer will they need to teach one another and say to one another, "Heed the Lord"; for all of them, from the least of them to the greatest shall heed Me—declares the Lord. (Jeremiah 31:31–34)

5. The Redeemer of Israel

Jeremiah's interest was in a new Covenant. Another prophet, Isaiah, had a vision that was at once more startling and more personal: there is to be a mediator, a redeemer for Israel sent by God Himself, and it this very person who speaks in the following passage.

Listen, O coastlands, to me,
And give heed, O nations afar:
The Lord appointed me before I was born,
He named me while I was in my mother's womb.
He made my mouth shaped like a sharpened blade,
He hid me in the shadow of His hand,
And He made me like a polished arrow;
He concealed me in His quiver.
And He said to me, "You are My servant,
Israel in whom I glory."
I thought, "I have labored in vain,
I have spent my strength for empty breath."
But my case rested with the Lord,
My recompense was in the hands of my God.
And now the Lord has resolved—
He who formed me in the womb to be His servant—
To bring back Jacob to Himself,
That Israel may be restored to Him.
And I have been honored in the sight of the Lord,
My God has been my strength.
For He has said:

"It is too little that you should be My servant
In that I raise up the tribes of Jacob
And restore the survivors of Israel:
I will also make you a light of nations,
That My salvation may reach the ends of the earth."
([Second] Isaiah 49:1–6)

6. The Suffering Servant

Here too there was much for the Christians to ponder.

Indeed, My servant shall prosper,
Be exalted and raised to great heights.
Just as the many were appalled at him—
So marred was his appearance, unlike that of man,
His form, beyond human semblance—
Just so he shall startle many nations.
Kings shall be silenced because of him,
For they shall see what has not been told them,
Shall behold what they never have heard.

Who can believe what we have heard?
Upon whom has the arm of the Lord been revealed?
For he has grown, by His favor, like a tree-crown,
Like a tree-trunk out of arid ground.
He had no form or beauty, that we should look at him:
No charm, that we should find him pleasing.

He was despised, shunned by men,
A man of suffering, familiar with disease.
As one who hid his face from us,
He was despised, we held him of no account.
Yet it was our sickness that he was bearing,
Our suffering that he endured.
We accounted him plagued,
Smitten and afflicted by God;
But he was wounded because of our sins,
Crushed because of our iniquities.
He bore the chastisement that made us whole,
And by his bruises we were healed.
We all went astray like sheep,
Each going his own way;

And the Lord visited upon him
The guilt of all of us.

He was maltreated, yet he was submissive,
He did not open his mouth;
Like a sheep being led to slaughter,
Like an ewe, dumb before those who shear her,
He did not open his mouth.
By oppressive judgment he was taken away,
Who could describe his abode?
For he was cut off from the land of the living
Through the sin of My people, who deserved the punishment.
And his grave was set among the wicked,
And with the rich, in his death—
Though he had done no injustice
And had spoken no falsehood.
But the Lord chose to crush him by disease,
That, if he made himself an offering for guilt,
He might see offspring and have long life,
And that through him the Lord's purpose might prosper.
Out of his anguish he shall see it;
He shall enjoy it to the full through his devotion.
My righteous servant makes the many righteous,
It is their punishment that he bears;
Assuredly, I will give him the many as his portion,
He shall receive the multitude as his spoil.
For he exposed himself to death
And was numbered among the sinners,
Whereas he bore the guilt of the many
And made intercession for sinners.
([Second] Isaiah 52:13–53:12)

7. The Return

Eventually, in the turning world of Near Eastern politics, the invincible Babylonians met their own doom. They were replaced by a new Iranian power, the Achaemenians, and with the change of dynasty in Iraq and Iran there was a change of circumstances for the Israelites as well.

In the first year of King Cyrus of Persia [538 B.C.E.], when the word of the Lord spoken by Jeremiah was fulfilled, the Lord roused the spirit of King Cyrus of Persia to issue a proclamation throughout his realm by word of mouth and in writing as follows:

Thus said King Cyrus of Persia: The Lord God of Heaven has given me all the kingdoms of the earth and has charged me with building Him a house in Jerusalem, which is in Judah. Anyone of you of all His people—may his God be with him, and let him go up to Jerusalem that is in Judah and build the House of the Lord God of Israel, the God that is in Jerusalem; and all who stay behind, wherever he may be living, let the people of his place assist him with silver, gold, goods, and livestock, beside the freewill offering to the House of God that is in Jerusalem. (Ezra 1:1–4)

8. The Cult of the Lord Restored

Among the first of the projects undertaken by the returnees was the restoration of the sacrificial worship of the God of Israel in the only place where that was now possible, on the Temple mount in Jerusalem.

When the seventh month arrived—the Israelites being settled in their towns—the entire people assembled as one man in Jerusalem. Then Jeshua son of Jozadak and his brother priests, and Zerubbabel son of Shealtiel and his brothers set to and built the altar of the God of Israel to offer burnt offerings upon it as is written in the Teaching of Moses, the man of God. They set up the altar on its site because they were in fear of the peoples of the land, and they offered burnt offerings upon it to the Lord, burnt offerings every morning and evening. Then they celebrated the festival of Tabernacles as is written, with its daily burnt offerings in the proper quantities, on each day as is prescribed for it, followed by the regular burnt offering and the offerings for the new moons and for all the sacred fixed times of the Lord and whatever freewill offerings were made to the Lord. From the first day of the seventh month they began to make burnt offerings to the Lord, though the foundation of the Temple of the Lord had not been laid. . . .

In the second year after their arrival at the House of God, at Jerusalem, in the second month, Zerubbabel son of Shealtiel and Jeshua son of Jozadak, and the rest of their brother priests and Levites, and all who had come from the captivity to Jerusalem . . . appointed Levites . . . to supervise the work. . . .

When the builders had laid the foundation of the Temple of the Lord, priests in their vestments with trumpets, and Levites sons of Asaph with cymbals were stationed to give praise to the Lord, as King David of Israel had ordained. . . . All the people raised a great shout extolling the Lord because the foundation of the House of the Lord had been laid. Many of the priests and Levites and the chiefs of the clans, the old men who had seen the first house, wept loudly at the sight of the founding of this house. Many others shouted joyously at the top of their voices. The people could not distinguish the shouts of joy from the people's weeping, for the people raised a great shout, the sound of which could be heard from afar. (Ezra 3:1–13)

9. The Second Temple

The cult of the Lord had been restored, but there was still no temple in Jerusalem, and the task of rebuilding it figures nowhere in the plans of Nehemiah, the chief political architect of the new Jerusalem, whose post was, however, a purely civil one. The temple initiative came from quite another source, the prophets Haggai and Zechariah, and with explicit permission of the Shah Darius.

Now you, Tattenai, governor of the province of Beyond the River (Euphrates), Shethar-bozenai, and your colleagues, the officials of the province of Beyond the River, stay away from that place. Allow the work of this House of God to go on; let the governor of the Jews and the elders of the Jews rebuild this House of God on its site.

Moreover, this Jewish temple in Jerusalem would be built with a subsidy from the imperial exchequer of Iran.

And I hereby issue an order concerning what you must do to help these elders of the Jews rebuild this House of God: the expenses are to be paid to these men with dispatch out of the resources of the king, derived from the taxes of the province of Beyond the River, so that the work not be stopped. They are to be given daily, without fail, whatever they need of young bulls, rams, or lambs as burnt offerings for the God of Heaven, and wheat, salt, wine, and oil, at the order of the priests in Jerusalem, so that they may offer pleasing sacrifices to the God of heaven and pray for the life of the king and his sons. . . .

Then Tattenai, (Achaemenian) governor of the province of Beyond the River, Shethar-bozenai, and their colleagues carried out with dispatch what King Darius had written. So the elders of the Jews progressed in the building, urged on by the prophesying of Haggai the prophet and Zechariah son of Iddo, and they brought the building (of the Temple) to completion under the aegis of the God of Israel and by the order of Cyrus and

Darius and King Artaxerxes of Persia. The house was finished on the third of the month of Adar in the sixth year of the reign of King Darius. (Ezra 6:6–15)

Thus we are given to believe that Zerubbabel's Temple stood where Solomon's had before it. We have no reason to think otherwise. But even though we are assured through Haggai that people old enough to remember Solomon's building found the new Temple not unlike the old (Haggai 2:3), it is difficult to think of this as anything but a validation of authenticity. Solomon's resources and ambitions in the tenth century B.C.E. were substantially greater than those of Zerubbabel in the fifth, and the Second Temple, like the rebuilt Jerusalem, must have reflected the straitened circumstances of the people who lived there, as those priests and Levites and elders whom we saw weeping in disappointment at the sight of the new Temple's foundations poignantly attest.

But a fresh start had been made in Jerusalem, and the hopes earlier expressed by Isaiah seemed to Zechariah, the prophet of this age who was present at the momentous beginnings, now at last close to fulfillment.

Thus said the Lord of Hosts: Take courage, you who now hear these words which the prophets spoke when the foundations were laid for the rebuilding of the Temple, the House of the Lord of Hosts.

Thus said the Lord: I have returned to Zion, and I will dwell in Jerusalem. Jerusalem will be called the City of Faithfulness, and the mount of the Lord of Hosts the Holy Mount.

Thus said the Lord of Hosts: There shall yet be old men and women in the squares of Jerusalem, each with staff in hand because of their great age. And the squares of the city shall be crowded with boys and girls playing in the squares. . . . I will rescue My people from the lands of the east and from the lands of the west, and I will bring them home to dwell in Jerusalem. They shall be My people, and I will be their God—in truth and sincerity. (Zechariah 8:3–8)

10. The Mosaic Law Renewed

Finally, the Mosaic constitution of the restored Jewish theocracy had once again to be promulgated, and it is here perhaps that Ezra, the prototype of the class of Jewish Torah scholars later called rabbis, enters the story of Jerusalem.

After these events, during the reign of King Artaxerxes of Persia, Ezra son of Seriah . . . came up from Babylon, a scribe expert in the Teaching of Moses which the Lord God of Israel had given, whose request the king had granted in its entirety, thanks to the benevolence of the Lord toward him. . . . For Ezra had dedicated himself to study the Teaching of the Lord so as to observe it, and to teach laws and rules to Israel. (Ezra 7:1–10)

When the seventh month arrived—the Israelites being (settled) in their towns—the entire people assembled as one man in the square behind the Water Gate, and they asked Ezra the scribe to bring the scroll of the Teaching of Moses with which the Lord had charged Israel. On the first day of the seventh month, Ezra the priest brought the Teaching before the congregation, men and women and all who could listen with understanding. He read from it, facing the square before the Water Gate, from the first light until midday, to the men and the women and those who could understand; the ears of all the people were given to the scroll of the Teaching.

Ezra the scribe stood upon a wooden tower made for the purpose. . . . Ezra opened the scroll in the sight of all the people, for he was above all the people; as he opened it, all the people answered, "Amen, Amen," with hands upraised. Then they bowed their heads and prostrated themselves before the Lord with their faces to the ground. Jeshua, Bani, Sherebiah, Jamin, Akkub, Shabbethai, Hodiah, Maaseiah, Kelita, Azariah, Jozabad, Hanan, Pelaiah, and the Levites explained the Teaching to the people, while the people stood in their places. They read from the scroll of the Teaching of God, translating it and giving the sense (in Aramaic); so they understood the reading. (Nehemiah 8:1–8)

On the twenty-fourth day of this month, the Israelites assembled, fasting, in sackcloth, and with earth upon them. Those of the stock of Israel separated themselves from all foreigners, and stood and confessed their sins and the iniquities of their fathers. Standing in their places, they read from the scroll of the teaching of the Lord their God for one-fourth of the day, and for another fourth they confessed and prostrated themselves before the Lord their God. . . .

". . . We make this pledge and put it in writing; And on the sealed copy (are subscribed) our officials, our Levites, and our priests. . . .

"And the rest of the people, the priests, the Levites, the gatekeepers, the singers, the temple servants, and all who separated themselves from the peoples of the lands to (follow) the Teaching of God, their wives, sons and daughters, all who know enough to understand, join with their noble brothers, and take an oath with sanctions to follow the Teaching of God, given through Moses the servant of God, and to observe carefully all the commandments of the Lord our Lord, His rules and laws." (Nehemiah 9:1–3; 10:1–30)

11. An Edict of Toleration

The Israelites had been restored to Palestine but not to sovereignty over that land. They were subjects of the Persian shah and then, in the wake of Alexander the Great's progress across Asia, a province to be fought over by his Greek successors in Egypt and Syria, the Ptolemies and Seleucids. The latter finally triumphed, and by 200 B.C.E. the Seleucid Antiochus III (223–187 B.C.E.) was firmly in control of Palestine, together with most of western Asia.

When Antiochus [III] the Great reigned over Asia it was the lot of the Jews to undergo great hardships through the devastation of their land, as did also the inhabitants of Coele-Syria. For while he was at war with Ptolemy Philopator and with his son Ptolemy, surnamed Epiphanes, and whether he was victorious or defeated, they experienced the same fate. . . . But not long afterward Antiochus defeated (the Egyptian general) Scopas in a battle near the sources of the Jordan [200 B.C.E.] and destroyed a greater part of his army. And later, when Antiochus took possession of the cities in Coele-Syria which Scopas had held, and Samaria, the Jews of their own will went over to him and admitted him to their city and made abundant provision for his entire army and his elephants; and they readily joined his forces in besieging the (Egyptian) garrison which had been left by Scopas in the citadel of Jerusalem. Accordingly, Antiochus, considering it just to requite the zeal and exertions of the Jews on his behalf, wrote to his governors and Friends (of the King), bearing witness to the Jews concerning the good treatment he had received at their hands and announcing the rewards which he had decided to give them on that account. (Josephus, *Antiquities* 12.3.3)

Josephus then reproduces Antiochus' letter, which carries us directly into the complex and often tortured relations between the Jerusalem Jews and their Greco-Macedonian sovereigns in Antioch.

King Antiochus to Ptolemy, greetings. Since the Jews, beginning from the time that we entered their territory, have testified to their zeal in our regard, and since, from our arrival in their city they have received us in a magnificent manner and came out to meet us with their senate [*gerousia*, literally Council of Elders], have contributed generously to the upkeep of our soldiers and our elephants, and have assisted us in captur-

ing the Egyptian garrison in the citadel (*akra*), we have judged it proper
that we too should respond to those good offices by restoring their city
destroyed by the misfortunes of war and repopulating it by bringing back
all those people dispersed from it.

*And like past sovereigns of the land of Israel, the Seleucids too would subsidize the
daily Temple offerings.*

First we have decided by reasons of piety to furnish for the sacrifices
a contribution of sacrificial offerings and wine and oil and incense to the
value of 20,000 drachmas of silver, and of flour of grain in sacred artabas
according to the measure of the country, 1,460 mediamni of wheat and
375 mediamni of salt. I wish all these contributions be furnished them as
I have commanded and that the work on the Temple be achieved, the
stoas and whatever else needs be built. Let wood be provided from both
Judea itself and from among the other peoples and from the Lebanon,
without being taxed. Likewise for the other things required to make the
restoration of the Temple outstanding.

All of that people will be governed according to their ancestral laws,
and their Council of Elders and priests and scribes of the Temple and the
sacred chanters will be exempt from the capitation tax, the crown tax and
that on salt. And so that the city might more quickly be repopulated, I
grant to those who now live in it and those who will return until the
month of Hyperberetaios to be exempt from tax for a period of three
years. Further we exempt them in the future from one-third of the taxes
in order to compensate them for their losses. As for those who have been
taken from the city and reduced to slavery, to them and their offspring
we grant their freedom and bid their goods be restored to them. (Josephus, *Antiquities* 12.3.3)

*Finally, the authority of Seleucid sovereignty was placed behind the proper observa-
tion of the Mosaic Law.*

Now these [Josephus continues] were the contents of the letter. And
out of reverence for the Temple he also published throughout the kingdom a grave and holy public notice with these terms. "It is prohibited
for any foreigner to go into the sanctuary forbidden to the Jews themselves, except for those who have been purified and are so permitted
according to the ancestral law. It is prohibited to bring into the city either
horse meat or the flesh of a mule or a wild or domesticated ass, of the
panther, the fox or the hare, or in general of any of the animals forbidden
to the Jews. It is prohibited bringing in their skins. Nor can they be raised
in the city. It is prohibited using any but traditionally butchered animals,

from among which it is also prescribed that the sacrifices for God be chosen. Whoever shall transgress any one of these (prohibitions) shall pay to the priests a fine of 3,000 silver drachmas." (Josephus, *Antiquities* 12.3.4)

12. The Hellenization of Jerusalem

Onto this apparently agreeable scene came in "that wicked man" Antiochus IV, surnamed, in the ordinary grandiose style of the times, "Epiphanes," the "God-Made-Manifest." The mise-en-scène is provided by the first Book of Maccabees:

Alexander (the Great) had reigned twelve years when he died [323 B.C.E.]. His generals took over the government, each in his own province. On his death they were all crowned as kings, and their descendants succeeded them for many years. They brought untold miseries upon the world.

A scion of this stock was that wicked man Antiochus Epiphanes, son of King Antiochus (III). He had been a hostage in Rome before he succeeded to the throne in the year 137 of the Greek era [175 B.C.E.]. At that time there appeared in Israel a group of renegade Jews who incited the people. "Let us enter into a covenant with the Gentiles round about," they said, "because disaster after disaster has overtaken us since we segregated ourselves from them." The people thought this a good argument, and some of them in their enthusiasm went to the king and received authority to introduce non-Jewish laws and customs. They built a sports stadium in Gentile style in Jerusalem. They removed the marks of their circumcision and they repudiated the holy Covenant. They intermarried with Gentiles and abandoned themselves to evil ways. (1 Maccabees 1: 7–16)

The author of the first Book of Maccabees had the advantage of considerable hindsight on the matter of Antiochus IV. But, as the text readily admits, the Greek king had neither planted the enthusiasm for things Greek among the Jews of Jerusalem nor even encouraged them to pursue that enthusiasm by introducing some of the hallmarks of urban Hellenism into the city. The initiative came from within, from the "Hellenizers" among the Jews in what was by then a large, populous, and prosperous city, as contemporary sources attest.

Jews were spreading all over the eastern Mediterranean, and their prosperity was shared by Jerusalem, or at least by the upper class constituted by the higher priesthoods and most intimately connected with the Holy City's chief and almost unique business, the Temple. And with prosperity came attraction to the life and the mores of the people who had brought it, the Hellenes. Not their gods, certainly, which every Jew despised, but that easily identified style that manifested itself in the art and the architecture that was beginning to fill the Near Eastern landscape and in that manner of life that was on prominent and attractive display in Alexandria, where many Jews now lived. Hellenism had no need of Antiochus Epiphanes to make its case: the Jews themselves reached out for it, and the Seleucid sovereign was happy to oblige.

13. Antioch-at-Jerusalem

The assimilation of the Jewish upper classes, particularly the priests, to the new Hellenism was complicated by a powerful rivalry for the chief post of that land, the High Priesthood. When High Priest Onias died, he was succeeded by his brother Jesus or Jeshua, who had Hellenized his name to Jason. How the matter was arranged is explained by Maccabees.

But when Seleucus was dead [in 175 B.C.E.] and had been succeeded by Antiochus, known as Epiphanes, Jason, Onias' brother, obtained the High Priesthood by corrupt means. He petitioned the king and promised him 360 talents in silver coin immediately and 80 talents from future revenues. In addition he undertook to pay another 150 talents for the authority to institute a sports stadium, to arrange for the education of young men there, and to enroll in Jerusalem a group to be known as "Antiochenes." The king agreed, and as soon as he had seized the High Priesthood, Jason made the Jews conform to the Greek way of life.

He set aside the royal privileges established for the Jews through the agency of John, the father of that Eupolemus who negotiated a treaty of friendship and alliance with the Romans. He abolished the lawful way of life and introduced practices which were against the law. He lost no time in establishing a sports stadium at the foot of the citadel itself, and he made the most outstanding of the young men assume the Greek athlete's hat. So Hellenism reached a high point with the introduction of foreign customs through the boundless wickedness of the impious Jason, no true High Priest. As a result, the priests no longer had any enthusiasm for their duties at the altar, but despised the Temple and neglected the sacrifices; and in defiance of the Law they eagerly contributed to the expenses of the wrestling school whenever the opening gong called them. They placed no honor on their hereditary dignities, but cared above everything for Hellenic honors. (2 Maccabees 4:7–16)

Josephus has his own, somewhat more political version of the same events, which now includes Jason's younger brother.

About this same time the High Priest Onias also died, and Antiochus gave the high priesthood to his brother, for the son whom Onias had left was still an infant. . . . Jesus, however—this was the brother of Onias—was deprived of the high priesthood when the king became angry with him and gave it to his youngest brother, named Onias. . . . Now Jesus changed his name to Jason while Onias was called Menelaus. And when the former High Priest Jesus rose up against Menelaus, who was appointed after him, the populace was divided between the two, the [pro–Seleucid] Tobiads being on the side of Menelaus, while the majority of the people supported Jason; and being hard pressed by him, Menelaus and the Tobiads withdrew, and going to Antiochus informed him that they wished to abandon their country's laws and the way of life prescribed by these and to follow the king's laws and adopt the Greek way of life. (Josephus, *Antiquities* 12.5.1, 2)

14. The Abomination of Desolation

About this time [that is, 170–169 B.C.E.] Antiochus undertook his second invasion of Egypt. . . . Upon a false report of Antiochus' death, Jason collected no less than a thousand men and made a surprise attack upon Jerusalem. The defenders on the wall were driven back and the city was finally taken; Menelaus took refuge in the citadel, and Jason continued to massacre his fellow citizens without pity. . . . He did not, however, gain control of the government; he gained only dishonor as the result of his plot, and returned again as a fugitive to Ammonite territory. . . .

When news of this reached the king (Antiochus), it became clear to him that Judea was in a state of rebellion. So he set out from Egypt in a savage mood, took Jerusalem by storm, and ordered his troops to cut down without mercy everyone they met and to slaughter those who took refuge in the houses. Young and old were massacred, girls and infants butchered. By the end of three days their losses had amounted to eighty thousand, and as many sold into slavery.

Not satisfied with this, the king had the audacity to enter the holiest Temple on earth, guided by Menelaus, who had turned traitor both to his religion and his country. He laid impious hands on the sacred vessels; his desecrating hands swept together the votive offerings which other kings had set up to enhance the splendor and fame of the shrine. (2 Maccabees 5:1–16)

1 Maccabees adds a few details on the spoliation of the Temple.

In his arrogance he entered the Temple and carried off the golden altar, the lampstand with all its equipment, the table for the Bread of the Presence, the sacred cups and bowls, the golden censers, the curtain and the crowns. He stripped off all the gold plating from the Temple front. He seized the silver, gold, and precious vessels, and whatever secret treasures he found, he took them all with him when he left for his own country. (1 Maccabees 1:21–24)

Sometime about 174 B.C.E. Antiochus had elevated Jerusalem to the high status of polis. In his anger at what seemed like a transparent act of treason committed while he was at war with Egypt, and after another disastrous foray into Egypt in 168, in the following year he degraded the city to the lowest and most humiliating rank of all, that of a military colony, in effect an occupied city under martial law. He then banned the very practice of Judaism.

Two years later the king sent to the towns of Judea a high revenue official, who arrived at Jerusalem with a powerful force. His language was friendly, but full of guile. For, once he had gained the city's confidence, he suddenly attacked it. He dealt it a heavy blow and killed many Israelites, plundering the city and setting it ablaze. He pulled down houses and walls on every side; women and children were made prisoners, and the cattle seized.

The City of David was turned into a citadel, enclosed by a high, stout wall with strong towers, and garrisoned by impious foreigners and renegades. Having made themselves secure, they accumulated arms and provisions, and deposited there the massed plunder of Jerusalem. There they lay in ambush, a lurking threat to the Temple and a perpetual menace to Israel. (1 Maccabees 1:29–36)

Moreover, he forbade them to offer the daily sacrifices which they used to offer to God in accordance with their law, and after plundering the entire city, he killed some of the people and some he took captive together with their women and children, so that the number of those taken alive came to ten thousand. And he burnt the finest parts of the city and pulling down the walls, built the Citadel in the Lower City; for it was high enough to overlook the Temple and it was for this reason that he fortified it with high walls and towers and stationed a Macedonian garrison there. Nonetheless, there remained in the Akra those of the people who were impious and of bad character and at their hands the citizens were destined to suffer terrible things. (Josephus, *Antiquities* 12.5.4)

The king then issued a decree throughout his empire: his subjects were all to become one people and abandon their own laws and religion.

The nations everywhere complied with the royal command, and many in Israel accepted the foreign worship, sacrificing to idols and profaning the sabbath. Moreover, the king sent agents with written orders to Jerusalem and the towns of Judea. Ways and customs foreign to the country were to be introduced. Burnt offerings, sacrifices and libations in the Temple were forbidden. . . .

Such was the decree which the king issued to all his subjects. He appointed superintendents over all of the people and instructed the towns of Judea to offer sacrifice, town by town. People thronged to their side in large numbers, every one of them a traitor to the law. (1 Maccabees 1:41–64)

This was a full-scale pogrom, indeed, an attempt to exterminate the Jewish religion, quite unlike anything Jerusalem had experienced before. And though there are trails of political clues across the acts of Antiochus, there can be no certainty that they lead to either the full or the true story of the events of 167 B.C.E. This is how they were read by one Jew, the prophetic author of the Book of Daniel.

At the appointed time, he [Antiochus] will again invade the south [that is, Egypt], but the second time will not be like the first. Ships from Kittim [Rome] will come against him. He will be checked, and will turn back, raging against the holy covenant. Having done his pleasure, he will then attend to those who forsake the holy covenant. Forces will be levied by him; they will desecrate the Temple, the fortress; they will abolish the regular offering and set up the appalling abomination. (Daniel 11:29–31)

And so in fact it happened.

    . . . King Antiochus sent an elderly Athenian to force the Jews to abandon their ancestral customs and no longer regulate their lives according to the laws of God. He was also commissioned to pollute the Temple at Jerusalem and dedicate it to Olympian Zeus, and to dedicate the sanctuary on Mount Gerizim to Zeus, God of Hospitality, following the practice of the local inhabitants.

This evil hit them hard and was a severe trial. The Gentiles filled the Temple with licentious revelry; they took their pleasure with prostitutes and had intercourse with women in the sacred precincts. They brought forbidden things inside, and heaped the altar with impure offerings prohibited by the law. It was forbidden either to observe the Sabbath or keep the traditional festivals, or to admit being a Jew at all. On the monthly celebration of the king's birthday, the Jews were driven by brute force to eat the entrails of the sacrificial victims; and on the feast of Dionysus they were forced to wear ivy wreaths and join the procession in his honor. (2 Maccabees 6:1–7)

On the 15th day of the month of Kislev in the year 145 [7 December 167 B.C.E.] the "Abomination of Desolation" was set up on the altar. Pagan altars were built throughout the towns of Judea; incense was offered at the doors of houses and in the streets. All scrolls of the Law which were found were torn up and burnt. Anyone discovered in possession of a Book of the Covenant, or conforming to the Law, was put to death by the king's sentence. . . .

On the twenty-fifth day of the month they offered sacrifice on the pagan altar which was on top of the altar of the Lord. (1 Maccabees 1: 54–60)

15. The Maccabean Restoration

The origins and early unfolding of the Maccabean rebellion against Seleucid oppression do not directly concern us here. Jerusalem continued to be held by a Syrian garrison and their Jewish sympathizers in the Akra. There was an early and brief Maccabean occupation of the Holy City, but permanent reappropriation awaited more convincing military triumphs over the Syrian forces, as occurred at Bethsura in 164 B.C.E. Only then could Jerusalem be entered and the Temple restored.

But Judas and his brothers said: "Now that our enemies have been crushed, let us go up to Jerusalem to cleanse the Temple and rededicate it." So the whole army was assembled and went up to Mount Sion. There they found the Temple laid waste, the altar profaned, the gates burnt down, the courts overgrown like a thicket or wooded hillside, and the priests' rooms in ruin. . . .

Then Judas detailed troops to engage the garrison of the citadel while he cleansed the Temple. He selected priests without blemish, devoted to the Law, and they purified the Temple, removing to an unclean place the stones which defiled it. They discussed what to do with the altar of burnt offering, which was profaned, and rightly decided to demolish it, for fear it might become a standing reproach to them because it had been defiled by the Gentiles. They therefore pulled down the altar and stored away the stones in a fitting place on the Temple hill, until a prophet should arise who could be consulted about them. They took unhewn stones, as the law commands, and built a new altar on the model of the previous one. They rebuilt the Temple and restored its interior, and consecrated the Temple courts. . . .

Then early on the twenty-fifth day of the ninth month, the month Kislev, in the year 148 [164 B.C.E.] sacrifice was offered as the Law commands on the newly made altar of burnt offerings. On the anniversary of the day when the Gentiles had profaned it, on that very day, it was rededicated, with hymns of thanksgiving, to the music of harps and lutes and cymbals. All the people prostrated themselves, worshiping and praising Heaven that their cause had prospered.

They celebrated the rededication of the altar for eight days; there was great rejoicing and they brought burnt offerings and sacrificed peace offerings and thank offerings. They decorated the front of the Temple with golden wreaths and ornamental shields. They renewed the gates and the priests' rooms, and fitted them with doors. There was great merrymaking among the people, and the disgrace brought on them by the Gentiles was removed.

Then Judas, his brothers, and the whole congregation of Israel decreed that the rededication of the altar should be observed with joy and gladness at the same season of each year, for eight days, beginning on the twenty-fifth of Kislev. (1 Maccabees 4:36–59)

16. A Muslim Tells the Story of Hanukka

One of the motives behind the writing of Maccabees may have been to popularize among Diaspora communities this feast of the "Purification of the Temple" and so to glorify the still new dynasty responsible for it. And despite its lack of biblical authority—the books of Maccabees were never included in the canon of the Bible— the festival of Hanukka, as it was called, did enjoy some measure of popularity, at least in Jerusalem, where it was celebrated in Jesus' day as the "Festival of Lights" (John 10:22).

Another measure of the success of Hanukka is the number of stories and legends that grew up around the event, like the "Acts of the Maccabean Martyrs" included in 2 Maccabees 6:9–7:42. This, for example, is how the Muslim scholar Biruni heard the story in the early eleventh century, when he included it in his Traces of the Past *in the section on "Festivals and Fasts of the Jews."*

The 25th of Kislev. Beginning of the feast *Hanukka*, that is, purification. It lasts eight days, during which they [that is, the Jews] light lamps at the door of the hall: on the first night one lamp for each inhabitant of the house, on the second night two lamps, on the third night three, etc., and finally eight lamps on the eighth night, by which they mean to express their thanks toward God from day to day for the purification and sanctification of Jerusalem.

The origin is this: Antiochus, the king of the Greeks, had subdued and maltreated them during a long period. It was his custom to violate the women, before they were led to their spouses, in a subterranean vault. From this vault two cords led outside, where two bells were fixed at their ends. When, then, he wanted a woman, he rang the right bell, and the woman entered; when he had done with her he rang the left bell and dismissed her. Further there was an Israelite who had eight sons, and a daughter whom another Israelite had demanded in marriage. Now when the young man asked to marry her, the father of the bride said: "Give me time, for I stand between two things. If we give my daughter to you, she will be dishonored by the cursed tyrant, and she will no longer be a lawful bride for you. And if she does not submit to Antiochus, he will make me perish." For this state of things he blamed and reviled his sons, who became greatly excited and angry. But the youngest of them jumped up, dressed himself like a woman, hid a dagger in his clothes, and went to the gate of the king, behaving like the whores. Now, the tyrant rang the right bell, and he was ushered into his presence; there being along with him, he killed him and cut off his head; then he rang the left bell and was let out, and stuck up the head somewhere. Therefore the Israelites celebrate a feast on that and the following (seven) days, corresponding to the number of the brothers of this youth. But God knows best. (Biruni, *Traces of the Past*) [BIRUNI 1879: 271–272]

17. The New Covenant at Qumran

Although the Covenant concluded by the Lord with Abraham—and through him, his descendants—was the charter document of the Children of Israel as the Chosen People, it was neither the first nor the last such contract made or renewed between God and the Israelites. In the pre-Exilic period Joshua son of Nun had presided over just such a renewal (see Chapter 1 above), and in more recent times we have seen how Ezra had presided over a formal covenantal renewal in Jerusalem and how Jeremiah had predicted other, more sweeping revisions of the agreement between the Lord and His people.

Christianity regarded itself as one such latter-day revision in the form of a "New Covenant"; but as we now know from the discovery of the Dead Sea Scrolls and their related documents, it was not the first. Whatever the exact identification of those Jewish sectaries who lived in community at Qumran near the Dead Sea, and whatever their precise relationship with the group Josephus and others call the "Essenes" or their fellow covenanters who produced the "Damascus Rule" at about the same time, it is certain that there were within the body of Palestinian Jews some priestly pietists who disagreed with the current interpretation of the Law on a number of points, including the ritual prescriptions governing Temple sacrifice. Their disagreement was sufficiently strong and deeply principled that it led them to separate themselves from the rest of the Jews and constitute themselves a true priestly Israel, the only participants in the New Covenant.

The Damascus Rule undertakes to describe, in its extremely allusive way, the events leading to this new dispensation. The "time of desolation," it appears likely, was the Hasmonean era, and the critical event in the schism may well have been the promotion of Jonathan in 152 B.C.E. to the position of High Priest by the Seleucid Alexander Balas.

And at the time of the desolation of the land there arose removers of the bond who led Israel astray. And the land was ravaged because they preached rebellion against the commandments of God given by the hand of Moses and of His holy anointed ones, and because they prophesied lies to turn Israel away from God. But God remembered the Covenant with the forefathers, and He raised from Aaron [that is, from among the hereditary priesthoods] men of discernment and from Israel [that is, from the lay community] men of wisdom, and He caused them to hear. And they dug the Well: "the well which the nobles of the people delved with the stave" (Num. 21:18).

This sectarian view of history rests, as often in both this document and the Qumran library, on a privileged reading of Scripture, in this instance of a text of Numbers, which the Damascus Rule directly proceeds to gloss.

The "Well" is the Law, and those who dug it were the converts of Israel who went out of the land of Judah to sojourn in the land of Damascus. God called them all "princes" because they sought Him, and their renown was disputed by no man. The "stave" is the Interpreter of the Law, of whom Isaiah said, "He made a tool for His work" (Isa. 54:16); and the "nobles of the people" are those who came to dig the "Well" with the staves with which "the stave" ordained that they should walk in all the age of wickedness—and without them they shall find nothing— until he comes who shall teach righteousness at the end of days.

None of those brought into the Covenant shall enter the Temple to light His altar in vain. They shall bar the door, inasmuch as God has said, "Who among you will bar its door?" And, "You shall not light My altar in vain" (Mal. 1:10). They shall take care to act according to the exact interpretation of the Law during the age of wickedness. They shall separate from the sons of the Pit, and shall keep away from the unclean riches of wickedness acquired by vow or anathema or from the Temple treasure; they shall not rob the poor of His people, to make widows their prey or of the fatherless their victim (Isa. 10:2). They shall distinguish between clean and unclean, and shall proclaim the difference between holy and profane. They shall keep the Sabbath day according to its exact interpretation, and the feasts and the Day of Fasting according to the findings of the members of the New Covenant of the land of Damascus. (*The Damascus Rule* 5–6) [VERMES 1968: 102–103])

One plausible interpretation of the "land of Damascus" is that it refers to the Qumran community. That community had, at any rate, a similar view of the New Covenant, whose ideals and renewal are described in the opening passages of the "Community Rule."

The Master shall teach the saints to live [according to] the Book of the Community Rule, that they may seek God with a whole heart and soul, and do what is right and good before Him as He commanded by the hand of Moses and all His servants the Prophets; that they may love all that He has chosen and hate all that He has rejected; that they may abstain from all evil and hold fast to all good; that they may practice truth, righteousness and justice upon earth and no longer stubbornly follow a sinful heart and lustful eyes, committing all manner of evil. . . .

All those who freely devote themselves to His truth shall bring all their knowledge, powers and possessions into the Community of God, that they may purify their knowledge in the truth of God's precepts and order their powers according to His ways of perfection and all their possessions according to His righteous counsel. They shall not depart from any command of God concerning their times; they shall be neither early nor late for their appointed times; they shall stray neither to the right nor the left of any of His true precepts. All who embrace the Community Rule shall enter into the Covenant before God to obey all His commandments so that they may not abandon him during the dominion of Satan because of fear or error or affliction.

On entering the Covenant, the Priests and the Levites shall bless the God of salvation and all His faithfulness, and all those entering the Covenant shall say after them "Amen, Amen!"

Then the Priests shall recite the favors God manifested in His mighty deeds and declare all His merciful grace to Israel, and all the Levites shall recite the iniquities of the children of Israel, all their guilty rebellions and sins during the dominion of Satan. And after them, all those entering the Covenant shall confess and say, "We have strayed! We have disobeyed!" (*Community Rule* 1) [VERMES 1968: 71–72]

What the Community Rule calls the "dominion of Satan" is the present age, from which the members of the community attempted to hold themselves apart. This evil will one day come to an end, and the truth will be restored.

But in the mysteries of His understanding, and in His glorious wisdom, God has ordained an end for falsehood, and at the time of the visitation He will destroy it forever. Then truth, which has wallowed in the ways of wickedness during the dominion of falsehood until the appointed time of judgment, shall arise in the world forever. God will then purify every deed of Man with His truth. He will refine for Himself the human frame by rooting out all spirit of falsehood from the bounds of the flesh. He will cleanse him of all wicked deeds with the spirit of holiness; like purifying waters He will shed upon him the spirit of truth to cleanse him of all abomination and falsehood. And he shall be plunged into the spirit of purification that he may instruct the upright in the knowledge of the Most High and teach the wisdom of the sons of heaven to the perfect way. For God has chosen them for an everlasting Covenant and all the glory of Adam shall be theirs. There shall be no more lies and all the works of falsehood will be put to shame. (*Community Rule* 4)

[VERMES 1968: 77–78]

18. Herod the Great
(37–4 B.C.E.)

The inglorious end of the glorious Maccabean beginning came a scant century later in the person of the two sons of Alexander Janneus (103–76 B.C.E.), the then reigning sovereign of the Hasmonean house, as the later royal Maccabees were known. Their names were Aristobulus and Hyrcanus, and their qualifications for ruling Judea were perhaps doubtful. The question was in any event moot, since the Romans by then held all the East in fief, and it was they who would choose and control the ruler of Israel. In the summer of 47 B.C.E. Julius Caesar came in person to Palestine and held audience with his Judean clients.

After listening to both (sons), Caesar declared Hyrcanus the better candidate for the High Priesthood and allowed Antipater [Hyrcanus' vizier] to choose his own office. Antipater left it to the bestower of the honor to decide its magnitude, and was appointed Commissioner of all Judea, with authority to rebuild the walls of the metropolis [that is,

Jerusalem]. These honors Caesar ordered to be engraved in the Capitol, to commemorate his own justice and Antipater's splendid services.

As soon as Antipater had escorted Caesar out of Palestine, he returned to Judea. There he began rebuilding the wall of the metropolis which Pompey had torn down [in 63 B.C.E.], and proceeded to suppress disturbances in various parts of the country, using in every case both threats and advice. . . . While he [Antipater] talked in this way he was organizing the country along his own lines, knowing that Hyrcanus was too lethargic and spineless to be a real king. Phasael, his eldest son, he appointed governor of Jerusalem and its district; the next one, Herod, he sent with equal authority into Galilee, though he was quite young. (Josephus, *War* 1.10.3–4)

Thus arrived Herod, aged twenty-six, on the stage of Jewish history, the middle son of an Idumean adventurer named Antipater who had risen by his own skill, cunning, and ambition to be effective ruler of the Jewish Temple state in Judea. In 43 B.C.E. Antipater was murdered by an Arab rival from the Transjordan. It took Herod five years to navigate a civil war in Rome and a Parthian invasion of Palestine and secure his father's place. In 39 B.C.E. he was nominated king of Judea by action of the Roman Senate, and two years later he besieged and captured Jerusalem and so took possession of his kingdom, which he ruled with loyalty to Rome and cruelty to his subjects until his death in 4 B.C.E.

The extraordinary Herod dominates much of Josephus' narrative in both the Antiquities *and the* Jewish War, *not without a certain admiration on the part of the historian.*

In the fifteenth year of his reign [or the eighteenth, according to the *Antiquities*; see below] Herod restored the existing Sanctuary (in Jerusalem) and around it enclosed an area double the former size, keeping no account of the cost and achieving a magnificence beyond compare. This could be seen particularly in the great colonnades that ran around the entire Temple and the fortress that towered over it to the north. The former were completely new structures, the latter an extremely costly reconstruction, as luxurious as a palace, and named Antonia in honor of Antony. Herod's own palace, built in the Upper city, consisted of two very large and very lovely buildings which made even the Sanctuary seem insignificant; these he named after his friends, one Caesareum, one Agrippeum. (Josephus, *War* 1.21.1)

If ever a man was full of family affection, that man was Herod. In memory of his father he founded a city, choosing a site in the loveliest plain in his kingdom with an abundance of rivers and trees and naming it Antipatris; and the fortress overlooking Jericho he refortified, making it outstandingly strong and beautiful, and dedicated it to his mother under the name of Cypros. To his brother Phasael he erected the tower in Jerusalem that took his name. . . . He also founded another city in the valley running north from Jericho and called it Phasaelis. . . .

After this spate of building he extended his generosity to a great many cities outside his boundaries. For Tripolis, Damascus and Ptolemais he provided gymnasia, for Byblos, a wall, for Beirut and Tyre, halls, colonnades, temples and marketplaces, for Sidon and Damascus, theaters, for the coastal Laodicea, an aqueduct, for Ascalon, baths, magnificent fountains, and cloistered quadrangles remarkable for both scale and craftsmanship; in other places he dedicated woods and parks. . . . And the wide street in Syrian Antioch, did he not pave—two and a quarter miles of it—with polished marble and to keep the rain off furnish it with a colonnade from end to end?

It may be argued that all these benefits were enjoyed only by the particular community favored; but his endowment of Elis was a gift not only to Greece in general but to every corner of the civilized world reached by the fame of the Olympic Games. Seeing that the games were declining for lack of funds and that the sole relic of ancient Greece was slipping away, he not only acted as president of the quadrennial meeting held when he happened to be on his way to Rome, but he also endowed them for all time with an income large enough to ensure that his presidency should never be forgotten. (Josephus, *War* 1.21.9–12)

19. Herod Rebuilds the Temple

It is not those other ecumenical works of that prodigious builder Herod that concern us here, but rather his chief legacy to his own Jewish subjects: the Temple in Jerusalem.

It was at this time [of Augustus' visit to Syria in 20 B.C.E.], in the eighteenth year of his reign, . . . that Herod undertook an extraordinary work, the reconstructing of the Temple of God at his own expense, enlarging its precincts and raising it to a more imposing height. For he believed that the accomplishment of this task would be the most notable of all the things achieved by him, as indeed it was, and would be great enough to assure his eternal remembrance. (Josephus, *Antiquities* 15.11.1)

And while the unlikelihood of his realizing his hope did not disturb (the people), they were dismayed by the thought that he might tear down the whole edifice and not have sufficient means to bring his project (of rebuilding it) to completion. . . . Since they felt this way, the king spoke encouragingly to them, saying that he would not pull down the Temple (of Zerubbabel) before having ready all the materials needed for its completion. And these assurances he did not belie. For he prepared a thousand wagons to carry the stones, selected 10,000 of the most skilled workmen, purchased priestly robes for a thousand priests and trained some as masons and others as carpenters, and began the construction only after all these preparations had been diligently made by him.

Moreover, according to the Mishna, the king arranged that the Temple liturgy was not disturbed at any time during the work.

Rabbi Eliezer said: I have heard a tradition that while they were building the Temple they made curtains for the Temple and curtains for the courtyards, but they built (the walls of) the Temple outside (the curtains), (the walls of the courtyards) they built within (the curtains). (M.Eduyoth 8:6)

Josephus' account of the construction of the Temple continues.

After removing the old foundations, he [Herod] laid down others, and upon these he erected the Temple, which was a hundred cubits in length . . . and twenty more in height, but in the course of time this dropped as the foundations subsided. And this part we decided to raise again in the time of Nero. The Temple was built of hard, white stones, each of which was about twenty-five cubits in length, eight in height and twelve in width. And the whole of it, as also in the Royal Portico, either side was the lowest, while the middle portion was the highest, so that it was visible at a distance of many stades to those who inhabited the country, especially those who lived opposite or happened to approach it. . . . And he surrounded the Temple with very large porticoes, all of which he made in proportion (to the Temple), and he surpassed his predecessors in spending money, so that it was thought that no one else had adorned the Temple so splendidly.

(The Temple sanctuary and its porticoes) were supported by a great wall and the wall itself was the greatest ever heard of by man. The hill was a rocky ascent that sloped gently up toward the eastern part of the city to the topmost peak. The hill our first king Solomon [or "our king Solomon first"] with God-given wisdom surrounded with great works above at the top. And below, beginning at the foot, where a deep ravine runs round it, he (Herod) surrounded it with enormous stones bound together with lead. He cut off more and more of the area within as (the wall) became greater in depth, so that the size and height of the structure, which was square, were immense, and the great size of the stones was seen along the front [that is, outside] surface, while the iron clamps in the inside assured that the joints would remain permanently united.

When the work reached the top of the hill, he leveled off the summit and filled in the hollow spaces near the walls, and made the upper surfaces smooth and even throughout. Such was the whole enclosure, having a circumference of four stades, each side taking up the length of a stade. Within this wall and on the very summit there ran another wall of stone, which had on the eastern ridge a double portico of the same length as the wall, and it faced the doors of the Temple, for this lay within it. This portico many of the earlier kings adorned. Round about the entire Temple were fixed the spoils taken from the barbarians, and all these King Herod dedicated, adding those which he took from the (Nabatean) Arabs. (Josephus, *Antiquities* 15.11.24)

Again, in the War:

Though the Temple . . . was seated on a strong hill, the level area on its summit originally barely sufficed for shrine and altar, the ground around it being precipitous and steep. But king Solomon, the actual founder of the Temple, having walled up the eastern side, a single portico was reared on this made ground; on its other sides the sanctuary remained exposed. In the course of the ages, however, through the constant additions of people to the embankment, the hilltop by this process of leveling up was widened. They further broke down the north wall and thus took in an area as large as the whole Temple area subsequently occupied. Then, after having enclosed the hill from its base on (the other) three sides, and accomplished a task greater than they could ever have hoped to achieve—a task upon which long ages were spent by them as well as all their sacred treasures, though replenished by the tributes offered to God from every quarter of the world—they built around the original block the upper courts and the lower Temple enclosure. The latter, where its foundations were lowest, they built up from a depth of three hundred cubits; at some spots this figure was exceeded. The whole depth of the foundations was not, however, apparent, for they filled up a considerable part of the ravines, wishing to level the narrow alleys of the town. Blocks of stone were used in building measuring forty cubits; for lavish funds and popular enthusiasm led to incredible enterprise, and a task seemingly interminable was through perseverance and in time actually achieved. (Josephus, *War* 5.5.1)

Josephus proceeds to describe the gates into the Temple complex, and the Mishna too
names and locates them.

In the western part of the court (of the Temple) there were four
gates. The first led to the palace over the intervening ravine, two others
led to the suburbs, and the last led to the other part of the (Upper) city,
from which it was separated by many steps going down into the ravine
and from here up again to the hill. For the city lay opposite the Temple,
being in the form of a theater and being bordered by a deep ravine along
its whole southern side. The fourth front of this (court), facing south, also
had gates in the middle, and had over it the Royal Portico, which had
three aisles extending in length from the eastern to the western ravine.
And it was a structure more noteworthy than any under the sun. For
while the depth of the ravine was great, and no one who bent over to look
into it from above could bear to look down to the bottom, the height of
the portico standing over it was so very great that anyone looking down
from its rooftop, combining the two elevations, he would become dizzy
and his vision would be unable to reach the end of so measureless a depth.
(Josephus, *Antiquities* 15.11.5)

There are five gates to the Temple Mount: the two Huldah Gates on
the south that served for coming in and for going out; the Kiponus gate
on the west that served for coming in and going out; the Tadi Gate on the
north which was not used at all; the eastern on which was portrayed [or
sculpted] the Palace of Shushan. Through this the High Priest who
burned the (Red) Cow and the heifer and all (the priests) who aided him
went forth to the Mount of Olives. (M.Middoth 1:3)

20. The Annexation of Judea to the Roman Empire

Whatever his own subjects thought of him, Herod was a useful and obliging client
to his Roman masters, not least for his capacity and willingness to maintain order,
if not peace, in his own turbulent kingdom. He cost the Romans little and gave a
substantial return. How substantial appeared immediately after his death in 4 B.C.E.
In his own plans for his succession, Herod's choice for Judea fell upon his son
Archelaus. As the ineffective Archelaus was preparing to go to Rome to secure his
appointment as king—"because Caesar was to have control of all the settlements
he [Herod] had made"—disturbances broke out in Jerusalem, and at his departure
the Roman governor of Syria had to intervene with a legion to quell them. Ar-
chelaus' appointment did not pass uncontested. A delegation of Jews went to Rome
and rehearsed Herod's crimes against the people.

. . . That, in short the Jews had borne more calamities from Herod, in a few years, than had their forefathers during all that interval of time that had passed since they had come out of Babylon, and returned home, in the reign of Xerxes. . . . Whereupon, they prayed that the Romans would have compassion upon the remains of Judea and not expose what was left of them to such as would barbarously tear them to pieces, and that they would join their country to (the province of) Syria and administer the government by their own commanders. (Josephus, *War* 2.6.2)

The Romans were willing to oblige on this occasion, and in 6 C.E. Judea was joined to the province of Syria and thereafter administered by a Roman prefect.

21. The View from the Diaspora

Elsewhere around the Mediterranean, where the Jews lived in colonies in the lands of others, they had passed, like those lands themselves, directly from Greek to Roman sovereignty. The largest of those Jewish communities that constituted what was called "the Diaspora" was in Egypt. We do not know a great deal about it; people appear to have prospered, particularly in Alexandria, though in a milieu that on occasion displayed profoundly anti-Jewish sentiments. One of the more violent outbursts took place in Alexandria in 38 C.E., when there were attacks upon the Jewish quarters: synagogues were broken into, statues of Emperor Caligula erected there, and the Jews officially denounced as "aliens and foreigners." Here Philo, the chief spokesman of the Alexandrian Jews and the head of a Jewish delegation to the emperor in 39 C.E., undertakes to set straight the record on the Jews for the benefit of his sovereign in Rome.

It was perfectly clear that the rumor of the overthrow of the synagogues beginning at Alexandria would spread at once to the rest of Egypt and speed from Egypt to the East and the nations of the East . . . and to the West and the nations of the West. For so populous are the Jews that no one country can contain them, and therefore they settle in very many of the most prosperous countries in Europe and Asia, both in the islands and on the mainland, and while they hold the Holy City where stands the sacred Temple of the Most High God to be their mother city, yet those which are theirs by inheritance from their fathers, grandfathers and ancestors even farther back, are in each case accounted by them to be their fatherland in which they were born and reared, while to some of them they have come at the time of their foundation as immigrants to the satisfaction of the founders. It was feared, then, that people everywhere might take their cue from Alexandria and outrage their Jewish fellow citizens by rioting against their synagogues and ancestral customs.

There follows a somewhat curious argument: if their synagogues are closed or destroyed, the Jews will have no place to thank their Roman benefactors appropriately!

Now the Jews, though naturally well-disposed for peace, could not be expected to remain quiet whatever happened, not only because with all men the determination to fight for their institutions outweighs even the danger to life, but also because they are the only people under the sun who, by losing their meetinghouses, were losing also what what they would have valued as worth dying many thousands of deaths, namely their means of showing reverence to their benefactors, since they no longer had the sacred buildings where they could set forth their thankfulness. And they might have said to their enemies, "You have failed to see that you are not adding to, but taking from, the honor given to our masters; and you do not understand that everywhere in the habitable world the religious veneration of the Jews for the Augustan house has its basis, as all may see, in the meetinghouses; and if we have these destroyed, no place, no method is left to us for paying this homage. If we neglect to pay it when our institutions permit, we should deserve the utmost penalty for not tendering our requital with all due fullness. But if we fall short because it is forbidden by our own laws, which Augustus also was well pleased to confirm, I do not see what offense, either small or great, can be laid to our charge. The only thing for which we might be blamed would be that we transgressed, though involuntarily, by not defending ourselves against defections from our customs. . . .

"What we have described is an act of aggression by bitterly hostile and crafty plotters in which the authors of the outrages would not appear to be acting unjustly and the sufferers could not oppose them in safety. For surely, my good sirs, there is no honor given by overthrowing the laws, disturbing ancestral customs, outraging fellow citizens, and teaching the inhabitants of other cities to disregard the claims of fellow feeling." (Philo, *Against Flaccus* 7.45–52)

22. Divine Wisdom

With the return from exile in the last decades of the sixth century B.C.E., *the historical narrative of the canonical books of the Bible comes to an end. Thereafter the continuous voice of prophetic history is stilled. What follow are accounts of partisan religious pleaders who did not find their way into the canon—like the various books of Maccabees—or made no pretense to that status—like the un-*

ashamedly secular Josephus, who preferred to follow in the steps of Thucydides rather than those of the authors of Kings.

The past was still open to contemplation, however, even revalorization, and one notable feature of that new understanding of God's working in history is reflected in the appearance of the personified figure of Divine Wisdom, who was present at creation and whose providential hand was guiding the destiny of the Children of Israel. We see it first in the canonical book called "The Proverbs of Solomon," whose author or editor passes over Law, Temple, and Priesthood to focus on a new theme:

> The Lord created me at the beginning of His course
> As the first of His works of old.
> In the distant past I was fashioned,
> At the beginning, at the origin of earth.
> There was still no deep when I was brought forth,
> No springs rich in water;
> Before [the foundation of] the mountains were sunk,
> Before the hills I was born.
> He had not yet made earth and fields,
> Or the world's first clumps of clay.
> I was there when He set the heavens into place;
> When He fixed the horizon upon the deep;
> When He made the heavens above firm,
> And the fountains of the deep gushed forth;
> When He assigned the sea its limits,
> So that its waters never transgress His command;
> When He fixed the foundations of the earth,
> I was with Him as a confidant,
> A source of delight every day,
> Rejoicing before Him at all times,
> Rejoicing in the inhabited world,
> Finding delight with mankind.
> (Proverbs 8:22–31)

Jesus ben Sira, sometime about 180 B.C.E., writes with the just cited text before him.

> Hear the praise of Wisdom from her own mouth,
> as she speaks with pride among her own people,
> before the assembly of the Most High
> and in the presence of the heavenly host:

"I am the Word which was spoken by the Most High;
it was I who covered the earth like a mist.
My dwelling place was in high heaven;
my throne was in a pillar of cloud.
Alone I made a circuit of the sky
and traversed the depths of the abyss.
The waves of the sea, the whole earth,
every people and nation are under my sway.
Among them all I looked for a home:
in whose territory was I to settle?
Then the Creator of the universe laid a command upon me:
my Creator decreed where I should dwell.
He said, "Make your home in Jacob;
find your heritage in Israel."
Before time began He created me,
and I shall remain forever.
In the sacred tent I ministered in His presence,
and so I came to be established in Sion.
Thus He settled me in the city He loved
and gave me authority in Jerusalem.
I took root among the people whom the Lord had honored
by choosing them to be his special possession.
There I grew like a cedar of Lebanon,
like a cypress on the slopes of Hermon,
like a date-palm at Engedi,
like roses at Jericho.
I drew like a fair olive tree in vale,
or like a plane tree planted beside the water. . . .

"Come to me, you who desire me,
eat your full of my fruit.
The memory of me is sweeter than syrup,
the possession of me is sweeter than the honey
dripping from the comb.
Whoever feeds on me will be hungry for more,
and whoever drinks from me will thirst for more.
To obey me is to be safe from disgrace;
those who work in wisdom will not go astray."
(Wisdom of Jesus ben Sira [Ecclesiasticus] 24:1–22)

23. The Vision of Daniel

The visionary style was not new in Israel—we have already seen an example in the Exilic prophet Ezekiel—but what was more typical, and urgent, was the transcendental quality of what these latter-day seers saw. They were experiencing a New Age, terrible and glorious in turn, a trial and a fulfillment of Israel on some level of experience far different from that of history.

One such work that was included in the Jewish canon was the prophecy attributed to a certain Daniel. The time purports to be that of the Exile, but the circumstances of the book are transparently those of the second century B.C.E., when the Greeks were in the land of Israel. The trials of Daniel at the court of Nebuchadnezzar take up the first six books of the work, at which point there is a somewhat abrupt shift into another mode:

In the first year of King Belshazzar of Babylon, Daniel saw a dream and a vision of his mind in bed; afterward he wrote down the dream. Beginning the account, Daniel related the following:

"In my vision at night, I saw the four winds of heaven stirring up the great sea. Four mighty beasts different from each other emerged from the sea. The first was like a lion but had eagles' wings. As I looked on, its wings were plucked off, and it was lifted off the ground and set on its feet like a man and given the mind of a man. Then I saw a second, different beast, which was like a bear but raised on one side, and with three fangs in its mouth among its teeth; it was told, "Arise, eat much meat!" After that, as I looked on, there was another one, like a leopard, and it had on its back four wings like those of a bird; the beast had four heads, and dominion was given to it. After that, as I looked on in the night vision, there was a fourth beast—fearsome, dreadful, and very powerful, with great iron teeth—that devoured and crushed, and stamped the remains with its feet. It was different from all the other beasts which had gone before it; and it had ten horns. While I was gazing upon these horns, a new little horn sprouted up among them; three of the older horns were uprooted to make room for it. There were eyes in this horn like those of a man, and a mouth that spoke arrogantly. As I looked on,

> Thrones were set in place,
> And the Ancient of Days took his seat.
> His garment was like lamb's wool.
> And the hair of his head was like lamb's wool.
> His throne was tongues of flame;
> Its wheels were blazing fire.

> A river of fire streamed forth before Him;
> Thousands upon thousands served Him;
> Myriads upon myriads attended Him;
> The court sat and the books were opened.

"I looked on. Then, because of the arrogant words that the horn spoke, the beast was killed as I looked on; its body was destroyed and it was consigned to the flames. The dominion of the other beasts was taken away, but an extension of life was given to them for a time and season. As I looked on, in the night vision,

> One like a human being
> Came with the clouds of heaven;
> He reached the Ancient of Days
> And was presented to Him.
> Dominion, glory, and kingship were given to him;
> All peoples and nations of every language must serve him.

> His dominion is an everlasting dominion that
>   shall not pass away.
> And his kingship, one that shall not be destroyed.

"As for me, Daniel, my spirit was disturbed within me and the vision of my mind alarmed me. I approached one of the attendants and asked him the true meaning of all this. He gave me this interpretation of the matter: 'These great beasts, four in number, (mean) four kingdoms will arise out of the earth; then holy ones of the Most High will receive the kingdom, and will possess the kingdom forever—forever and ever.' Then I wanted to ascertain the true meaning of the fourth beast, which was different from them all, very fearsome, with teeth of iron, claws of bronze that devoured and crushed, and stamped the remains; and of the ten horns on its head; and of the new one that sprouted, to make room for which three fell—the horn that had eyes, and a mouth that spoke arrogantly, and which was more conspicuous than its fellows. (I looked on as that horn made war with the holy ones and overcame them, until the Ancient of Days came and judgment was rendered in favor of the holy ones of the Most High, for the time had come, and the holy ones took possession of the kingdom.) This is what he said: 'The fourth beast (means)—there will be a fourth kingdom upon the earth which will be different from all the other kingdoms; it will devour the whole earth, tread it down, and crush it. And the ten horns (mean)—from that kingdom, ten kings will arise, and after them another will arise. He will be different from the former ones, and will bring low three kings. He will speak words against the Most High, and will harass the holy ones of the Most High. He will think of changing times and laws, and they will be delivered into his power for a time, times, and half a time. Then the court will sit and his dominion will be taken away, to be destroyed and abolished for all time. The kingship and dominion and grandeur belonging to all the kingdoms under heaven will be given to the people of the holy ones of the Most High. Their kingdom shall be an everlasting kingdom, and all dominions shall serve and obey them.' Here the account ends. I, Daniel, was very alarmed by my thoughts, and my face darkened; and I could not put the matter out of my mind." (Daniel 7:1–28)

Here, then, is a vision not of the End Time but of a historical resolution, though mediated in heaven. The vision is allegorical and supplies its own interpretation— "These great beasts, four in number, [mean] four kingdoms"—at least to the extent of telling us that the context is political. Which kingdoms are meant, we are left to guess. Most commentators have supposed that the reference is to the Babylonian, Median, Persian, and Greek kingdoms and that within the latter the "little horn" is Antiochus Epiphanes.

This is plausible, and it would seem equally plausible that by the "Ancient in Years" is meant God Himself. Daniel does not ask and the anonymous interpreter offers no explanation of the "One like a human being / Came with the clouds of heaven," to whom "Dominion, glory and kingship" were given. Here too, however, it seems likely from the text that the "saints" of the people of Israel are thus personified.

24. Jewish Voices in the First Christian Century

One way of bringing a new understanding to the now classical texts of the biblical canon was to retell them in the disguise of one of the earlier prophets, as was done in the book called Jubilees, in those attributed to Enoch, Baruch, and Ezra, and in those circulated under the name of Solomon. All of these anonymous authors concealed under older names were addressing the present, of course. In some cases they attempted to peer into the future, since one of the predominant modes of post-Exilic literature—when it was not dispensing a mild terrestrial wisdom, often in the current Hellenic style, or a more transcendental appeal to a personified Divine Wisdom—was "unveiling" the future in the form of visions of the End Time.

The historical Baruch was a contemporary of Jeremiah, best known for having written down that latter prophet's utterances. But in the first century of the Christian era the name became a popular magnet for apocalypses, and a number of them circulated under his name. One of them, preserved only in Syriac and generally called 2 Baruch, is of special interest in that it represents a Jewish voice, or rather a number of Jewish voices, contemporary to Paul, the destruction of Jerusalem, and the growth of the Christian movement.

Whatever happens then will happen to the whole earth; so that all who are alive will experience it. For at that time I will protect only those who are found in those days in this land. And it shall be that when all is accomplished that was to come to pass in the twelve periods before the end, the Messiah shall then begin to be revealed. And Behemoth shall appear from his place and Leviathan shall ascend from the sea—those two great monsters I created on the fifth day of creation and have kept until then; and then they shall serve as food for all that survive. . . . And those who have been hungry will rejoice; and also, they shall see marvels every day. . . .

And it shall come to pass after this, when the time of the presence of the Messiah on earth has run its course, that he will return in glory to the heavens. Then all who have died and have set their hopes on him will rise again. And it shall come to pass at that time that the treasuries will be opened in which is preserved the number of the souls of the righteous, and they will come out, and the multitude of souls will appear together in one single assembly; and those who are first will rejoice and those who are last will not be cast down. For each of them will know that the predetermined end of the times has come. But the souls of the wicked, when they see all this, will be the more discomforted. For they will know that their torment is upon them and that their perdition has arrived. (2 Baruch 29–30)

Another such work was the so-called Psalms of Solomon, written about the time Pompey and the Romans took and sacked Jerusalem in 63 B.C.E.

Behold, O Lord, and raise up for them their king, the son of David.
For the time You did foresee, O God, that he may reign over Israel
                  Your servant.
And gird him with strength, that he may shatter unrighteous rulers
And purify Jerusalem of the nations which trample her down in
                  destruction.
In wisdom, in righteousness, may he expel sinners from the inheritance.
May he smash the sinners' arrogance like a potter's vessel.
With a rod of iron may he break in pieces all their substance:
 May he destroy the lawless nations by the word of his mouth.
So that, at his rebuke, nations before him;

And may he reprove sinners by the word of their own hearts.
And he shall gather together a holy people, whom he shall lead
        in righteousness,
And he shall judge the tribes of the people which has been sanctified
        by the Lord his God.
And he shall not permit unrighteousness to lodge any more in
        their midst,
Nor shall there dwell with them any man with knowledge of wickedness,
For he shall know them, that they are all sons of their God. . . .

And he shall be a righteous king, taught by God, over them,
And there shall be no unrighteousness in his days in their midst,
For all shall be holy and their king the anointed Lord. . . .

He will bless the people of the Lord with wisdom and joy,
And he himself is pure from sin, so that he may rule a great people,
That he may rebuke rulers, and remove sinners by the might of his word.
And during his days he shall not be weakened, relying upon his God;
For God created him strong in the holy spirit,
And wise in prudent counsel, together with strength and righteousness.
And the blessing of the Lord is with him providing strength,
And he shall not be weakened.
His hope is upon the Lord;
Who then can prevail against him?
(Psalms of Solomon 17:23–39)

25. The Son of Man

The first Book of Enoch is a composite that includes a number of visions, with one of them, the second, expressed in the form of parables. These are difficult to date, but for all their later popularity with Christians, they appear to have been composed well before the time of Jesus and perhaps as long as a century or more before his day. This is how the second vision begins.

The second vision which he saw, the vision of wisdom, which Enoch the son of Jared, the son of Mahalel, the son of Cainan, the son of Enosh, the son of Seth, the son of Adam, saw. And this is the beginning of the words of wisdom which I raised my voice to speak and say to those who dwell on the dry ground: Hear me, you men of old, and see, you who come after, the words of the Holy One which I will speak before the Lord of Spirits. It would have been better to have said these things before, but from those who come after we will not withhold the beginning of wisdom. Until now there has not been given by the Lord of Spirits such wisdom as I have now received in accordance with my insight, in accordance with the wish of the Lord of Spirits by whom the lot of eternal life has been given me. And three Parables were imparted to me, and I raised my voice and said to those who dwell on the dry ground. (1 Enoch 37:1–5)

All three parables are filled with Messianic associations, where the titles of "The Anointed One," "The Righteous One," "The Elected One" are all applied to him. In addition, the second and third bear a number of references to the more unusual "Son of Man," the same designation that appears to be used in a Messianic context in the Gospel of Mark.

And at that hour that Son of Man was named in the presence of the Lord of Spirits, and his name was named before the Head of Days. Even before the sun and the constellations were created, before the stars of the heaven were made, his name was named before the Lord of Spirits. He will be a staff to the righteous and the holy, that they may lean on him and not fall, and he shall be the light of the nations, and he will be the hope of those who grieve in their hearts. All who dwell upon the dry ground will fall down and worship before him, and they will bless, and praise, and celebrate with psalms the name of the Lord of Spirits. And because of this he was chosen and hidden before him, before the world was created, and forever. But the wisdom of the Lord of Spirits has revealed him to the holy and righteous, for he has kept safe the lot of the righteous, for they have hated and rejected this world of iniquity, and all its works and ways they have hated in the name of the Lord of Spirits; for in his name they are saved, and he is the one who will require their lives. (1 Enoch 48:2–7)

And they had great joy, and they blessed and glorified and exalted because the name of that Son of Man has been revealed to them. And he sat on the throne of his glory, and the whole judgment was given to the Son of Man, and he will cause the sinners to pass away and be destroyed from the face of the earth. And those who have led astray the world will be bound in chains, and will be shut up in the assembly place of their destruction, and all their works will pass away from the face of the earth. And from then on there will be nothing corruptible, for that Son of Man has appeared, and has sat on the throne of his glory, and everything evil will pass away and go from before him; and the word of that Son of Man will be strong before the Lord of Spirits. This is the third Parable of Enoch. (1 Enoch 69:26–29)

And from the end of the third parable:

And that angel came to me and greeted me with his voice and said to me: "You are the Son of Man who was born to righteousness, and righteousness remains over you, and the righteousness of the Head of Days will not leave you." And he said to me, "He proclaims peace to you in the name of the world which is to come; for from there peace has come out from the creation of the world; and so you will have it for ever and for ever and ever. And all will walk according to your way, inasmuch as righteousness will never leave you; with you will be their dwelling, and with you their lot, and they will never be separated from you for ever and ever and ever. And so there will be length of days with that Son of Man, and the righteous will have peace and an upright way in the name of the Lord of Spirits for ever and ever." (1 Enoch 71:14–17)

26. The Rabbis Discuss the Messiah

Many of these freewheeling apocalyptic writings run down in time to about 200 C.E., when the Mishna was being put together as the authoritative codex of the Jewish Oral Law. Tracts like Baruch and Enoch are visionary, poetical, and often ecstatic, while the rabbis represented in the Mishna, and those who sat down in the yeshivas or academies to study it, were primarily concerned with the prescriptions of the Law. Their interests, if not their methods, occasionally converged, however. One such point of convergence is the question of the Messiah. Rabbi Judah's Mishna does not pay a great deal of formal attention to the issue, but one passage in that text dealing with "the world to come" prompted Messianic speculation by the next generation of rabbis in a Mishnaic text that we will see again in Chapter 5 below in a different context.

All Israelites have a share in the world to come, for it is written, "Your people also shall be all righteous, they shall inherit the land forever; the branch of My planting, the work of My hands that I might be glorified" (Isa. 60:21). And these are they who have no share in the world that is to come: he that says that there is no resurrection of the dead prescribed in the Law, and he that says that the Law is not from heaven, and an Epicurean [that is, a skeptic or doubter]. Rabbi Akiba says: Also he that reads non-canonical books, or that utters a charm over a wound. . . . Abba Saul says: Also he that pronounces the Name (of God) with its proper letters. (M.Sanhedrin 10:1)

The discussion of this in the Babylonian Talmud winds about until it at length reaches the Messianic question.

Rabbi Nahman said to Rabbi Isaac, "Have you heard when the Bar Nafle [possibly the "Son of the Clouds" of Dan. 7:13] will come?" "Who is Bar Nafle?" he asked. "Messiah," he answered. "Do you call Messiah Bar Nafle?" "Even so," he rejoined, "as it is written, 'In that day I will raise up a tabernacle of David that is fallen [in Hebrew *ha-nofeleth*, of the same root as "Nafle"]' (Amos 9:11)." He replied, "Thus has Rabbi Yohanan said: 'In the generation when the Son of David [that is, the Messiah] will come, scholars will be few in number, and as for the rest, their eyes will fail through sorrow and grief. Multitudes of troubles and evil decrees will be promulgated anew, each new evil coming with haste before the other has ended.' " (BT.Sanhedrin 96b–97a)

Thus we are launched on a long discussion not so much of the character, personality, or even the work of the Messiah as of the characteristics of the Messianic era and when that time might be expected to come. The discourse goes on.

Our Rabbis taught: In the seven-year cycle at the end of which the Son of David will come—in the first year this verse will be fulfilled: "And I will cause it to rain on one city and cause it not to rain on another city" (Amos 4:7); in the second the arrows of hunger will be sent forth; in the third, a great famine, in the course of which men, women and children, pious men and saints, will die and the Torah will be forgotten by its students; in the fourth, partial plenty; in the fifth, great plenty, when men will eat, drink and rejoice; in the sixth, heavenly sounds; in the seventh, wars, and at the conclusion of the seven-year cycle the Son of David will come." Rabbi Joseph demurred: But so many such seven-year cycles have passed, yet he has not come! Abaye retorted: Were there then heavenly sounds in the sixth and wars in the seventh? Moreover, have they been in this order?

It has been taught, Rabbi Judah said: In the generation when the Son of David comes, the House of Assembly will be for harlots, Galilee in ruins, Gablan lie desolate, the border inhabitants wander about from city to city, receiving no hospitality, the wisdom of the scribes in disfavor, God-fearing men despised, people dog-faced, and truth entirely lacking, as it is written, "Yes, truth fails and he that departs from evil makes himself a prey" (Isa. 59:15).

There may have been some attempt at a historical identification of these rather generalized circumstances, but they are not included in the text. At some points, however, there may have been more specific events behind the words, as in this remark, which may reflect the spread of Christianity, "heresy," through the Roman Empire, the "kingdom" of the text, or even the whole world.

It has been taught, Rabbi Nehemiah said: In the generation of Messiah's coming impudence will increase, esteem be perverted, the wine yield its fruits and yet wine be dear, and the Kingdom will be converted to heresy, with none to rebuke them. This supports Rabbi Isaac, who said: The Son of David will not come until the whole world is converted to the belief of the heretics. Raba said: What verse proves this? "It [that is, the leprosy] is all turned white; he is clean" (Lev. 13:13).

Here the reference to the Hasmoneans, the Herodians, and the revolt of Bar Kokhba in 132–135 C.E. is unmistakable.

It has been taught: Rabbi Nathan said: This verse pierces and descends to the very abyss: "For the vision is yet for an appointed time, but at the end it shall speak and not lie; though he tarry, yet wait for him, because it will surely come; it will not tarry" (Hab. 2:3). Not as our Masters, who interpreted the verse "until a time and times and the dividing of time" (Dan. 7:25); nor as Rabbi Simlai, who expounded the verse "You feed them with the bread of tears, and give them tears to drink a third time" (Ps. 80:6); nor as Rabbi Akiba, who expounded the verse "Yet once, it is a little while and I will shake the heavens and the earth" (Hag. 2:6); but the first dynasty [that is, the Hasmoneans] shall last seventy years, the second [the Herodian] fifty-two, and the reign of Bar Koziba [or Bar Kokhba] two and a half years.

But there was, after all, no great certainty, and even a certain display of wit.

Rab said: The world was created only on David's account. Samuel said: On Moses' account. Rabbi Yohanan said: For the sake of the Messiah. What is the Messiah's name? The School of Rabbi Shilah said: His name is Shiloh, for it is written, "Until Shiloh comes" (Gen. 49:10). The School of Rabbi Yannai said: His name is Yinnon, for it is written, "His name shall endure forever; before the sun, his name was Yinnon" (Ps. 72:17). The School of Rabbi Haninah maintained: His name is Haninah, as it is written, "Where I will not give you Haninah" (Jer. 16:13). Others say: His name is Menahem the son of Hezekiah, for it is written, "Because Menahem [or "The Comforter"], who would relieve my soul, is far away" (Lam. 1:16).

This last suggestion—that the Messiah was, not will be, Menahem the son of Hezekiah—carries us into an entirely new position: there will be no future Messiah because he has already come.

Rabbi Hillel said: There shall be no Messiah for Israel because they have already enjoyed him in the days of Hezekiah. Rabbi Joseph said: May

God forgive him (for saying so). Now when did Hezekiah flourish? During the first Temple. Yet Zechariah, prophesying in the days of the second [that is, after the Exile], proclaimed: "Rejoice greatly, O daughter of Sion, O daughter of Jerusalem; behold, the king comes to you! He is just and, having salvation, lowly; and riding upon an ass, and upon a colt, the foal of an ass" (Zech. 9:9). (BT. Sanhedrin 97a–99a)

It is tempting to think that here too the spread of Christianity, with its own Messianic claims, had influenced the rethinking of the Messianic question by Rabbi Hillel. This opinion that the Messiah had already come did not in any event find a great deal of support in either rabbinical or later circles, but it does bring us full circle to the beginnings of Messianic speculation in Israel. The time of troubles from which release would come may well have been the Assyrian invasion at the end of the seventh century B.C.E., as we have seen, and Hezekiah may indeed have been Isaiah's candidate for the instrument of that release. A millennium later the troubles were still political, though they now bore a Roman face, and a savior-king was just as urgently required.

27. The Rabbis Preach the Suffering Redeemer

The Pesikta Rabbati is an assembly of rabbinic meditations on the Torah lessons read in the synagogue throughout the year on the Sabbath. Although this collection was not finally put together until Islamic times, the material in it is mostly Talmudic. The homiletic approach, it is obvious, is not very different from that taken by the discussions of the Messiah in the Talmud itself. We begin with the Sabbath lesson.

> Arise, shine, for your Lord is come,
> And the glory of the Lord is risen upon you.
> For behold, darkness will cover the earth,
> And gross darkness the peoples; but upon you
> The Lord will arise, and His glory shall be
> Seen upon you. (Isa. 60:1–2)

These words are to be considered in the light of what David king of Israel was inspired by the Holy Spirit to say: "For with You is the fountain of life; in Your light do we see light" (Ps. 36:10). . . . What is meant by "in Your light we see light"? What light is it that the congregation of Israel looks for as from a watchtower? It is the light of the Messiah, of which it is said, "And God saw the light and it was good" (Gen. 1:4). This verse proves that the Holy One, blessed be He, contemplated the Messiah and his works before the world was created, and then under His throne of glory put away the Messiah until the time of the generation in which he will appear.

Satan asked the Holy One, blessed be He: Master of the universe, for whom is the light which is put away under Your throne of glory? God replied: For him who will turn you back and put you to utter shame. Satan said: Master of the universe, show him to me. God replied: Come and see him. And when he saw him, Satan was shaken, and he fell upon his face and said: Surely this is the Messiah who will cause me and the counterparts in heaven of the princes of the earth's nations to be swallowed up in Gehenna. . . . In that hour all princely counterparts of the nations in agitation will say to Him: Master of the universe, who is this through whose power we are to be swallowed up? What is his name? What kind of being is he?

The Holy One, blessed be He, will reply: He is the Messiah, and his name is Ephraim, My true Messiah, who will pull himself up straight and will pull up straight his generation, and who will give light to the eyes of Israel and deliver his people; and no nation or people will be able to withstand him. . . .

(At the time of the Messiah's creation) the Holy One, blessed be He, will tell him in detail what will befall him: There are souls that have been put away with you under My throne, and it is their sins which will bend you down under a yoke of iron and make you like a calf whose eyes grow dim with suffering and will choke your spirit as with a yoke; because of the sins of those souls your tongue will cleave to the roof of your mouth. Are you willing to endure such things?

The Messiah will ask the Holy One, blessed be He: Will my suffering last many years? The Holy One, blessed be He, will reply: Upon your life and the life of My head, it is a period of seven years which I have decreed for you. But if your soul is sad at the prospect of your suffering, I shall at this moment banish those sinful souls. The Messiah will say: Master of the universe, with joy in my soul and gladness in my heart I take this suffering upon myself, provided that not one soul in Israel perish; that not only those who are alive to be saved in my days, but also those who are dead, who died from the days of Adam up to the time of the redemption; and that not only those to be saved in my days, but also those who died as abortions; and that not only those to be saved in my days, but all those whom You have thought to create but were not created. Such are the things I desire, and for these I am ready to take upon myself (whatever You decree).

The following passage from the same section seems to be from a later stratum of comment and to refer to contemporary events, possibly sometime just before the Muslim conquest of the Near East in the seventh century C.E.

Rabbi Isaac taught: In the year in which the king Messiah reveals himself, all the kings of the nations of the earth will be at strife with one another. The king of Persia will make war against the king of Arabia, and this king of Arabia will go to Edom and take counsel of the Edomites [who are usually the Romans or Byzantines in this context]. Thereupon the king of Persia will again lay the whole world waste. . . . And Israel, agitated and frightened, will say: Where shall we go, where shall we come? God will reply: My children, be not afraid, the time of your redemption is come. And this latter redemption will not be like your previous redemption, for following your previous redemption you suffered anguish and enslavement by the kingdoms; as for this redemption— following this one you will have no anguish or enslavement by the kingdoms.

Our Masters taught: When the Messiah appears, he will come stand on the roof of the Temple and will make a proclamation to Israel, saying: Meek ones, the day of your redemption is come. And if you do not believe me, behold my light which rises upon you, as it is said, "Arise, shine, for your light is come, and the glory of the Lord is risen upon you." And it has risen only upon you and not the nations of the earth, as it is said, "For behold, darkness shall cover the earth, and gross darkness the peoples; but upon you the Lord shall rise, and His glory shall be seen upon you." (*Pesikta Rabbati* 36:1–2) [PESIKTA RABBATI 1968: 2:676–683]

28. A Seventh-Century Messianic Apocalypse

There may indeed have been heightened Messianic expectations at the beginning of the Muslim era, just as there were at the time of the Roman occupation of Palestine. Among the debris of documents preserved in the storeroom of the medieval synagogue of Cairo is a poem that provides an apocalyptic vision of what it was like when the Arabs—here, as often, the "Ishmaelites"—suddenly descended on the Holy City in the seventh century. It is couched in the familiar opaque language of apocalypses, but the references are sufficiently clear—to the Byzantines or Romans as "Edomites," for example—to enable us to date it very close to 638 C.E.:

On that day when the Messiah, son of David, will come
To a downtrodden people
These signs will be seen in the world and will be brought forth:

Earth and heaven will wither,
And the sun and the moon will be blemished,
And the dwellers in the Land (of Israel) will be struck silent.

The king of the West and the king of the East
Will be ground one against the other,
And the armies of the king of the West will hold firm in the Land.
And a king will go forth from the land of Yoqtan [Arabia]
And his armies will seize the Land,
The dwellers of the world will be judged
And the heavens will rain dust on the earth,
And winds will spread in the Land.
Gog and Magog will incite one another
And kindle fear in the heart of the Gentiles.
And Israel will be freed of all their sins
And will no more be kept far from the house of prayer.

Blessings and consolations will be showered on them,
And they will be engraved on the Book of Life.
The Kings from the land of Edom will be no more,
And the people of Antioch will rebel and make peace
And Ma῾uziya [Tiberias] and Samaria will be consoled,
And Acre and Galilee will be shown mercy.
Edomites and Ishmaelites will fight in the valley of Acre
Till the horses sink in blood and panic.
Gaza and her daughters will be stoned
And Ascalon and Ashod will be terror-stricken.

Israel will go forth from the City and turn eastwards,
And taste no bread for five and four days.
And their Messiah will be revealed and they will be consoled.
And they will share pleasant secrets with their King
And they will raise praises to their King;
And all the wicked will not rise up in the Judgment.

(LEWIS 1976: 198)

29. Later Messianic Thinking

The rabbis of the Babylonian schools of the fourth and fifth centuries C.E. were somewhat vague on the functions of the Messiah to come. The destructive events of 70–135 C.E., when the city of Jerusalem was twice retaken and sacked by a Roman army, made the arrival of a political savior for Israel seem increasingly implausible at best; and after the followers of Jesus the Messiah left the body of the Jewish community and began to enjoy enormous success among the Gentiles, Messianic expectations among the Jews had necessarily to reshape themselves. Some of that rethinking may have quietly occurred among the generations of scholars who completed the Talmuds, but that was by no means the end of it. This, for example, is how the question of the Messiah of Israel appeared first to Saadya (d. 942 C.E.), the gaon, or head, of the yeshiva in Iraq, and then to Maimonides, writing toward the end of the twelfth century C.E., also within Islam. The Christian claims are not very far from their thoughts and in both instances are addressed directly. First, Saadya:

There are so-called Jews who assert that the prophetic promises and messages of comfort were all fulfilled at the time of the Second Temple and have been entirely abrogated in that nothing remains of their promise. These people base their opinion on a fundamentally wrong conception. They say that the emphatic assurances of salvation which we find in the Scripture [that is, in the Prophets] . . . were all given on condition that the obedience of the people would be complete. They said that this was similar to the promise which our teacher Moses gave to Israel . . . and that on account of their sins their kingdom came to an end and vanished; in the same way, some of the Messianic promises, they say were fulfilled at the time of the Second Temple [that is, in the era after the Exile] and then vanished, whereas others did not come to pass at all on account of the sins of the people.

In the first part of his refutation of this position Saadya attacks the notion that the promises of salvation to Israel, whether before the Exile or after, were in any way "stipulated" or "conditioned." He then turns to the notion that the Messianic Age has in fact occurred.

(1) In the Messianic Age it is expected that all creatures will believe in God and proclaim His unity, as it is said, "And the Lord shall be king over all the earth; and in that day shall the Lord be one and His Name One" (Zech. 14:9), but do we not see them still clinging to their errors and their denial of God? (2) In the Messianic Age the faithful are supposed to be free and not forced to pay tribute in money and food to other nations, as it says, "The Lord has sworn by His right hand. . . . Surely I will no more give your grain to be food for your enemies; and strangers shall not drink your wine for which you have labored" (Isa. 62:8). But do we not see that every nation is compelled to pay tribute and obedience to the nation to which it is subject? (3) In the Messianic Age we expect the abolition of wars between men and complete disarmament, as it says, "And they shall beat their swords into plowshares, and their spears into

pruning hooks; nation shall not lift up sword against nation, neither shall they learn war any more" (Isa. 2:4). But do we not see the nations fighting and contending with each other more violently than ever before? Should one try to explain that the Scripture only means to say that there will be no more wars under the banner of religion, is it not the fact that religious wars and quarrels are today more intensive than ever? (4) In the Messianic Age animals are expected to live peacefully one beside the other, the wolf feeding the lamb, the lion eating straw, and the young child playing with a snake and a basilisk . . . (Isa. 11:6–9), whereas we see that the evil nature of wild animals is still the same and they have not changed in any way. Again, should someone explain that Scripture only means to say that the wicked people will live peacefully alongside the virtuous, the facts are precisely to the contrary. For nowadays the tyranny and violence of the strong against the weak are more ruthless than ever before.

All these facts prove conclusively that the prophetic messages of comfort have not yet been fulfilled. Our refutation of the opinion held by the people we have referred to applies also to the Christians. (Saadya, *Book of Doctrines and Beliefs* 8.3) [SAADYA 1945: 175–179]

Maimonides, two and a half centuries later, on the same subject:

King Messiah will arise and restore the kingdom of David to its former state and original sovereignty. He will rebuild the sanctuary (of the Temple) and gather the dispersed of Israel. All the ancient laws will be reinstituted in his days; sacrifices will again be offered; the Sabbatical and Jubilee years will again be observed in accordance with the commandments set forth in the Law.

He who does not believe in the restoration or does not look forward to the coming of the Messiah denies not only the teachings of the prophets but also those of the Law and Moses our Teacher, for Scripture reaffirms the rehabilitation of Israel, as it is said: "Then the Lord your God will turn your captivity, and have compassion on you and will return and gather you . . . and the Lord your God will bring you into the land which your fathers possessed" (Deut. 30:3–5). These words stated in Scripture include all that the prophets said (on the subject). They recur in the section treating of Balaam (Num. 22–24). The prophecy in that section bears upon the two Messiahs: the first, namely David, who saved Israel from the hand of their enemies; and the later Messiah, a descendent of David, who will achieve the final salvation of Israel. . . .

Do not think that King Messiah will have to perform signs and wonders, bring anything new into being, revive the dead, or do similar things. It is not so. Rabbi Akiba was a great sage, a teacher of Mishna, yet he was also the armor bearer of Bar Kozba [or Bar Koziba or Kokhba, the leader of the Jewish insurrection of 135 C.E.]. He affirmed that the latter was King Messiah; he and all the wise men of his generation shared this belief until Bar Kozba was slain in (his) iniquity, when it became known he was not the Messiah. Yet the rabbis had not asked him for a sign or a token. The general principle is: This Law of ours with its statutes and ordinances is not subject to change. It is for ever and all eternity; it is not to be added to or taken away from. . . .

If there arises a king from the house of David who meditates on the Torah, occupies himself with the commandments, as did his ancestor David, observes the precepts prescribed in the Written and Oral Law, prevails upon Israel to walk in the way of Torah and repair its breaches, and fights the battles of the Lord, it may be assumed that he is the Messiah. If he does these things and (further) succeeds, rebuilds the sanctuary on its site and gathers the dispersed of Israel, he is beyond all doubt the Messiah.

The text then continues, though this passage is removed in some of the versions of the Mishneh Torah.

But if he does not meet with success, or is slain, it is obvious that he is not the Messiah promised in the Torah. He is to be regarded like all the other wholehearted and worthy kings of the house of David who died and whom the Holy One, blessed be He, raised up to test the multitude, as it is written, "And some of them that are wise shall stumble, to refine among them, and to purify, and to make white, even to the end of the end; for it is yet for the time appointed" (Dan. 11:35).

Even of Jesus of Nazareth, who imagined that he was the Messiah and was put to death by the court, Daniel had prophesied, as it is written, "And the children of the violent among your people shall lift themselves up to establish the vision, but they shall stumble" (Dan. 11:14). For has there ever been a greater stumbling than this? All the prophets affirmed that the Messiah would redeem Israel, save them, gather their dispersed, and confirm the commandments. But he caused Israel to be destroyed by their sword, their remnant to be dispersed and humiliated. He was instrumental in changing the Torah and causing the world to err and service another besides God.

But it is beyond the human mind to fathom the designs of the Creator, for our ways are not His ways, neither are our thoughts His thoughts. All these matters relating to Jesus of Nazareth and the Ish-

maelite [that is, Muhammad] who came after him, only served to clear the way for King Messiah, to prepare the whole world to worship God with one accord, as it is written, "For then will I turn to the peoples a pure language, that they may call upon the name of the Lord to serve Him with one consent" (Zeph. 3:9). Thus the Messianic hope, the Torah, and the commandments have become familiar topics, topics of conversation (among the inhabitants) of the far isles and many peoples, uncircumcised of heart and flesh. These are discussing these matters and the commandments of the Torah. Some say, "These commandments were true, but have lost their validity and are no longer binding"; others declare that they had an esoteric meaning and were not intended to be taken literally, that the Messiah has already come and revealed their their occult significance. But when the true King Messiah will appear and succeed, be exalted and lifted up, they will forthwith recant and realize that they have inherited naught but lies from their fathers, that their prophets and forebears have led them astray. (Maimonides, *Mishneh Torah* 14.11)
[MAIMONIDES 1965]

Let no one think that in the days of the Messiah any of the laws of nature will be set aside, or any innovation introduced into creation. The world will follow its normal course. The words of Isaiah, "And the wolf will dwell with the lamb, and the leopard lie down with the kid" (11:6), are to be understood figuratively, meaning that Israel will live securely among the wicked of the heathens, who are likened to wolves and leopards. . . . They will accept the true religion, and will neither plunder nor destroy, and together with Israel earn a comfortable living in a legitimate way, as it is written, "And the lion shall eat straw with the ox" (Isa. 11:7). All similar expressions used in connection with the Messianic age are metaphorical. In the days of King Messiah the full meaning of these metaphors and their allusions will become clear to all. . . .

Some of our sages say that the coming of Elijah will precede the advent of the Messiah. But no one is in a position to know the details of this and similar things until they come to pass. They are not explicitly stated by the prophets. Nor have the rabbis any traditions with regard to these matters. They are guided solely by what the scriptural texts seem to apply. Hence there is divergence of opinion on the subject. Be that as it may, neither the exact sequence of those events nor the details thereof constitute religious dogmas. No one should occupy himself with the legendary themes or spend much time on homiletic statements bearing on this and like subjects. . . .

The Sages and the prophets did not long for the days of the Messiah that Israel might exercise dominion over the world, or rule over the heathens, or be exalted by the nations, or that it might eat and drink and rejoice. Their aspiration was that Israel might be free to devote itself to the Law and its wisdom, with no one to oppress or disturb it, and thus be worthy of life in the world to come. (Maimonides, *Mishneh Torah* 14.12) [MAIMONIDES 1965]

30. A Muslim Savant Makes His Own Calculations on the Era of the Messiah

The first and most famous of the beginnings of antiquity is the fact of the creation of mankind. But among those who have a book of divine revelation, such as the Jews, Christians and Magians, and their various sects, there exists such a difference of opinion as to the nature of this fact, and as to the question of how to date from it, the like of which is not allowable for eras. Everything, the knowledge of which is connected with the beginning of creation and the history of bygone generations, is mixed up with falsifications and myths, because it belongs to a far remote age, because a long interval separates us from it, and because the student is incapable of keeping it in memory and of fixing it. God says, "Have they not got the stories about those who were before them? None but God knows them" (Quran 9:71). Therefore it is becoming not to admit any account of a similar subject, if it is not attested by a book whose correctness can be relied upon, or from a tradition for which the conditions of authenticity, according to the prevalent opinion, furnish grounds for belief.

On this note of exasperation the Muslim scientist Biruni (d. 1048 C.E.), whom we have already heard on the subject of Hanukka, opens his study of the chronology of ancient nations. The beginning of the world was indeed buried in the remote past; but as Biruni was well aware, it was ideology as much as chronology that was at work in determining the date of creation.

The Jews and the Christians differ widely on this subject (of the era of creation); for, according to the doctrine of the Jews, the time between Adam and Alexander is 3,448 years, while according to the Christian doctrine, it is 5,180 years. The Christians reproach the Jews with having diminished the number of years with the view of making the appearance of Jesus fall in the middle of the seven millennia, which are according to their view, the time of the duration of the world, so as not to coincide with the time at which, as the prophets after Moses had prophesied, the birth of Jesus from a pure virgin at the end of time would take place. . . .

The Jews expect the coming of the Messiah, who was promised to them at the end of 1,335 years after Alexander, expecting it like something which they know for certain. . . . This expectation was based on the assumption that the beginning of this era [that is, the era of Alexander the Great] coincided with the time when the sacrifices were abolished, when no more divine revelation was received, and no more prophets were sent. Then they referred to the Hebrew word of God in the fifth book of the Torah (Deut. 31:18), "I, God, shall be concealing my being until that day." And they counted the (numerical value of) letters of the words for "be concealing," which gives the sum of 1,335. This they declared to be the time during which no inspiration from heaven was received and the sacrifices were abolished, which is what is meant by God's "concealing" Himself. . . .

In order to support what they maintain, they quote two passages in the book of Daniel: "Since the time when the sacrifice was abolished until impurity comes to destruction it is 1,290 (days)" (Dan. 12:11), and the next following passage (Dan. 12:12), "Therefore happy the man who hopes to reach to 1,335 (days)." Some people explain the difference of 45 years in these two passages so as to refer the former (1,290) to the beginning of the rebuilding of Jerusalem, and the latter (1,335) to the time when the rebuilding would be finished. According to other, the first number is the date of the birth of the Messiah, while the latter is the date of his public appearance.

Further, the Jews say, when Jacob bestowed his blessing on Judah (Gen. 49:10), he informed him that the rule would always remain with his sons till the coming of him to whom the rule belongs. So in these words he told him that the rule would remain with his descendants until the appearance of the expected Messiah. And now the Jews add that this is really the case; that the rule has not been taken from them. For the *Resh Galuta*, that is, the "Chief of the Exiles" who had been banished from their homes in Jerusalem, is the master of every Jew in the world, the ruler whom they obey in all countries, whose order is carried out under most circumstances.

As to what the Jews think of the continuance of rule in the family of Judah, and which they transfer to the leadership of the exiles, we must remark that if was correct to extend the word "rule" to similar leadership by way of analogy, the Magians, the Sabians and others would partake of this, and neither the other Israelites nor other nations would be exempt therefrom. Because no class of men, not even the lowest, are without a sort of rule and leadership with relation to others who are inferior to them.

As to that which they derive from the book of Daniel . . . the first passage, "since the time when the sacrifices were abolished . . . is 1,290," admits of being referred, first, to the first destruction of Jerusalem; and, secondly, to the second destruction, which happened, however, 385 years *after* the accession of Alexander. Therefore the Jews have not the slightest reason to commence (the calculations on the coming of the Messiah) with that date which they have announced [that is, the era of Alexander the Great]. (Biruni, *Traces of the Past*) [BIRUNI 1879: 16–21]

3. The Good News of Jesus Christ

1. What Is the Good News?

From Paul, servant of Christ Jesus, Apostle by God's call, set apart for the service of the Good News. This Good News God announced before in Sacred Scriptures through His prophets. It is about His Son: on the human level he was born of David's stock, but on the level of the spirit, the Holy Spirit, he was declared Son of God by a mighty act in that he rose from the dead: it is about Jesus Christ our Lord. (Paul, *To the Romans* 1:1–4)

For Paul, the "Good News" was precisely that: the announcement of an event. But for the early Christians that same "Good News"—in Greek, euangelion; in English, the Gospel—was something more. It was the text, or rather, the four texts or books that proclaimed the event on early and good authority: the books of Matthew and John, disciples of Jesus; of Mark, a follower of Peter; and of Luke, the companion of Paul. They are our chief sources on the life and teachings of Jesus of Nazareth.

2. The Genealogy of Jesus

The bloodlines of Jesus of Nazareth are given in two of those four Gospels that record the main outlines of his life and teachings. In Luke 3:23–38 his genealogy is carried back to Adam. In Matthew, who was concerned with establishing Jesus' Messianic credentials, Jesus' ancestors are traced back to David, from whose line the Messiah will come, and then eventually to Abraham, the father of all believers.

A table of the descent of Jesus Christ, son of David, son of Abraham.

Abraham was the father of Isaac, Isaac of Jacob, Jacob of Judah and his brothers, Judah of Perez and Zarah—their mother was Tamar—Perez of Hezron, Hezron of Ram, Ram of Amminadab, Amminadab of

Nahshon, Nahshon of Salma, Salma of Boaz—his mother was Rahab—Boaz of Obed—his mother was Ruth—Obed of Jesse, and Jesse was the father of King David.

David was the father of Solomon—his mother had been the wife of Uriah—Solomon of Rehoboam, Rehoboam of Abijah, Abijah of Asa, Asa of Jehoshaphat, Jehoshaphat of Joram, Joram of Azariah, Azariah of Jotham, Jotham of Ahaz, Ahaz of Hezekiah, Hezekiah of Menasseh, Menasseh of Amon, Amon of Josiah, and Josiah was the father of Jeconiah and his brothers at the time of the deportation to Babylon.

After the deportation Jeconiah was the father of Shealtiel, Shealtiel of Zerubbabel, Zerubbabel of Abiud, Abiud of Eliakim, Eliakim of Azor, Azor of Zadok, Zadok of Achim, Achim of Eliud, Eliud of Eliezer, Eliezer of Matthan, Matthan of Jacob, Jacob of Joseph, the husband of Mary, who gave birth to Jesus called Messiah.

There were fourteen generations in all from Abraham to David, fourteen from David until the deportation to Babylon, and fourteen from the deportation to the Messiah. (Matthew 1:1–17)

3. Two Miraculous Conceptions: John and Jesus

In all three of the Synoptic Gospels—Matthew, Mark, and Luke—the figure of John, called "the Baptizer," precedes the adult Jesus onto the scene in Palestine. Luke, in fact, gives a circumstantial account of the birth of John before he describes Jesus' own nativity.

In the days of Herod, king of Judea [37–4 B.C.E.], there was a priest named Zechariah, of the division of the priesthood called after Abijah. His wife was also of priestly descent; her name was Elizabeth. Both of them were upright and devout, blamelessly observing all the commandments and ordinances of the Lord.

Once, when it was the turn of his division and he was there to take part in the divine service, it fell to his lot, by priestly custom, to enter the sanctuary of the Lord and offer incense; and the whole congregation was at prayer outside. It was the hour of the incense offering. There appeared to him an angel of the Lord, standing at the right of the altar of incense. At this sight Zechariah was startled, and fear overcame him. But the angel said to him, "Do not be afraid, Zechariah; your prayer has been heard; your wife Elizabeth will bear a son, and you shall name him John. Your heart will thrill with joy, and many will be glad that he was born, for he will be great in the eyes of the Lord. He will never touch wine or strong drink. From his very birth he will be filled with the Holy Spirit; and he will bring back many Israelites to the Lord their God. He will go before him as a forerunner, possessed by the spirit and power of Elijah, to reconcile father and child, to convert the rebellious to the ways of the righteous, to prepare a people that will be fit for the Lord."

Zechariah said to the angel, "How can I be sure of this? I am an old man and my wife is well on in years."

The angel replied, "I am Gabriel; I stand in attendance upon God, and I have been sent to speak to you and bring you this good news. But now listen: you will lose your powers of speech and remain silent until the days when these things happen to you, because you have not believed me, though at their proper time my words will be proved true. . . ."

When his period of duty was completed Zechariah returned home. After this his wife Elizabeth conceived, and for five months she lived in seclusion, thinking, "This is the Lord's doing; now at last He has deigned to take away my reproach from among men."

In the sixth month the angel Gabriel was sent from God to a town in Galilee called Nazareth, with a message for a girl betrothed to a man named Joseph, a descendant of David; the girl's name was Mary. The angel went in and said to her, "Greetings, most favored one! The Lord is with you." But she was deeply troubled by what he said and wondered what this greeting might mean. Then the angel said to her, "Do not be afraid, Mary, for God has been gracious to you; you shall conceive and bear a son, and you shall give him the name Jesus. He will be great; he will bear the title 'Son of the Most High'; the Lord God will give him the throne of his ancestor David, and he will be king over Israel forever; his reign shall never end." "How can this be?" Mary said; "I am still a virgin." The angel answered, "The Holy Spirit will come upon you, and the power of the Most High will overshadow you; and for that reason the holy child to be born from you will be called 'Son of God.' Moreover, your kinswoman Elizabeth has herself conceived a son in her old age; and she who was reputed barren is now in her sixth month, for God's promises can never fail." "Here am I," said Mary; "I am the Lord's servant; as you have spoken, so be it." And the angel left. (Luke 1:5–38)

4. The Quranic Versions

The Quranic account of Jesus begins with the birth of Mary, here identified as the daughter of Imran. In Numbers 26:58–59 Imran is the name of the father of Moses, Aaron, and their sister Mary, and so there may be some confusion here between the mother of Jesus and the sister of Moses.

Remember when the wife of Imran said: "O Lord, I offer You what I carry in my womb in dedication to your service, accept it for You hear all and know every thing."

And when she had given birth to the child, she said, "O Lord, I have delivered but a girl"—but God knew better what she had delivered; the boy could not be as that girl was—"I have named her Mary, (she said) and I give her into Your keeping. Preserve her and her children from Satan the ostracized."

Her Lord accepted her graciously and she grew up with excellence, and was given into the care of Zechariah. Whenever Zechariah came to see her in the chamber, he found her provided with food, and he asked: "Where did this come from, O Mary?" And she said, "From God who gives food in abundance to whomsoever He will."

Then Zechariah prayed to his Lord: "O Lord, bestow on me offspring, virtuous and good, for You answer all prayers." Then the angels said to him as he stood in the chamber in prayer: "God sends you good tidings of John, who will confirm a thing from God and be noble, continent, and a prophet, and one of those who are upright and do good."

He said: "O Lord, how can I have a son when I am old and my wife is barren?" "Thus," came the answer, "God does as He wills." And Zechariah said: "Give me a token, O Lord, My Lord." "The token will be," was the reply, "that you will speak to no man for three days except by signs; and remember your Lord much, and pray at evening and sunrise."

The angels said: "O Mary, indeed God has favored you and made you immaculate, and has chosen you from all the women of the world. So adore your Lord, O Mary, and pay homage and bow with those who bow in prayer."

This is news of the Unknown that We send you, for you were not there when they cast lots with quills to determine who would take care of Mary, nor when they disputed it. When the angels said: "O Mary, God gives you news of a thing from Him, for rejoicing, (news of one) whose name will be Messiah, Jesus son of Mary, illustrious in this world and the next, and one among the honored, who will speak to the people when in the cradle and in the prime of life, and will be among the upright and the doers of good."

She said: "How can I have a son, O Lord, when no man has touched me?" He said: "That is how God creates what He wills. When He decrees a thing, He says 'Be!' and it is. And He will teach him the Law and the judgment, and the Torah and the Gospel." (Quran 3:35–48)

And again:

Commemorate Mary in the Book. When she withdrew from her family people to a place in the east, and took cover from them. We sent a spirit of Ours to her who appeared before her in the concrete form of a man.

"I seek refuge in the Merciful from you, if you fear Him," she said. He replied: "I am only a messenger from your Lord (sent) to bestow a good son on you." "How can I have a son," she said, "when no man has touched me, nor am I sinful?" He said: "Thus will it be. Your Lord said: 'It will be easy for Me,' that 'We shall make him a sign for men and a blessing from Us.' This is a thing already decreed."

When she conceived him she went away to a distant place. (Quran 19:16–22)

5. The Question of the Virgin Birth

This is the story of the birth of the Messiah. Mary his mother was betrothed to Joseph. Before their wedding she found that she was with child by the Holy Spirit. Being a man of principle, and at the same time wanting to save her from exposure, Joseph desired to have the marriage contract set aside quietly. He had resolved on this when an angel of the Lord appeared to him in a dream. "Joseph, son of David," said the angel, "do not be afraid to take Mary home with you as your wife. It was by the Holy Spirit that she conceived this child. She will bear a son; and you shall give him the name Jesus for he shall save the people from their sins." All this happened to fulfill what the Lord declared through the prophet, "The virgin will conceive and bear a son and he shall be called Emmanuel" (Isa. 7:14), a name which means "God is with us." Rising from sleep Joseph did as the angel had directed him; he took Mary home to be his wife but had no intercourse with her until her son was born. (Matthew 1:18–25)

If Muslims were quite prepared to accept this account of the miraculous conception of Jesus as presented in the Gospel of Matthew, Jews were not. The rabbis, whenever they do mention Jesus, maintain that he was the illegitimate son of a quite human father; and, as will be seen, even some heretical Jewish-Christian groups likewise denied the Virgin Birth. The only place where we can get close to an actual Jewish and Christian discussion of the issue is in the Dialogue with Trypho, *written by the Gentile Christian Justin in the middle of the second century* C.E. *The arguments, drawn from philology and comparative religion, are placed by Justin in Rabbi Trypho's mouth, of course, but they are plausibly genuine.*

Trypho responded, "The passage [from Isa. 7:14 cited in Matthew's text above] does not say, 'Behold a virgin shall conceive in the womb and bring forth a son,' but rather 'Behold, a young woman shall conceive . . .' The whole prophecy is to be applied to Hezekiah, and it can be demonstrated that the events happened to Hezekiah according to the prophecy [see Chapter 2 above]. And in the myths of those who are called the Greeks it is related that Perseus was born of Danae while she was a virgin after he who is called Zeus among them had flowed into her in the form of a stream of gold. You should be ashamed of peddling the same tales as the Greeks; you should say rather that this Jesus was a human being born as a human being from human beings, and if you are attempting to demonstrate from the Scriptures that he is the Christ [that is, the Messiah], you should say that he earned the appointment as Christ by his perfect behavior in obedience to the Law, but in no event should you dare to tell fairy tales, in which case you are convicted of the same futility as the Greeks."

I replied to this . . . "Be assured, Trypho, that the very stories which the one who is called the devil deceitfully caused to be told among the Greeks, just as he operated through the sages of Egypt and the false prophets in the time of Elijah, have confirmed my understanding and faith in the Scriptures. For when they say that Dionysus was born as the son of Zeus as the result of his intercourse with Semele, and when they tell us that this same Dionysus was the inventor of wine, and that he was torn to pieces and rose again and went up to heaven, and when they introduce an ass into his mysteries, do I not recognize that he has imitated the prophecy spoken beforehand by the Patriarch Jacob and recorded by Moses (Gen. 49:11–12)?"

"When those who pass down the mysteries of Mithras [Justin continues] maintain that he was born from a rock and call the place a cave where they initiate into their traditions those who believe in him, do I not perceive that in this case they are imitating the saying of Daniel that 'A stone cut without hands from a great mountain' (Dan. 2:34), and a similar passage in Isaiah (33:16), the whole of whose utterances they attempted to imitate? For they have arranged that words encouraging right conduct should be spoken in their rites?" (Justin, *Dialogue with Trypho*)

6. The Birth of Jesus in Bethlehem

In those days a decree was issued by the Emperor Augustus for a registration to be made throughout the Roman world. This was the first registration of its kind; it took place when Quirinius was governor of Syria. For this purpose everyone made his way to his own town; and so Joseph went up to Judea from the town of Nazareth in Galilee, to register at the city of David, called Bethlehem, because he was of the house of David by descent; and with him went Mary, who was betrothed to him. She was expecting a child, and while they were there the time came for her baby to be born, and she gave birth to a son, her firstborn. She wrapped him in his swaddling clothes and laid him in a manger, because there was no room for them to lodge in the house. (Luke 2:1–7)

Eight days later the time came to circumcise him, and he was given the name Jesus, the name given by the angel before he was conceived. Then after their purification had been completed in accordance with the Law of Moses, they brought him up to Jerusalem to present him to the Lord, as prescribed in the Law of the Lord: "Every firstborn male shall be deemed to belong to the Lord" (Lev. 12:1–8), and also to make the offering as stated in the Law, "a pair of turtle doves or two young pigeons."

There was at that time in Jerusalem a man called Simeon. This man was upright and devout, one who watched and waited for the restoration of Israel, and the Holy Spirit was upon him. It had been disclosed to him by the Holy Spirit that he would not see death until he had seen the Lord's Messiah. Guided by the spirit he came into the Temple, and when the parents brought in the child Jesus to do for him what was customary under the Law, he took him in his arms, praised God and said:

"This day, Master, You give your servant his discharge in peace; now your promise is fulfilled. For I have seen with my own eyes the deliverance which You have made ready in full view of all the nations: A light that will be a revelation to the heathen and glory to your people Israel."

The child's father and mother were full of wonder at what was being said about him. Simeon blessed them and said to Mary, his mother, "This child is destined to be a sign which men reject; and you too will be pierced to the heart. Many in Israel will stand or fall because of him, and thus the secret thoughts of men will be laid bare."

... When they had done everything prescribed by the Law of the Lord, they returned to Galilee to their own town of Nazareth. The child grew big and strong and full of wisdom and God's favor was upon him. (Luke 2:21–40)

The last sentence is all we know of Jesus from the time of his circumcision until the point, some three decades later, when he makes his first public appearance in the life of Israel. It occurs at a ford of the river Jordan, and the protagonist of the scene is a Jewish revivalist named John.

7. John and the Baptism of Jesus

About that time John the Baptist appeared as a preacher in the Judean wilderness; his theme was: "Repent, for the kingdom of Heaven is upon you." It was of him that the prophet Isaiah spoke (Isa. 40:3) when he said, "A voice crying aloud in the wilderness, 'Prepare a way for the Lord; clear a straight path for him.'"

John's clothing was a rough coat of camel's hair, with a leather belt around his waist, and his food was locusts and honey. They flocked to him from Jerusalem, from all Judea, and the whole Jordan valley, and were baptized by him in the River Jordan, confessing their sins."

When he saw many of the Pharisees and Sadducees coming for baptism he said to them: "You vipers' brood! Who warned you to escape from the coming tribulation? Then prove your repentance by the fruit it bears, and do not presume to say to yourselves 'We have Abraham as our father.' I tell you that God can make children of Abraham out of these stones here. Already the axe is laid to the roots of the trees; and every tree that fails to produce good fruit is cut down and thrown into the fire. I baptize you with water, for repentance; but the one who comes after me is mightier than I. I am not fit to take off his shoes. He will baptize you with the Holy Spirit and with fire. His shovel is ready in his hand and he will winnow his threshing floor; the wheat he will gather into his granary; but he will burn the chaff on a fire that can never go out."

Then Jesus arrived at the Jordan from Galilee and came to John to be baptized by him. John tried to dissuade him. "Do you come to me?" he said. "I need rather to be baptized by you." Jesus replied: "Let it be so for the present; we do well to conform in this way with all that God requires." John then allowed him to come. After baptism Jesus came up out of the water at once, and at that moment heaven opened; he saw the Spirit of God descending like a dove to alight upon him; and a voice from heaven was heard saying, "This is my Son, my Beloved, on whom my favor rests." (Matthew 3:1–17)

We can follow the career of John to its end, since both the Gospels and Josephus supply details. Of John, Josephus says the following.

He was a good man and exhorted the Jews to lead righteous lives, practice justice toward one another and piety toward God, and so to join in baptism. In his view this was a necessary preliminary if baptism was to be acceptable to God. They must not use it to gain pardon for the sins they have committed, but as a consecration of the body, implying that the soul was thoroughly purified beforehand by right behavior. When many others joined the crowds about him, for they were greatly moved on hearing his words, Herod (Antipas; 4 B.C.E.–39 C.E.) feared that John's great influence over the people would lead to a rebellion—for they seemed already willing to do anything he might advise. Herod decided therefore that it would be much better to strike first and to be rid of him before his work led to an uprising than to wait for an upheaval, become involved in a difficult situation and see his mistake. Accordingly John was sent as a prisoner to (the fortress) Machaerus . . . because of Herod's suspicious temper, and was there put to death. (Josephus, *Antiquities* 18.5.2)

8. The Ministry Begins

When he heard that John had been arrested (by Herod Antipas), Jesus withdrew to Galilee; and leaving Nazareth he went and settled in Capernaum on the Sea of Galilee, in the district of Zebulun and Naphtali. This was to fulfill the passage in the prophet Isaiah (9: 1–2) which tells of "the land of Zebulun, the land of Naphtali, the Way of the Sea, the land beyond Jordan, heathen Galilee," and says, "The people that lived in darkness saw a great light; light dawned on the dwellers of the land of death's dark shadow."

From that day Jesus began to proclaim his message: "Repent, for the kingdom of Heaven is upon you."

Jesus was walking by the Sea of Galilee when he saw two brothers, Peter and his brother Andrew, casting a net into the lake, for they were fishermen. Jesus said to them, "Come with me, and I will make you fishers of men." And at once they left their nets and followed him.

He went on, and saw another pair of brothers, James son of Zebedee and his brother John; they were in the boat with their father Zebedee, overhauling their nets. He called them and at once they left their boat and followed him.

He went round the whole of Galilee teaching in the synagogues, preaching the gospel of the Kingdom, and curing whatever illness or infirmity there was among the people. His fame reached the whole of Syria, and sufferers from every kind of illness, racked with pain, possessed by devils, epileptic or paralyzed, were all brought to him and he cured them. Great crowds followed him, from Galilee and the Ten Towns, from Jerusalem and Judea and the Transjordan. (Matthew 4:12–35)

9. The Family of Jesus

Not much is said of the family of Jesus in the Gospels, but on a few occasions early in his public ministry we are given brief, sometimes surprising glances at his household.

On the third day there was a wedding at Cana in Galilee. The mother of Jesus was there, and Jesus and his disciples were guests also. The wine gave out, so Jesus' mother said to him, "They have no wine left." He said, "Your concern, mother, is not mine. My hour has not yet come." His mother said to the servants, "Do whatever he tells you." There were six stone water jars standing near, of the kind used for Jewish rites of purification; each held from twenty to thirty gallons. Jesus said to the servants, "Fill the jars with water," and they filled them to the brim. "Now draw some off," he said, "and take it to the steward of the feast"; and they did so. The steward tasted the water, now turned into wine, not knowing the source, though the servants who had drawn the water knew. He hailed the bridegroom and said, "Everyone serves the best wine first, and waits until the guests have drunk freely before serving the poorer sort; but you have kept the best wine till now."

This deed at Cana in Galilee is the first of the signs by which Jesus revealed his glory and led his disciples to believe in him. (John 2:1–11)

He entered a house; and once more such a crowd collected round that they had no chance to eat. When his family heard of this, they set out to take charge of him; for people were saying that he was out of his mind. (Mark 3:20–21)

"I tell you this [Jesus said], no sin, no slander is beyond forgiveness for men; but whoever slanders the Holy Spirit can never be forgiven; he is guilty of eternal sin." He said this because they had declared that he was possessed by an unclean spirit. Then his mother and his brothers arrived, and remaining outside sent in a message asking him to come out to them. "Your mother and your brothers are outside asking for you." He replied,

"Who is my mother, who are my brothers?" And looking around at those who were sitting in the circle about him, he said, "Here are my mother and my brothers. Whoever does the will of God is my brother, my sister, my mother." (Mark 3:28–35)

He left that place and went to his home town (of Nazareth) accompanied by his disciples. When the Sabbath came he began to teach in the synagogue, and the large congregation that heard him were amazed and said, "Where does he get it from?" and "What wisdom is this that has been given him?" and "How does he work such miracles? Is not this the carpenter, the son of Mary, the brother of James and Joseph and Judas and Simon? And are not his sisters here with us?" So they fell foul of him. Jesus said to them, "A prophet will always be held in honor except in his home town, and among his kinsmen and his own family." He would work no miracles there, except that he put his hands on a few sick people and healed them; and he was taken aback by their want of faith. (Mark 6:1–6)

The plain sense of this latter passage is that Jesus had brothers and sisters, all presumably younger, if we accept the Gospel account of his birth. Church tradition did not understand it so, however. At some point—it is difficult to say precisely when—it began to be affirmed not only that Mary was a virgin before and even in the birth of Jesus, as the Gospels state, but also that she remained so for the rest of her life. Leo, bishop of Rome (440–461 C.E.), put it this way in one of his sermons.

Christ was born by a new birth, conceived of a virgin, born of a virgin, without benefit of the concupiscence of paternal flesh and without injury to maternal integrity. By origin different but in nature similar, it was brought about not by normal human usage but by the divine power that a virgin conceived him, and a virgin bore him and a virgin she remained. (Leo, *Sermon* 22.2)

There are earlier attestations to this belief about the mother of Jesus, and at least one of them was elicited by an opposing point of view. A certain Helvidius maintained that Jesus indeed had brothers and sisters according to the flesh, James, the first head of the church in Jerusalem, being notable among them. The assertion brought this reply from the Latin theologian and biblical scholar Jerome in 383 C.E.

We believe that God was born of a virgin because that is what we read; that Mary married after that birth we do not believe because that we do not read. Nor do we assert this in order to condemn marriage; indeed virginity itself is one of the fruits of marriage. . . . You say that Mary did not remain a virgin (after the birth of Jesus); I prefer to say that Joseph himself was a virgin through Mary, so that from a virginal union a virgin son was born. (Jerome, *Against Helvidius* 19)

10. Jesus the Healer

A substantial part of the Gospels is given over to an account of the years that Jesus spent in Galilee preaching his message of the Kingdom in public and private and performing miraculous acts, most of them healing, that began to attract attention to him in ever-widening circles.

That day, in the evening, he [Jesus] said to them [his disciples], "Let us cross over to the other side of the lake (of Galilee)." So they left the crowd and they took him with them in the boat where he had been sitting, and there were other boats accompanying him. A heavy squall came on and the waves broke over the boat until it was all but swamped. Now he was asleep in the stern on a cushion; they roused him and said, "Master, we are sinking! Do you not care?" He awoke, rebuked the wind and said to the sea, "Hush! Be still!" The wind dropped and there was a dead calm. He said to them, "Why are you such cowards? Have you no faith even now?" They were awestruck and said to one another, "Who can this be? Even the wind and the sea obey him."

So they came to the other side of the lake, into the country of the Gerasenes. As he stepped ashore, a man possessed by an unclean spirit came up to him from among the tombs where he had been dwelling. He could no longer be controlled. Even chains were useless; he had often been fettered and chained up, but he had snapped his chains and broken the fetters. No one was strong enough to master him. And so, unceasingly, night and day, he would cry aloud among the tombs and on the hillsides and cut himself with stones. When he saw Jesus in the distance, he ran and flung himself down before him, shouting loudly, "'What do you want with me, Jesus, Son of the Most High God? In God's name do not torment me," for Jesus was already saying to him, "Out, unclean spirit, come out of this man." Jesus asked him, "What is your name?" "My name is Legion," he said, "there are so many of us." And he begged hard that Jesus would not send them out of the country.

Now there happened to be a large herd of pigs feeding on the hillside, and the spirits begged him, "Send us among the pigs and let us go into them." He gave them leave, and the unclean spirits came out and went into the pigs. And the herd of about two thousand rushed over the edge into the lake and were drowned. The men in charge of them took to their heels and carried the news to the town and the countryside, and the people came out to see what had happened. They came to Jesus and saw the madman who had been possessed by the legion of devils sitting there clothed and in his right mind; and they were afraid. The spectators told them how the madman had been cured and what had happened to the pigs. Then they begged Jesus to leave the district. . . .

As soon as Jesus had returned by boat to the other shore, a great crowd once more gathered round him. While he was still by the lakeside, the president of one of the synagogues came up, Jairus by name, and when he saw him, he threw himself down at his feet and pleaded with him. "My little daughter," he said, "is at death's door. I beg you to come and to lay your hands on her and to cure her and save her life." So Jesus went with him, accompanied by a great crowd that pressed upon him.

Among them was a woman who had suffered from hemorrhages for twelve years; and in spite of long treatment by many doctors on which she had spent all she had, there had been no improvement. On the contrary, she had grown worse. She had heard what people were saying about Jesus, so she came up behind in the crowd and touched his cloak. For she said to herself, if I touch even his clothes I shall be healed. And then and there the source of her hemorrhages dried up and she knew in herself that she was cured of her trouble. At the same time, Jesus, aware that power had gone out of him, turned round in the crowd and asked, "Who touched my clothes?" His disciples said to him, "You see the crowd pressing upon you and yet you ask 'Who touched me?'" Meanwhile he was looking around to see who had done it. And the woman, trembling with fear when she grasped what had happened to her, came and fell at his feet and told him the whole truth. He said to her, "My daughter, your faith has cured you. Go in peace, free forever from this trouble."

While he was still speaking, a message came from the president's house, "Your daughter is dead. Why trouble the Rabbi further?" But Jesus, overhearing the message as it was delivered, said to the president of the synagogue, "Do not be afraid; only have faith." After this he allowed no one to accompany him, except Peter and James and James' brother John. They came to the president's house, where they found a great commotion, with loud crying and wailing. So he went in and said to them, "Why the crying and commotion? The child is not dead; she is asleep." And they only laughed at him. But after turning all the others out, he took the child's father and mother and his own companions and went in where the child was lying. Then, taking hold of her hand, he said to her "*talitha, qum*," which means "Get up, my child." Immediately the girl got up and walked about—she was about twelve years old. At that they were beside themselves in amazement. He gave strict orders to let no one hear about it, and told them to give her something to eat. (Mark 4:33–5:43)

11. The Public Preacher

When he [Jesus] saw the crowds he went up the hill. There he took his seat, and when his disciples had gathered round him, he began to address them, and this is the teaching he gave:

How blest are those who know their need of God; the kingdom of Heaven is theirs.

How blest are the sorrowful; they shall find consolation.

How blest are those of gentle spirit; they shall have the earth for their possession.

How blest are those who hunger and thirst to see right prevail; they shall be satisfied.

How blest are those who show mercy; mercy shall be shown to them.

How blest are those whose hearts are pure; they shall see God.

How blest are the peacemakers; God shall call them His sons.

How blessed are those who have suffered persecution for the cause of right; the kingdom of Heaven is theirs.

How blest are you when you suffer insults and persecution and every kind of calumny for my sake. Accept it with gladness and exultation, for you have a reward in heaven; in the same way they persecuted the prophets before you.

You are the salt to the world. And if the salt becomes tasteless, how is its saltness to be restored? It is now good for nothing except to be thrown away and trodden underfoot.

You are light for all the world. A town that stands on a hill cannot be hidden. When a lamp is lit, it is not put under a bushel but on the lampstand, where it gives light to everyone in the house. And you, like the lamp, must shed light among your fellows, so that, when they see the good you do, they may give praise to your Father in heaven. (Matthew 5:1–16)

"Not everyone who calls me 'Lord, Lord,' will enter the kingdom of Heaven, but only those who do the will of my heavenly Father. When that day comes, many will say to me, 'Lord, Lord, did we not prophesy in your name, cast out devils in your name, and in your name perform many miracles?' Then I will tell them to their face, 'I never knew you; out of my sight, you and your wicked ways!' " . . .

When Jesus had finished this discourse the people were astounded at his teaching; unlike their own teachers, he taught with a note of authority. (Matthew 7:21–29)

12. The Parables of the Kingdom

On another occasion he began to teach by the lakeside. The crowd that gathered round him was so large that he had to get into a boat on the lake, and there he sat, with the whole crowd on the beach right down to the water's edge. And he taught them many things in parables. . . .

When he was alone the Twelve and others who were around him questioned him about the parables. He replied, "To you the secret of the kingdom of God has been given; but to those who are outside, everything comes by way of parables, so that, as Scripture says (Isa. 6:9–10), they may look and look and see nothing, they may hear and hear but understand nothing; otherwise they would turn to God and be forgiven."

He said, "The kingdom of God is like this. A man scatters seed on the land; he goes to bed at night and wakes up in the morning, and the seed sprouts and grows, he knows not how. The ground produces a crop by itself, first the blade, then the ear, then the full-grown grain in the ear. But as soon as the crop is ripe he plies the sickle because harvest time has come."

He also said, "How shall we picture the kingdom of God, or by what parable shall we describe it? It is like the mustard seed, which is smaller than any seed in the ground at its sowing, but once sown, it springs up and grows taller than any other plant, and forms branches so large that the birds can settle in its shade."

With many such parables he would give them his message, so far as they were able to receive it. He never spoke to them except in parables; but privately to his disciples he explained everything. (Mark 4:1–14)

13. Jesus' Instructions to His Disciples

Then he called his twelve disciples to him and gave them authority to cast out unclean spirits and to cure every kind of ailment and disease.

These are the names of the twelve Apostles: first Simon, also called Peter, and his brother Andrew; James, son of Zebedee, and his brother John; Philip and Bartholomew, Thomas and Matthew the tax gatherer; James son of Alpheus; Thaddeus, Simon, a member of the Zealot party [or, a man zealous for the Law], and Judas Iscariot, the man who betrayed him.

These twelve Jesus sent out with the following instructions: "Do not take the road to Gentile lands, and do not enter any Samaritan town; but go rather to the lost sheep of the house of Israel. And as you go, proclaim the message: 'The kingdom of Heaven is upon you.' Heal the sick, raise the dead, cleanse lepers, cast out devils. You received without cost; give without charge. . . .

"Whoever will acknowledge you, I will acknowledge him before my Father in heaven, and whoever disowns me before men, I will disown him before my Father in heaven.

"You must not think that I have come to bring peace to the earth. I have not come to bring peace but a sword. I have come to set a man against his father, a daughter against her mother, a son's wife against his mother-in-law; and a man will find his enemies under his own roof. No man is worthy of me who cares more for a father or a mother than for me; no man is worthy of me who cares for son or daughter; no man is worthy of me who does not take up his cross and follow in my footsteps. By gaining his life, a man will lose it; by losing his life for my sake, he will gain it. . . ."

When Jesus had finished giving his twelve disciples their instructions, he left that place and went to teach and preach in neighboring towns. (Matthew 10:1–11:1)

14. The Demand for Signs

Both Jesus and Muhammad were asked for signs to validate their message. Neither was very eager to comply.

At this some of the doctors of the Law and the Pharisees said, "Master, we would like you to show us a sign." He answered: "It is a wicked, godless generation that asks for a sign. And the only sign that will be given it is the sign of the prophet Jonah. Jonah was in the sea monster's belly for three days and three nights, and in the same way the Son of Man will be three days and three nights in the bowels of the earth. At the Judgment, when this generation is on trial, the men of Nineveh will appear against it and ensure its condemnation, for they repented at the teaching of Jonah." (Matthew 12:38–40)

And Muhammad:

They say: "How is it no signs were sent down to him from his
Lord?" Say: "The signs are with God. I am only a warner, plain and
simple." (Quran 29:50)

*The issue raised in this verse was subsequently taken up by the Quranic commen-
tators.*

"The signs are with God": This means that God sends down from
among them only what He wishes, and if He had wanted to send down
the sign which they demanded, then he would have done so.

"I am only a warner": This means that I, Muhammad, am commis-
sioned to warn and to make this warning clear through the sign [that is,
the Quran] which has been given to me. It is not for me to choose among
God's signs, so that it would be in my power to say, "Send down to me
one of this kind and not one of that kind!" Besides, I know that each sign
has a lasting purpose, and each sign is as good as that of anyone else in this
regard. (Zamakhshari, *The Unveiler*, ad loc.)

15. The Bread of Life

*Jesus did in fact point to a sign, one that provoked a strong response not only from
his opponents but even from his followers.*

They said "What sign can you give us to see, so that we may believe
you? What is the work you do? Our ancestors had manna to eat in the
desert; as Scripture says, 'He gave them bread from heaven to eat.' " Jesus
answered, "I tell you this; the truth is not that Moses gave you the bread
from heaven, but that my Father gives you the real bread from heaven.
The bread that God gives comes down from heaven and brings life to the
world." They said to him, "Sir, give us this bread now and always." Jesus
said to them, "I am the bread of life. Whoever comes to me shall never
be hungry, and whoever believes in me shall never be thirsty. But you, as
I said, do not believe, though you have seen. All that the Father gives me
will come to me, and the man who comes to me I will never turn away.
I have come down from heaven, to do not my own will but the will of
Him who sent me. It is his will that I should not lose even one of all that
He has given me, but raise them all up on the Last Day. For it is my
Father's will that everyone who looks upon the Son and puts his faith in
him shall possess eternal life; and I will raise him up on the Last Day."

At this the Jews began to murmur disapprovingly because he said "I
am the bread which came down from heaven." They said, "Surely this is

Jesus son of Joseph; we know his father and his mother. How can he now say 'I have come down from heaven'?" Jesus answered, "Stop murmuring among yourselves. No man can come to me unless he is drawn by the Father who sent me; and I will raise him up on the Last Day. It is written in the prophets: 'And they shall all be taught by God.' Anyone who has listened to the Father and learns from him comes to me. I do not mean that anyone has seen the Father. He who has come from God has seen the Father and he alone. In truth, in very truth, I tell you, the believer possesses eternal life. Your forefathers ate the manna in the desert and they are dead. I am speaking of the bread that comes down from heaven; if anyone eats this bread he shall live forever. Moreover, the bread which I will give you is my own flesh; I give it for the life of the world."

This led to a fierce dispute among the Jews. "How can this man give us his flesh to eat?" they said. Jesus replied, "In truth, in very truth I tell you, unless you eat the flesh of the Son of Man and drink his blood, you can have no life in you. Whoever eats my flesh and drinks my blood possesses eternal life, and I will raise him up on the Last Day. My flesh is real food; my blood is real drink. Whoever eats my flesh and drinks my blood dwells continually in me and I dwell in him. As the living Father sent me, and I live because of the Father, so he who eats me shall live because of me. This is the bread which came down from heaven; and it is not like the bread which our fathers ate: they are dead, but whoever eats this bread will live forever."

This was spoken in synagogue when Jesus was teaching in Capernaum. Many of his disciples on hearing it exclaimed, "This is more than we can stomach! Why listen to such talk?" Jesus was aware that his disciples were murmuring about it and asked them, "Does this shock you? What if you see the Son of Man ascending to the place where he was before? The spirit alone gives life; the flesh is of no avail. The words which I have spoken to you are both spirit and life. And yet there are some of you who have no faith." For Jesus knew all along who were without faith and who was to betray him. So he said, "This is why I told you that no one can come to me unless it has been granted to him by the Father."

From that time many of his disciples withdrew and no longer went about with him. So Jesus asked the Twelve, "Do you also want to leave me?" Simon Peter answered him, "Lord, to whom shall we go? Your words are words of eternal life. We have faith and we know you are the Holy One of God." (John 6:30–69)

16. The Heavenly Table in the Quran

In the Gospel, as we have seen, the doubters of Jesus' role and mission ask for a heavenly sign and cite Moses' reception of manna in the desert as just such a sign. In the Quran too a sign is demanded of Jesus.

Said Jesus son of Mary: "O God our Lord, send down a table well laid out with food from the skies so that this day may be a day of feast for the earlier among us and the later, and a token from You. Give us our (daily) bread, for you are the best of all givers of food."

And God said: "I shall send it down to you; but if any of you disbelieve after this, I shall inflict such punishment on him as I never shall inflict on any other creature." (Quran 5:114–115)

The Muslim commentators on the Quran were uncertain of the exact meaning of this passage, as indeed are we. What, for example, is the meaning of "may be a day of feast"? Tabari (d. 923 C.E.), one of the earliest and most abundant of the Islamic exegetes, explains the disagreement and offers his solutions.

The commentators are in disagreement concerning the interpretation of God's words "which may be a day of feast." Some think that the meaning is: Send down upon us a table and we will henceforth take the day on which it comes down as a feast day which we and our descendants will hold in esteem. . . . Others think the meaning is: Send down upon us a table from which we will all eat together. . . . Still others say that when God here speaks of a feast day, it is meant not in the sense of a festival but in the sense of a benefit which God is vouchsafing us, and an argument and a proof as well. Among these interpretations, that which comes nearest to being correct is the one which includes the following meaning: Send down upon us a table which will be a feast day for us, in that we will pray and worship our Lord on the day that it comes down, just as the people used to do on their feast days. Thus the meaning which we affirm corresponds to the normal usage that people associate with the word "feast day" in their speech and not with the interpretation that reads it "a benefit from God," since the meaning of God's speech is always to be be interpreted as lying closer to the ordinary manner of speaking of the one who makes the request than to some significance inaccessible or unknown to the speaker. . . .

The commentators likewise disagree on whether or not the table was (actually) sent down (from heaven) and concerning what was on it. Some say that it was sent down with fish and other food and that the people ate from it. Then, after its descent, the table was taken up again because of (certain) innovations they (that is, the Christians) introduced in their relationship to God. . . . Others say that it came down with fruit from Paradise. . . . Still others say that on it lay every kind of food except meat. . . . Still others hold that that God did not send down a table to the Children of Israel. Those who maintain this view have another disagreement among themselves. Many say that this may be nothing more than a figure that God has offered to His creatures to inhibit their demanding (divine) signs from the prophets of God. . . .

In our view, however, the correct interpretation is as follows: God (actually) sent down the table to those who asked Jesus to request it from his Lord. We hold this because of the information we have received on this point from the Messenger of God, his companions, and after them the exegetes. . . . Furthermore, God breaks no promise, and there will not be any contradiction in what He announces. Thus God announced in His Book that He will fulfill the request of His prophet Jesus when He says: "In truth I do send it down on you." . . . As to what was on the table, it is correct to say that there was (some kind of) food on it. It could have been fish and bread, or it could have been fruit from Paradise. There is no advantage in knowing exactly what it was, nor is there any harm in not knowing, as long as the conclusions drawn from the verse correspond with the external wording of the revelation. (Tabari, *Commentary*, *ad loc.*)

One fairly consistent Muslim interpretation of the miracle of the Table was to associate it with the multiplication of the loaves and fishes, here told in Matthew's version.

When he heard what had happened Jesus withdrew privately by boat to a lonely place; but the people heard of it and came after him in crowds by land from the towns. When he came ashore, he saw a great crowd; his heart went out for them, and he cured those of them who were sick. When it grew late the disciples came up to him and said: "This is a lonely place and the day has gone; send the people off to the villages to buy themselves food." He answered: "There is no need for them to go; give them something to eat yourselves." "All we have here," they said, "is five loaves and two fishes." "Let me have them," he replied. So he told the people to sit down on the grass; then, taking the five loaves and the two fishes, he looked up to heaven, said the blessing, broke the loaves and gave them to the disciples; and the disciples gave them to the people. They all ate to their hearts' content; and the scraps left over, which they picked up, were enough to fill twelve great baskets. Some five thousand men shared in this meal, to say nothing of women and children. (Matthew 14:13–21)

Some early Muslim authorities offered their own versions of the miracle of the Table.

Muqatil and al-Kalbi say that God answered Jesus, on whom be peace, saying: "Behold, I am sending it down to you as you requested, but whosoever eats of that food and does not believe, I will make him an example and a curse and a warning to those who will come after." They said, "We agree," so Jesus summoned Simon, the brass worker, who was the most worthy of the Apostles, and asked, "Have you any food?" He answered, "I have two small fishes and six loaves." Jesus said, "Give them to me." Then Jesus broke them into little bits and said, "Sit down in the meadow in rows of ten persons a row." Then Jesus stood up and prayed to God Most High, and God answered him, sending down blessing on them, so that they became excellent bread and excellent fish. Then Jesus arose and went and began to distribute to each row what his fingers could carry. Then he said, "Eat in the name of God," and straightway the food became so plentiful that it was up to their knees. So they ate what God willed, and there was still some left over, even though the people numbered five thousand and more. Then all the people said, "We bear witness that you are the servant of God and His Messenger." (Tha ͑alibi, *Stories of the Prophets*)

17. Two Alien Encounters

One of the issues that would exercise the early community of Jesus' followers, as we shall see, was the question of carrying his message and extending his redemptive role into the world of the non-Jew. On at least two occasions in his life Jesus had extended contact with such non-Jews in a didactic context, one a Gentile woman in the region of Tyre and Sidon and the other a Samaritan woman at a well near Shechem.

Jesus then withdrew to the region of Tyre and Sidon. And a Canaanite woman from those parts came up to him crying out, "Sir! Have pity on me, Son of David; my daughter is tormented by a devil." But he said not a word in reply. His disciples came and urged him, "Send her away; see how she comes shouting after us." Jesus replied, "I was sent to the lost sheep of the house of Israel, and to them alone." But the woman came and fell at his feet and cried, "Help me, sir." To this Jesus replied, "It is not right to take the children's bread and throw it to the dogs." "True, sir," she answered; "and yet the dogs eat the scraps that fall from the master's table." Hearing this Jesus replied, "Woman, what faith you

have! Be it as you wish." And from that moment her daughter was restored to health. (Matthew 15:21–28)

Since the fall of the Kingdom of Israel to the Assyrians in 721 C.E. and the
resettlement of pagans in the region of Samaria, the natives of that region were not
accepted by the Judeans as true Jews. As a result, they built their own temple atop
Mount Gerizim near Shechem. Most Jews avoided the region and its hostile inhabi-
tants by passing between Judea and Galilee via the Transjordan, but on this occasion
Jesus and his disciples took the more direct route northward.

A report now reached the Pharisees: "Jesus is winning and baptizing
more disciples than John"; although in fact it was only the disciples who
were baptizing and not Jesus himself. When Jesus learned this, he left
Judea and set out once more for Galilee. He had to pass through Samaria,
and on his way came to a Samaritan town called Sychar [that is,
Shechem], near the plot of ground which Jacob gave to his son Joseph and
the spring called "Jacob's Well." It was about noon and Jesus, tired after
his journey, sat down by the well.

The disciples had gone away to the town to buy food. Meanwhile a
Samaritan woman came to draw water. Jesus said to her, "Give me a
drink." The Samaritan woman said, "What! You, a Jew, ask a drink of
me, a Samaritan woman?" Jews and Samaritans, it should be noted, do
not use vessels in common. Jesus answered her, "If only you knew what
God gives and who it is that is asking you for a drink, you would have
asked him and he would have given you living water." "Sir," the woman
said, "you have no bucket and this well is deep. How can you give me
'living water'? Are you a greater man than Jacob our ancestor, who gave
us the well and drank from it himself, he and his sons, and his cattle too?"
Jesus said, "Everyone who drinks this water will be thirsty again, but
whoever drinks the water that I shall give him will never suffer thirst any
more. The water that I shall give him will be an inner spring always
welling up for eternal life." "Sir," said the woman, "give me that water,
and then I shall not be thirsty, nor have to come all this way to draw."

Jesus replied, "Go home, call your husband and come back." She
answered, "I have no husband." "You are right," said Jesus, "in saying
that you have no husband, for, although you have had five husbands, the
man with whom you are now living is not your husband; you told me the
truth there." "Sir," she replied, "I can see that you are a prophet. Our
fathers worshiped on this mountain, but you Jews say that the temple
where God should be worshiped is in Jerusalem." "Believe me," said
Jesus, "the time is coming when you will worship the Father neither on

this mountain nor in Jerusalem. You Samaritans worship without knowing what you worship, while we worship what we know. It is from the Jews that salvation comes. But the time approaches, indeed it is already here, when those who are real worshipers will worship the Father in spirit and in truth. Such are the worshipers whom the Father wants. God is spirit, and those who worship Him must worship in spirit and truth." The woman answered, "I know that Messiah—that is, Christ—is coming. When he comes he will tell us everything." Jesus said, "I am he, I who am speaking to you now." (John 4:1–26)

18. Peter's Confession of Jesus' Messiahship

Jesus' self-confession of his Messiahship in Samaria had its sequel in another, equally dramatic event.

When he came to the territory of Caesarea Philippi, Jesus asked his disciples, "Who do men say that the Son of Man is?" They answer, "Some say John the Baptist, others Elijah, others Jeremiah, or one of the prophets." "And you," he asked, "who do you say I am?" Simon Peter answered: "You are the Messiah, the Son of the Living God." Then Jesus said, "Simon, son of Jonah, you are favored indeed! You did not learn that from mortal man; it was revealed to you by my heavenly Father. And I say this to you: You are Peter, the Rock; and on this rock I will build my church and the powers of death will never conquer it. I will give you the keys of the kingdom of Heaven; what you forbid on earth will be forbidden in heaven; and what you allow on earth will be allowed in heaven." He then gave his disciples strict orders not to tell anyone that he was the Messiah. (Matthew 16:13–21)

19. The Last Days of Jesus

They were on the road, going up to Jerusalem, Jesus leading the way; and the disciples were filled with awe, while those who followed behind were afraid. He took the Twelve aside and began to tell them what was to happen to him. "We are now going to Jerusalem," he said, "and the Son of Man will be given up to the chief priests and the doctors of the Law. They will condemn him to death and hand him over to the foreign power. He will be mocked and spat upon, flogged and killed; and three days afterwards he will rise again." (Mark 10:32–34)

So begins Jesus' final visit to Jerusalem. Although he had been to the Holy City on occasion—how often or for how long is difficult to say on the Gospel evidence—he had labored during most of his brief career in his native region of Galilee. But as the end that he had anticipated approached sometime about 30 C.E., it would be played out not in the towns around the Sea of Galilee but in the heart and center of Judaism, in Jerusalem, and the Roman prefect Pilate would be one of its chief actors. And with Jesus' final journey to Jerusalem to celebrate the Passover, so moves the focus of the four Gospels that chronicle his ministry and his teaching to that same city.

They were now nearing Jerusalem; and when they reached Bethphage at the Mount of Olives, Jesus sent two disciples with these instructions: "Go to the village opposite, where you will at once find a donkey tethered with her foal beside her; untie them and bring them to me. If anyone speaks to you, say 'Our Master needs them' and he will let you take them at once." This was to fulfill the prophecy which says: "Tell the daughter of Sion, 'Here is your king, who comes to you in gentleness, riding on an ass, riding on the foal of a beast of burden.' "

It is Passover, and Jerusalem is filled with people from the other towns of Judea, from Galilee, and from the entire Diaspora.

The disciples went and did as Jesus had directed, and brought the donkey and her foal; they laid their cloaks on them and Jesus mounted. Crowds of people carpeted the road with their cloaks, and some cut branches from the trees to spread in his path. Then the crowd that went ahead and the others that came behind raised the shout: "Hosanna to the Son of David! Blessings on him who comes in the name of the Lord! Hosanna in the heavens!"

When he entered Jerusalem the whole city went wild with excitement. "Who is this?" people asked, and the crowd replied, "This is the prophet Jesus, from Nazareth in Galilee."

Jesus then went into the Temple and drove out all who were buying and selling in the Temple precincts; he upset the tables of the money-changers and the seats of the dealers in pigeons; and said to them: "Scripture says, 'My House shall be called a house of prayer,' but you are making it a robbers' cave." (Matthew 21:1–17)

John continues the story.

His disciples recalled the words of Scripture, "Zeal for thy house will destroy me." The Jews challenged Jesus: "What sign," they asked, "can you show us as authority for your action?" "Destroy this Temple," Jesus replied, "and in three days I will raise it again." They said, "It has taken forty-six years to build this Temple. Are you going to raise it again in three days?" But the Temple he was speaking of was his body. After his resurrection his disciples recalled what he had said, and they believed the Scripture and the words that Jesus had spoken. (John 2:17–22)

As he was leaving the Temple, one of his disciples exclaimed, "Look, Master, what huge stones! What fine buildings!" Jesus said to him, "You see these great buildings? Not one stone will be left upon another; all will be thrown down." (Mark 13:1–2)

"O Jerusalem, Jerusalem, Jerusalem, the city that murders the prophets and stones the messengers sent to her! How often have I longed to gather your children, as a hen gathers her brood under her wings; but you would not let me. Look, look! There is your Temple, forsaken by God. And I tell you, you shall never see me until the time when you say 'Blessings on him who comes in the name of the Lord.' " (Matthew 23:37–39)

20. The Plot against Jesus

According to John, the events leading to the arrest and execution of Jesus were set in train somewhat before the last Passover. Jesus was in Bethany, where he had raised Lazarus, the brother of Martha and Mary, from the dead (John 11:1–44).

Now many of the Jews who had come to visit Mary and had seen what Jesus did, put their faith in him. But some of them went off to the Pharisees and reported what he had done. Thereupon the chief priests and the Pharisees convened a meeting of the Council. "What action are we taking?" they said. "This man is performing many signs. If we leave him alone like this the whole populace will believe in him. Then the Romans will come and sweep away our Temple and our nation." But one of them, Caiaphas, who was High Priest that year, said, "You know nothing whatever; you do not use your judgment; it is more to your interest that one man should die for the people than that the whole nation should be destroyed." He did not say this of his own accord, but as the High Priest in office that year, he was prophesying that Jesus would die for the nation—would die not for the nation alone but to gather together the scattered children of God. So from that day on they plotted his death. (John 11: 45–53)

The Jewish Passover was now at hand, and many people went up from the country to Jerusalem to purify themselves before the festival. They looked out for Jesus, and as they stood in the Temple they asked one another, "What do you think? Perhaps he is not coming to the festival." Now the chief priests and the Pharisees had given orders that anyone who knew where he was should give information, so that they might arrest him. [And Mark adds: "It must not be during the Passover," they said, "or we should have rioting among the people."] (John 11:55–57)

21. "I Am in the Father and the Father Is in Me"

On the evening of Thursday, the day for the preparation for Passover (or somewhat earlier, according to John), Jesus gathered with his disciples in an upper room in Jerusalem to celebrate the Passover Seder with them. The meal marked, among other things, the institution of the Eucharist. The Synoptics' account is quite brief, but John includes in his narrative of Jesus' last supper a long and moving discourse to his disciples. It follows immediately upon the departure of Judas, the Apostle who was to betray him.

When he had gone out Jesus said, "Now the Son is glorified, and in him God is glorified. If God is glorified in him, God will also glorify him in Himself; and He will glorify him now. My children, for a little longer I am with you; then you will look for me, and as I told the Jews, so I tell you now, where I am going you cannot come. I give you a new commandment: love one another; as I have loved you, so you are to love one another. If there is this love among you, then all will know you are my disciples. . . .

"Set your troubled hearts at rest. Trust in God always; trust also in me. There are many dwelling places in my Father's house; if it were not so, I should have told you; for I am going there on purpose to prepare a place for you. And if I go and prepare a place for you, I shall come again and receive you to myself, so that where I am you may be also; and my way there is known to you." Thomas said, "Lord, we do not know where you are going, so how can we know the way?" Jesus replied, "I am the way; I am the truth and I am the life; no one comes to the Father except by me.

"If you knew me you would know my Father too. From now on you do know Him; you have seen Him." Philip said to him, "Lord, show us the Father and we ask no more." Jesus answered, "Have I been all this time with you, Philip, and you still do not know me? Anyone who has seen me has seen the Father. Then how can you say 'Show us the Father'? Do you not believe that I am in the Father and the Father is in me? I am not myself the source of the words I speak to you: it is the Father who dwells in me doing His own work. Believe me when I say that I am in the Father and the Father is in me; or else accept the evidence of the deeds themselves. In truth, in very truth I tell you, he who has faith in me will do what I am doing; and he will do greater things still because I am going to the Father. Indeed anything you ask in my name I will do, so that the Father may be gloried in the Son. If you ask anything in my name, I will do it.

"If you love me you will obey my commands; and I will ask the Father and He will give you another to be your Advocate, who will be with you forever, the Spirit of truth. The world cannot receive him, because the world neither sees nor knows him; but you know him because he dwells with you and is in you. I will not leave you bereft; I am coming back to you. In a little while the world will see me no longer, but you will see me; because I live, you too will live; then you will know that I am in my Father, and you in me and I in you. The man who has received my commands and obeys them, he it is who loves me; and he who loves me will be loved by my Father; and I will love him and disclose myself to him. . . .

"Peace is my parting gift to you, my own peace, such as the world cannot give. Set your troubled hearts at rest, and banish your fears. You hear me say 'I am going away, and coming back to you.' If you loved me you would be glad to hear that I was going to the Father, for the Father is greater than I. I have told you now, beforehand, so that when it happens you may have faith." (John 13:31–14:29)

22. "This Is My Commandment . . . "

"I am the real vine, and my Father is the gardener. Every barren branch of mine He cuts away; and every fruiting branch he cleans, to make it more fruitful still. You have already been cleansed by the word I have spoken to you. Dwell in me, as I in you. No branch can bear fruit by itself, but only if it remains united with the vine; no more can you bear fruit unless you remain united with me.

"I am the vine, and you are the branches. He who dwells in me, as I dwell in him, bears much fruit; for apart from me you can do nothing. He who does not dwell in me is thrown away like a withered branch. The withered branches are heaped together, thrown on the fire, and burnt.

"If you dwell in me, and my words dwell in you, ask what you will and you shall have it. This is my Father's glory, that you may bear fruit in plenty and so be my disciples. As the Father has loved me, so I have loved you. Dwell in my love. If you heed my commands, you will dwell in my love, as I have heeded my Father's commands and dwell in His love.

"I have spoken thus to you, so that my joy may be in you, and your joy complete. This is my commandment: love one another as I have loved you. There is no greater love than this, that a man should lay down his life for his friends. You are my friends, if you do what I command you. I call you servants no longer; a servant does not know what his master is about. I have called you friends because I have disclosed to you everything that I heard from my Father. You did not choose me; I chose you; I appointed you to go on and bear fruit, fruit that shall last, so that the Father may give you all that you ask in my name. This is my commandment to you: love one another." (John 15:1-17)

23. "The Victory Is Mine; I Have Conquered the World"

"Till now I have been using figures of speech; a time is coming when I shall no longer use figures but tell you of the Father in plain words. When that day comes you will make your request in my name, and I do not say that I shall pray to the Father for you, for the Father loves you Himself, because you have loved me and believed that I came from God. I came from the Father and came into the world. Now I am leaving the world again and going to the Father." His disciples said, "Why this is plain speaking; this is no figure of speech. We are certain now that you know everything, and do not need to be questioned; because of this we believe that you have come from God."

Jesus answered, "Do you now believe? Look, the hour is coming, has indeed already come, when you are all to be scattered, each to his home, leaving me alone. Yet I am not alone, because the Father is with me. I have told you all this that you may find peace. In the world you will have trouble. But courage! The victory is mine; I have conquered the world." (John 16:25-33)

24. The Arrest of Jesus

When the meal was finished, Jesus and his disciples left. It was by then late Thursday evening.

After singing the Passover Hymn, they went out to the Mount of Olives. . . . When they reached a place called Gethsemane, he [Jesus] said to his disciples, "Sit here while I pray." And he took Peter and James and John with him. Horror and dismay came over him and he said to them, "My heart is ready to break with grief; stop here and stay awake." Then he went forward a little and threw himself upon the ground, and prayed that, if it were possible, this hour might pass him by. "Abba, Father," he said, "all things are possible to you; take this cup away from me. Yet, not what I will, but You will."

He came back and found them asleep; and he said to Peter, "Asleep, Simon? Were you not able to stay awake for one hour? Stay awake, all of you, and pray that you may be spared the test. The spirit is willing but the flesh is weak." Once more he went away and prayed. On his return he found them asleep again, for their eyes were heavy; and they did not know how to answer him. A third time he came and said to them, "Still sleeping? Still taking your ease? Enough! The hour has come. The Son of Man is betrayed to sinful men. Up, let us go forward! My betrayer is upon us."

Suddenly, while he was still speaking, Judas, one of the Twelve, appeared, and with him a crowd armed with swords and cudgels, sent by the chief priests, lawyers and elders. Now the traitor had agreed with them upon a signal. "The one I kiss is your man; seize him and get him safely away." When he reached the spot, he stepped forward at once and said to Jesus, "Rabbi," and kissed him. Then they seized him and held him fast. One of the party drew his sword and struck at the High Priest's servant, cutting off his ear. Then Jesus spoke. "Do you take me for a bandit, that you have come out with swords and cudgels to arrest me? Day after day I was within your reach as I taught in the Temple, and you did not lay hands on me. But let the Scriptures be fulfilled." Then the disciples all deserted him and ran away.

Among those following was a young man with nothing on but a linen cloth. They tried to seize him; but he slipped out of the linen cloth and ran away naked. (Mark 14:26–52)

25. The Sanhedrin Trial

Jesus was led off under arrest to the house of Caiaphas the High Priest where the lawyers and elders were assembled. . . . The chief priests and the elders tried to find some allegation against Jesus on which a death sentence could be based; but they failed to find one, though many came forward with false evidence. Finally two men alleged that he had said "I can pull down the Temple of God and rebuild it in three days." At this the High Priest rose and said to him, "Have you no answer to the charge that these witnesses bring against you?" But Jesus kept silence. The High Priest then said, "By the living God I charge you to tell us: Are you the Messiah, the Son of God?" Jesus replied, "The words are yours. But I tell you this: from now on, you will see the Son of Man seated at the right hand of God and coming on the clouds of heaven." At these words the High Priest tore his robes and exclaimed, "Blasphemy! Need we call further witnesses? You have heard the blasphemy. What is your opinion?" "He is guilty," they answered; "he should die." Then they spat in his face and struck him with their fists; and others said, "Now, Messiah, if you are a prophet, tell us who hit you." (Matthew 26:30–50)

The meeting at the house of the High Priest may have been a preliminary hearing, at least according to Luke, who puts the formal Sanhedrin trial early on the next day, Friday.

When day broke, the elders of the nation, chief priests and doctors of the Law assembled, and he was brought before their Council. "Tell us," they said, "are you the Messiah?" "If I tell you," he replied, "you will not believe me; and if I ask questions, you will not answer. But from now on the Son of Man will be seated at the right hand of Almighty God." "You are the Son of God, then?" they all said, and he replied, "It is you who say I am." They said, "Need we call further witnesses? We have heard it ourselves from his own lips." (Luke 22:66–71)

The Mishnaic tractate called "Sanhedrin" devotes considerable detail to the procedures to be followed in cases held before that body, though we cannot be certain which, if any of them, were operative in Jesus' own day nearly two centuries earlier.

In non-capital cases they hold the trial during the daytime and the verdict may be reached during the night; in capital cases they hold the trial during the daytime and the verdict also must be reached during the daytime. In non-capital cases the verdict, whether of acquittal or of conviction, may be reached the same day; in capital cases a verdict of acquittal may be reached the same day, but a verdict of conviction not until the following day. Therefore trials may not be held on the eve of the Sabbath or on the eve of a festival day. (M.Sanhedrin 4:1)

And on the charge of blasphemy:

The Lord spoke to Moses and said, Take the man who blasphemed out of the camp. Everyone who heard him shall put a hand on his head, and then all the community shall stone him to death. You shall say to the Israelites: When any man whatever blasphemes his God, he shall accept responsibility for his sin. Whoever utters the name of the Lord shall be put to death: all the community shall stone him; alien or native, if he utters the Name, he shall be put to death. (Leviticus 24:13–16)

The blasphemer is not culpable unless he pronounces the Name itself. Rabbi Joshua ben Karha says: On every day (of the trial) they examined the witnesses with a substituted name, (such as) "May Yosi smite Yosi." When sentence was to be given they did not declare him guilty of death (on the grounds of evidence given) with the substituted name but they sent out all the people and asked the chief among the witnesses and said to him, "Say expressly what you heard," and he says it; and the judges stand up on their feet and rend their garments, and they may not mend them again. And the second witness says, "I also heard the like," and the third says, "I also heard the like." (M.Sanhedrin 7:5)

26. Jesus before Pilate

John's chronology of the events of the arrest and execution of Jesus is somewhat different from that presented by the Synoptics. Here, for example, it is clear that the events were taking place before the Passover Supper; according to the Synoptics, Jesus had taken that meal with his disciples before his arrest.

From Caiaphas Jesus was led into the Governor's headquarters. It was now early morning, and the Jews themselves stayed outside the headquarters to avoid defilement, so that they could eat the Passover meal. So Pilate went out to them and asked, "What charge do you bring against this man?" "If he were not a criminal," they replied, "we should not have brought him before you." Pilate said, "Take him away and try him by your own law." The Jews answered, "We are not allowed to put any man to death." Thus they ensured the fulfillment of the words by which Jesus indicated the manner of his death. (John 18:28–32)

If the response given in John does not address itself to the specific charges, Luke's narrative does, beginning immediately after the Friday morning trial before the Sanhedrin.

With that the whole assembly [that is, of the Sanhedrin] rose, and they brought him before Pilate. They opened the case against him by saying, "We found this man subverting our nation, opposing the payment of taxes to Caesar and claiming to be Messiah, a king." Pilate asked him, "Are you the king of the Jews?" He replied, "The words are yours." Pilate then turned to the chief priests and the crowd. "I find no case for this man to answer." But they insisted: "His teaching is causing disaffection among the people all through Judea. It started from Galilee and has spread as far as this city."

When Pilate heard this, he asked if the man was a Galilean, and on learning that he belonged to Herod's [Antipas'] jurisdiction, he remitted the case to him. When Herod saw Jesus he was greatly pleased; having heard about him, he had long been wanting to see him and had been hoping to see some miracle performed by him. He questioned him at some length without getting any reply; but the chief priests and lawyers appeared and pressed the case against him vigorously. Then Herod and his troops treated him with contempt and ridicule and sent him back to Pilate dressed in a gorgeous robe. That same day Herod and Pilate became friends; till then there had been a standing feud between them. (Luke 23:1–12)

Pilate, perhaps in an effort to confront the crowd with an unacceptable alternative, offers the release of either Jesus or a notorious criminal called Bar Abbas, "who had committed murder in the recent uprising" (Mark 15:7), possibly the one mentioned in Luke 13:1–2.

At the festival season it was the Governor's custom to release one prisoner chosen by the people. There was then in custody a man of some notoriety, called Jesus Bar Abbas. When they were assembled, Pilate said to them, "Which would you like me to release to you—Jesus Bar Abbas, or Jesus called the Messiah?" For he knew that it was out of malice that they had brought Jesus before him.

While Pilate was sitting in court a message came to him from his wife: "Have nothing to do with this innocent man; I was much troubled on his account in my dreams last night."

Meanwhile the chief priests and elders had persuaded the crowd to ask for the release of Bar Abbas and to have Jesus put to death. So when the Governor asked, "Which of the two do you wish me to release to you?" they said, "Bar Abbas." "Then what am I to do with Jesus who is called Messiah?" asked Pilate; and with one voice they answered, "Crucify him!" "Why, what harm has he done?" Pilate asked; but they shouted all the louder, "Crucify him!"

Pilate could see that nothing was being gained and a riot was start-ing; so he took water and washed his hands in the full view of the people, saying, "My hands are clean of this man's blood; see to that yourselves." And with one voice the people cried, "His blood be upon us and upon our children." He then released Bar Abbas to them; but he had Jesus flogged and handed over to be crucified. Pilate's soldiers then took Jesus into the governor's headquarters, where they collected the whole company round him. They stripped him and dressed him in a scarlet mantle; and plaiting a crown of thorns they placed it on his head, with a cane in his right hand. Falling on their knees before him they jeered at him: "Hail, King of the Jews!" They spat on him, and used the cane to beat him about the head. When they had finished their mockery, they took off the mantle and dressed him in his own clothes. (Matthew 27:24–31)

Once more Pilate came out and said to the Jews, "Here he is; I am bringing him out to let you know that I find no case against him"; and Jesus came out, wearing the crown of thorns and the purple cloak. "Be-hold the man!" said Pilate. The chief priests and their henchmen saw him and shouted, "Crucify him! Crucify him!" "Take him and crucify him yourselves," said Pilate; "for my part, I find no no case against him." The Jews answered, "We have a law, and by that law he ought to die because he has claimed to be the Son of God."

When Pilate heard that, he was more afraid than ever, and going back into his headquarters, he asked Jesus, "Where have you come from?" But Jesus gave him no answer. "Do you refuse to speak to me?" said Pilate. "Surely you know that I have authority to release you, and I have authority to crucify you?" "You would have no authority at all over me," Jesus replied, "if it had not been granted to you from above; and therefore the deeper guilt lies with the man who handed me over to you." From that moment Pilate tried to release him; but the Jews kept shouting, "If you let this man go, you are no friend to Caesar; any man who claims to be king is defying Caesar." When Pilate heard what they were saying, he brought Jesus out and took his seat on the tribunal at the place known as "The Pavement"—"Gabbatha" in the language of the Jews. It was the eve of Passover, about noon. Pilate said to the Jews, "Here is your king." They shouted, "Away with him! Crucify him!" "Crucify your king?" said Pilate. "We have no king but Caesar," the Jews replied. Then at last, to satisfy them, he handed Jesus over to be crucified. (John 19:4–16)

27. The Crucifixion

Jesus was now taken in charge and carrying his own cross, went out to the Place of the Skull, as it is called—or, in the Jews' language "Golgotha"—where they crucified him, and with him two others ["bandits," Mark calls them], one on the right, one on the left, and Jesus between them. And Pilate wrote an inscription to be fastened on the cross; it read, "Jesus of Nazareth, King of the Jews." This inscription was read by many Jews, because the place where Jesus was crucified was not far from the city, and the inscription was in Hebrew, Latin and Greek. . . . The soldiers, having crucified Jesus, took possession of his clothes, and divided them into four parts, one for each soldier, leaving out the tunic. (John 19:17–23)

The passersby hurled abuse at him: they wagged their heads and cried, "You would pull the Temple down, would you, and build it in three days? Come down from the cross and save yourself, if you are indeed the Son of God." So too the chief priests with the lawyers and elders mocked at him. "He saved others," they said, "but he cannot save himself. King of Israel indeed! Let him come down now from the cross, and then we will believe him. Did he trust in God? Let God rescue him, if he wants him—for he said he was God's Son." Even the bandits who were crucified with him taunted him in the same way.

From midday a darkness fell over the whole land, which lasted until three in the afternoon; and about three Jesus cried aloud "*Eli, Eli, lema sabachthani?*" which means "My God, my God, why hast thou forsaken me?" Some of the bystanders, on hearing this, said, "He is calling Elijah." One of the soldiers then ran at once and fetched a sponge, which he soaked in sour wine, and held it to his lips at the end of a cane. But the others said, "Let us see if Elijah will come to save him." Jesus again gave a loud cry and breathed his last. At that moment the curtain of the Temple was torn in two from top to bottom. There was an earthquake, the rocks split and the graves opened, and many of God's saints were raised from sleep; and coming out of their graves after his resurrection they entered the Holy City where many saw them. (Matthew 27:39–53)

Because it was the eve of Passover, the Jews were anxious that the bodies should not remain on the cross for the coming Sabbath, since that Sabbath was a day of great solemnity. So they requested Pilate to have the legs broken and the bodies taken down. The soldiers accordingly came to the first of his fellow victims and to the second, and they broke their legs.

But when they came to Jesus they found that he was already dead, so they did not break his legs. But one of the soldiers stabbed his side with a lance, and at once there was a flow of blood and water. (John 19:31–34)

28. Josephus on Jesus

The Jewish Antiquities *of the Jewish historian Flavius Josephus, who wrote after the destruction of Jerusalem in 70 C.E., cover most of the events that took place in Palestine during the lifetime of Jesus. In the Greek manuscripts of that work there occurs in Book 17 a passage concerning Jesus.*

About this time there lived Jesus, a wise man, if indeed one ought to call him a man. For he was one who wrought surprising feats and was a teacher of such people as accept the truth gladly. He won over many Jews and many of the Greeks. He was the Messiah. When Pilate, upon hearing him accused by men of the highest standing among us, had condemned him to be crucified, those who had in the first place come to love him did not cease. On the third day he appeared to them restored to life. For the prophets of God had prophesied these and many other marvelous things about him. And the tribe of the Christians, so called after him, has still up to now not disappeared. (Josephus, *Antiquities* 17.3.3)

This celebrated passage, with its open acknowledgment of Jesus' Messiahship and its not very subtle Christian coloring throughout, has long provoked suspicion that either a complete forgery or a series of interpolations had taken place. The latter is not an unlikely possibility, particularly in the light of such latter-day versions as the following, found in a tenth-century Arab Christian historian, Agapius of Manbij, who is patently quoting from the Antiquities *and may have had before him the authentic text of Josephus. It was one, at any rate, closer to what we might imagine Josephus and not a Christian author to have written.*

Similarly Josephus the Hebrew. For he says in the treatises that he has written on the governance of the Jews:

"At this time there was a wise man who was called Jesus. And his conduct was good, and (he) was known to be virtuous. And many people from among the Jews and the other nations became his disciples. Pilate condemned him to be crucified and to die. And those who had become his disciples did not desert his discipleship. They reported that he had appeared to them three days after his crucifixion and that he was alive; accordingly, he was perhaps the Messiah concerning whom the prophets have recounted wonders." (Agapius, *Kitab al-ʿUnwan*, 239–240)

[PINES 1971: 16]

29. The Rabbis on the Life and Death of Jesus

The life and death of Jesus of Nazareth did not pass completely unnoticed in the rabbinic writings, though the references are generally oblique and were for the most part excised from later editions of the Talmuds and related texts. The following remarks on Ben Stada or Ben Pandera, elsewhere identified as "Jeshua ben Pandera," are not atypical of the kinds of passages that have been identified, not without argument, as references to Jesus.

"He who cuts upon his flesh." It is a tradition that Rabbi Eliezer said to the Wise, "Did not Ben Stada bring spells from Egypt in a cut which was upon his flesh?" They said to him, "He was a fool and they do not bring a proof from a fool." Ben Stada is Ben Pandera. Rab Hisda said, "The husband was Stada, the paramour was Pandera." The husband was Pappos ben Yehudah, the mother was Stada. The mother was Miriam, the dresser of women's hair, as they say in Pumbeditha, "Such a one has been false to her husband." (BT.Sanhedrin 67a)

These allusions, particularly as they refer to the death of Jesus, most often occur in the context of the Mishnaic treatise "Sanhedrin," which is concerned with that tribunal's jurisdiction and procedures in capital cases.

In regard to all who are worthy of death according to the Torah, they do not use concealment against them, except in the case of the deceiver. How do they deal with him? They put two disciples of the wise in the inner chamber and he sits in the outer chamber, and they light the lamp so that they shall see him and hear his voice. And thus they did to Ben Stada in Lydda; two disciples of the wise were chosen for him, and they brought him to the Beth Din and stoned him. [Or, as in B.Sanhedrin 67b, "they hung him on the eve of Passover."] (Tosefta Sanhedrin 10:11)

And it was taught: On the eve of the Passover Jeshua [the Nazarene] was hanged. For forty days before the execution took place a herald went forth and cried, "He is going forth to be stoned because he has practiced sorcery and enticed Israel to apostasy. Anyone who can say anything in his favor, let him come and plead on his behalf." And since nothing was brought forward in his favor, he was hanged on the eve of Passover. Ulla retorted, "Do you suppose that he was one for whom a defense could be made? Was he not an enticer, concerning whom Scripture says, 'Neither shall you spare, neither shall thou conceal him' (Deut. 13:9). With Jeshua however it was different, for he was connected with the government [or royalty—that is, influential]." (BT.Sanhedrin 43a)

The following comment, attributed to the second-century Rabbi Meir, may also, despite the lack of names, refer to Jesus' crucifixion.

Rabbi Meir used to say, What is the meaning of "For a curse of God is he that is hung" (Deut. 21:23)? [It is like the case of] two brothers, twins, who resembled each other. One ruled over the whole world, the other took to robbery. After a time the one who took to robbery was caught, and they crucified him on a cross. And everyone who passed to and fro said, "It seems that the king is crucified." Therefore it is said "A curse of God is he that is hung." (Tosefta Sanhedrin 9:7)

30. The Quranic Account of the Crucifixion

For Muslims, who regard Jesus as one of the greatest of the prophets, the alleged crucifixion did not occur—not, at any rate, with Jesus as the victim.

And (the Jews were punished) because they said: "We killed the Christ, Jesus son of Mary, who was an apostle of God"; but they neither killed him nor crucified him, though it so appeared to them. Those who disagree in the matter are only lost in doubt. They have no knowledge of it other than conjecture, for surely they did not kill him. (Quran 4:157–158)

The classical Muslim exegetical tradition on the Quran's account of the alleged crucifixion of Jesus is represented by al-Baydawi (d. 1286 C.E.), and it illustrates the somewhat uncertain attempts to explain what actually occurred in Jerusalem during that Passover in 30 C.E.

There is a story that a group of Jews insulted Jesus and his mother, whereupon he appealed to God against them. When God transformed those (who had insulted them) into monkeys and swine, the Jews took counsel to kill Jesus. Then God told Jesus that He would raise him up to heaven, and so Jesus said to his disciples: "Who among you will agree to take a form similar to mine and die (in my place) and be crucified and then go (straight) to paradise?" A man among them offered himself, so God changed him into a form resembling Jesus', and he was killed and crucified.

Others say that a man pretended (to be a believer) in Jesus' presence but then went off and denounced him, whereupon God changed the man into form similar to that of Jesus, and then he was seized and crucified. (Baydawi, *Commentary*, *ad loc.*)

The thesis was not a Muslim innovation. It had been put forward by the Christian Gnostic Valentinus sometime about 140 C.E.

So Jesus did not suffer (on the cross), but a certain Simon of Cyrene was constrained to bear his cross for him, and it was Simon who was crucified in ignorance and error, since he had been transformed by Jesus to look like himself, so that people thought he was Jesus, while Jesus took on the appearance of Simon and stood by and mocked them. (Ireneus, *Against the Heresies* 1:24.4)

31. The Burial

We return to the Gospel accounts of the events immediately following Jesus' execution.

After that Pilate was approached by Joseph of Arimathea, a disciple of Jesus, but a secret disciple for fear of the Jews, who asked to be allowed to remove the body of Jesus. Pilate gave the permission so Joseph came and took the body away. He was joined by Nicodemus, the man who had first visited Jesus by night, who brought with him a mixture of myrrh and aloes, more than half a hundredweight. They took the body of Jesus and wrapped it, with the spices, in strips of linen cloth according to Jewish burial customs. Now at the place where he had been crucified there was a garden, and in the garden a new tomb, not yet used for burial. There, because the tomb was near at hand and it was the eve of the Jewish Sabbath, they laid Jesus. (John 19:38–42)

So Joseph bought a linen sheet, took him down from the cross and wrapped him in the sheet. Then he laid him in a tomb cut out of the rock, and rolled a stone against the entrance. And Mary of Magdala and Mary the mother of Joseph were watching and saw where he was laid. (Mark 15:46–47)

32. The Resurrection

The account of the Resurrection, or rather, the testimony that the Resurrection had occurred, is quite brief in all four of the Gospels.

When the Sabbath was over, Mary of Magdala, Mary the mother of James, and Salome brought aromatic oils intending to go and anoint him; and very early on the Sunday morning, just after sunrise, they came to the tomb. They were wondering among themselves who would roll away the stone for them from the entrance of the tomb, when they looked up and saw that the stone, huge as it was, had been rolled back already. They went into the tomb, where they saw a youth sitting on the right-hand side, wearing a white robe; and they were dumbfounded. But he said to them, "Fear nothing; you are looking for Jesus of Nazareth, who was crucified. He has been raised again; he is not here; look, there is the place where they laid him. But go and give this message to his disciples and Peter: 'He is going before you into Galilee; there you will see him, as he told you.'" Then they went and ran away from the tomb, beside themselves with terror. They said nothing to anybody, for they were afraid.

When he had risen from the dead early on Sunday morning he appeared first to Mary of Magdala, from whom he had formerly cast out seven devils. She went and carried the news to his mourning and sorrowful followers, but when they were told that he was alive and that she had seen him, they did not believe it. (Mark 16:1–11)

Matthew is somewhat more circumstantial.

Next day, the morning after that same Friday, the chief priests and the Pharisees came in a body to Pilate: "Your excellency," they said, "we recall how that imposter said while he was still alive, 'I am to be raised again after three days.' So will you give orders for the grave to be made secure until the third day? Otherwise his disciples may come, steal the body, and then tell the people that he has been raised from the dead; and the final deception will be worse than the first." "You may have your guard," said Pilate; "go and make it secure as best you can." So they went and made the grave secure; they sealed the stone and left the guard in charge.

The Sabbath was over, and it was about daybreak on Sunday, when Mary of Magdala and the other Mary came to look at the grave. Suddenly there was a violent earthquake; an angel of the Lord descended from heaven; he came to the stone and rolled it away, and sat himself down on it. His face shone like lightning; his garments were white as snow. At the sight of him the guards shook with fear and lay like the dead.

The angel then addressed the women: "You," he said, "have nothing to fear. I know you are looking for Jesus, who was crucified. He is not here; he has been raised again, as he said he would be. Come and see the place where he was laid, and then go quickly and tell his disciples: 'He has been raised from the dead and is going before you into Galilee; there you will see him.' That is what I had to tell you."

They hurried away from the tomb in awe and great joy, and ran to tell his disciples. Suddenly Jesus was there in their path. He gave them his greeting, and they came up and clasped his feet, falling prostrate before him. Then Jesus said to them, "Do not be afraid. Go and take word to my brothers that they are to leave for Galilee. They will see me there."

The women had started on their way when some of the guard went into the city and reported to the chief priests everything that had happened. After meeting with the elders and conferring together, the chief priests offered the soldiers a substantial bribe and told them to say, "His disciples came by night and stole his body, while we were asleep." They added, "If this should reach the Governor's ears, we will put matters right with him and see that you do not suffer." So they took the money and did as they were told. This story became widely known, and is current in Jewish circles to this day. (Matthew 27:62–28:15)

33. The Ascension

Luke begins his Acts of the Apostles by referring his patron, a certain Theophilus, back to his earlier work, the Gospel!

In the first part of my work, Theophilus, I wrote all that Jesus did and taught from the beginning until the day when, after giving instructions through the Holy Spirit to the apostles whom he had chosen, he was taken up to heaven. He showed himself to these men after his death and gave ample proof that he was alive: over a period of forty days he appeared to them and taught them about the kingdom of God. While he was in their company he told them not to leave Jerusalem. "You must wait," he said, "for the promise made by my Father, about which you have heard me speak: John, as you know, baptized with water, but you will be baptized with the Holy Spirit, and within the next few days.

". . . You will bear witness for me in Jerusalem, and all of Judea and Samaria, and away to the ends of the earth." When he had said this, as they watched, he was lifted up, and a cloud removed him from their sight. . . . Then they returned to Jerusalem from the hill called Olivet, which is near Jerusalem, no farther than a Sabbath day's journey. Entering the city they went to the room upstairs where they were lodging: Peter and John and James and Andrew, Philip and Thomas, Bartholomew and Matthew, James son of Alpheus and Simon the Zealot and Judas son of James. All these were constantly at prayer together, and with them a group of women, including Mary the mother of Jesus, and his brothers. (Acts 1:1–14)

34. Peter on Jesus as the Messiah

Almost immediately after the Ascension, the Apostles took to the streets of Jerusalem and began to announce that the recently executed Jesus of Nazareth was risen from the dead and was indeed the Messiah. The Acts of the Apostles has preserved an early version of that message as preached by Peter to his fellow Jews in Jerusalem.

The God of Abraham, Isaac and Jacob, the God of our fathers, has given the highest honor to his servant Jesus, whom you committed to trial and repudiated in Pilate's court—repudiated the one who was holy and righteous when Pilate had decided to release him. You begged as a favor the release of a murderer, and killed him who had led the way to life. But God raised him from the dead; of that we are witnesses. . . .

And now, my friends, I know quite well that you acted in ignorance, and so did your rulers; but this is how God fulfilled what he had foretold in the utterances of the prophets: that his Messiah should suffer. Repent then and turn to God, so that your sins may be wiped out. Then the Lord may grant you a time of recovery and send you the Messiah that he has already appointed, that is, Jesus. He must be received into heaven until the time of universal restoration comes, of which God spoke by his holy prophets. Moses said, "The Lord God will raise a prophet for you from among yourselves as he raised me; you shall listen to everything he says to you, and anyone who refuses to listen to that prophet must be extirpated from Israel" (Deut. 18:15–19). And so said all the prophets, from Samuel onwards; with one voice they all predicted this present time.

You are the heirs of the prophets: you are within the Covenant which God made with your fathers, when he said to Abraham, "And in your offspring all the families on earth shall find blessing." When God raised up his Servant, he sent him to you first, to bring you blessings by turning every one of you from your wicked ways. (Acts 3:13–26)

35. Jesus Explained to the Pagans

Peter spoke to believing Jews familiar with the general tenor of their own Scriptures and willing at least to entertain the notion that Jesus was the fulfillment of the promises made in those Scriptures. Among a pagan audience the matter was quite different, as Paul discovered when he reached Athens. The time is in the fifties of the first century C.E.

Now while Paul was waiting for them [that is, his traveling compan-
ions] at Athens, he was exasperated to see how the city was filled with
idols. So he argued in the synagogue with the Jews and Gentile worshipers, and also in the city square every day with the casual passersby. And
some of the Epicurean and Stoic philosophers joined issue with him.
Some said, "What can this charlatan be trying to say?"; others, "He
would appear to be a propagandist for foreign deities"—this because he
was preaching about Jesus and Resurrection. So they took him and
brought him before the Court of the Areopagus and said, "May we know
what this new doctrine is that you propound? You are introducing ideas
that sound strange to us, and we should like to know what they mean."
Now the Athenians in general and the foreigners there had no time for
anything but talking or hearing about the latest novelty.

Then Paul stood up before the Court of the Areopagus and said:
"Men of Athens, I see that in everything that concerns religion you are
uncommonly scrupulous. For as I was going round looking at the objects
of your worship, I noticed among other things an altar bearing the inscription 'To an Unknown God.' What you worship and do not know,
that is what I now proclaim. The God who created the world and everything in it, and who is Lord of heaven and earth, does not live in shrines
made by men. It is not because He lacks anything that He accepts service
at men's hands, for He is Himself the universal giver of life and breath and
all else. He created every race of men of one stock, to inhabit the whole
earth's surface. He fixed the epochs of their history and the limits of their
territory. They were to seek God and, it might be, touch and find Him;
though indeed He is not far from each one of us, for in Him we live and
move, in Him we exist; as some of your own poets have said, 'We are also
His offspring.' As God's offspring, then, we ought not to suppose that the
deity is like an image in gold or silver or stone, shaped by human craftsmanship and design. As for the times of ignorance, God has overlooked
them; but now He commands mankind, all men everywhere, to repent,
because He has fixed the day on which He will have the world judged, by
a man of His own choosing; of this He has given assurance to all by raising
him from the dead."

When they heard about the raising of the dead, some scoffed; and
others said, "We will hear you on this subject some other time." And so
Paul left the assembly. (Acts 17:16–33)

Paul's was a public speech, delivered under the limitations of time and place by a
man not notoriously patient of such limitations. The same case was made to the

pagans from a somewhat different angle by the converted philosopher Justin in the
more expansive context of a literary Apologia *addressed to the Roman emperor. The*
date is now about a century after Paul stood before the Athenians.

There were among the Jews certain men who were prophets of God,
through whom the prophetic spirit published beforehand things that
were to come to pass before they happened. And their prophecies, as they
were spoken and when they were uttered, the kings who were among the
Jews at those times carefully preserved in their possession, after they had
been arranged by the prophets themselves in their own Hebrew language.
. . . They are also in the possession of all Jews throughout the world. . . .
In these books of the prophets we found the coming of Jesus our Christ
foretold, born of a virgin, growing up to manhood, and healing every
disease and every sickness, and raising the dead, and being hated and
unrecognized and crucified, and dying, and rising again and ascending
into heaven, and both being in fact and called the Son of God, and that
certain persons should be sent by him to every race of men to publish
these things, and that rather among the Gentiles (than among the Jews)
men would believe in him. And he was predicted before he appeared, first
5,000 years before, and again 3,000, then 2,000, then 1,000, and yet again
800; for according to the succession of generations prophets after prophets arose.

Though we have many other prophecies, we say nothing of them,
judging these sufficient for the persuasion of those who have ears capable
of hearing and understanding; and considering also that that these persons are able to see that we do not make assertions for which we are
incapable of bringing forth proof, like those fables that are told of the
reputed sons of Zeus. For why should we believe of a crucified man that
he is the firstborn of the Unbegotten God and himself will pass judgment
on the whole human race unless we found testimonies concerning him
published before he came and was born as a man and unless we saw that
things had happened exactly so? (Justin, *Apology* 1.31.53)

36. Jesus, Messiah of Israel?

That some Jews, perhaps many, accepted the Messianic claims made by Jesus and
then by his followers on his behalf is manifest from the spread of his community first
in Palestine and then through the Diaspora synagogues where those claims were
preached and argued. That many more Jews did not accept them is equally clear
from the rift that developed between the Jewish community at large and the "Chris-

tians," as they came to be called, who had sprung from its midst. And although a Jewish polemicist might derisively dismiss the Christians' developing theology of Jesus as the Son of God, the case that Jesus of Nazareth was in fact the Messiah promised to and long awaited by the Children of Israel was made out of the Jewish Scriptures themselves and so had to be treated more carefully. The Jewish response to the Messianic claims on behalf of Jesus of Nazareth can be gauged from these much later remarks by the medieval Jewish scholar Maimonides.

But if he (who claims to be the Messiah) does not meet with success, or is slain, it is obvious that he is not the Messiah promised in the Torah. He is to be regarded like all the other wholehearted and worthy kings of the house of David who died and whom the Holy One, blessed be He, raised up to test the multitude, as it is written, "And some of them that are wise shall stumble, to refine among them, and to purify, and to make white, even to the end of the end; for it is yet for the time appointed" (Dan. 11:35).

Even of Jesus of Nazareth, who imagined that he was the Messiah and who was put to death by the court, Daniel had prophesied, as it is written, "And the children of the violent among your people shall lift themselves up to establish the vision, but they shall stumble" (Dan. 11:14). For has there ever been a greater stumbling than this? All the prophets affirmed that the Messiah would redeem Israel, save them, gather their dispersed, and confirm the commandments. But he caused Israel to be destroyed by the sword, their remnant to be dispersed and humiliated. He was instrumental in changing the Torah and causing the world to err and serve another besides God. (Maimonides, *Mishneh Torah* 14.11) [MAIMONIDES 1965]

Maimonides could also be more direct, and more polemical, as in his Letter to the Yemen.

There arose a new sect which combined the two previously mentioned methods (of foiling the will of God), namely, conquest and polemic, into one, because it believed that this procedure would be the more effective in removing every trace of the Jewish nation and its religion. And so it determined to make its own claim to prophecy and to found a new faith, contrary to our divine religion, and to contend that it too was God-given. It hoped by this to sow doubts and confusion, since one (religion) is opposed to the other, and yet both supposedly emanate from a divine source, which would lead to the destruction of both religions. Such is the remarkable plan contrived by a man who is both envious and dangerous. He will attempt to kill his enemy and to save his own life, but when he finds it impossible to attain both objectives, he will contrive a plan that will kill them both.

The first to have adopted this sort of plan was Jesus the Nazarene, may his bones be ground to dust! He was a Jew by reason of the fact that his mother was a Jewess, even though his father was a Gentile. For in accordance with the principle of our law, a child born of a Jewess and a Gentile, or a Jewess and a slave, is legitimate. And so it is only figuratively that Jesus is called illegitimate. He constrained people to believe he was a prophet sent by God to clarify problems in the Torah, and that he was the Messiah who had been predicted by every seer. He interpreted the Torah and its precepts in such a fashion as to lead to their total annulment, to the abolition of all its commandments and to violation of its prohibitions. The sages, of blessed memory, since they become aware of his plans before his reputation spread among our people, meted out to him an appropriate punishment.

Daniel had already referred to him [that is, Jesus] when he predicted the downfall of a wicked and heretic man among the Jews who would seek to destroy the Law, claim prophecy for himself, pretend to work miracles and claim that he is the Messiah, as it is written, "Also the children of the impudent among your people shall make bold to claim prophecy, but they shall fall" (Dan. 11:14). (Maimonides, *Letter to the Yemen*)

37. A Muslim Has Some Arithmetic Problems

We have seen in Chapter 2 above that the Muslim scientist Biruni (d. 1048 C.E.) had difficulties with the Jews' calculations on the date of their expected Messiah. He has no fewer with the Christians' arithmetic.

These are the doubts and difficulties which beset the assertions of the Jews. Those, however, which attach to the schemes of the Christians are even more numerous and conspicuous. For even if the Jews granted to them that the coming of the Messiah would take place seventy "weeks of years" (Dan. 9:24) after the vision of Daniel, we must remark that the appearance of Jesus the son of Mary did not take place at that time. The reason is this: The Jews agree to fix the interval between the exodus of the Israelites from Egypt and the era of Alexander at 1,000 complete years. From passages in the books of the Prophets they have inferred that the interval between the exodus from Egypt and the building of Jerusalem is 480 years; and the interval between the building and the destruction by

Nebuchadnezzar 410 years, and that it remained in a ruined state for 70 years. Now this gives the sum of 960 years (after the exodus) as the date for the vision of Daniel, and as a remainder of the above-mentioned millennium, 40 years. Further, Jews and Christians unanimously suppose that the birth of Jesus son of Mary took place in the year 304 of the era of Alexander. Therefore, if we use their own chronology, the birth of Jesus the son of Mary took place 344 years after the vision of Daniel and the rebuilding of Jerusalem, that is, about 49 "weeks of years." From his birth till the time when he began preaching are four and a half more. Hence it is evident that the birth of Jesus precedes the date which they have assumed (as the time of the birth of the Messiah). (Al-Biruni, *Traces of the Past*) [BIRUNI 1879: 21]

38. A Jewish Reflection on the Christians' Role in History

In the same passage of the Mishneh Torah *where he addressed Jesus' Messianic claims, Maimonides turned briefly to the larger question of God's purpose in permitting the spread of such claims.*

But it is beyond the human mind to fathom the designs of the Creator, for our ways are not His ways, neither are our thoughts His thoughts. All these matters relating to Jesus of Nazareth and the Ishmaelite (that is, Muhammad) who came after him, only served to clear the way for King Messiah, to prepare the whole world to worship God with one accord, as it is written, "For then will I turn to the peoples a pure language, that they may call upon the name of the Lord to serve Him with one consent" (Zeph. 3:9). Thus the Messianic hope, the Torah, and the commandments have become familiar topics, topics of conversation (among the inhabitants) of the far isles and many peoples, uncircumcised of heart and flesh. They are discussing these matters and the commandments of the Torah. Some say, "These commandments were true, but have lost their validity and are no longer binding"; others declare that they had an esoteric meaning and were not intended to be taken literally; that the Messiah has already come and revealed their their occult significance. But when the true King Messiah will appear and succeed, be exalted and lifted up, they will forthwith recant and realize that they have inherited naught but lies from their fathers, that their prophets and forebears have led them astray. (Maimonides, *Mishneh Torah* 14.11)

39. John on Jesus as the Word of God

The case for and against Jesus as the Messiah of Israel was one argued by and for Jews. But the claims by and about Jesus did not end there, as the opening verses of the Gospel of John reveal.

When all things began, the Word already was. The Word dwelt with God, and what God was, the Word was. The Word, then, was with God at the beginning, and through him all things came to be; no single thing was created without him. All that came to be was alive with his life, and that life was the light on men. The light shines on in the dark, and the darkness has never mastered it.

There appeared a man named John, sent from God; he came as a witness, to testify to the light, that all might become believers through him. He was not himself the light; he came to bear witness to the light. The real light which enlightens every man was even then coming into the world.

He was in the world; but the world, though it owed its being to him, did not recognize him. He entered his own realm, and his own did not receive him. But to all who did receive him, to those who have yielded him their allegiance, he gave the right to become children of God, not born of any human stock, or by the fleshly desire of an earthly father, but the offspring of God Himself. So the Word became flesh; he came to dwell among us, and we saw his glory, such glory as befits the Father's only Son, full of grace and truth. (John 1:1–14)

40. A Muslim Interpretation of John

Although there were other differences among the three religions, this assertion of the divinity of Jesus in the opening lines of John's Gospel appeared to Jews and Muslims to repudiate the monotheism that stood at the very heart of the faith of Abraham. The Jew would reject the claim simply: there was no need to deal with the Gospel as such. The Muslim's task, on the other hand, was exegetical: to defend the Gospel, which was authentic revelation, but refute the Christians' understanding of it as a proclamation of Jesus' divinity. The task was taken up by the Muslim theologian al-Ghazali (d. 1111 C.E.), onetime professor of Islamic law in Baghdad.

We now turn to a final point and shall examine one of the critical points upon which Christians rely to prove the Divinity of Jesus, upon whom be peace, the opening verses of John's Gospel: "In the beginning was the Word" and so on and so forth, to the end of the passage: "And the Word was made flesh and dwelt among us, and we beheld his glory."

Ghazali's approach to this text is to demonstrate that the expression "the Word," which the Christians apply to Jesus throughout the passage, applies rather to God understood with the attributes of knowledge or speech. This Ghazali can do with relative ease in the opening verses of John. What must then be navigated, however, is the closing formula of the passage: "And the Word was made flesh." Here Ghazali resorts to allegorical interpretation.

The "Word" in their system stands for the essence regarded as an attribute of knowledge or speech. . . . It therefore indicates the essence qualified by knowledge or speech. This usage is by no means peculiar to God; a dubious expression, however confused it may be, may quite properly and accurately be used to denote each particular thing to which it is applied. So "the Word" can be employed to connote the essence as defined by knowledge or speech, without any implication of the essence having the attribute of corporeality or being dissociated from that attribute. Consequently, at the beginning of the passage the expression "the Word" is applied to the knower as dissociated from corporeality in fact, that is, to God; while at the end of this passage the same term is also applied to the knower or the speaker as possessing the attribute of corporeality in fact, that is to say, to God's Messenger. Therefore the phrase "and the Word became flesh" means that the God-Knower had previously been called "the Word" in a manner dissociated from corporeality, but now that same term was being applied to a knower possessing the attribute of corporeality, to wit, the Messenger. . . .

. . . It is established that it is the Truth, glorious be His Name, who lightens with His Light "every man who comes" and unveils for him every secret; that much is clearly stated in this text: "to bear witness of the Light. That was the true Light that lights every man." The phrase "He was in the world" may well qualify "the Light," and also the Truth, glorious is His name; for Almighty God's guidance, His making clear every secret and His unveiling every ambiguity—that has never ceased to dwell in the world. The words "and the world was made by him" qualify the Truth, blessed be His Name; that has been explicitly stated at the beginning of the chapter: "All things were made by Him."

I should like to know what grounds there are for taking this to refer to Jesus, upon whom be peace, in the face of the clear statement occurring at the beginning of the chapter, describing God: "and without Him was not anything made that was made." The words "he came to his own" mean "to the Truth's own appeared His Light, to wit, His guidance and direction; since it is by His Light that every man is guided to follow the right path. . . ."

"To them He gave the power to become sons of God": it would have been more natural to say "to become His sons," only the writer avoided that, preferring the explicit mention of the revered Name God, because of the noble relationship, in order to make a deeper impression on the souls of his readers. After that he said: "even to them that believe in His name, who were born, not of blood, nor of the will of the flesh, nor of the will of man, but of God," meaning that this sonship by virtue of which they obtained that noble relationship was not of the order of those sonships which are apt to result from the wills of men and their attention to women, with the resultant formation of flesh and blood, but rather the meaning is that the extreme nearness and compassion of God towards them. Finally, the writer connects up again with the beginning of the chapter, making it clear that it is a property of the Word, from which the idea of the Knower is derived, to be applied, whether that Knower is dissociated from corporeality, such as the Essence of the Creator, or not dissociated, as with the essence of the Messenger. (Ghazali, *The Elegant Refutation*) [ARBERRY 1964: 300–306]

41. Paul on Jesus as the Image and the Son of God

Thus Ghazali was at some pains to separate the Father, who created all, from the "son," Jesus, who is His messenger. Christians felt no such constraint, of course, and Paul and the author of Hebrews were eager to explain all the nuances of the relationship between the Father and His only begotten Son.

He rescued us from the domain of the darkness and brought us away into the kingdom of his dear Son, in whom our release is secured and our sins forgiven. He is the image of the invisible God; his is the primacy over all created things. In him everything in heaven and on earth was created, not only things visible but also the invisible order of thrones, sovereignties, authorities and powers; the whole universe has been created through him and for him. And he exists before everything and all things are held together in him. He is, moreover, the head of the body, the Church. He is its origin, the first to return from the dead, to be in all things alone supreme. For in him the complete being of God, by God's own choice, came to dwell. Through him God chose to reconcile the whole universe to himself, making peace through the shedding of his blood upon the cross—to reconcile all things, whether on earth or in heaven, through him alone. (Paul, *To the Colossians* 1:13–20)

When in former times God spoke to our forefathers, He spoke in fragmentary and varied fashion through the prophets. But in these latter days He has spoken to us in the Son whom He made heir to the whole universe and through whom He created all orders of existence: the Son who is the effulgence of God's splendor and the stamp of God's very being, and sustains the universe by his word of power. When he had brought about the purgation of sins, he took his seat at the right hand of Majesty on high, raised as far above the angels as the title he has inherited is above theirs. For God never said to any angel, "Thou art My Son; this day have I begotten thee," or again, "I will be Father to him and he will be My son" (Ps. 110:1). (Hebrews 1:1–6)

The divine nature was his from the first; but he did not prize his equality with God, but made himself nothing, assuming the nature of a slave. Bearing the human likeness, revealed in human shape, he humbled himself, and in obedience accepted even death—death on a cross. Therefore God raised him to the heights and bestowed on him the name above all names, that at the name of Jesus every knee should bow—in heaven, on earth, and in the depths—and every tongue should confess "Jesus Christ is Lord," to the glory of God the Father. (Paul, *To the Philippians* 2:6–11)

42. The Second Adam

Christians saw the New Covenant foreshadowed on almost every page of the Old. According to Paul, one of the earliest of those biblical prototypes of Jesus was Adam. He uses the comparison to make two different points, one spiritual and one moral.

If there is such a thing as an animal body, there is also a spiritual body. It is in this sense that Scripture says, "The first man, Adam, became an animate man," whereas the last Adam has become a life-giving spirit. Observe, the spiritual does not come first; the animal body comes first, and then the spiritual. The first man was made "of the dust of the earth"; the second man is from heaven. The man made of dust is the pattern of all men of dust, and the heavenly man is the pattern of all the heavenly. As we have worn the likeness of the man born of dust, so we shall wear the likeness of the heavenly man. (Paul, *To the Corinthians* 1.15:44–49)

Again, in his letter to the Romans, contrasting the Old Law and the New, the rule of sin and the rule of grace, Paul enlarges on the theology of redemption.

It was through one man that sin entered the world, and through sin death, and thus death pervaded the whole human race, inasmuch as all men have sinned. For sin was already in the world before there was law, though in the absence of law no reckoning is kept of sin. But death held sway from Adam to Moses, even over those who had not sinned as Adam did, by disobeying a direct command—and Adam foreshadows the Man who was to come.

But God's grace is out of all proportion to Adam's wrongdoing. For if the wrongdoing of that one man brought death upon so many, its effect is vastly exceeded by the grace of God and the gift that came to so many by the grace of the one man, Jesus Christ. And again, the gift of God is not to be compared in its effect with that one man's sin. For the judicial action, following upon the one offense, issued in a verdict of condemnation, but the act of grace, following upon so many misdeeds, issued in a verdict of acquittal. For if by the wrongdoing of that one man death established its reign, through a single sinner, so much more shall those who receive in far greater measure God's grace and His gift of righteousness, live and reign through the one man, Jesus Christ. (Paul, *To the Romans* 5:12–17)

43. Jesus Christ, God and Man and Mediator between Them

John's meditation on Jesus as the pre-existent Word of God and Paul's on Jesus as the second Adam are brought together in this work of Ireneus, bishop of Lyons about 175 C.E.

Since it has been clearly demonstrated that the Word, which existed in the beginning with God, and by whom all things were made, who was also present with the human race, was in these latter days, according to the time appointed by the Father, united to His own workmanship, having been made a man subject to suffering, every objection is set aside on the part of those who say "If Christ were born at that time, He did not exist before that time." For I have shown that the Son of God did not then begin to be, since he existed with his Father always; but when he was incarnate, and was made man, he began afresh the long line of human beings, and furnished us in a brief and comprehensive fashion with salvation; so that what we had lost in Adam, namely to be according to the image and likeness of God, that we might recover in Jesus Christ.

Jesus caused human nature to cleave to and become one with God, as we have said. For if man had not overcome the adversary of man, the enemy would not have been legitimately overcome. And again, if God had not given salvation, we could not have had it securely. And if man had not been united to God, he could never have become a partaker in incorruptibility. For it was incumbent upon the mediator between God and man, by his relationship to both, to bring about a friendship and concord, and to present man to God and to reveal God to man. For in what way could we be partakers of the adoption of sons if we had not received from him, through the Son, that fellowship that refers to himself, if the Word, having been made flesh, had not entered into communion with us? Wherefore he passed through every stage of life, restoring to all communication with God. (Ireneus, *Against the Heresies* 3.18.1.7)

44. Muhammad on Jesus

While still in Mecca, before his emigration to Medina in 622 C.E., Muhammad was often engaged by his opponents in polemical disputations. One such, reported in his Life, *had to do with Jesus.*

Ask him (a certain Abdullah suggested), "Is everything which is worshiped besides God in Gehenna along with those who worship it? We (Quraysh) worship angels; the Jews worship Uzayr [that is, Ezra]; and the Christians worship Jesus Son of Mary." Al-Walid and others with him in the assembly marveled at Abdullah's words and thought that he had argued convincingly. When the Apostle (Muhammad) was told of this he said, "Everyone who wishes to be worshiped to the exclusion of God will indeed be with those who worship him. But they worship only satans and those whom they [the satans] have ordered to be worshiped. So God revealed (the verses) 'Those who have received kindness from Us in the past will be removed far from it (the pains of damnation) and will not hear its sound and they abide eternally in their heart's desire' (Quran 21: 101). This refers to Jesus Son of Mary and Uzayr and those rabbis and monks who have lived in obedience to God, whom the erring people worship as lords beside God. . . ."

Then He [that is, God] mentions Jesus Son of Mary (in the Quran) and says, "He was nothing but a slave to whom We showed favor and made him an example to the Children of Israel. If We had wished We could have made (even) for you angels to act as vice-regents in the earth. Verily, there is knowledge of the Final Hour, so doubt not about it but follow Me. This is an upright path" (Quran 43:59–61), that is, the signs which I gave him (Jesus) in raising the dead and healing the sick, therein is sufficient proof of (his) knowledge of the Final Hour. God is saying, "Doubt not about it but follow Me. This is an upright path." (*Life* 236–237) [IBN ISHAQ 1955: 163–164]

Apart from the Quran, Jesus appears in a variety of contexts in the teachings of Muhammad. Here, for example, is a tradition reported of the Prophet, one that provides a kind of doctrinal summary of the beliefs of the Muslim, with considerable emphasis on Jesus.

It is narrated on the authority of Ubadah ibn Samit that the Messenger of God, may peace be upon him, observed: He who has said: "There is no god but the God, that He is One and there is no associate with Him, that Muhammad is His servant and His Messenger, that the Anointed One (that is, Christ) is His servant and the son of His slave girl, and he (Christ) is His Word, which He communicated to Mary, and is His Spirit, that Paradise is a fact and Hell is a fact," him God will cause to enter Paradise through which of its eight doors he would like. (Muslim, *Sahih* 1.11.43)

45. Pentecost and the Descent of the Holy Spirit

We return to the account of the Acts of the Apostles immediately following the Ascension of Jesus.

While the day of Pentecost [that is, the Jewish feast of Weeks, fifty days after the Passover when Jesus was executed] was running its course they were all together in one place when suddenly there came from the sky a noise like that of a strong driving wind, which filled the whole house where they were sitting. And there appeared to them tongues like flames of fire, dispersed among them and resting on each one. And they were all filled with the Holy Spirit and began to talk in other tongues, as the Spirit gave them power of utterance.

Now there were living in Jerusalem devout Jews drawn from every nation under heaven; and at this sound the crowd gathered, all bewildered because each one heard his own language spoken. They were amazed and in their astonishment exclaimed, "Why these are all Galileans, are they not, these men who are speaking? Parthians, Medes, Elamites; inhabitants of Mesopotamia, of Judea and Cappadocia, of Pontus and Asia, of Phrygia and Pamphylia, of Egypt and the districts of Libya round Cyrene; visitors from Rome, both Jews and proselytes, Cretans and Arabs, we hear them telling in our own tongues the great things God has done." (Acts 2:1–11)

46. A Muslim Account of Pentecost

Wahb [an early convert to Islam] and others among the People of the Book say that when God raised Jesus, on whom be peace, to Himself, he remained in heaven seven days. Then God said to him: "Behold, your enemies the Jews have precluded you from (keeping) your promise to your companions, so descend to them and give them your testament. Go down also to Mary Magdalen for there is no one who has wept for you or grieved for you as she has. Go down, therefore, to her and announce yourself to her, that she may be the first one to find you. Then bid her gather the Apostles to you so that you may send them out into the world as preachers summoning to God Most High. . . .

When God bade Jesus descend to her seven days after his ascension, he went down to her and the mountain blazed with light as he came down. Then she gathered to him the Apostles, whom he sent out into the world as summoners to God. After this God took him up (again), clothed him with feathers, dressed him in light, and removed from him his desire for food and drink. So he flew about with the angels around the Throne, being of human and angelic kind, earthly and heavenly. Then the Apostles dispersed to where he had bidden each one of them to go. The night in which he descended is the night which the Christians celebrate. They say that he sent Peter to Rome, Andrew and Matthew to the land where the inhabitants eat men, Thomas and Levi to the Orient, Philip and Judas to Qayrawan and Africa, John to Ephesus, the place of the Companions of the Cave (Quran 18), the two James to Jerusalem, which is Aelia, the land of the Holy House, Bartholomew to Arabia, that is, to the Hejaz, Simon to the land of the Berbers. Each one of the Apostles who was thus sent out was made able to speak the language of those to whom Jesus sent him. (Tha'alibi, *Stories of the Prophets*) [JEFFERY 1962: 594–595]

47. The Apostles Examined by the Sanhedrin

The account in the Acts of the Apostles of events in Jerusalem after the Ascension of Jesus continues.

They [the disciples of Jesus] used to meet by common consent in Solomon's Portico (of the Temple), no one from outside their number venturing to join with them. But people in general spoke highly of them, and more than that, numbers of men and women were added to their ranks as believers in the Lord. In the end the sick were actually carried out into the streets and laid there on beds and stretchers, so that even the shadow of Peter might fall on one or another as he passed by. And the people from the towns round about Jerusalem flocked in, bringing those who were ill or harassed by unclean spirits, and all of them were cured.

Then the High Priest and his colleagues, the Sadducean party as it then was, were goaded into action by jealousy. They proceeded to arrest the Apostles, and put them in official custody.

The Apostles are released by a miracle, but the Temple gendarmerie take them into custody once again.

So they brought them and stood them before the Council [or Sanhedrin, that is, "the full senate of the Israelite nation"] and the High Priest began his examination. "We expressly ordered you," he said, "to desist from your teaching in that name, and what has happened? You have filled Jerusalem with your teaching, and you are trying to make us responsible for that man's death." Peter replied for himself and the Apostles. "We must obey God rather than men. The God of our fathers raised up Jesus whom you have done to death by hanging him on a gibbet. He it is whom God has exalted by his own hand as leader and savior, to grant Israel repentance and forgiveness of sins. And we are witnesses to all this, and so is the Holy Spirit given by God to those who are obedient to him."

This touched them to the raw, and they wanted to put them to death. But a member of the Council rose to his feet, a Pharisee named Gamaliel, a teacher of the Law held in high regard by all the people [and one of Paul's mentors; see below]. He moved that the men be put outside for a while. Then he said, "Men of Israel, be cautious in deciding what to do with these men. . . . Leave them alone. For if this idea of theirs or its execution is of human origin, it will collapse; but if it is from God, you will never be able to put them down, and you risk finding yourselves at war with God."

They took his advice. They sent for the Apostles and had them flogged; then they ordered them to give up speaking in the name of Jesus, and discharged them. So the Apostles went out of the Council rejoicing that they had been found worthy to suffer indignity for the sake of the Name. And every day they went steadily on with their teaching in the

Temple and in private houses, telling the good news of Jesus the Messiah. (Acts 5:12–42)

48. The "Hellenists"

During this period, when disciples were growing in number, there was disagreement between those who spoke Greek and those who spoke the language of the Jews. The former party complained that their widows were being overlooked in the daily distribution. . . . (So) they elected Stephen, a man full of faith and the Holy Spirit, Philip, Prochorus, Nicanor, Timon, Parmenas, and Nicolas of Antioch, a former convert to Judaism. These they presented to the apostles, who prayed and laid hands on them. The word of God now spread more and more widely; the number of disciples in Jerusalem went on increasing rapidly, and very many of the priests adhered to the Faith. Stephen, who was full of grace and power, began to work great miracles and signs among the people. But some members of the synagogue called the Synagogue of the Freedmen, comprising Cyrenians and Alexandrians and people from Cilicia and Asia, came forward and argued with Stephen, but could not hold their own against the inspired wisdom with which he spoke. (Acts 6:1–10)

49. Stephen and Paul

Precisely one of those "Hellenists," Greek-acculturated Jews from the Diaspora, provoked the next crisis for the followers of Jesus in Jerusalem. The performance of signs and wonders might inspire admiration, astonishment, and even belief, but Stephen's long and critical catechesis of the Jewish elders in Jerusalem aroused somewhat different feelings.

This (speech of Stephen's) touched them to the raw and they ground their teeth with fury. But Stephen, filled with the Holy Spirit, and gazing intently up to heaven, saw the glory of God, and Jesus standing at God's right hand. "Look," he said, "there is a rift in the sky. I can see the Son of Man standing at God's right hand!" At this they gave a great shout and stopped their ears. Then they made one rush at him, and flinging him out of the city, set about stoning him. The witnesses laid their coats at the feet of a young man named Saul. So they stoned Stephen, and as they did so, he called out, "Lord Jesus, receive my spirit." Then he fell on his knees and cried aloud, "Lord, do not hold this sin against them," and with that he died. And Saul was among those who approved of his murder. (Acts 7:54–8:1)

50. The Conversion of Paul

Christianity thus had its first martyr. More important, there appears dramatically and for the first time the figure of Paul, here still called Saul. His well-known conversion through a vision of Jesus on the road to Damascus followed, as described in Acts 9 and again, with added autobiographical detail, in Acts 22.

"I am a true-born Jew [Paul explained to a hostile crowd collected in the Temple at Jerusalem], a native of Tarsus in Cilicia. I was brought up in this city, and as a pupil of Gamaliel I was thoroughly trained in every point of our ancestral law. I have always been ardent in God's service, as you are all today, and so I began to persecute this movement to the death, arresting its followers, men and women alike, and putting them in chains. For this I have as witnesses the High Priest and the whole Council of Elders. I was given letters from them to our fellow Jews at Damascus, and had started out to bring the Christians there to Jerusalem as prisoners for punishment; and this is what happened.

"I was on the road and nearing Damascus, when suddenly about midday a great light flashed from the sky all around me and I heard a voice saying to me, 'Saul, Saul, why do you persecute me?' I answered, 'Tell me, Lord, who you are.' 'I am Jesus of Nazareth,' he said, 'whom you are persecuting.' My companions saw the light but did not hear the voice that spoke to me. 'What shall I do, Lord?' I said, and the Lord replied, 'Get up and continue your journey to Damascus; there you will be told of all the tasks that are laid upon you.' As I had been blinded by the brilliance of that light, my companions led me by the hand, and so I came to Damascus." (Acts 22:1–11)

As the days mounted up, the Jews (of Damascus) hatched a plot against his life; but their plans became known to Saul. They kept watch on the city gates day and night so that they might murder him. But his converts took him one night and let him down by the wall, lowering him in a basket. When he reached Jerusalem he tried to join the body of the disciples there; but they were all afraid of him, because they did not believe that he was really a convert. Barnabas, however, took him by the hand and introduced him to the apostles. . . . Saul now stayed with them, moving about freely in Jerusalem. He spoke out openly and boldly in the name of the Lord, talking and debating with the Greek-speaking Jews. But they planned to murder him, and when the brethren learned of this they escorted him to Caesarea and saw him off to Tarsus. (Acts 9:23–30)

That is the version of Paul's coming to Jerusalem in Acts. Paul's own account in his letters is considerably different.

You have heard what my manner of life was when I was still a practicing Jew: how savagely I persecuted the Church of God and tried to destroy it; and how in the practice of our national religion I was outstripping many of my Jewish contemporaries in my boundless devotions to the traditions of my ancestors. But then in his good pleasure God, who had set me apart from birth and called me through his grace, chose to reveal his Son to me and through me, in order that I might proclaim him among the Gentiles. When that happened, without consulting any human being, without going up to Jerusalem to see those who were Apostles before me, I went off at once to Arabia, and afterwards returned to Damascus. Three years later did I go up Jerusalem to get to know Cephas [Peter]. I stayed with him for a fortnight, without seeing any of the other Apostles, except James, the Lord's brother. What I write is plain truth; before God I am not lying. (Paul, *To the Galatians* 1:13–20)

51. The Gospel According to Peter

One of the earliest explanations of Jesus and his message occurs early in the Acts of the Apostles, where Peter is invited to Caesarea.

At Caesarea there was a man named Cornelius, a centurion of the Italian Cohort, as it was called. He was a religious man, and he and his whole family joined in the worship of God. He gave generously to help the Jewish people, and was regular in his prayers to God. (Acts 10:1–2)

Peter, summoned by a vision, accompanies Cornelius' servants to Caesarea.

Cornelius was expecting them and had called together his relatives and close friends. When Peter arrived, Cornelius came to meet him and bowed to the ground in deep reverence. But Peter raised him up to his feet and said, "Stand up; I am a man like anyone else." Still talking with him he went in and found a large gathering. He said to them, "I need not tell you that a Jew is forbidden by his religion to visit or associate with a man of another race; yet God has shown clearly that I must not call any man profane or unclean. That is why I came here without demur when you sent for me." (Acts 10:17–29)

Peter then unfolds the "Good News of Jesus."

I now see how true it is that God has no favorites, but that in every nation the man who is God-fearing and does what is right is acceptable to Him. He sent his word to the Israelites and gave the good news of peace through Jesus Christ, who is Lord of all. I need not tell you what happened lately all over the land of the Jews starting from Galilee after the baptism proclaimed by John. You know about Jesus of Nazareth, how God anointed him with the Holy Spirit and with power. He went about doing good and healing all who were oppressed by the devil, for God was with him. And we can bear witness to what he did in the Jewish country-side and in Jerusalem. He was put to death by hanging on a gibbet; but God raised him to life on the third day, and allowed him to appear, not to the whole people, but to witnesses whom God had chosen in advance—to us who ate and drank with him after he rose from the dead. He commanded us to proclaim him to the people and affirm that he is the one who has been designated by God as the judge of the living and the dead. It is to him that all the prophets testify, declaring that everyone who trusts him receives forgiveness of sins through his name. (Acts 10:34–43)

52. The Gentile Issue

The issue raised by Peter's consorting with Gentiles, even with the God-fearing and sympathetic Cornelius, did not simply disappear. Peter was called to account on his return to Jerusalem: "You have been visiting men who are uncircumcised, and sitting at table with them!" (Acts 11:3). Only after he told the brethren about his vision were their misgivings temporarily allayed.

"Hardly had I begun speaking," Peter explained, "when the Holy Spirit came upon them, just as upon us at the beginning. Then I recalled what the Lord had said: 'John baptized with water, but you will be baptized with the Holy Spirit.' God gave them no less of a gift than He gave us when we put our trust in the Lord Jesus Christ. Then how could I possibly stand in God's way?"

When they heard this their doubts were silenced. They gave praise to God and said, "This means that God has given life-giving repentance to the Gentiles also." (Acts 11:16–18)

Now certain persons who had come down (to Antioch) from Judea began to teach the brotherhood that those who were not circumcised in accordance with the Mosaic practice could not be saved. That brought them into fierce dissension and controversy with Paul and Barnabas. And so it was arranged that these two and some others from Antioch should go up to Jerusalem and see the apostles and elders about this question. . . .

When they reached Jerusalem they were welcomed by the church and the apostles and elders, and reported all that God had done through them. Then some of the Pharisaic party who had become believers came forward and said, "They must be circumcised and told to keep the Law of Moses."

The question was discussed at length. Peter expressed a preference for the lenient view; then James, "the brother of the Lord," speaks.

My judgment therefore is that we should impose no irksome restrictions on those of the Gentiles who are turning to God but instruct them by letter to abstain from things polluted by contact with idols, from fornication, from anything that has been strangled and from blood. Moses, after all, has never lacked for spokesmen in every town for generations past; he is read in the synagogues Sabbath by Sabbath. (Acts 15:1–21)

53. Jews and Gentiles

Paul gives his own, more personal reflections on these same events in his letter to the Galatians.

These men of repute (in the Jerusalem church) did not prolong the consultation, but on the contrary acknowledged that I had been entrusted with the Gospel for Gentiles as surely as Peter had been entrusted with the Gospel for Jews. For God whose action made Peter an Apostle to the Jews, also made me an Apostle to the Gentiles. Recognizing, then, the favor thus bestowed on me, those reputed pillars of our society, James, Cephas [that is, Peter] and John, accepted Barnabas and myself as partners, and shook hands upon it, agreeing that we should go to the Gentiles while they went to the Jews. All they asked was that we should keep their poor in mind, which was the very thing I made it my business to do.

But when Cephas came to Antioch, I opposed him to his face, because he was clearly in the wrong. For until certain persons came from James (in Jerusalem) he was taking his meals with Gentile Christians; but when they came he drew back and began to hold himself apart, because he was afraid of the advocates of circumcision. The other Jewish Christians showed the same lack of principle; even Barnabas was carried away and played false like the rest. But when I saw that their conduct did not square with the truth of the Gospel, I said to Cephas, before the whole congregation, "If you, a Jew born and bred, live like a Gentile and not like a Jew, how can you insist that Gentiles must live like Jews?"

We ourselves are Jews by birth, not Gentiles and sinners. But we know that that no man is justified by doing what the Law demands, but only through faith in Christ Jesus; so we too have put our faith in Jesus Christ, in order that we might be justified through this faith and not through deeds dictated by law; for by such deeds, Scripture says, no mortal man shall be justified.

If now, in seeking to be justified in Christ, we ourselves no less than the Gentiles turn out to be sinners against the Law, does that mean that Christ is an abettor of sin? No, never! No, if I start building up a system which I have pulled down, then it is that I show myself up as a transgressor of the Law. For through the Law I died to law—to live for God. I have been crucified with Christ: the life I live is not my life, but the life which Christ lives in me; and my present bodily life is lived by faith in the Son of God, who loved me and gave himself up for me. I will not nullify the grace of God; if righteousness comes by Law, then Christ died for nothing. (Paul, *To the Galatians* 2:6–21)

54. Paul's Mission
and God's Hidden Purpose

As we shall see, this issue of Jews and Gentiles will have a long history in the Christian Church. Aquinas was still pondering these particular events in Acts and Galatians in the thirteenth century. Paul too had reason to give them thought later in his apostolic career.

I, Paul, who in the cause of you Gentiles am now the prisoner of Jesus Christ—for surely you have heard how God has assigned the gift of his grace to me for your benefit. It was by a revelation that His secret was made known to me. I have already written a brief account of this, and by reading it you may perceive that I understand the secret of Christ. In former generations this was not disclosed to the human race; but now it has been revealed by inspiration to his dedicated apostles and prophets, that through the Gospel the Gentiles are the joint heirs with the Jews, part of the same body, sharers together in the promise made in Christ Jesus. Such is the gospel of which I was made a minister, by God's gift, bestowed unmerited on me in the working of his power.

To me, who am less than the least of all God's people, He has granted by His grace the privilege of proclaiming to the Gentiles the good news of the unfathomable riches of Christ, and of bringing to light how this hidden purpose was to be put into effect. It was hidden for long ages in God the creator of the universe, in order that now, through the Church, the wisdom of God in all its varied forms might be made known to the rulers and authorities in the realms of heaven. This is in accord with his age-long purpose, which He achieved in Christ Jesus our Lord. (Paul, *To the Ephesians* 3:1–11)

55. The Arrest of Paul

After the community meeting in Jerusalem, Paul departs for a long round of mission-ary visits through the eastern Mediterranean. Finally, he and Luke, who is now using "we" in the account in Acts, reach Jerusalem.

So we reached Jerusalem where the brotherhood welcomed us gladly. Next day Paul paid a visit to James; we were with him, and all the elders attended. He greeted them, and then described in detail all that God had done among the Gentiles through his ministry. When they heard this they [James and the elders] gave praise to God. Then they said to Paul, "You see, brother, how many thousands of converts we have amongst the Jews, all of them staunch upholders of the Law. Now they have been given certain information about you: it is said that you teach all the Jews in the Gentile world to turn their backs on Moses, telling them to give up circumcising their children and following our way of life. What is the position, then? They are sure to hear that you have arrived. You must therefore do as we tell you. We have four men here who are under a vow; take them with you and go through the ritual purification with them, paying their expenses, after which they may shave their heads. Then everyone will know there is nothing in the stories that were told about you, but that you are a practicing Jew and keep the Law yourself." ... So Paul took the four men and next day, having gone through the ritual purification with them, he went into the Temple to give notice of the date when the period of purification would end and the offering be made for each of them. (Acts 21:15–26)

But just before the seven days were up, the Jews from the province of Asia saw him in the Temple. They stirred up the whole crowd, and seized him, shouting, "Men of Israel, help, help! This is the fellow who spreads his doctrine all over the world, attacking our people, our Law, and this sanctuary. On top of all this he has brought Gentiles into the Temple and profaned this holy place." For they had previously seen Tro-phimus the Ephesian with him in the city and assumed that Paul had brought him into the Temple.

The whole city was in turmoil, and people came running from all directions. They seized Paul and dragged him out of the Temple; and at once the doors [of the Court of the Israelites] were shut. While they were clamoring for his death, a report reached the officer commanding the cohort (in the Fortress Antonia) that all Jerusalem was in an uproar. He immediately took a force of soldiers with their centurions and came down on the rioters at the double. As soon as they saw the commandant and his troops they stopped beating Paul. The commandant stepped forward, arrested him and ordered him to be shackled with two chains. He then asked who the man was and what he had been doing. Some in the crowd shouted one thing, some another. As he could not get at the truth because of the hubbub, he ordered him to be taken into the barracks. When Paul reached the steps [up to the Antonia], he had to be carried by the soldiers because of the violence of the crowd. For the whole crowd was at their heels yelling "Kill him!"

Just before Paul was taken into the barracks he said to the commandant, "May I have a word with you?" The commandant said, "So you speak Greek, do you? Then you are not the Egyptian who started a revolt some time ago and led a force of four thousand terrorists into the wilds?" Paul replied, "I am a Jew, a Tarsian from Cilicia, a citizen of no mean city. I ask your permission to speak to the people." When permission had been given, Paul stood on the steps and with a gesture called for the attention of the people. As soon as quiet was restored, he addressed them in the Jewish language: "Brothers and fathers, give me a hearing while I make my defense before you." When they heard him speaking to them in their own language, they listened more quietly. "I am a true-born Jew," he said, "a native of Tarsus in Cilicia. I was brought up in this city, and as a pupil of Gamaliel I was thoroughly trained in every point of our ancestral law." (Acts 21:7–22:4)

Paul proceeds to describe his conversion and his return from Damascus to Jerusalem, when he had another vision of Jesus, who said, "Go, I am sending you far away to the Gentiles."

Up to this point they had given him a hearing but now they began shouting, "Down with him! A scoundrel like that is better dead!" And as they were yelling and waving their cloaks and flinging dust in the air, the commandant ordered him to be brought into the barracks and gave instructions to examine him by flogging and find out what reason there was for such an outcry against him. But when they tied him up for the lash, Paul said to the centurion who was standing there, "Can you legally flog a man who is a Roman citizen and moreover who has not been found guilty?" When the centurion heard this, he went and reported it to the commandant. "What do you mean to do?" he said. "This man is a Roman citizen." The commandant came to Paul. "Tell me, are you a Roman citizen?" he asked. "Yes," said he. The commandant rejoined, "It cost me a large sum to acquire citizenship." Paul said, "But it was mine by birth." Then those who were about to examine him withdrew hastily, and the commandant himself was alarmed when he realized that Paul was a Roman citizen and that he had put him in irons. (Acts 22:22–29)

The commandant of the Antonia garrison planned to have a hearing before the Sanhedrin in Jerusalem, but threats to Paul's life caused him to send the prisoner under heavy escort to Caesarea to the governor Felix. The date was sometime shortly before 60 C.E., and it marked the end of Paul's association with Jerusalem.

56. The Great War Begins

In 64 C.E., Gessius Florus, the last Roman prefect for Judea and the unwitting provocateur of the destruction of the Holy City, takes up his post. From the beginning, Florus had little understanding of or sympathy with his subjects in Judea, who were in fact never very far from sedition. The trouble began when a number of Jews were arrested in Caesarea.

The citizens of Jerusalem, though they took this affair badly, yet they restrained their passion. But Florus acted as if he had been hired to fan the war into flame, and sent some men to take seventeen talents out of the sacred treasure (of the Temple), on the pretense that Caesar required them. At this the people became immediately disturbed and ran in a body to the Temple with great shouting and called upon Caesar by name and begged him to free them from the tyranny of Florus. Some of the more seditious cried out against Florus himself and blamed him severely. They carried about a basket and solicited small change for him, as if he were a poor man without possessions. Far from being ashamed of his greed for money, he became further enraged and was provoked to get even more. Instead of going to Caesarea, as he ought to have done, and damping the flames of war there . . . he marched quickly with a force of cavalry and infantry against Jerusalem, that he might gain his objective by force of Roman arms and drain the city dry.

Once in the city Florus summoned the elders and leaders of the Jews and demanded the guilty be handed over to him. Apologies were made, and they protested, "it was no wonder that in so great a crowd there should be some rasher than they ought to have been and, by reason of their age, foolish as well."

Florus was all the more provoked at this, and called out aloud from his soldiers to loot the Upper Market, and to slay whomever they met there. The soldiers, who found this order of their commander agreeable to their own sense of greed, plundered not only the (public) place where they were sent but broke into houses and killed the inhabitants. The citizens fled down the alleys and the soldiers killed those they caught and looted in every way conceivable. They also arrested many of the peaceable citizens and brought them before Florus, whom he first had whipped and then crucified. (Josephus, *War* 2.14.6–9)

This was in April or May 66 C.E., the beginning of a long-postponed and now increasingly inevitable confrontation between the Romans and the Jews of Jerusalem. The critical moment was at hand.

Eleazer, the son of Ananias the High Priest, a very bold young man, who was also at that time the superintendent of the Temple, persuaded those who were officiating in the divine services to accept no gift or sacrifice on behalf of any foreigner. And this was the true beginning of our war with the Romans, for they rejected the sacrifice of Caesar on this account. When many of the high priests and leaders begged them not to omit this sacrifice, which was customary for them to offer for their rulers, they would not be persuaded. (Josephus, *War* 2.17.2)

When the (Jewish) leaders in Jerusalem perceived that the sedition was too difficult for them to put down, and that the danger that would arise from the Romans would descend in the first place upon their shoulders, they tried to clear themselves and sent representatives, some to Florus . . . and others to Agrippa . . . and they requested that both of them should come with an army to the city and cut off the revolt while it was still possible. Now this terrible message was good news to Florus, and since it was his intent that there should be a war, he gave no answer to the delegates. But Agrippa was equally solicitous for the rebels and for those against whom the war would be fought; he wanted to save the Jews for the Romans and the Temple for the Jews. He was also aware that a war would not be to his own advantage and so he sent 2,000 horsemen to the assistance of the people. . . .

At this the (Jewish) leaders and the high priests, as well as those others who wanted peace, took courage and seized the Upper City, since the rebels had already occupied the Lower City and the Temple.

The next day Agrippa's cavalry are driven out of the Upper City by the rebels.

... [They] set fire to the house of Ananias the High Priest and to the palace of Agrippa and Berenice. After which they spread the fire to the place where the archives were kept and quickly burned the due bills belonging to creditors and so dissolved the obligation of paying debts. This was done to gain the allegiance of the many who profited thereby and to persuade the poorer citizens to join the insurrection with impunity against the wealthy.

The next day they ... made an assault upon the Antonia and besieged the garrison within it for two days, and then took the garrison and slew them and set the citadel on fire, after which they marched against the palace [that, is Herod's former palace, the Roman pretorium] where the king's soldiers had fled. (Josephus, *War* 2.17.4–7)

57. Fugitives from the City

Finally, all the forces of resistance, Roman and Agrippan, are driven from Jerusalem, and the city rests entirely in the possession of the rebels. Others had departed as well, among them the small community of Christians in Jerusalem.

The members of the Jerusalem church, by means of an oracle given by revelation to acceptable persons there, were ordered to leave the country before the war (of 66–70 C.E.) began and settle in a town in the Peraea (in the Transjordan) called Pella. To Pella those who believed in Christ migrated from Jerusalem; and as if holy men had abandoned the royal metropolis of the Jews and the entire Jewish land, the judgment of God at last overtook them for the abominable crimes against Christ and His Apostles, completely blotting out that wicked generation from among men. (Eusebius, *Church History* 3.5)

Somewhat later in the war:

Now when Vespasian came to destroy Jerusalem, he said to the inhabitants, "Fools, why do you seek to destroy this city and why do you seek to burn the Temple? For what do I ask you but that you send me one bow or one arrow and I shall go away from you?" They then said to him, "Even as we went forth against the first two who were here before you and slew them, so shall we go forth against you and slay you."

And when Rabban Yohanan ben Zakkai heard this, he sent for the men of Jerusalem and said to them, "My children, why do you destroy this city, and why do you seek to destroy the Temple? For what is it that he asks of you?" ...

Vespasian had men stationed inside the walls of Jerusalem. Every word which they overheard they would write down, attach it to an arrow and shoot it over the wall, saying that Rabban Yohanan ben Zakkai was one of the emperor's friends.

Now after Rabban Yohanan ben Zakkai had spoken to them one day, two days, and three days, and they would still not listen to him, he sent for his disciples, Rabbi Eliezer and Rabbi Joshua.

"My sons," he said, "arise and take me out of here. Make a coffin for me that I may lie in it."

Rabbi Eliezer took the head of the coffin and Rabbi Joshua took hold of the foot, and they began carrying him as the sun set until they reached the gates of Jerusalem. "Who is this?" the gatekeepers demanded. "It is a dead man," they replied. "Do you not know that the dead may not be held overnight in Jerusalem?" "If it is a dead man," the gatekeepers said to them, "take him out." So they took him out. (*The Fathers According to Rabbi Nathan* 4) [ABOTH RABBI NATHAN 1955: 35–36]

Thus Rabbi Yohanan ben Zakkai, who eventually went on to Jabneh to found the academy from which much of rabbinic Judaism was later to flow, escaped, like the Christian elders, from a Jerusalem destined for ruin and so preserved intact institutions that would return there at a later date and shape the spiritual reconstruction of the city and, indeed, the entire Jewish tradition.

4. Muhammad, the Prophet of God

1. Muhammad's Descent from Adam

Like the Synoptic Gospels' presentation of Jesus, the standard Muslim life of Muhammad, the Life of the Apostle of God, *which was composed out of earlier materials by Ibn Ishaq (d. 768 C.E.) and then re-edited by Ibn Hisham (d. 843 C.E.), begins with a genealogy, here, as in Luke 3:23–38, stretching back to the father of all mankind.*

This is the book of the life of the Messenger of God:

Muhammad was the son of Abdullah, son of Abd al-Muttalib, whose name was Shayba, son of Hashim, whose name was Amr, son of Abd al-Manaf, whose name was al-Mughira, son of Qusayy, whose name was Zayd, son of Kilab, son of Murra, son of Ka'b, son of Lu'ayy, son of Ghalib, son of Fikr, son of Malik, son of al-Nadr, son of Kinana, son of Khuzayma, son of Mudrika, whose name was Amir, son of Ilyas, son of Mudar, son of Nizar, son of Ma'add, son of Adnan, son of Udd or Udad, son of Muqawwam, son of Nahur, son of Tayrah, son of Ya'rub, son of Yashjub, son of Nabit, son of Ishmael, son of Abraham, the Friend of the Compassionate One, son of Tarih, who is Azar, son of Nahur, son of Sarugh, son of Ra'u, son of Falikh, son of Aybar, son of Shalikh, son of Arfakhshad, son of Shem, son of Noah, son of Lamk, son of Matthuselah, son of Enoch, who is the prophet Idris, according to what is alleged, though God knows best, he was the first of the sons of Adam to whom prophecy and writing with a pen were given, son of Yard, son of Mahlil, son of Cain, son of Yanish, son of Seth, son of Adam. (Ibn Ishaq, *Life* 3) [IBN ISHAQ 1955: 3]

2. The Birth of the Prophet

After this prelude on the remote past, the standard life of the Prophet sets the historical scene by laying out various traditions about early Mecca: how Abraham and Ishmael came to build the House of the Lord there and how Ishmael's descendants were forced to leave the place and lapsed back into paganism. After some additional material on south Arabia, the narrative turns directly to the birth of the Prophet.

It is alleged in popular stories, and only God knows the truth, that Amina, daughter of Wahb, mother of God's Apostle, used to say when she was pregnant with God's Apostle, that a voice said to her, "You are pregnant with the lord of this people, and when he is born say 'I put him in the care of the One away from the evil of every envyer'; then call him Muhammad." As she was pregnant with him she saw a light come forth from her by which she could see the castles of Busra in Syria. Shortly afterwards Abdullah, the Apostle's father, died while his mother was still pregnant. (*Life* 102) [IBN ISHAQ 1955: 69]

The Messenger was born on Monday, the 12th of First Rabi^c in the Year of the Elephant [570 C.E.]. . . . Salih b. Ibrahim . . . said that his tribesmen said that Hassan ibn Thabit said: "I was a well-grown boy of seven or eight, understanding all that I heard, when I heard a Jew calling out at the top of his voice from the top of a fort in Yathrib [Medina] 'O company of Jews!' until they all came together and called out 'Confound you! What is the matter?' He answered, 'Tonight has a star risen under which Ahmad is to be born.'"

After his birth his mother (Amina) sent to tell his grandfather Abd al-Muttalib that she had given birth to a boy and asked him to come and look at him. When he came she told him what she had seen when she conceived him and what was said to her and what she was ordered to call him. It is alleged that Abd al-Muttalib took him before (the idol) Hubal in the middle of the Ka'ba, where he stood and prayed to God, thanking him for this gift. Then he brought him out and delivered him to his mother, and he tried to find foster mothers [or wet nurses] for him. (*Life* 103) [IBN ISHAQ 1955: 70]

Finally the boy Muhammad undergoes a purification at the hands of more than human agents, then is weighed and found worthy of his future role.

Thawr ibn Yazid . . . told me that some of the Apostle's companions asked him to tell them about himself. He said: "I am what Abraham my father prayed for and the good news of my brother Jesus. When my mother was carrying me she saw a light proceeding from her which showed her the castles of Syria. I was suckled among the Banu Saʿd ibn Bakr, and while I was with a (foster) brother of mine behind our tents shepherding the lambs, two men in white raiment came to me with a gold basin full of snow. Then they seized me and opened my belly, extracted my heart and split it; then they extracted a black drop from it and threw it away; then they washed my heart and my belly with the snow until they had thoroughly cleaned them. Then one said to the other, weigh him against ten of his people; they did and I outweighed them. Then they weighed me against a hundred and then a thousand and I outweighed them. He said 'Leave him alone, for by God, if you weigh him against all his people he would outweigh them.' " (*Life* 106) [IBN ISHAQ 1955: 72]

3. The Christian Monk Bahira Identifies Muhammad

When Muhammad was six, his mother, Amina, died, whereupon he was sent to live with his grandfather. Two years later Abd al-Muttalib died as well, and Muhammad was then put into the care of his paternal uncle, Abu Talib. Thus we are introduced in a somewhat offhand manner to the commercial climate of Mecca in which Muhammad would continue to share for most of his adult life. The point of the story is other, however. In the passage cited above the Prophet's birth was acknowledged by a Jew, who saw his sign in the stars; here a Christian monk recognizes Muhammad in the flesh as the one of whom Scripture had spoken.

Abu Talib had planned to go on a merchant caravan to Syria, and when all preparations had been made for the journey, the Messenger of God, so they allege, attached himself closely to him so that he took pity on him and said that he would take him with him. . . . When the caravan reached Busra in Syria there was a monk there in his cell by the name of Bahira, who was well versed in the knowledge of the Christians. . . . They had often passed by him in the past and he never spoke to them or took any notice of them until this year, and when they stopped near his cell he made a great feast for them . . . and sent word to them, "I have prepared food for you, O men of Quraysh, and I should like you all to come, great and small, bond and free." One of them said to him, "By God, Bahira, something extraordinary has happened today; you used not to treat us so, and we have often passed by you. What has befallen you today?" He answered, "You are right in what you say, but you are my guests and I wish to honor you and give you food so that you may eat."

So they gathered together with him, leaving the Messenger of God behind with the baggage under the tree, on account of his extreme youth. When Bahira looked at the people he did not see the mark which he knew and found in his books, so he said, "Do not let one of you remain behind and not come to my feast." . . . One of the men of Quraysh said, "By al-Lat and al-Uzza, we are to blame for leaving behind the son of Abdullah ibn Abd al-Muttalib." Then he got up and embraced him and made him sit with the people. When Bahira saw him he stared at him closely, looking at his body and finding traces of his description (in the Christian books). When people had finished eating and had gone away, Bahira got up and said to him, "Boy, I now ask you by al-Lat and al-Uzza to answer my question." Now Bahira said this only because he had heard his people swearing by these goddesses. They allege that the Messenger of God said to him, "Do not ask me by al-Lat and al-Uzza, for by God nothing is more hateful to me than those two." Bahira answered, "Then, by God, tell me what I ask"; he replied, "Ask me what you like," so he began to question him about what happened in his waking and in his sleep, and his habits and affairs generally, and what the Messenger of God told him coincided with what Bahira knew of his description. Then he looked at his back and saw the seal of prophethood between his shoulders in the very place described in his book.

When he had finished he went to his uncle Abu Talib . . . and said, "Take your nephew back to his country and guard him carefully against the Jews, for, by God! if they see him and know about him what I know, they will do him evil; a great future lies before this nephew of yours, so take him home quickly." (*Life* 115–116) [IBN ISHAQ 1955: 79–81]

4. The Scriptural Prediction of the Coming of the Prophet of Islam

The boy Muhammad's identification and acknowledgment by the Christian monk Bahira was a popular story in Islam, and the motif of the future holy man identified in the child can be paralleled from the infancy and boyhood accounts of Moses and Jesus, among others. Although such stories may be no more than the stuff of legend, there is a similar but theologically quite different question that is proposed for meditation by the Quran itself, namely, God's own foreshadowing of the coming of His prophet Muhammad in Scripture. It is God who speaks here.

Those who follow the messenger, the unlettered Prophet, described in the Torah and the Gospel, who bids things noble and forbids things vile, makes lawful what is clean, and prohibits what is foul, who relieves them of their burdens and the yoke that lies upon them, those who believe and honor and help him, and follow the light sent with him, are those who will attain their goal. (Quran 7:157)

In this first passage God in the Quran makes explicit though unspecified reference to the Bible and the Gospels as announcing the coming of a future prophet, "whose name shall be Ahmad." In another passage the same sentiments are expressed from the mouth of Jesus.

And when Jesus son of Mary said: "O Children of Israel, I am sent to you by God to confirm the Torah (sent) before me, and to give you good tidings of an apostle who will come after me, whose name is Ahmad (the praised one)." Yet, when he has come to them with clear proofs, they say: "This is only magic." (Quran 61:6)

On the second of these passages, the classical Quranic commentaries have this to say.

According to Ka'b al-Ahbar [a rabbi who was an early convert to Islam and the attributed source of much of the material on Judaism in the early Islamic tradition], it is related that the disciples of Jesus asked: "O Spirit of God, will there be another religious community after us?" and that Jesus then said: "Yes, the community of Ahmad. It will comprise people who are wise, knowing, devout and pious, as if they were all prophets in religious knowledge. They will be content with modest sustenance from God, and He will be pleased with a modest conduct on their part." (Zamakhshari, *The Unveiler*, ad loc.)

"... whose name is Ahmad ... ": that is, Muhammad. The meaning is: My [that is, Jesus'] religion exists by reason of holding on firmly to the books of God and His prophets. And so Jesus mentions (only) the very first of the well-known books, concerning which the earlier prophets rendered judgment, and only that prophet who (as the last) constitutes the seal of those who are sent by God. (Baydawi, *Commentary*, ad loc.)

The Muslim scientist and chronologer Biruni (d. 1048 C.E.) argues the case somewhat more rigorously in his Traces of the Past. His point of departure is the chief biblical proof-text for the Muslims' contention that Muhammad had been foretold in earlier Scripture, namely this passage in Isaiah.

God ordered him to set a watchman on the watchtower, that he might declare what he should see. Then he said: I see a man riding on an ass and a man riding on a camel. And one of them came forward crying and speaking: Babylon is fallen, and its graven images are broken. (Isaiah 21:6–9)

Biruni begins:

This is a prophecy regarding the Messiah, the "man riding on an ass," and regarding Muhammad, the "man riding on a camel," because in consequence of the latter's appearance, Babylon has fallen, its idols have been broken, its castles have been shattered, and its empire has perished. There are many passages in this book of Isaiah predicting Muhammad, being rather hints (than explicit texts), but easily admitting of a clear interpretation. And despite all this, the Jews' obstinacy in clinging to their error induces them to devise and maintain things which are not acknowledged by men in general, to wit, that the "man riding on a camel" is Moses and not Muhammad. But what connection have Moses and his people with Babylon? And did that happen to Moses and to his people after him which happened to Muhammad and his companions in Babylon? By no means! If the Jews had escaped one by one from the Babylonians, they would have considered it a sufficient prize to return (to their country), even though in a desperate condition.

This testimony (of Isaiah) is confirmed in the fifth book of Moses, which is called Deuteronomy: "I will raise them up a prophet like yourself from among their brethren, and will put My word in his mouth. And he shall speak to them all that I command him. And whoever will not heed the word of him who speaks in My name, I shall take revenge on him" (Deut. 21:6–9). Now I should like to know whether there are other brethren of the sons of Isaac except the sons of Ishmael? If they say that the brethren of the sons of Israel are the children of Esau, we ask only: Has there been raised among *them* a man like Moses—in the times after Moses—of the same description and resembling him?

Does not also the following passage from the same book, of which this is a translation, bear testimony to Muhammad: "The Lord came from Mount Sinai, and rose up to us from Seir, and He shone from Mount Paran, accompanied by ten thousand saints at His right hand" (Deut. 33:2)? The terms of this passage are hints for the establishing of the proof that the (anthropomorphic) descriptions inherent in them cannot be referred to the essence of the Creator, nor to His qualities, He being high above such things. His coming from Mount Sinai means His secret conversation with Moses there; His riding up from Seir means the appearance of the Messiah; and His shining forth from Paran, where Ishmael grew up and married, means the coming of Muhammad from there as the last of the founders of religions, accompanied by legions of saints, who were sent down from heaven to help, being marked with certain badges. He who refuses to accept this interpretation, for which all evidence has borne testimony, is required to prove what kinds of mistakes there are in it. "But he whose companion is Satan, woe to him for such a companion" (Quran 4:42). (al-Biruni, *Traces of the Past*)

[BIRUNI 1879: 22–23]

5. Maimonides Replies

The issue of the scriptural predictions of the coming of Muhammad as a prophet, and the related one of the Jews and Christians tampering with those texts, was to be a rich source of polemic among Muslims, Christians, and Jews. The Christians had built their case for the Messiahship of Jesus on biblical prophecy, and in the passage just cited the Quran invokes just such a foretelling on the part of another postbiblical prophet, Jesus son of Mary. But that evidence merely opened the discussion. If the Bible had foretold the coming of Jesus, had it not also foreshadowed the Prophet of Islam? Where? On the basis of Quran 7:156–157 Muslims had of necessity to argue that it had, and it was their search for confirmatory texts that lay behind this response of the Spanish scriptural scholar and philosopher Maimonides (d. 1204 C.E.), written to his fellow Jews in the Yemen and reassuring them that the Muslim claim was absurd.

In your letter you mention that the emissary [apparently a Jewish apostate to Islam] has incited a number of people to believe that several verses in Scripture allude to the Madman [Muhammad], such as "multiply exceedingly" (Gen. 17:20); "he shone forth from Mount Paran" (Deut. 33:2); "a prophet from the midst of you" (Deut. 18:15); and the promise to Ishmael, "I will make him a great nation" (Gen. 17:20). These arguments have been rehashed so often that they have become nauseating. It is not enough to declare that they are altogether feeble; more, to cite these verses as proofs is ridiculous and absurd in the extreme. For these are not matters that can confuse the minds of anyone. Neither the untutored multitude, nor even the very apostates who delude others with them, believe in them or entertain any illusions about them. Their purpose in citing these verses is to win favor in the eyes of the Gentiles by demonstrating that they believe the statement in the Quran that Muhammad was mentioned in the Torah. But the Muslims themselves put no faith in their arguments: they neither accept nor cite them, because they are manifestly so fallacious.

Inasmuch as the Muslims could not find a single proof in the entire Bible, nor any reference, nor even a possible allusion to their prophet which they could utilize, they were compelled to accuse us, saying, "You have altered the text of the Torah and expunged from it every trace of the name of Muhammad." They could find nothing stronger than this ignominious argument, the falseness of which is easily demonstrated to one and all by the following facts. First, the Scripture was translated into Syriac, Greek, Persian and Latin hundreds of years before the appearance of Muhammad. Second, there is a uniform tradition regarding the text of the Bible both in the East and in the West, with the result that no differences in the text exist at all, not even in the vocalization, for they are all correct. Nor do any differences affecting the meaning exist. The motive for their accusation lies, therefore, in the absence of any allusion to Muhammad in the Torah. (Maimonides, *Letter to the Yemen*)

6. Marriage with Khadija

We return to Ibn Ishaq's Life of the Apostle of God.

The Messenger of God grew up, God protecting and keeping him from the vileness of heathenism because He wished to honor him with Apostleship, until he grew up to be the finest of his people in manliness, the best in character, most noble in lineage, the best neighbor, the most kind, truthful, reliable, the furthest removed from filthiness and corrupt morals, through loftiness and nobility, so that he was known among his people as "the trustworthy" because of the good qualities which God had implanted in him. (*Life* 117) [IBN ISHAQ 1955: 81]

Next we are introduced to Khadija, Muhammad's longtime and, for as long as she lived, his only wife. The motifs of Muhammad the successful and the acknowledged future holy man continue to be entwined in the narrative.

Khadija was a merchant woman of dignity and wealth. She used to hire men to carry merchandise outside the country on a profit-sharing basis, for the Quraysh were a people given to commerce. Now when she heard about the Prophet's truthfulness, trustworthiness and honorable character, she sent for him and proposed that he should take her goods to Syria and trade with them, while she would pay him more than she paid others. He was to take a lad called Maysara. The Messenger of God accepted the proposal and the two set forth until they came to Syria.

The Messenger stopped in the shade of a tree near a monk's cell, when the monk came up to Maysara and asked him who the man was resting under the tree. He told him he was of the Quraysh, the people who held the sanctuary (in Mecca), and the monk exclaimed: "None but a prophet ever sat beneath this tree."

Then the Prophet sold the goods he had brought and bought what he wanted to buy and began the return journey to Mecca. The story goes that at the height of noon, when the heat was intense as he rode his beast, Maysara saw two angels shading the Messenger from the sun's rays. When he brought Khadija her property she sold it and it amounted to double or thereabouts. Maysara for his part told her about the two angels who had shaded him and of the monk's words.

Now Khadija was a determined, noble and intelligent woman possessing the properties with which God willed to honor her. So when Maysara told her those things she sent to the Messenger of God and—so the story goes—said "O son of my uncle, I like you because of our relationship and your high reputation among your people, your trustworthiness and good character and truthfulness." Then she proposed marriage. Now Khadija at that time was the best-born woman in the Quraysh, of the greatest dignity, and also the richest. All the people were eager to get possession of her wealth if were possible. . . .

The Messenger of God told his uncles of Khadija's proposal, and his his uncle Hamza ibn Abd al-Muttalib went with him to Khuwaylid ibn Asad and asked for her hand and he married her. She was the mother of all the Apostle's children except Ibrahim, namely, al-Qasim [whence he was known as Abu al-Qasim], al-Tahir, al-Tayyib, Zaynab, Ruqayya, Umm Kulthum and Fatima. Al-Qasim, al-Tayyib and al-Tahir died in the time of paganism. All his daughters lived into Islam and embraced it, and migrated with him to Medina. (*Life* 119–121) [IBN ISHAQ 1955: 82–83]

7. The Ka'ba Rebuilt

The center of the pre-Islamic religious cult in Mecca (later incorporated into Islamic ritual as well) was the Ka'ba or "cube," a square building in the midst of the sacred precinct or haram. *It had a black meteoric rock embedded in one of its corners.*

The Quraysh decided to rebuild the Ka'ba when the Messenger was thirty-five years of age. They were planning to roof it and feared to demolish it, for it was made of loose stones about a man's height, and they wanted to raise it and roof it because men had stolen part of the treasure of the Ka'ba which used to be in a well in the middle of it. . . .

Now a ship belonging to a Greek merchant had been cast ashore at Jedda and became a total wreck. They took its timbers and got ready to roof the Ka'ba (with them). It happened that in Mecca there was a Copt who was a carpenter, so everything they needed was at hand. . . . The people were afraid to demolish the temple, however, and withdrew in awe from it. Al-Walid ibn al-Mughira said, "I will begin the demolition." So he took a pick ax, went up to it, saying the while, "O God, do not be afraid, O God, we intend only what is best." Then he demolished the part at the two corners. That night the people watched, saying, "We will look out; if he is struck down, we won't destroy any more of it and will restore it as it was; but if nothing happens to him, then God is pleased with what we are doing and we will demolish it." In the morning al-Walid returned to the work of demolition and the people worked with him until they got down to the foundation of Abraham (Quran 2:127). They came upon green stones like camel's humps joined to one another. . . . I was told that the Quraysh found in the corner a writing in Syriac. They could not understand it until a Jew read it for them. It was as follows: "I am God, the Lord of the Bakka. I created it on the day that I created heaven and earth and formed the sun and the moon, and I surrounded it with seven pious angels. It will stand while its two mountains stand, a blessing to its people with milk and water," and I was told that they found in the *maqam* [a stone, and a shrine, sacred to Abraham in Islamic tradition] a writing, "Mecca is God's holy house, its sustenance comes to it from three directions; let its people not be the first to profane it. . . ."

The tribes of Quraysh gathered stones for the building, each tribe collecting them and building by itself until the building was finished up to the (location of the) black stone, where controversy arose, since each tribe wanted to lift it into its place, until they went their several ways formed alliances and got ready for battle.

They agree to accept the arbitration of the next man to enter into the sanctuary. It was Muhammad.

When they saw him they said, "This is the trustworthy one. We are satisfied. This is Muhammad." When they came to him and they informed him of the matter he said, "Give me a cloak," and when it was brought to him he took the black stone and placed it inside it and said that each tribe should take hold of an end of the cloak and lift it together. They did this so that when they got it into position he placed it with his own hand, and then building went on above it. (*Life* 122–125) [IBN ISHAQ 1955: 84–86]

8. The Religion of Abraham

It seems likely that the stories of Abraham's association with Mecca were circulating before the Quran began making reference to them. How or when that connection

*came to be, we cannot even guess, since there is no evidence that Jews or Christians
lived in Muhammad's native city. But there were some type of monotheists there, or
so the Arab tradition informs us, though the word used to describe them, hanif,
remains somewhat mysterious.*

One day when the Quraysh had assembled on a feast day to venerate
and circumambulate the idol to which they offered sacrifices, this being
a feast which they held annually, four men drew apart and agreed to
keep their counsel in the bonds of friendship. There were Waraqa ibn
Nawfal, Ubaydallah ibn Jahsh, Uthman ibn al-Hawarith and Zayd ibn
Amr. They were of the opinion that their people had corrupted the
religion of their father Abraham, and that the stone they went around was
of no account; it could neither hear, nor see, nor hurt, nor help. "Find for
yourselves a religion," they said, "for by God you have none." So they
went their several ways in the lands, seeking the Hanifiyya, the religion
of Abraham.

Waraqa attached himself to Christianity and studied its Scriptures
until he had completely mastered them. Ubaydallah went on searching
until Islam came; then he migrated with the Muslims to Abyssinia, taking
with him his wife who was a Muslim, Umm Habiba. When he arrived
there he adopted Christianity, parted from Islam, and died a Christian in
Abyssinia. . . . Uthman ibn al-Hawarith went to the Byzantine emperor
and became a Christian. He was given a high office there. Zayd ibn Amr
stayed as he was: he accepted neither Judaism or Christianity. He abandoned the religion of his people and abstained from idols, animals that
had died, and things offered to idols. He forbade the killing of infant
daughters, saying that he worshiped the God of Abraham, and he publicly
rebuked his people for their practices. (*Life* 143–144) [IBN ISHAQ 1955: 98–99]

9. Muhammad's Call and First Revelation

*Like the hanifs, Muhammad too may have been a man struggling toward belief—
until God once again intervened in history. Our source is the Prophet's biographer,
Ibn Ishaq.*

When Muhammad the Messenger of God reached the age of forty
[ca. 610 C.E.], God sent him in compassion to mankind as "a bearer of
good news and a warner to all men" (Quran 34:28). Now God had made
a covenant with every prophet whom He had sent before him that he
should believe in Him, testify to His truth, and help Him against His
adversaries, and He required of them that they should transmit that to

everyone who believed in them and they carried out their obligations in that respect. . . .

Al-Zuhri related from Urwa ibn Zubayr that Aisha told him that when God desired to honor Muhammad and have mercy on His servants by means of him, the first sign of prophethood vouchsafed to the Messenger was true visions, resembling the brightness of daybreak, which were shown to him in his sleep. And God, she said, made him love solitude so that he liked nothing better than to be alone.

Abd al-Malik ibn Abdullah, who had a retentive memory, related to me from a certain scholar that the Apostle, at the time when God willed to bestow His grace upon him and endow him with prophethood, would go forth for his affair and journey far afield until he reached the glens of Mecca and the valleys where no house was in sight; and not a stone or a tree that he passed but would say, "Peace unto you, O Messenger of God." And the Messenger would turn to his right and his left and look behind him and he would see naught but trees and stones. Thus he stayed seeing and hearing so long as it pleased God that he should stay. Then Gabriel came to him with the gift of God's grace while he was on (Mount) Hira in the month of Ramadan.

. . . Ubayd ibn Umayr related . . . that the Messenger would pray in seclusion on Hira every year for a month to practice *tahannuth* as was the custom of the Quraysh in heathen days. *Tahannuth* is religious devotion. . . .

Wahb ibn Kaysan told me that Ubayd told him: Every year during that month the Messenger would pray in seclusion and give food to the poor that came to him. And when he completed the month and returned from his seclusion, even before entering his house he would go to the Ka'ba and walk around it seven times or as often as it pleased God. Then he would go back to his house.

(Thus it went) until in the year when God sent him, in the month of Ramadan when God willed concerning him what He willed of His grace, the Messenger set forth for (Mount) Hira as was his custom, and his family was with him. When it was the night on which God honored him with his mission and showed mercy on His servants thereby, Gabriel brought him the command of God. "He came to me," said the Messenger of God, "while I was asleep, with a coverlet of brocade on which was some writing, and said, 'Recite!' I said, 'What shall I recite?' He pressed me with it so tightly that I thought it was death; then he let me go and said 'Recite!' I said, 'What shall I recite?' He pressed me with it a third time so that I thought it was death and said 'Recite!' I said, 'What then shall I recite?'—and this I said only to deliver myself from him, lest he should do the same to me again. He said:

> 'Recite: In the name of your Lord who created,
> Who created man from an embryo.
> Recite: Your Lord is the most beneficent,
> Who taught by the pen,
> Taught man what he did not know.' "
> (Quran 96:1–5)

According to Ibn Ishaq's account, then, the verses included in the Quran as Sura or Chapter 96 constituted the earliest of the revelations given to Muhammad. But the matter of the earliest revelation is not so certain. The narrative continues.

So I recited it and he departed from me. And I awoke from my sleep, and it was as though these words were written on my heart. When I was midway on the mountain, I heard a voice from heaven saying, "O Muhammad, thou art the Messenger of God and I am Gabriel." I raised my head toward heaven to see who was speaking, and behold, there was Gabriel with feet astride the horizon saying, "O Muhammad, thou art the Messenger of God and I am Gabriel." . . . And I continued standing there, neither advancing nor turning back until Khadija sent her messengers in search of me, and they gained the high ground above Mecca and returned to her all the while I was standing in the same place. Then he parted from me and I from him, returning to my family. (*Life*, 150–153)

[IBN ISHAQ 1955: 104–106]

This last incident is echoed in the Quran, though in a slightly different form.

> So he acquired poise and balance,
> And reached the highest pinnacle.
> Then he drew near and drew closer
> Until a space of two bow arcs or less remained,
> When He revealed to His votary what He revealed.
> (Quran 53:6–10)

The events of this critical moment in the life of the Prophet are described in various forms in the traditions circulating in the early Islamic community.

Muhammad ibn Umar informed us . . . on the authority of Aisha: The beginning of the revelations to the Apostle of God, may God bless him, was in the form of true dreams. . . . They came to him like daybreak. She said: he remained in this condition for as long as God willed. He liked solitude; nothing was dearer to him. He would retire to the cave of Hira taking provisions for several nights, after which he returned to his family. Then he would come to Khadija to take provisions again until the truth dawned on him while he was in the cave of Hira.

Muhammad ibn Umar informed us ... on the authority of Ibn Abbas: When, at that time, the Apostle of God, may God bless him, was at Ajyad, he saw an angel, with one foot on the other, in the horizon, and calling: "O Muhammad. I am Gabriel, O Muhammad. I am Gabriel." The Apostle of God, may God bless him, was terrified. Whenever he raised his head toward the heaven he saw him; so he returned hastily to Khadija and conveyed this information to her. He said: "O Khadija! By God, I never hated anything so much as idols and soothsayers; and I am afraid that I shall myself become a soothsayer. ..."

She informs him he has nothing to fear.

Yahya ibn Abbad said ... I think on the authority of Ibn Abbas: "In truth the Prophet, may God bless him, said; 'O Khadija, I hear sounds and see light and I fear I am mad.' "

Once again Khadija assures him he has nothing to fear on this score. There is still another version, once again from Muhammad ibn Umar, that derives finally from the authority of Ibn Abbas.

In truth, after the first revelation to the Apostle of God, may God bless him, that came at Hira, the coming of revelations remained suspended for a few days. Since he did not see Gabriel he was much grieved; he went to Thabir and at another time to Hira with the intention of throwing himself down. When the Apostle of God, may God bless him. was intending to do this from one of these mountains, he heard a sound coming from heaven. The Apostle of God, may God bless him, paused for a moment because of the thunderous sound, then he raised his head and behold, it was Gabriel seated in a chair between the earth and the sky. He was saying: "O Muhammad, you are truly the Apostle of God and I am Gabriel." The Apostle of God, may God bless him, returned and God had cooled his eye and strengthened his heart; thereafter revelations followed one after the other. (Ibn Saʿd, *Tabaqat* I/1 129–130)

We return to Ibn Ishaq's version of events. Waraqa ibn Nawfal, it will be recalled, was earlier identified as one of the hanifs. He now re-enters the account at a crucial point.

And I came to Khadija and sat by her thigh and drew close to her. She said, "O Abu al-Qasim, where have you been? By God, I sent my messengers in search of you, and they reached the high ground above

Mecca and returned to me (without seeing you)." Then I told her what I had seen, and she said, "Rejoice, O son of my uncle, and be of good heart. Verily, by Him in whose hand is Khadija's soul, I have hopes that you will be the prophet of this people." Then she rose and gathered her garments about her and set forth to her cousin Waraqa ibn Nawfal, who had become a Christian and read the Scriptures and learned from those that follow the Torah and the Gospel. And when she related to him what the Messenger of God told her he had seen and heard, Waraqa cried, "Holy! Holy! Holy! Verily, by Him in whose hand is Waraqa's soul, if you have spoken to me the truth, O Khadija, there has come to him the greatest *Namus* [Gk. *nomos*, law, likely the Torah, though not understood as such by the tradition] who came to Moses previously, and behold, he is the prophet of this people. Bid him be of good heart." So Khadija returned to the Prophet of God and told him what Waraqa had said. (*Life* 153–154) [IBN ISHAQ 1955: 106–107]

10. Sadness, Doubt, Consolation

Muhammad, for his part, was not so certain of what had befallen him. The traditional Life *leaves little doubt that it was Khadija who supported him through this difficult period of doubt and hesitation.*

Khadija believed in him and accepted as true what he had brought from God, and helped him in his work. She was the first to believe in God and His Messenger and in the truth of his message. By her, God lightened the burden of His Prophet. He had never met with contradiction and charges of falsehood (before), which saddened him, but God comforted him by her when he went home. She strengthened him, lightened his burden, proclaimed his truth, and belittled men's opposition. May God Almighty have mercy on her!

. . . Then the revelations stopped for a time so that the Messenger of God was distressed and grieved. Then Gabriel brought him the Sura of the Morning (Sura 93), in which his Lord, who had so honored him, swore that He had not forsaken him and did not hate him. God said, "By the morning and the night, when it is still, thy Lord has not forsaken or hated thee," meaning that He has not left you, forsaken you or hated you after having loved you. "And verily, the latter end is better for you than the beginning," that is, what I have for you when you return to Me is better than the honor which I have given you in the world. "And the Lord will give you and satisfy you," that is, of victory in this world and reward in the next. "Did he not find you an orphan and give you refuge, going astray and guided you, found you poor and made you rich?" God thus told him how He had begun to honor him in his earthly life, and His kindness to him as an orphan and wandering astray, and His delivering him from all that by His compassion.

"Do not oppress the orphan and do not repel the beggar," that is, do not be a tyrant or proud or harsh or mean toward the weakest of God's creatures. "Speak of the kindness of thy Lord," that is, tell about the kindness of God in giving you prophecy, mention it and call men to it.

So the Messenger began to mention secretly God's kindness to him and to his servants in the matter of prophecy to everyone among his people whom he could trust. (*Life* 155–156) [IBN ISHAQ 1955: 111–112]

11. The Conversion of Ali

This was not yet public preaching, but Muhammad's own firm conviction and the urgency of his message began to have its effect, although at first in a limited circle. Ali, the son of Abu Talib and cousin of the Prophet, and later one of the great heroes of Islam, embraced the new faith. But the reaction of his father illustrates the enormous social difficulty of a Meccan rejecting the "tradition of his fathers" for the new "tradition of the Prophet."

Ali was the first male to believe in the Apostle, to pray with him and to believe in his divine message, when he was a boy of ten. God favored him in that he was brought up in the care of the Messenger before Islam began. . . .

A traditionist mentioned that when the time of prayer came the Messenger used to go out to the glens of Mecca accompanied by Ali, who went unbeknown to his father, and his uncles and the rest of the people. There they used to pray the ritual prayers and return at nightfall. This went on as long as God intended that it should, until one day Abu Talib came upon them while they were praying and said to the Apostle, "O nephew, what is this religion which I see you practicing?" He replied, "O uncle, this is the religion of God, His angels, His Apostles, and the religion of our father Abraham." Or, as he said, "God sent me as a Messenger to mankind, and you, my uncle, most deserve that I should teach you the truth and call you to guidance, and you are the most worthy to respond and help me," or words to that effect. His uncle replied, "I cannot give up the religion of my fathers which they followed, but by God, you shall never meet anything to distress you so long as I live." They (also) mention that he said to Ali, "My boy, what is this religion of yours?" He answered, "I believe in God and the Messenger of God, and I declare that what he has brought is true, and I pray to God with him and follow him." (*Life* 158–160) [IBN ISHAQ 1955: 114]

12. The Earliest Public Preaching of Islam

People began to accept Islam, both men and women, in large numbers until the fame of it was spread throughout Mecca, and it began to be talked about. Then God commanded His Messenger to declare the truth of what he had received and to make known his commands to men and to call them to Him. Three years had elapsed from the time that the Messenger concealed his state until God commanded him to publish His religion, according to information which has reached me. Then God said, "Proclaim what you have been ordered and turn aside the polytheists" (Quran 15: 94). And again, "Warn your family, your nearest relations, and lower your wing to the followers who follow you" (Quran 26:214–215). And "Say, I am the one who warns plainly" (Quran 15:9). (*Life* 166) [IBN ISHAQ 1955: 117]

The 114 suras or chapters of the Quran were eventually arranged pretty much in reverse order of their length, and so it is difficult to be exact about the precise sequence or chronology of the revelations to Muhammad. There is, however, general agreement among both Muslim and non-Muslim scholars on some of the earliest of them, and they offer an insight into the tenor and tone of the Prophet's preaching to his contemporaries in Mecca.

> You, enfolded in your mantle!
> Arise and warn!
> Glorify your Lord,
> Purify your inner self,
> And banish all trepidation.
> Do not bestow favors in expectation of return,
> And persevere in the way of your Lord.
> For when the trumpet blows
> It will be a day of distress,
> Dolorous for the unbelievers.
> Leave him to Me alone whom I created,
> And gave him abundant wealth
> And sons always present by his side,

And made things easy for them.
Yet he wants that I should give him more.
Never! He is refractory of our signs.
I shall inflict on him hardship,
For he had thought and calculated.
May he be accursed, how he planned!
May he be accursed, how he plotted!
Then he looked around,
And frowned and puckered his brow,
Then turned his back and waxed proud,
And said: "This is nothing but the magic of old,
Nothing more than the speech of a man!"
I will cast him into the fire of Hell.
What do you think Hell-fire is?
It leaves nothing, nor does it spare;
It glows and burns the skin. . . .
(Quran 74:1–29)

I call to witness the early hours of the morning,
And the night when dark and still,
Your Lord has neither left you, nor despises you.
What is to come is better for you than what has gone before;
For your Lord will certainly give you, and you will be content.
Did He not find you an orphan, and take care of you?
Did He not find you perplexed and show you the way?
Did He not find you poor and enrich you?
So do not oppress the orphan,
And do not drive the beggar away,
And keep recounting the favors of your Lord.
(Quran 93)

Say: O you unbelievers,
I do not worship what you worship,
Nor do you worship Who I worship;
Nor will I worship what you worship,
Nor will you worship Who I worship.
To you your way; to me my way.
(Quran 109)

Say: He is God, the one the most unique,
God the immanently indispensable.

He has begotten no one, and is begotten of none.
There is no one comparable to Him.
(Quran 112)

Have you seen him who denies the Day of Judgment?
It is he who pushes the orphan away,
And does not induce others to feed the needy.
Woe to those who pray,
But who are oblivious in their moral duties,
Who dissimulate,
And withhold the necessities (from others).
(Quran 107)

I call to witness the heavens and the night star—
How will you comprehend what the night star is?
It is the star that shines with a piercing brightness—
That over each soul there is a guardian.
Let man consider what he was made of:
He was created of spurting water
Issuing from between the backbone and the ribs.
God has certainly the power to bring him back (from the dead).
The day all secrets are examined
He will have no strength or helper.
So I call to witness the rain-producing sky,
And the earth which opens up,
That this Quran is a distinctive word
And no trifle.
They are hatching up a plot, (Muhammad,)
But I too am devising a plan.
So bear with unbelievers with patience and give them a respite
                    for a while.
(Quran 86)

Recite, in the name of your Lord who created,
Created man from an embryo;
Recite! For your Lord is most beneficent,
Who taught by the pen,
Taught man what he did not know.
And yet, but yet man is rebellious,
For he thinks he is sufficient in himself.
Surely your returning is to your Lord.

Have you seen him who restrains
A votary when he turns to his devotions?
Have you thought that if he denies and turns away,
Does he not know that God sees?
And yet indeed if he does not desist We shall drag him by the
        forelock,
By the lying, the sinful forelock!
So let him summon his associates,
And we shall call the guards of Hell!
Beware! Do not obey him, but bow in adoration and draw near
        (to your Lord).

    (Quran 96)

The Message of these early suras of the Quran is clear and direct: God, who created
the world and mankind, will require an accounting from His creation on the Last
Day. The insolent, the worldly, the greedy will be cast into Hell; the generous and
obedient will be rewarded with Paradise. The appropriate human response, then, is
submission—in Arabic islam—to the will of God and the directions of His Prophet.

13. The Opposition of the Quraysh

Since the Quraysh have been united,
United to fit out caravans winter and summer.
Let them worship the Lord of this House,
Who provided them against destitution, and gave them security
        from fear.

    (Quran 106)

The earliest Meccan Muslims—literally, "those who have submitted," the same
term used of Abraham and his descendants—did not include many of the powerful
first families of Mecca, those same Quraysh who sent forth their summer and winter
caravans to trade in Syria and the Yemen. The Meccan merchant aristocracy contin-
ued to be what it had always been in living memory: the worshipers of idols, a great
many of which were collected in the haram, *or sacred enclosure that surrounded the*
*Ka*ʿ*ba in the midst of Mecca.*

When the Messenger openly displayed Islam as God ordered him,
his people did not withdraw or turn against him, so far as I have heard,
until he spoke disparagingly of their gods. When he did that they took
great offense and resolved unanimously to treat him as an enemy, except
those whom God had protected by Islam from such evil, but they were
a despised minority. Abu Talib his uncle treated the Messenger kindly and

protected him, the latter continuing to obey God's commands, nothing turning him back. When the Quraysh saw that he would not yield to them and insulted their gods and that his uncle treated him kindly and stood up in his defense and would not give him up to them, some of their leading men went to Abu Talib. . . . They said, "O Abu Talib, your nephew has cursed our gods, insulted our religion, mocked our way of life and accused our forefathers of error. Either you must stop him or you must let us get at him, for you yourself are in the same position as we are in opposition to him and we will rid you of him." He gave them a conciliatory reply and a soft answer and they went away.

The Messenger continued on his way, making public God's religion and calling men to it. In consequence his relations with the Quraysh deteriorated and men withdrew from him in enmity. They were always talking about him and inciting one another against him. Then they went to Abu Talib a second time and said, "You have a high and lofty position among us, and we have asked you to put a stop to your nephew's activities but you have not done so. By God, we cannot endure that our fathers should be reviled, our customs mocked and our gods insulted. Until you rid us of him we will fight the pair of you until one side perishes," or words to that effect. Thus saying, they went off. Abu Talib was deeply distressed at the breach with his people and their enmity, but he could not desert the Messenger and give him up to them.

Mecca was still very much a tribal society, and the message of Muhammad inevitably raised the specter of schisms running across the complex lines of patronage and clientage in the city.

Then the Quraysh incited people against the companions of the Messenger who had become Muslims. Every tribe fell upon the Muslims among them, beating them and seducing them from their religion. God protected His Messenger from them through his uncle, who, when he saw what the Quraysh were doing, called upon the Banu Hashim and the Banu al-Muttalib to stand with him in protecting the Apostle. This they agreed to do, with the exception of Abu Lahab, the accursed enemy of God. (*Life* 166–170) [IBN ISHAQ 1955: 118–120]

14. The Prophet Characterized

When the annual fair was due, a number of the Quraysh came to al-Walid ibn al-Mughira, who was a man of some standing, and he addressed them in these words: "The time of the fair has come round again, and representatives of the Arabs will come to you and they will have heard about this fellow of yours. So agree on one opinion (concerning him) without dispute so that none may contradict the other." They replied, "You give us your opinion about him." He said, "No, you speak and I will listen." They said, "He is a seer." Al-Walid said, "By God, he is not, for he has not the unintelligent murmuring and rhymed speech of the seer." "Then he is possessed," they said. "No, he is not that," al-Walid replied. "We have seen possessed people and here is no choking, spasmodic movements and whispering." "Then he is a poet," they said. "No, he is no poet," al-Walid said, "for we know poetry in all its forms and meters." "Then he is a sorcerer." "No, we have seen sorcerers and their sorcery, and here is no blowing and no knots." "Then what are we to say, O Abu Abd al-Shams?" they asked. He replied, "By God, his speech is sweet, his root is a palm tree whose branches are fruitful and everything you have said would be recognized as false. The nearest thing to such in your saying is that he is a sorcerer, who has brought a message by which he separates a man from his father or from his brother, or from his wife, or from his family." (*Life* 171) [IBN ISHAQ 1955: 121]

15. Attempted Negotiations

Islam began to spread in Mecca among men and women of the tribes of the Quraysh, though the Quraysh were imprisoning and seducing as many of the Muslims as they could. A traditionist told me from Saʿid ibn Jubayr and from Ikrima, freedman of Abdullah ibn Abbas, that the leading men of every clan of the Quraysh . . . decided to send for Muhammad and to negotiate and argue with him so that they could not be held to blame on his account in the future. When they sent for him the Messenger of God came quickly because he thought that what he had (earlier) said to them had made an impression, for he was most zealous for their welfare and their wicked ways pained him. When he came and sat down with them, they explained that they had sent for him in order that they could talk together. No Arab had ever treated his tribe as he had treated them, and they repeated the charges which have been mentioned on several occasions. If it was money he wanted, they would make him richest of them all; if it was honor, he should be their prince; if it was sovereignty, they would make him king; if it was a spirit that had got possession of him, then they would exhaust their means in finding medicine to cure him.

These broad promises were likely neither sincere nor altogether practical, but they attest to the magnitude of the threat that Muhammad was thought to pose to the social and commercial equilibrium of Mecca, a city that had combined trade and pilgrimage to its shrine into a profitable enterprise.

The Messenger replied that he had no such intention. He sought not money nor honor nor sovereignty, but God had sent him as an Apostle, and revealed a book to him, and commanded him to become an announcer and a warner. He had brought the message of his Lord and given them good advice. If they took it, then they would have a portion of this world and the next; if they rejected it, he could only patiently await the outcome until God decided between them, or words to that effect.

"Well, Muhammad," they said, "if you won't accept any of our propositions, you know that no people are more short of land and water and live a harder life than we, so ask your Lord, who sent you, to remove us from these mountains which shut us in, and to straighten out our country for us, and to open up in it rivers like those of Syria and Iraq, and to resurrect for us our forefathers—and let there be among those who are resurrected Qusayy ibn Kilab, for he was a true shaykh—so that we may ask them whether what you say is true or false." . . . He replied that he had not been sent to them with such an object. He had conveyed to them God's message and they could either accept it with advantage or reject it and await God's judgment. They said that if he could not do that for them, let him do something for himself. Ask God to send an angel with him to confirm what he said and to contradict them; to make him gardens and castles and treasures of gold and silver to satisfy his obvious wants, since he stood in the street as they did and he sought a livelihood as they did. . . . He replied that he would not do it, and would not ask for such things, for he was not sent to do so, and he repeated what he had said before. . . . They said, "Did not your Lord know that we would sit with you and ask you these questions, so that He might come to you and instruct you how to answer, and tell you what He was going to do with us, if we did not accept your message? Information has reached us that you are taught by this fellow in al-Yamama called al-Rahman ["The Compassionate"], and by God we will never believe in the Rahman. Our conscience is clear, by God, we will not leave you and our treatment of you until either we destroy you or you destroy us." (*Life* 187–189)
[IBN ISHAQ 1955: 133–134]

16. Persecution and Emigration to Abyssinia

Then the Quraysh showed the enmity to all those who followed the Apostle; every clan which included Muslims attacked them, imprisoning and beating them, allowing them no food or drink, and exposing them to the burning heat of Mecca so as to seduce them from their religion. Some gave way under pressure of persecution and others resisted them, being protected by God. . . . It was that evil man Abu Jahl who stirred up the Meccans against them. When he heard that a man had become a Muslim, if he was a man of social importance and had relations to defend him, he (merely) reprimanded him and poured scorn on him, saying, "You have forsaken the religion of your father who is better than you. We will declare you a blockhead and brand you a fool and destroy your reputation." If he was a merchant he said, "We will boycott your goods and reduce you to beggary." If he was a person of no social importance, he beat him and incited the people against him. (*Life* 205–207)

[IBN ISHAQ 1955: 143–145]

When the Messenger saw the affliction of his companions and, though he (himself) escaped it because of his standing with God and his uncle Abu Talib, he could not protect them, he said to them: "If you were to go to Abyssinia it would be better for you, for the king (there) will not tolerate injustice and it is a friendly country, until such time as God shall relieve you from your distress." Thereupon his companions went to Abyssinia, being afraid of apostasy and fleeing to God with their religion. This was the first *hijra* [emigration] in Islam.

The choice of Abyssinia across the Red Sea as a place of refuge for the beleaguered Muslims is somewhat surprising, but only because we are so scantily instructed by our sources on the larger commercial connections of Mecca. Abyssinia had long since embraced Christianity, a religion to which Muhammad may have felt an affinity. But Abyssinia was also a rising commercial exporter in the shifting international trade of the sixth and seventh centuries, and the tiny band of Muslim expatriates may well have been sent there to explore commercial possibilities. Whatever the case, the Quraysh sent their own deputation to convince the Christian king of Abyssinia, called the Negus, to send the Muslims back. The Negus holds a public hearing on the matter and requests an explanation of Islam.

When they [the Muslims] came into the royal presence, they found the king had summoned his bishops with their sacred books exposed around him. He asked them what was the religion for which they had forsaken their people, without entering into his religion or any other. Abu

Ja'far ibn Abi Talib answered, "O King, we were an uncivilized people, worshiping idols, eating corpses, committing abominations, breaking natural ties, treating guests badly, and our strong devoured our weak. Thus we were until God sent us a Messenger whose lineage, truth, trustworthiness and clemency we know. He summoned us to acknowledge God's unity and to worship Him and renounce the stones and images which our fathers formerly worshiped. He commanded us to speak the truth, be faithful to our engagements, mindful of the ties of kinship and kindly hospitality, and to refrain from crimes and bloodshed. He forbade us to commit abominations and to speak lies, and to devour the property of orphans, and to vilify chaste women. He commanded us to worship God alone and not to associate anything with Him, and he gave us orders about prayer, almsgiving and fasting. We confessed his truth and believed in him, and we followed him in what he had brought from God, and we worshiped God alone without associating aught with Him. We treated as forbidden what he forbade and as lawful what he declared lawful. . . ."

The Negus asked if they had with them anything which had come from God. When Ja'far said he had, the Negus commanded him to read it to him, so he read him a passage from the sura called "Mary" (19). The Negus wept until his beard was wet and the bishops wept until their scrolls were wet, when they heard what was read to them. Then the Negus said, "Of a truth, this and what Jesus brought have come from the same niche. You two (Quraysh) may go, for by God, I will never give them [the Muslims] up and they shall not be betrayed. (*Life* 208–220)
[IBN ISHAQ 1955: 146–148]

17. A Famous Conversion

Abdullah ibn Abi Najih, the Meccan, from his companions Ata and Mujahid, or other narrators, said that the conversion of Umar [Umar ibn al-Khattab, the second Caliph, 634–644 C.E.], according to what he himself used to say, happened thus:

"I was far from Islam. I was a winebibber in the heathen period, used to love it and rejoice in it. We used to have a meeting place in al-Hazwara where the Quraysh used to gather. . . . I went out one night, making for my boon companions in that gathering, but when I got there, there was no one present, so I thought it would be a good thing if I went to so-and-so, the wineseller, who was selling wine in Mecca at that time, in the hope that I might get something to drink from him. I could not find him either, so I thought it would be a good thing if I went around the

Ka'ba seven or seventy times. So I came to the sanctuary intending to go round the Ka'ba, and there was the Messenger standing praying. As he prayed he faced Syria [that is, Jerusalem], putting the Ka'ba between himself and Syria. His position was between the black stone and the southern corner. When I saw him I thought it would be a good thing if I could listen to Muhammad so as to hear what he said. If I came near to listen to him I would frighten him, so I came from the direction of the Hijr [a low stone porch near the Ka'ba] . . . until I stood facing him in the path of his direction of prayer, there being nothing between us but the covering of the Ka'ba.

"When I heard the Quran my heart was softened and I wept, and Islam entered into me; but I remained in my place until the Messenger had finished his prayer. Then he went away. . . . I followed him until he got between the house of Abbas and Ibn Azhar, where I overtook him. When he heard my voice he recognized me and supposed that I had followed him only to ill treat him, so he repelled me, saying 'What has brought you here at this hour?' I replied that I had come to believe in God and His Messenger and what he had brought from God. He gave thanks to God and said, 'God has guided you.' Then he rubbed my breast and prayed that I might be steadfast. Afterwards I left him. He went into his house." (*Life* 227–230) [IBN ISHAQ 1955: 157–158]

18. The Boycott

When the Quraysh perceived that the Apostle's companions had settled in a land in peace and safety and that the Negus had protected those who had sought refuge with him, and that Umar had become a Muslim and that he and Hamza were on the side of the Messenger and his companions, and that Islam had begun to spread among the tribes, they came together and decided among themselves to write a document in which they would put a boycott on the Banu Hashim and the Banu Muttalib that no one should marry their women or give women for them to marry; and that no one should either buy from them or sell to them, and when they agreed on that they wrote it in a deed. Then they solemnly agreed on the points and hung the deed up in the middle of the Ka'ba to remind them of their obligations.

The point does not appear to have been so much to starve Muhammad and his followers into submission as to exclude them from the commercial life of that very commercial city.

... Meanwhile the Messenger was exhorting his people night and day, secretly and publicly, openly proclaiming God's command without fear of anyone. His uncle and the rest of the Banu Hashim gathered round him and protected him from the attacks of the Quraysh, who when they saw they could not get at him, mocked and laughed and disputed with him. The Quran began to come down concerning the wickedness of the Quraysh and those who showed enmity to him, some by name and some only referred to in general. (*Life* 230–233) [IBN ISHAQ 1955: 159–161]

19. Muhammad's Night Journey

Deceived by false reports of the conversion of the Quraysh, many of the emigrants return from Abyssinia. Although the Quraysh showed no signs of relenting on religious grounds, their boycott against the Banu Hashim and the Banu Muttalib did in effect collapse. It is at this point that the Life *inserts the account of the famous "Night Journey" of the Prophet referred to in Sura 17:1 of the Quran.*

Glory be to Him who took His votary by night from the Sacred Mosque to the distant Mosque, whose precincts We have blessed, that We may show him some of Our signs. Verily, He is the all-hearing and all-seeing.

The Life *fills out the details.*

The following account reached me from Abdullah b. Mas'ud and Abu Sa'id al-Khudri and Aisha the Prophet's wife and Mu'awiya b. Abi Sufyan and al-Hasan al-Basri and Ibn Shihab al-Zuhri and Qatada and other traditionists as well as Umm Hani, daughter of Abu Talib. It is pieced together in the story that follows, each one contributing something of what he was told about what had happened when the Prophet was taken on the Night Journey. The matter of the place of the journey and what is said about it is a searching test and a matter of God's power and authority wherein is a lesson for the intelligent, and guidance and mercy and strengthening to those who believe. It was certainly an act of God by which He took him by night in whatever way He pleased to show him signs which He willed him to see so that he witnessed His mighty sovereignty and power by which He does what He wills to do.

Though there may have been, as this text hints, some hesitations about the destination of this journey by night, there soon developed a consensus that the "distant shrine" of Quran 17:1 was in fact the site of the former Temple in Jerusalem.

According to what I have heard, Abdullah ibn Mas'ud used to say: Buraq [the steed that carried Muhammad; see below], whose every stride carried it as far as its eye could reach and on which earlier prophets had ridden, was brought to the Messenger and he was mounted on it. His companion (Gabriel) went with him to see the wonders between heaven and earth, until he came to Jerusalem's Temple. There he found Abraham the Friend of God, Moses and Jesus assembled with a company of prophets and prayed with them. Then he was brought three vessels containing milk, wine and water respectively. The Messenger said: "I heard a voice saying when these were offered to me, If he takes the water he will be drowned and his people also; if he takes the wine he will go astray and his people also; and if he tastes the milk, he will be rightly guided and his people also. So I took the vessel containing the milk and drank it. Gabriel said to me, 'You have been rightly guided, and so will your people be, Muhammad.' "

In the manner of Arab historians, Ibn Ishaq provides another version of the same event, this one from Hasan al-Basri [d. 728 C.E.], a purported eyewitness to some of the circumstances, though he must have been a very small child at the time.

I was told that al-Hasan al-Basri said that the Messenger of God said: "While I was sleeping in the Hijr [a kind of semicircular stone porch close by the Ka'ba], Gabriel came and stirred me with his foot. I sat up but saw nothing and lay down again. He came a second time and stirred me with his foot. I sat up but saw nothing and lay down again. He came to me the third time and stirred me with his foot. I sat up and he took hold of my arm and I stood beside him and he brought me out to the door of the shrine and there was a white animal, half mule and half donkey with wings on its side with which it propelled its feet, putting down each forefoot at the limit of its sight, and he mounted me on it. Then he went out with me, keeping close by my side."

In his story al-Hasan continued: "The Messenger and Gabriel went their way until they arrived at the shrine at Jerusalem. There he found Abraham, Moses and Jesus among a company of the prophets. The Messenger acted as their leader in prayer. . . . Then the Messenger returned to Mecca and in the morning he told the Quraysh what had happened. Most of them said: 'By God, this is a plain absurdity! A caravan takes a month to go to Syria and a month to return and can Muhammad do the return journey in one night?' At this many Muslims gave up their faith; some went to Abu Bakr and said: 'What do you think of your friend now, Abu Bakr? He alleges he went to Jerusalem last night and prayed there and came back to Mecca.' Abu Bakr replied that they were lying about the Apostle. But they replied that he was at that very moment in the shrine telling the people about it. Abu Bakr said: 'If he says so, then it must be true. And what is so surprising in that? He tells me that communications from God from heaven to earth come to him in an hour of a day or night and I believe him, and that is more extraordinary than that at which you boggle!'

"Abu Bakr then went to the Messenger and asked him if these reports were true, and when he said they were, he asked him to describe Jerusalem to him." Al-Hasan said that [as a small child] he was lifted up so that he could see the Messenger speaking as he told Abu Bakr what Jerusalem was like. Whenever Muhammad described a part of it, Abu Bakr said: "That's true. I testify that you are the Messenger of God!" until he had completed the description, and then the Messenger said: "And you, Abu Bakr, are the Witness to Truth."

But the entire incident of the Night Journey was, as Ibn Ishaq had warned at the outset, a grave trial of faith for some of the early Muslims.

Al-Hasan continued: "God sent down the verse (Quran 13:62) concerning those who had left Islam on this account: 'We made you a vision which we showed you only for a test to men and the accursed tree in the Quran. We put them in fear, but it only adds to their heinous error.' " Such is al-Hasan's story. (*Life* 263–265) [IBN ISHAQ 1955: 181–182]

This celebrated Night Journey, a frequent subject of Islamic art and legend, is the cornerstone of Muslim attachment to Jerusalem.

20. The Death of Khadija and Abu Talib (619 C.E.)

Khadija and Abu Talib died in the same year, and with Khadija's death troubles followed fast on each other's heels, for she had been a faithful support for him in Islam, and he used to tell her all his troubles. With the death of Abu Talib he lost a strength and stay in his personal life and a defense and protection against his tribe. Abu Talib died some three years before he migrated to Medina (in 622 C.E.), and it was then that the Quraysh began to treat him in an offensive way which they would not have dared to follow in his uncle's lifetime. (*Life* 276–277)

[IBN ISHAQ 1955: 191]

Muhammad had married Khadija in 595 C.E., when he was twenty-five and she forty. She bore him a number of sons, all of whom died in infancy, and four daughters—Zaynab, Ruqayya, Umm Kulthum, and Fatima. In the years that followed Khadija's death, and when he was in his fifties, Muhammad married Sawda, Abu Bakr's daughter Aisha, Umar's daughter Hafsa, Hind, Zaynab daugh-

ter of Jahsh, Umm Salama, Juwayriyya, Ramla or Umm Habiba, Safiyya, and Maymuna. None of them bore him children, however, though he had a son, Ibrahim, by his Coptic concubine, Mary. Ibrahim too died in infancy.

21. The Pledge at Aqaba

Help was suddenly proferred from an unexpected source: by visitors from the oasis of Yathrib, some 275 miles to the north of Mecca. Yathrib, later named "The medina [city] of the Prophet," or simply Medina, was an agricultural settlement of mixed Arab and Jewish population. Here, too, as had happened earlier, the Jews were quick to recognize and possibly appropriate (or reject) the Prophet of Islam.

When God wished to display His religion openly and to glorify His Prophet and to fulfill His promise to him, the time came when he met a number of "Helpers" [that is, future converts to Islam at Medina] at one of the (Meccan) fairs. . . . They said that when the Messenger met them he learned by inquiry that they were of the (tribe of the) Khazraj and were allies of the Jews (there). He invited them to sit with him and he expounded to them Islam and recited the Quran to them. Now God had prepared the way for Islam in that they [the Khazraj] lived side by side with the Jews (of Medina), who were people of the Scriptures and knowledge, while they themselves were polytheists and idolaters. They had often raided them in their district and whenever bad feelings arose the Jews used to say to them, "A Prophet will be sent soon. His day is at hand. We shall follow him and kill you by his aid just as Ad and Iram perished." So when they [the Khazraj] heard the Apostle's message they said to one another, "This is the very Prophet of whom the Jews warned us. Don't let them get to him before us!" Thereupon they accepted his teaching and became Muslims, saying, "We have left our people, for no tribe is so divided by hatred and rancor as they. Perhaps God will unite them through you. So let us go to them and invite them to this religion of yours; and if God unites them in it, then no man will be mightier than you." Thus saying they returned to Medina as believers.

In the following year twelve "Helpers" attended the fair and met at al-Aqaba (a place near Mecca)—this was the first Aqaba—where they gave the Messenger the "pledge of women" (cf. Quran 60:12). . . . "I was present at Aqaba [one of the participants reported]. There were twelve of us and we pledged ourselves to the Prophet after the manner of women and that was before (the obligation of) war was enjoined, the undertaking being that we should associate nothing with God; we should not steal; we should not commit fornication; nor kill our offspring; we should not

slander our neighbors; we should not disobey him (Muhammad) in what
was right. If we fulfilled this, paradise would be ours; if we committed any
of these sins, it was for God to punish or forgive us as He pleased. . . ."

(The next year) the Muslim "Helpers" came to the fair with the
pilgrims of their people who were polytheists. They met the Messenger
at Aqaba during the days following upon the day of the (Hajj) sacrifice,
when God intended to honor them and to help His Messenger and
strengthen Islam and to humiliate heathenism and its devotees. . . .
Ma'bad ibn Ka'b told me that his brother Abdullah had told him that his
father Ka'b ibn Malik said: ". . . We slept that night among our people
in the caravan until, when a third of the night had passed, we went
stealing softly like sandgrouse to our appointment with the Messenger as
far as the gully by al-Aqaba. There were seventy-three men with two of
our women. . . . We gathered together in the gully, waiting until the
Messenger came with his uncle al-Abbas, who was at that time a polythe-
ist, though he wanted to be present at his nephew's business and make
certain that he received a firm guarantee.

"When we sat down al-Abbas was the first to speak and said: 'O
people of Khazraj—the Arabs used that term to cover the tribes of both
the Khazraj and the Aws. You know Muhammad's situation among us.
We have protected him from his own people who think as we do about
him. He lives in honor and safety among his people, but he will turn to
you and join you. If you think you can be faithful to what you promised
him and protect him from his opponents, then assume the burden you
have undertaken. But if you think you will betray and abandon him after
he has gone out with you, then leave him now, for he is safe where he is.'
We replied, 'We have heard what you say. You speak, O Apostle, and
choose for yourself and for your Lord what you wish.'

"The Messenger spoke and recited the Quran and invited me to God
and recommended Islam, and then said: 'I invite your allegiance on the
basis that you protect me as you would your women and children.' Al-
Bara took his hand and said: 'By Him who sent you with the truth, we will
protect you as we protect our women. We give our alliance and we are
men of war possessing arms which have been passed on from father to
son.' While al-Bara was speaking, Abu al-Haytham ibn al-Tayyihan inter-
rupted him and said: 'O Apostle, we have ties with other men—he meant
the Jews—and if we sever them, perhaps when we have done that and
God will have given us victory, will you return to your people and leave
us?' The Messenger smiled and said, 'No, blood is blood and blood not to

be paid for is blood not to be paid for. I am of you and you are of me. I will war against those who war against you and be at peace with those at peace with you.' " (*Life* 288–297) [IBN ISHAQ 1955: 198–204]

22. A Turn to Armed Resistance

The Messenger had not been given permission to fight or allowed to shed blood before the second (pledge of) Aqaba. He had simply been ordered to call men to God and to endure insult and forgive the innocent. The Quraysh had persecuted his followers, seducing some from their religion and exiling others from their country. They had to choose whether to give up their religion, be mistreated at home, or to flee the country, some to Abyssinia, others to Medina.

When the Quraysh became insolent toward God and rejected His gracious purpose, accused His Prophet of lying, and ill treated and exiled those who served Him and proclaimed His unity, believed in His Prophet and held fast to His religion, He gave permission for His Messenger to fight and protect himself against those who wronged them and treated them badly.

The first verse which was sent down on this subject from what I have heard from Urwa ibn al-Zubayr and other learned persons was:

"Permission is granted those (to take up arms) who fight because they were oppressed. God is certainly able to give help to those who were driven away from their homes for no other reason than that they said 'Our Lord is God.' And if God had not restrained some men through some others, monasteries, churches, synagogues and mosques, where the name of God is honored most, would have been razed. God will surely help those who help Him. —Verily, God is all-powerful and all-mighty— Those who would be firm in devotion, pay the tithe, and enjoin what is good and forbid what is wrong, if we give them authority in the land. But the result of things rests with God." (Quran 22:39–41)

The meaning is: "I have allowed them to fight only because they were unjustly treated, while their sole offense against men is that they worship God. When they are in the ascendent they will establish prayer, pay the poor tax, enjoin kindness and forbid iniquity, that is, the Prophet and his companions, all of them." Then God sent down to him (the verse): "Fight so there is no more persecution," that is, until no believer is seduced from his religion, "and the religion is God's," that is, until God alone is worshiped. (Quran 2:193).

This permission to fight, to turn from passive to active resistance to the Quraysh, was no trifling matter, as its divine sanction shows. The Quraysh's commercial enterprises were protected by their own religiously sanctioned prohibitions against violence and bloodshed during the months of pilgrimage and the annual fairs that were connected with it.

When God had given permission to fight, and this clan of the "Helpers" had pledged their support to him in Islam and to help him and his followers, and the Muslims had taken refuge with them, the Messenger commanded his companions to emigrate to Medina and to link up with their brethren the "Helpers." "God will make for you brethren and houses in which you may be safe." So they went out in companies, and the Messenger stayed in Mecca waiting for the Lord's permission to leave Mecca and migrate to Medina. (*Life* 313–314) [IBN ISHAQ 1955: 212–213]

23. The Emigration to Medina
(622 C.E.)

The arrangements were now complete, and the emigration of Muslims to Mecca began, though gradually and with great caution.

After his companions had left, the Messenger stayed at Mecca waiting for permission to emigrate. Except for Abu Bakr and Ali, none of his supporters were left but those who were under restraint and those who had been forced to apostatize. The former kept asking the Messenger for permission to emigrate and he would answer, "Don't be in a hurry; it may be that God will give you a companion." Abu Bakr hoped that it would be Muhammad himself.

When the Quraysh saw that the Messenger (now) had a party and companions not of their tribe and outside their territory, and that his companions had migrated to join them, and knew that they had settled in a new home and had gained protectors, they feared that the Messenger might join them, since they knew that he had decided to fight them. So they assembled in their council chamber, the house of Qusayy ibn Kilab, where all their important business was conducted, to take counsel what they should do in regard to the Apostle, for they were now in fear of him.

As with the Pharisaic opposition to Jesus, we are at a loss to explain why the Quraysh should have so feared Muhammad and his few followers. In both instances there may have been more than meets the eye or than the sources could or would tell us. With Jesus, the hidden background may well have been political; here, equally likely, it was commercial. The Quraysh not only feared for their souls; Muhammad was perceived as a potentially dangerous rival to the prosperity of the Mecca Trading Company.

(After a discussion of various possibilities) Abu Jahl said that he had a plan that had not been suggested hitherto, namely that each clan should provide a young, powerful, well-born aristocratic warrior; that each of them should be equipped with a sharp sword; and that each of them should strike a blow at him and kill him. Thus they would be relieved of him, and the responsibility for his blood would lie on all the clans. The Banu Abd al-Manaf could not fight them all and would accept the blood money to which they would all contribute. . . . Having come to a decision, the people dispersed.

Then Gabriel came to the Messenger and said, "Do not sleep tonight on the bed on which you usually sleep." Before much of the night had passed they [the deputized assassins] assembled at his door waiting for him to go to sleep so they might fall upon him. When the Messenger saw what they were doing, he told Ali to lie on his bed and wrap himself in his green Hadrami mantle; for no harm would befall him. He himself used to sleep in that mantle. . . .

According to what I have been told, none knew when the Messenger left except Ali and Abu Bakr and the latter's family. I have heard that the Messenger told Ali about his departure and ordered him to stay behind in Mecca in order to return goods which men had deposited with the Apostle, for anyone in Mecca who had property which he was anxious about left it with him because of his notorious honesty and trustworthiness.

When the Messenger decided to go he came to Abu Bakr and the two of them left by a window in the back of the latter's house and made for a cave on Thawr, a mountain below Mecca. Having entered, Abu Bakr ordered his son Abdullah to listen to what people were saying and to come to them by night with the day's news. . . . The two of them stayed in the cave for three days. When the Quraysh missed the Messenger they offered a hundred she-camels to anyone who would bring them back. During the day Abdullah was listening to the plans and conversations and would come at night with the news.

After three days in hiding, Muhammad and Abu Bakr ride in secrecy to Medina.

Muhammad ibn Ja'far ibn al-Zubayr from Urwa ibn al-Zubayr from Abd al-Rahman ibn Uwaymir ibn Sa' told me, saying, Men of my tribe who were the Apostle's companions told me: "When we heard that the Messenger had left Mecca and we were eagerly expecting his arrival, we used to go out after morning prayers to the lava tract beyond our land to await him. This we did until there was no more shade left, then we went indoors in the hot season. On the day the Messenger arrived we had sat as we always had until there being no more shade we went inside, and it was then that the Prophet arrived. The first to see him was a Jew. He had seen what we were in the habit of doing and that we were expecting the arrival of the Apostle, and he called out at the top of his voice, 'O Banu Qayla, your luck has come!' So we went out to greet the Apostle, who was in the shadow of a palm tree with Abu Bakr, who was of like age. Now most of us had never seen the Messenger and as the people crowded around him they did not know him from Abu Bakr until the shade left him and Abu Bakr got up with his mantle and shielded him from the sun, and then we knew."

Ali stayed in Mecca for three days and nights until he restored the deposits which the Prophet held. This done, he joined the Messenger and (also) lodged at Kulthum's house. . . . The Messenger ordered that a mosque be built and he stayed with Abu Ayyub until the mosque and his houses were completed. The Messenger joined in the activity to encourage the Muslims to work and both the (Meccan) "Emigrants" and the (Medinese) "Helpers" labored hard. . . . The Messenger stayed in Medina from the month of First Rabi' to Safar of the following year until his mosque and his quarters were built. This tribe of the "Helpers" all accepted Islam, and every house of the "Helpers" accepted Islam except Khatma, Waqif, Wa'il and Umayya who were Aws Allah, a clan of the Aws who clung to their paganism. (*Life* 323–340) [IBN ISHAQ 1955: 221–230]

24. The Constitution of Medina

Included in Ibn Ishaq's Life of the Prophet *is a document that purports to record the political arrangements contracted between Muhammad and his partisans and the citizens of Medina. There is little reason to doubt its authenticity, since it constitutes Medina the kind of "protected" enclave found elsewhere in Arabia, though here not around a shrine, as at Mecca, for example, but on the authority of a recognized holy man. The contracting parties agreed to recognize Muhammad as their leader and to accept his judgments. In so doing, they were acknowledging, as was the Prophet himself, that they were one community, or* umma, *not yet uniquely composed of Muslims but committed to defend its joint interests, or what was now defined to be the common good.*

The Messenger wrote a document concerning the "Emigrants" and the "Helpers" in which he made a friendly agreement with the Jews and

established them in their religion and their property, and stated the recip-
rocal obligations as follows: In the Name of God, the Compassionate, the
Merciful. This is a document from Muhammad the Prophet (concerning
the relations) between the believers and Muslims of the Quraysh and
Yathrib [Medina], and those who followed them and joined them and
labored with them. They are one community to the exclusion of all men.
The Quraysh emigrants according to their present custom shall pay all the
blood money within their number and shall redeem their prisoners with
the kindness and justice common among believers. . . .

A believer shall not take as an ally the freedman of another Muslim
against him. The God-fearing believers shall be against the rebellious or
him who spreads injustice or sin or enmity or corruption between believers. A believer shall not slay a believer for the sake of an unbeliever, nor
shall he aid an unbeliever against a believer. God's protection is one, the
least of them may give protection to a stranger on their behalf. Believers
are friends one to the other to the exclusion of outsiders. To the Jew who
follows us belongs help and equality. He shall not be wronged nor his
enemies aided. The peace of believers is indivisible and no separate peace
shall be made when believers are fighting in the way of God. Conditions
must be fair and equitable to all. . . .

The Jews must bear their expenses and the Muslims their expenses.
Each must help the other against anyone who attacks the people of this
document. They must seek mutual advice and consultation, and loyalty
is a protection against treachery. A man is not liable for his ally's misdeeds. The wronged must be helped. The Jews must pay with the believers so long as war lasts. Yathrib [Medina] shall be sanctuary for the people
of this document. . . . If any dispute or controversy should arise it must
be referred to God and to Muhammad the Messenger of God. (*Life* 341–
343) [IBN ISHAQ 1955: 231–233]

25. Jewish Opposition

*Almost as soon as the Prophet and his followers had settled down in Medina, or
Yathrib, as it was still called at that time, his relations with the Jews of the place
began to deteriorate. Soon after his first great victory over his Meccan rivals at Badr
Wells, the conflict with the Jews turned to open warfare, as we shall see. But
commercial, religious, and psychological differences may have surfaced even before.
Muhammad, after all, claimed to be a prophet in the tradition of Moses and the
Torah. In the Jewish community of Medina he encountered, perhaps contrary to his
own expectations, a rebuff from the contemporary partisans of that same tradition.*

About this time the Jewish rabbis showed hostility to the Messenger in envy, hatred and malice, because God had chosen His Messenger from the Arabs. They were joined by men from (the Arab tribes of) al-Aws and al-Khazraj who had obstinately clung to their heathen religion. They were hypocrites, clinging to the polytheism of their fathers, denying the resurrection; yet when Islam appeared and their people flocked to it they were compelled to accept it to save their lives. But in secret they were hypocrites whose inclination was toward the Jews because these latter considered the Messenger a liar and strove against Islam.

It was the Jewish rabbis who used to annoy the Prophet with questions and introduce confusion, so as to confound the truth with falsity. The (verses of the) Quran used to come down in reference to questions of theirs, though some of the questions about what was allowed and forbidden came from the Muslims themselves. . . . The first hundred verses of the Sura of the Cow (2:1–100) came down in reference to these Jewish rabbis and the hypocrites of the Aws and Khazraj, according to what I have been told, and God knows best. (*Life* 351)

[IBN ISHAQ 1955: 239–240]

26. A Turning Away from the Jews

There follows in the Life *(363–400 [IBN ISHAQ 1955: 247–270]) an extended situational exegesis of Sura 2 of the Quran, which is Islam's most considerable meditation on the Jewish past and the newly revealed Islamic present in God's plan for mankind. Included in this same sura is a radical new development in the liturgical life of Muhammad and his followers.*

The foolish will now ask and say: "What has made the faithful turn them away from the direction of prayer toward which they used to pray?" Say: "To God belongs the East and the West, and He guides who so wills to the path that is straight."

Thus We have made you a community of the middle path that you act as witness over man, the Prophet is witness over you. We decreed the prayer-direction to which you faced before that We may know who follow the Apostle and who turn away in haste. It [that is, the change in the direction of prayer] was a hard test, except for those who were guided by God. But God will not suffer your faith to go to waste, for God is to men full of mercy and grace.

We have seen you turning your face to the heavens. We shall turn you toward a prayer-direction that will please you. So turn toward the

Holy Mosque, and turn toward it wherever you be. And those who are recipients of the Book surely know that this is the truth from their Lord, and God is not negligent of all that you do.

Even though you bring all the proof to the People of the Book, they will not face to the direction you turn to, nor you theirs, nor will they follow each other's direction. And if you follow their whims after all the knowledge that has reached you, then surely you will be among the transgressors. (Quran 2:142–145)

There was little agreement among the Muslim Quranic commentators on how to construe these verses on the change of the Muslims' direction of prayer. The standard Commentary of Tabari (d. 923 C.E.), for example, gives the reader a number of choices, no one of them greatly different from the others.

On the authority of Iqrima and Hasan al-Basri: The first command to be abrogated in the Quran was that concerning the direction of prayer. This was because the Prophet (first) preferred the Rock of the Holy House of Jerusalem, which was the prayer-direction of the Jews. The Prophet faced it for seventeen months (after his arrival in Medina) in the hope that the Jews would believe in him and follow him. Then God said: "Say: 'To God belongs the East and the West. . . .' "

Al-Rabi' ibn Anas relates on the authority of Abu al-Aliya: The Prophet of God was given his choice of turning his face (in prayer) toward whichever direction he wished. He chose the Holy House in Jerusalem so that the People of the Book might be conciliated. This was his prayer-direction for sixteen months (after his arrival in Medina); all the while, however, he kept turning his face toward the heavens until God turned him toward the House [that is, the Ka'ba].

It is related, on the other hand, on the authority of Ibn Abbas: When the Apostle of God migrated to Medina, most of whose inhabitants were Jews, God ordered him to (pray) with his face toward Jerusalem, and the Jews were glad. The Prophet faced that way for someting more than ten months, but he loved the prayer-direction of Abraham [that is, the Ka'ba]. So he used to pray to God and gaze into the heavens until God sent down (the verse), "We have seen you turning your face toward heaven" (2:144). The Jews became suspicious and said, "What has turned them away from the direction of prayer toward which they used to pray?" And so God sent down (the verse), "Say: To God belongs the East and the West." (Tabari, *Commentary, ad loc.*)

All these reports attempt to reconcile the Quranic verses with what was understood to be the position of Muhammad vis-à-vis the Jews of Medina. It was not the only way of approaching the problem, of course. Nisaburi (d. 1327 C.E.) illustrates the more "spiritual" reading of history favored by Sufi authors.

It is because the servant must turn his face toward and serve Him. It is also in order that unity and harmony among the people and faith may be established. It is as though the Exalted One says, "O man of faith! You are my servant, the Kaʿba is My House and the prayers are My service. Your heart is My Throne and Paradise is My noble abode. Turn your face toward My house and your heart to Me, so that I may grant you My noble abode." The Jews faced the west, which is the direction of the setting lights. . . . The Christians faced the east, which is the direction of the rising of lights . . . but the people of faith faced the manifestation of lights, which is Mecca. From Mecca is Muhammad, and from him were lights created, and for his sake the circling spheres were set on their course. The west is the prayer-direction of Moses and the east is the prayer-direction of Jesus; between them is the prayer-direction of Abraham and Muhammad, for the best of things is that which is in the middle position. (Nisaburi, *Marvels of the Qurʾan* 3.8)   [AYOUB 1984: 169]

27. The Battle at the Badr Wells

Once established in Medina, the Prophet turned his attention to the Quraysh of Mecca. Following some preliminary skirmishes, the first major confrontation took place at the wells of Badr near Medina in 624 C.E. When Muhammad received news of the passage there of a Quraysh caravan, "he summoned the Muslims and said, 'This is the Quraysh caravan containing their property. Go out and attack it; perhaps God will give it as prey.' The people answered his summons, some eagerly, others reluctantly because they had not thought that the Messenger would go to war" (Life 428 [IBN ISHAQ 1955: 289]). The Quraysh heard of the intended attack and mobilized their own forces, thus setting up a major confrontation between the Muslims and their opponents at Mecca. During the preliminaries, when Muhammad was positioning his forces, the following interesting incident is reported.

Al-Hubab ibn al-Mundhir ibn al-Jamuh said to the Apostle: "Is this the place which God has ordered you to occupy, so that we can neither advance nor withdraw from it, or is it a matter of opinion and military tactics?" When Muhammad replied that it was the latter al-Hubab pointed out to him that this was not the place to stop but that they should go on to the water hole nearest the enemy and halt there, stop up the wells beyond it and construct a cistern for themselves so that they would have plenty of water. . . . The Messenger agreed that it was an excellent plan and it was immediately carried out. (*Life* 439)   [IBN ISHAQ 1955: 296–297]

The fighting begins, and at first it goes badly for the outnumbered Muslims. The Prophet rallies his troops with this promise.

Then the Messenger went forth to the people and incited them, saying, "By God in whose hand is the soul of Muhammad, no man will be slain this day fighting against them (the Quraysh) with steadfast courage, advancing and not retreating, but God will cause him to enter Paradise." (*Life* 445) [IBN ISHAQ 1955: 300]

The Muslims were victorious, with a great effect on their own and the Quraysh's morale for the rest of the struggle between them. The jubilation that followed was tempered only by a quarrel about the distribution of the rich spoils.

They ask you (O Muhammad), about the spoils of war. Say: The spoils of war belong to God and the Apostle, so keep your duty to God and adjust the matter of your difference and obey God and his Apostle, if you are true believers. (Quran 8:1)

Thus the event is referred to in the opening verse of Sura 8, called "The Spoils." Most of the sura is in fact devoted to the events surrounding the battle of Badr and is interpreted at length in the Life *(476–485 [IBN ISHAQ 1955: 321–327]).*

28. The Affair of the Banu Qaynuqaᶜ

After the success at Badr, the issue of the Jews of Medina surfaced once again, or at least as it concerned one tribe of them, the Banu Qaynuqaᶜ.

Meanwhile there was the affair of the Banu Qaynuqaᶜ. The Messenger assembled them in their market and addressed them as follows: "O Jews, beware lest God bring upon you the vengeance He brought upon the Quraysh and become Muslims. You know I am the Prophet who has been sent—you will find that in your Scriptures and God's covenant with you." They replied, "O Muhammad, you seem to think that we are your people. Do not deceive yourself because you encountered a people with no knowledge of war and got the better of them; for by God, if we fight you, you will find that we are real men!"

A freedman of the family of Zayd ibn Thabit from Saᶜid ibn Jubayr from Iqrima from Ibn Abbas told me that the latter said that the following verses came down about them: "Say to those who disbelieve: You will be vanquished and gathered to Hell, an evil resting place. You have already had a sign in the two forces which met," that is, the Apostle's companions at Badr and the Quraysh. "One force fought in the way of God; the other, disbelievers, thought they saw double their own force with their very

eyes. God strengthens with His help whomever He wills. Verily in that is
an example for the discerning" (Quran 3:12–13).

Asim ibn Umar ibn Qatada said that the Banu Qaynuqaʿ were the
first of the Jews to break their agreement with the Messenger and to go
to war (with him), between Badr and (the battle of) Uhud, and the
Messenger besieged them until they surrendered unconditionally. Abdullah ibn Ubayy went to him when God put them in his power and said, "O
Muhammad, deal kindly with my clients"—the Banu Qaynuqaʿ were
allies of Khazraj—but the Messenger put him off. He repeated the words
and the Messenger turned away from him, whereupon Abdullah thrust
his hand into the collar of the Apostle's robe; the Messenger was so angry
that his face became almost black. He said, "Confound you, let me go."
Abdullah answered, "No, by God, I will not let you go until you deal
kindly with my clients. Four hundred men without mail and three hundred mailed protected me from all my enemies; would you cut them
down in one morning? By God, I am a man who fears that circumstances
may change." The Messenger said, "You can have them."

. . . (Thus) when the Banu Qaynuqaʿ fought against the Messenger
Abdullah ibn Ubayy espoused their cause and defended them, but Ubada
ibn al-Samit, who had the same alliance with them as had Abdullah, went
to the Messenger and renounced all responsibility for them in favor of
God and His Apostle, saying, "O Messenger of God, I take God and His
Messenger as my friends, and I renounce my agreement and friendship
with these unbelievers." It was concerning him and Abdullah ibn Ubayy
that this passage from the Sura of the Table came down: "O you who
believe, take not Jews and Christians as friends. They are friends one of
another. Who of you takes them as friends is one of them. God will not
guide the unjust people. You can see those in whose heart there is sickness," that is, Abdullah ibn Ubayy when he said "I fear a change of
circumstances." Acting hastily in regard to them, they say we fear a
change of circumstances may overtake us. Perhaps God will bring victory
or an act from Him so that they will be sorry for their secret thoughts,
and those who believe will say, Are these those who swore by God their
most binding oath that they were surely with you? As for God's words,
"Verily God and His Messenger are your friends, and those who believe,
who perform prayer, give alms and bow down in homage," they refer to
Ubada taking God and His Messenger and the believers as his friends and
renouncing his agreement and friendship with the Banu Qaynuqaʿ:
"Those who take God and His Messenger and the believers as friends,

they are God's party, they are victorious" (Quran 3:51–56). (*Life* 545–547) [IBN ISHAQ 1955: 363–364]

29. The Battle of Uhud

The triumph of Badr was followed in the next year by a full-scale attack of three thousand foot soldiers and two hundred cavalry mustered by the Quraysh for an assault on Medina. The severe setback that resulted for the Muslims is commemorated as the Battle of Uhud.

The Muslims were put to flight and the enemy slew many of them. It was a day of trial and testing in which God honored several with martyrdom, until the enemy got at the Messenger, who was struck with a stone so that he fell on his side and one of his teeth was smashed, his face gashed and his lip injured. The man who wounded him was Utba ibn Abi Waqqas. (*Life* 571) [IBN ISHAQ 1955: 380]

According to what Salih ibn Kaysan told me, Hind, the daughter of Utba, and the women with her stopped to mutilate the Apostle's dead companions. They cut off their ears and noses and Hind made them into anklets and collars. . . . She cut out Hamza's liver and chewed it, but she was not able to swallow it and threw it away. Then she mounted a high rock and shrieked at the top of her voice:

> "We have paid you back for Badr
> And a war that follows a war is always violent.
> I could not bear the loss of Utba
> Nor my brother and his uncle and my firstborn.
> I have slaked my vengeance and fulfilled my vow. . . ."

When (the Quraysh leader) Abu Sufyan wanted to leave, he went to the top of the mountain and shouted loudly, saying, "You have done a fine work. Victory in war goes by turns: today is in exchange for the day of Badr. Show your superiority, Hubal," that is, vindicate your religion. The Messenger told Umar to go up and answer him and say, "God is most high and most glorious. We are not equal: our dead are in paradise, yours are in hell." At this answer Abu Sufyan said to Umar, "Come up here to me." The Messenger told him to go and see what Abu Sufyan was up to. When he came Abu Sufyan said, "I adjure you by God, Umar, have we killed Muhammad?" "By God, you have not, he is listening to what you are saying right now," Umar replied. Abu Sufyan said, "I regard you as more truthful and reliable than Ibn Qami'a," referring to the latter's claim that he had killed Muhammad. (*Life* 581–583) [IBN ISHAQ 1955: 385–386]

30. The Deportation of the Banu al-Nadir

Just as in the sequel of Badr, when Muhammad turned to the Jewish tribe of the Qaynuqa, so the direct or indirect consequence of Uhud was the expulsion of a second Jewish tribe from the Medina association, the Banu al-Nadir. In this case the provocation was the report of a threat by members of the Banu al-Nadir against the Prophet's life. The response was prompt and direct: an assault on their redoubts in the Medina oasis.*

The Jews took refuge in their forts and the Messenger ordered the palm trees should be cut down and burnt. And they [the Banu al-Nadir] called out to him, "O Muhammad, you have prohibited wanton destruction and blamed those guilty of it. Why then are you cutting down and burning our palm trees?" Now there were a number of the (Arab tribe of the) Banu Awf ibn al-Khazraj . . . who had sent to the Banu al-Nadir saying, "Stand firm and protect yourselves, for we will not betray you. If you are attacked we will fight with you and if you are turned out we will go with you." Accordingly they waited for the help they had promised, but they [the Banu Awf] did nothing and God cast terror into their hearts. The Banu al-Nadir then asked the Messenger to deport them and to spare their lives on condition that they could retain all their property which they could carry on camels, armor excepted, and he agreed. So they loaded their camels with what they could carry. Men were destroying their houses down to the lintel of the door, which they put on the back of their camels and went off with it. Some went to Khaybar and others went to Syria. . . .

Abdullah ibn Abi Bakr told me that he was told that the Banu al-Nadir carried off their women and children and property with tambourines and pipes and singing girls playing behind them. . . . They went with such pomp and splendor as had never been seen in any tribe in their days. They left their property to the Messenger and it became his personal possession to dispose of as he wished. He divided it among the first emigrants (from Mecca to Medina), to the exclusion of the "Helpers." . . .

Concerning the Banu al-Nadir, the Sura of the Exile (59) came down in which is recorded how God wreaked his vengeance on them and gave His Messenger power over them and how He dealt with them. (*Life* 652–654) [IBN ISHAQ 1955: 437–438]

31. The Battle of the Trench (627 C.E.)

A number of Jews who had formed a party against the Apostle . . . went to the Quraysh at Mecca and invited them to join them in an attack upon the Messenger so they could get rid of him together. The Quraysh said, "You, O Jews, are the first people of Scripture and know the nature of our dispute with Muhammad. Is our religion the best or is his?" They replied that certainly the Quraysh's religion was better than Muhammad's and had a better claim to be in the right. And it was in this connection that God sent down (the verses of the Quran): "Have you not considered those to whom a part of Scripture was given and yet believe in idols and false deities and say to those who disbelieve, these are more rightly guided than those who believe? . . . We gave the family of Abraham the Scripture and the wisdom and We gave them a great kingdom and some of them believed in it and some of them turned from it, and hell is sufficient for (their) burning" (Quran 4:51–54).

These words (of the Jews) rejoiced the Quraysh and they responded gladly to their invitation to fight the Apostle, and they assembled and made their preparations. Then that company of Jews went off to Ghatafan of Qays Aylan and invited them to fight the Messenger and told them that they would act in concert with them and that the Quraysh had followed their lead in the matter; so they too joined in with them. . . .

When the Messenger heard of their intention he drew a trench around Medina and worked at it himself, encouraging the Muslims with hope of reward in heaven. The Muslims worked very hard with him, but the disaffected held back and began to hide their real object by working slackly and stealing away to their families without the Apostle's permission or knowledge.

When the Messenger had finished the trench, the Quraysh came and encamped where the torrent beds of Ruma meet between al-Juruf and Zughaba with ten thousand of their black mercenaries and their followers from the Banu Kinana and the people of Tihama. Ghatafan too came with their followers from Najd and halted at Dhanab Naqma toward the direction of Uhud. The Messenger and the Muslims came out with three thousand men having Sal' at their backs. He pitched his camp there with the trench between him and his foes, and he gave orders for the women and children to be taken up to the forts (of the oasis). . . .

The situation became serious and fear was everywhere. The enemy came at them from above and below until the believers imagined vain things and disaffection was rife among the disaffected, to the point that Mu'attib ibn Qushayr said, "Muhammad used to promise that we would eat the treasures of Khusraw and Caesar and today not one of us can feel safe going to the privy!" It reached such a point that Aws ibn al-Qayzi, one of the Banu Haritha ibn al-Harith, said to the people, "Our houses are exposed to the enemy"—this he said before a large gathering of his people—"so let us go out and return to our home, for it is outside Medina." The Messenger and the polytheists remained (facing each other) twenty days and more, nearly a month, without fighting except for some shooting with arrows and the siege. (*Life* 669–676) [IBN ISHAQ 1955: 450–454]

Muhammad and his followers were dispirited, but the morale in the camp of the Quraysh was at an even lower pitch. Soon the alliance began to disintegrate. In the end the siege was broken off, and the attackers returned to their homes.

32. The Banu Qurayza

One of the reasons for the failure of the siege at the trench was the unwillingness of the remaining Jewish tribe of the oasis, the Banu Qurayza, to take an active part in the Quraysh assault. On the Muslim side, however, restraint was not construed as sympathy.

According to what al-Zuhri told me, at the time of the noon prayers Gabriel came to the Messenger wearing an embroidered turban and riding on a mule with a saddle covered with a piece of brocade. He asked the Messenger if he had abandoned fighting, and when he said he had, Gabriel said that the angels had not yet laid aside their arms and that he had just come from pursuing the enemy. "God commands you, Muhammad, to go to the Banu Qurayza. I am about to go to them and shake their stronghold. . . ."

The Messenger besieged them for twenty-five nights until they were sore pressed and God cast terror into their hearts. . . . And when they felt sure that the Messenger would not leave them until he had made an end to them, (their leader) Ka'b ibn Asad said to them: "O Jews, you can see what has happened to you. I offer you three alternatives. Take which you please. We will follow this man and accept him as true, for by God it is plain to you that he is a prophet who has been sent and that it is he that you find mentioned in your Scripture; and then your lives, your property, your women and children will be saved." They said, "We will never abandon the laws of the Torah and never change it for another." He said, "Then if you will not accept this suggestion, let us kill our wives and children and send men with their swords drawn against Muhammad and his companions, leaving no encumbrances behind us, and let God decide between us and Muhammad. If we perish, we perish, and we shall not leave children behind us to cause anxiety. If we conquer, we can acquire other wives and children." They said, "Should we kill those poor creatures? What would be the good of life when they were dead?" He said, "Then if you will not accept this suggestion, tonight is the eve of the Sabbath and it may well be that Muhammad and his companions will feel secure from us, so come down and perhaps we can take Muhammad and his companions by surprise." They said, "Are we to profane our Sabbath and do on the Sabbath what those before us of whom you well know did and were turned into apes?" He answered, "Not a single man among you from the day of your birth has ever passed a night resolved to do what he knows ought to be done."

Then the Banu Qurayza sent to the Messenger saying, "Send us Abu Lubaba (of the Banu Aws) . . . for they were allies of the Aws, that we may consult him." So the Messenger sent him to them, and when they saw him they got up to meet him. The women and children went up to him weeping in his face, and he felt pity for them. They said, "O Abu Lubaba, do you think we should submit to Muhammad's judgment?" He said "Yes," but pointed his hand to his throat, signifying slaughter. Abu Lubaba (later) said, "My feet had not moved from the spot before I knew that I had been false to God and His Apostle." Then he left them and did not go to the Messenger but bound himself to one of the pillars in the mosque saying, "I will not leave this place until God forgives me for what I have done," and he promised that he would never go to the Banu Qurayza and would never be seen in a town in which he had betrayed God and His Apostle.

When the Aws, the former patrons of the Banu Qurayza, somewhat hesitantly asked for leniency—they recalled what had happened in the case of the other Jewish clients at Medina—Muhammad asked them if they would be content if one of their own number passed judgment on the Banu Qurayza. They said they would. A certain Saʿd ibn Muʿadh was chosen.

Saʿd said: "I give judgment that the men should be killed, the property divided, and the women and children taken as captives. . . ."

Then the Banu Qurayza surrendered themselves and the Messenger confined them in the quarter of Bint al-Harith, a woman of the Banu al-Najjar. Then the Messenger went out to the market of Medina—which is still the market today—and dug trenches in it. Then he sent for them and struck off their heads in those trenches as they were brought out to him in batches. Among them was the enemy of God Huyayy ibn Aktab and Ka'b ibn Asas their chief. There were 600 or 700 in all, though some put the figure as high as 800 or 900. As they were being taken out in batches to the Apostle, they asked Ka'b what he thought would be done to them. He replied, "Will you never understand? Don't you see that the summoner never stops and those who are taken away never return? By God, it is death!" This went on until the Messenger made an end to them. (*Life* 684–690) [IBN ISHAQ 1955: 641–464]

33. The Affair at Hudaybiyya

The Messenger stayed in Medina during the months of Ramadan and Shawwal (in 628 C.E.) and then went out on the 'umra (or lesser pilgrimage) in Dhu al-Qa'da with no intention of making war. He called together the Arabs and the neighboring bedouin to march with him, fearing that the Quraysh (in Mecca) would oppose him with arms or prevent his visiting the shrine, as they actually did. Many of the Arabs held back from him, and he went out with the Emigrants and the Helpers and such of the Arabs as stuck to him. He took the sacrificial victims with him and donned the pilgrim garb so that all would know that he did not intend war and that his purpose was to visit the shrine and venerate it. . . .

In his tradition al-Zuhri said: When the Messenger had rested (at Hudaybiyya near Mecca), Budayl ibn Warqa al-Khuza'i came to him with some men of the Khuza'a and asked him what he had come for. He told them he had not come for war but to go on pilgrimage and visit the sacred precincts. . . . Then they returned to the Quraysh and told them what they had heard; but the Quraysh suspected them and spoke roughly to them, "He may not come out wanting war, but by God, he will never come in here against our will nor will the Arabs ever see that we allowed it." The Khaza'a were in fact the Apostle's confidants, both the Muslims and the non-Muslims among them, and they kept him informed of everything that went on in Mecca. . . .

. . . Then they (the Quraysh of Mecca) sent Urwa ibn Mas'ud al-Thaqafi to the Apostle. . . . He came to the Messenger and sat before him and said: "Muhammad, you have collected a mixed people together and then brought them against your own people to destroy them? By God, I think I see you deserted by these people here tomorrow." Now Abu

Bakr was sitting behind the Messenger and he said, "Go suck al-Lat's tits! Should we desert him?" . . . Then Urwa began to take hold of the Apostle's beard as he talked to him. Al-Mughira ibn Shuʿba was standing by the Apostle's head clad in mail and he began to hit Urwa's hand as he held the Apostle's beard saying, "Take your hand away from the Apostle's face before you lose it!" Urwa said, "Confound you, how rough and rude you are!" The Messenger smiled and when Urwa asked who the man was he told him that it was his brother's son Urwa ibn Shuʿba, and Urwa said, "You wretch, it was only yesterday that I was wiping your behind!"

The Messenger told him what he told the others, namely that he had not come out for war. Urwa then got up from the Apostle's presence, having noted how his companions treated him. Whenever he performed his ablutions, they ran to get the water he used; if he spat, they ran to it; if a hair of his head fell out, they ran to pick it up. So he returned to the Quraysh and said, "I have seen Khusraw in his kingdom and Caesar in his kingdom and the Negus in his kingdom, but never have I seen a king among a people like Muhammad is among his companions."

Muhammad decided to try a more direct approach: to send one of his own followers into Mecca to convince the Quraysh of his peaceful intentions. The one chosen was Uthman, the future third Caliph of Islam (644–656 C.E.) and a man well connected in Mecca.

As Uthman entered or was about to enter Mecca, Aban ibn Saʿid met him and carried him in front of him (on his mount) and gave him protection until he could convey the Apostle's message to them. Having heard what Uthman had to say, the Quraysh said: "If you wish to circumambulate the shrine, then go ahead." He for his part said he would not until Muhammad did so, and so the Quraysh kept him prisoner with them. The Messenger and the Muslims were informed, however, that Uthman had been killed.

Abdullah ibn Abi Bakr told me that when the Messenger heard that Uthman had been killed, he said that he would not leave until they fought the enemy, and he summoned the men to pledge themselves to this. The pledge of al-Ridwan took place under a tree. Men used to say that Muhammad took their pledge unto death, but Jabir ibn Abdullah said that it was not a pledge unto death but an undertaking not to run away. . . . Then the Messenger heard that the news about Uthman was false. (*Life* 741–746) [IBN ISHAQ 1955: 499–504]

34. The Armistice

. . . Then the Quraysh sent Suhayl ibn Amr to the Messenger with instructions to make peace with him on condition that he returned (to Medina) this year so that none of the Arabs could say that he had made a forcible entry. . . . After a long discussion peace was made and nothing remained but to write the document. Umar leaped up and went to Abu Bakr saying, "Is he not God's Messenger and are we not Muslims, and are not they polytheists?" to which Abu Bakr agreed, and he went on, "Then why should we agree to what is demeaning to our religion?" Abu Bakr replied, "Follow what he says, for I bear witness that he is God's Apostle." Umar said, "And so do I." Then he went to the Messenger and put the same questions, to which the Messenger answered, "I am God's slave and His Apostle. I will not go against His commandment and He will not make me a loser." Umar used to say (afterwards), "I have not ceased giving alms and fasting and praying and freeing slaves because of what I did that day and for fear of what I had said, when I hoped that (my plan) would be better."

Then the Messenger summoned Ali and told him to write, "In the name of God, the Compassionate, the Merciful." Suhayl said, "I do not recognize this; write rather, In thy name, O God." The Messenger told Ali to write the latter and he did so. Then he said, "Write: This is what Muhammad, Messenger of God, has agreed with Suhayl ibn Amr." Suhayl said, "If I confessed that you were God's Messenger I would not have fought you. Write your own name and the name of your father." The Messenger said, "Write: This is what Muhammad ibn Abdullah has agreed with Suhayl ibn Amr: they have agreed to lay aside war for ten years during which men can be safe and refrain from hostilities on condition that if anyone comes to Muhammad without the permission of his guardian he will return him to them; and if anyone of those with Muhammad returns to the Quraysh they will not return him to him. We will not show enmity one to another and there shall be no secret reservation or bad faith. He who wishes to enter into a bond or agreement with Muhammad may do so and whoever wishes to enter into a bond or agreement with the Quraysh may do so."

The Messenger then went on his way back (to Medina), and when he was halfway the Sura of the Victory came down: "We have given you a signal victory that God may forgive you your past sin and the sin which is to come and may complete His favor upon you and guide you on an upright path" (Quran 48:1–2). . . .

No previous victory in Islam was greater than this. There was nothing but battle when men met; but when there was an armistice and war was abolished and men met in safety and held discussion, none talked about Islam intelligently without entering it. In those two years double or more than double as many entered Islam as ever before. (*Life 746–751*) [IBN ISHAQ 1955: 504–507]

35. Khaybar and Fadak

There followed almost immediately a raid upon the Jewish oasis of Khaybar in the north. The resistance was determined but unavailing, and the terms of the capitulation were not lost on the occupants of Fadak, another nearby oasis.

The Messenger besieged the people of Khaybar in their two forts al-Watih and al-Salalim until when they could hold out no longer they asked him to let them go and spare their lives, and he did so. Now the Messenger had already taken possession of all their property . . . except what belonged to these two forts. When the people of Fadak heard of what had happened they sent to the Messenger asking him to let them go (as well) and to spare their lives and they would leave him their property, and he did so. . . . When the people of Khaybar surrendered on these conditions they asked the Messenger to employ them on the property, with a half share of (future) produce, saying, "We know more about it than you and are better farmers." The Messenger agreed to this arrangement on the condition that "if we wish to expel you, we will expel you." He made a similar arrangement with the men of Fadak, except that Khaybar became war spoils for all the Muslims, while Fadak was the personal property of the Messenger because they had not attacked it with horses and camels. (*Life 763–764*) [IBN ISHAQ 1955: 515–516]

36. The Pilgrimage Fulfilled

When the Messenger returned from Khaybar to Medina he stayed there from the first Rabi until Shawwal, sending out raiding parties and expeditions. Then in Dhu al-Qa da—the month in which the polytheists had prevented him from making the pilgrimage (in the preceding year)—he went out to make the "fulfilled pilgrimage" in place of the lesser pilgrimage from which they had excluded him. Those Muslims who had been excluded with him went out in A.H. 7 [February 629 C.E.] and when the Meccans heard it, they got out of his way. . . .

. . . The Messenger married Maymuna daughter of al-Harith on that journey when he was on pilgrimage. (His uncle) al-Abbas gave her to him in marriage [and probably became a Muslim at the same time]. The Messenger remained three days in Mecca. Huwaytib ibn Abd al-Uzza with a few Quraysh came to him on the third day because the Quraysh had entrusted him with the duty of sending the Messenger out of Mecca. They said, "Your time is up, so get out from among us." The Messenger answered, "How would it harm you if you were to let me stay and I gave a wedding feast among you and prepared food and you came too?" They replied, "We don't need your food, so get out." So the Messenger went out and left Abu Rafi' his client in charge of Maymuna until he brought her to him in Sarif. (*Life* 788–790) [IBN ISHAQ 1955: 530–531]

37. "The Truth Has Come and Falsehood Has Passed Away"

The breaking of the armistice concluded between Muhammad and the Quraysh of Mecca at Hudaybiyya in 628 C.E. came about not through the principals themselves but by an altercation between two of their bedouin allies. The violation might have been settled in other ways perhaps—the Quraysh appeared willing to negotiate— but in 630 Muhammad judged the occasion fit and the time appropriate for settling accounts with the polytheists of Mecca once and for all.

The Messenger ordered preparations to be made for a foray and Abu Bakr came in to see his daughter (and Muhammad's wife) Aisha as she was moving some of the Apostle's gear. He asked her if the Messenger had ordered her to get things ready and she said he had and that her father had better get ready too. She told him that she did not know where the troops were going, however. Later the Messenger informed the men that he was going to Mecca and ordered them to make preparations. He said, "O God, take their eyes and ears from the Quraysh that we may take them by surprise in their land," and the men got themselves ready. (*Life* 808) [IBN ISHAQ 1955: 544]

The surprise prayed for by Muhammad was granted him, along with other good fortune: Abu Sufyan, the Quraysh leader, was captured by chance before the Muslims reached Mecca and persuaded, despite continuing doubts, to save himself and embrace Islam. The Meccans' will to resist was at a low ebb.

The Messenger had instructed his commanders when they entered Mecca only to fight those who resisted them, except for a small number [perhaps only four] who were to be killed even if they were found beneath the curtains of the Ka'ba itself. . . . The Messenger after arriving in Mecca, once the populace had settled down, went to the shrine and went round it seven times on his camel, touching the black stone with a stick which he had in his hand. This done, he summoned Uthman ibn Talha and took the keys of the Ka'ba from him, and when the door was opened for him, he went in. There he found a dove made of wood. He broke it in his hands and threw it away. . . . (According to another account) the Messenger entered Mecca on the day of the conquest and it contained 360 idols which Iblis [or Satan] had strengthened with lead. The Messenger was standing by them with a stick in his hand, saying, "The truth has come and falsehood has passed away" (Quran 17:81). Then he pointed at them with his stick and they collapsed on their backs one after another.

When the Messenger had prayed the noon prayer on the day of the conquest (of Mecca), he ordered that all the idols which were around the Ka'ba should be collected and burned with fire and broken up. . . . The Quraysh had put pictures in the Ka'ba, including two of Jesus son of Mary and of Mary, on both of whom be peace. Ibn Shihab said: Asma the daughter of Shaqr said that a woman of the Banu Ghassan had joined in the pilgrimage of the Arabs and when she saw a picture of Mary in the Ka'ba she said: "My father and my mother be your ransom! (Mary), you are surely an Arab woman!" The Messenger ordered that the pictures be erased, except those of Jesus and Mary.

A traditionist told me that the Messenger stood at the door of the Ka'ba and said: "There is no god but God alone; He has no associates. He has made good His promise and helped His servant. He alone has put to flight the confederates. Every claim of privilege or blood or property are abolished by me except the custody of the shrine and the watering of the pilgrims. . . . O Quraysh, God has taken from you the haughtiness of paganism and its veneration of ancestors. Man springs from Adam and Adam from dust." Then he recited them this verse: "O men, we created you male and female and made you into peoples and tribes that you may know one another; in truth, the most noble of you in God's sight is the most pious . . . " to the end of the passage (Quran 49:13). Then he added, "O Quraysh, what do you think I am about to do to you?" They replied, "Good, for you are a noble brother, son of a noble brother." He said, "Go your way; you are freed." (Life 818–821) [IBN ISHAQ 1955: 550–553]

38. Consolidation of Gains

Troops were despatched to the neighborhood of Mecca to smash the others idols revered in the holy places around that holy city. Then suddenly there came the last real challenge to Muhammad's political supremacy: a bedouin confederation mustered its last forces and marched against the Prophet. The encounter occurred at a place called Hunayn. Although at first there was panic in the Muslim ranks, their numerical superiority finally prevailed, and the bedouin were routed.

God has given you victory on many fields, and on the day of Hunayn, when you exulted in your numbers, though they availed you nothing, and the earth, vast as it was, was straitened for you. Then you turned back in flight. Then God sent down His peace of reassurance on His Messenger and upon the believers, and sent down hosts you could not see, and punished those who did not believe. Such is the reward of disbelievers. (Quran 9:25–26)

Even before the occupation of Mecca, Muhammad had been casting his net of raids and expeditions in an ever wider arc. After the battle of Hunayn, toward the end of that same eventful year of 630 C.E. (his last surviving son, the infant Ibrahim, born of the Egyptian Christian concubine named Mary, also died in that year), he prepared his troops for an expedition northward and deep across the frontiers of the Byzantine Empire to the town of Tabuk. Although it may have revealed to Muhammad the weakness of his international rivals, the raid was not an entirely successful enterprise in its organization or in its fulfillment, as many passages in Sura 9 of the Quran testify.

39. A Miracle of Muhammad

One event reported on the course of Muhammad's long journey into Byzantine territory is worth noting. Although it occurs in the canonical collection of traditions concerning the Prophet, it is not entirely typical. Contrary to most of the accounts of his life and deeds, this report attributes to Muhammad superhuman powers, albeit they are displayed at the quite explicit urging of Umar.

It is narrated either on the authority of Abu Hurayra or that of Abu Sa'id Khudri. The narrator A'mash has narrated this tradition with a little bit of doubt (about the original source). He [that is, the narrator] said: During the time of the Tabuk expedition (provisions) ran short and the men (of the army) suffered starvation. They said: Messenger of God, would you permit us to slay our camels? We would eat them and use their fat. The Messenger of God, may peace be upon him, said: Do as you please. He [the narrator] said: Then Umar came and said: Messenger of God, if you do that, the riding animals would become short. But (rather) summon them along with the provisions left to them. Then invoke God's blessings on them. It is hoped God will bless them. The Messenger of God replied in the affirmative.

He [the narrator] said: He called for a leather mat to be used as a tablecloth and spread it out. Then the people came, along with the remaining portions of their provisions. He [the narrator] said: One was coming with a handful of sorghum, another with a handful of dates, still another with a portion of bread, till small quantities of these were collected on the tablecloth. He [the narrator] said: Then the Messenger of God invoked blessings (on them) and said: Fill your utensils with these provisions. He [the narrator] said: They filled the vessels to the brim with them, and no one among the army was left even with a single empty vessel. He [the narrator] said: They ate their fill and there was still a surplus. Upon this the Messenger of God, may peace be upon him, remarked: I bear testimony that there is no god but the God and I am the Messenger of God. The man who meets his Lord without entertaining any doubt about these two (truths) would never be kept away from Paradise. (Muslim, *Sahih* 1:11.42)

40. The Submission of the Idolaters

Upon Muhammad's return from this far-reaching raid to the north, the bedouin continued to make their peace, political and religious, with him, though with some caution:

In deciding their attitude to Islam the Arabs were only waiting to see what happened to this clan of the Quraysh and the Apostle. For the Quraysh were the leaders and guides of men, the people of the sacred shrine (of Mecca), and the pure stock of Ishmael son of Abraham; and the leading Arabs did not contest this. It was the Quraysh who had declared war on the Messenger and opposed him; and when Mecca was occupied and the Quraysh became subject to him and he subdued them to Islam, and the Arabs knew they could not fight the Messenger or display enmity toward him, they entered into God's religion "in batches" as God said, coming to him from all directions. (*Life* 933)   [IBN ISHAQ 1955: 628]

Submission to the Prophet of Islam and his God was not always simple or easy, since the social, political, and psychological price of disavowing the customs of their own past was a large one. The Thaqif, for example, were willing to "make their submis-

sion and accept Islam on the Apostle's conditions provided they could get a document guaranteeing their land and their people and their animals." They got their document, but that was by no means the end of the matter.

Among the things they asked the Messenger was that they should be allowed to retain their idol al-Lat undestroyed for three years. The Messenger refused and they continued to ask him for a year or two (grace), and he refused. Finally they asked for a month (dispensation) after their return home, but he refused to agree to any set time. All that they wanted, as they were trying to show, was to be safe from their fanatics and women and children by leaving al-Lat, and they did not want to frighten their people by destroying her until they had (all) accepted Islam. The Messenger refused this, but he sent Abu Sufyan and al-Mughira to destroy her (for them). They also asked him that he would excuse them from prayer and that they would not have to break the idol with their own hands. The Messenger said: "We excuse you from breaking your idols with your own hands, but as for prayer, there is no good in a religion which has no prayers." They said that they would perform them, though they were demeaning. (*Life* 916) [IBN ISHAQ 1955: 613–614]

41. A Primer on Islam

As each new tribe embraced Islam, their duties and responsibilities as Muslims had to be spelled out for them. One case in particular gives us an opportunity to observe what was understood as "Islam" in those days.

Now the Messenger had sent to them [the Banu al-Harith, Christians of the city of Najran in the Yemen] . . . Amr ibn Hazm to instruct them in religion and to teach them the customary practice (*sunna*) and the institutions of Islam and to collect their alms. And he wrote Amr a letter in which he gave him his orders and injunctions as follows:

"In the Name of God, the Compassionate, the Merciful. This is a clear announcement from God and His Apostle. O you who believe, be faithful to your agreements. The instructions of Muhammad the Prophet, the Messenger of God, to Amr ibn Hazm when he sent him to the Yemen. He orders him to observe piety toward God in all his doings for God is with those who are pious and who do well; and he commanded him to behave with truth as God commanded him; and that he should give people the good news and command them to follow it and to teach men the Quran and instruct them in it and to forbid men to do wrong so that none but the pure should touch the Quran, and he should instruct men in their privileges and obligations and be lenient with them when they behave aright and severe on injustice, since God hates injustice and has forbidden it. 'The curse of God is on the evildoers' (Quran 5:1).

"Give men the good news of paradise and the way to earn it, and warn them of hell and the way to earn it, and make friends with men so that they may be instructed in religion. Teach men the rites of the pilgrimage (hajj), its customs and its obligation and what God has ordered about it: the greater pilgrimage is the hajj and the lesser pilgrimage is the ʿumra. Prohibit men from praying in one small garment, unless it be a garment whose ends are doubled over their shoulders, and forbid men from squatting in one garment which exposes their person to the air, and forbid them to twist the head of the hair on the back of the neck (in a pigtail).

"If there is a quarrel between men, forbid them to appeal to tribes and families, and let their appeal be to God. And those who do not appeal to God but to tribes and families, let them be smitten with the sword until their appeal is to God. Command men to perform the ablutions, their faces, their hands to the elbows and their feet to the ankles, and let them wipe their heads as God ordered. And command prayer at the proper time with bowing, prostration and humble reverence: prayer at daybreak; at noon when the sun declines; in the afternoon when the sun is descending; at evening when the night approaches, not delaying it until the stars appear in the sky; later at the beginning of the night. Order them to hasten to the mosques when they are summoned, and to wash when they go to them.

"Order them to subtract from the booty God's fifth and whatever alms are enjoined on the Muslims from land: a tenth of what the fountains water and the sky waters and a twentieth of what the bucket waters; and for every ten camels (they own), two sheep; and for every twenty camels, four sheep; for every forty cows, one cow; for every thirty cows, a bull or a cow calf; for every forty sheep at grass, one sheep. This is what God enjoined on the believers in the matters of alms (zakat). He who adds thereto, it is a merit to him.

"A Jew or a Christian who becomes a sincere Muslim of his own accord and obeys the religion of Islam is a believer with the same rights and the same obligations. If one of them holds fast to his own religion, he is not to be turned from it. Every adult (non-Muslim), male or female, bond or free, must pay a gold dinar or its equivalent in clothes. He who does this has the guarantee of God and His Apostle; he who withholds it is the enemy of God and His Messenger and all believers." (*Life* 961–962) [IBN ISHAQ 1955: 646–648]

42. The Farewell Pilgrimage

At the beginning of the year 632 C.E., the year of his death, Muhammad went on his final pilgrimage. The details were lovingly cherished, since they served as the foundation of all future performances of this ritual, which is a solemn obligation upon all Muslims. Ibn Ishaq passes over these in his Life; *he reproduces instead what turned out to be the Prophet's final discourse.*

In the beginning of Dhu al-Qaʿda the Messenger prepared to make the pilgrimage and ordered his men to get ready. Abd al-Rahman ibn al-Qasim from his father, from Aisha, the Prophet's wife, told me that the Messenger went on pilgrimage on the 25th of Dhu al-Qaʿda (20 February 632 C.E.).

(In its course) the Messenger showed the men the rites and taught them the customs of the Pilgrimage. He made a speech in which he made things clear. He praised and glorified God, then he said: "O men, listen to my words. I do not know whether I shall ever meet you in this place again after this year. Your blood and your property are sacrosanct until you meet your Lord, as this day and this month are holy. You will surely meet your Lord and He will ask you of your works. I have told you so. He who has a pledge, let him return it to him who entrusted it to him; all usury is abolished, but you have your capital. Wrong not and you shall not be wronged. . . . All blood shed in the period of paganism is to be left unavenged. . . . Satan despairs of ever being worshiped in your land, but if he can be obeyed in anything short of worship, he will be pleased in matters you may be disposed to think of little account, so beware of him in your religion. . . .

"You have rights over your wives and they have rights over you. You have the right they should not defile your bed and that they should not behave with open unseemliness. If they do, God allows you to put them in separate rooms and to beat them, though not with severity. If they refrain from these things, they have the right to their food and clothing with kindness. Lay injunctions on women kindly, for they are your prisoners, having no control of their persons. You have taken them only in trust from God, and you have the enjoyment of their persons by the words of God. So understand my words, O men, for I have told you. I have left you something with which, if you hold fast to it, you will never fall into error, a plain indication, the Book of God and the practices of His Prophet, so give good heed to what I say.

"Know that every Muslim is a Muslim's brother, and that (all) the Muslims are brethren. It is only lawful to take from a brother what he gives you willingly, so wrong not each other. O God, have I not told you?" (*Life* 968–969) [IBN ISHAQ 1955: 650–651]

43. Muhammad's Illness and Death
(June 632 C.E.)

Abdullah ibn Umar from Ubayd al-Jubayr, from Abdullah ibn Amr ibn al-As, from Abu Muwayhiba, a freedman of the Apostle, said: In the middle of the night the Messenger sent for me and told me that he was ordered to pray for the dead in this cemetery and that I was to go with him. I went, and when he stood among them he said: "Peace upon you, O people of the graves! Happy are you that you are so much better off than men here. Dissensions have come like waves of darkness one after the other, the last being worse than the first." Then he turned to me and said, "I have been given the choice between keys of the treasuries of this world and a long life here followed by Paradise, or meeting my Lord and Paradise (at once)." I urged him to choose the former, but he said he had chosen the latter. Then he prayed for the dead and went away. Then it was that the illness through which God took him began . . .

Al-Zuhri said that Abdullah ibn Ka'b ibn Malik told him that the messenger said on the day that he asked God's forgiveness for the men of the battle of Uhud, "O Emigrants, behave kindly to the Helpers, for other men increase but they in the nature of things cannot grow more numerous. They were my constant comfort and support. So treat their good men well and forgive those of them who were remiss." Then he came down and entered his house and his pain increased until he was exhausted. Then some of his wives gathered to him, Umm Salama and Maymuna, and some of the wives of the Muslims, among them Asma daughter of Umays, and his uncle Abbas was with him, and they agreed to force him to take some of the medicine. Abbas said, "Let me force him," but it was they who did it. When he recovered he asked . . . why they had done that. His uncle said, "We were afraid that you would get pleurisy." He replied, "That is a disease God would not afflict me with." . . .

Al-Zuhri said, Hamza ibn Abdullah ibn Umar told me that Aisha said: "When the Prophet became seriously ill, he ordered the people to tell Abu Bakr to superintend the prayers. Aisha told him that Abu Bakr was a delicate man with a weak voice who wept much when he read the Quran. He [Muhammad] repeated his order nonetheless and I repeated my objections. He said, 'You are like Joseph's companions; tell him to preside at prayers.' My only reason for saying what I did was that I wanted (my father) Abu Bakr to be spared this task, because I knew the people would never like a man who occupied the Apostle's place and would blame him for every misfortune that occurred, and I wanted Abu Bakr spared that."

Al-Zuhri said that Anas ibn Malik told him that on the Monday on which God took His Messenger he went out to the people as they were praying the morning prayer. The curtain was lifted and the door opened and out came the Messenger and stood at the door of Aisha's room. The Muslims were almost seduced from their prayers at seeing him, and he motioned to them that they should continue their prayers. The Messenger smiled with joy when he marked their demeanor at prayer, and I never saw him with a nobler expression than he had on that day. Then he went back and the people went away thinking that the Messenger had recovered from his illness. . . .

Ya'qub ibn Utba from al-Zuhri from Urwa from (Muhammad's wife) Aisha said: The Messenger came back to me from the mosque that day and lay on my lap. A man of Abu Bakr's family came in to me with a toothpick in his hand. The Messenger looked at it in such a way that I knew he wanted it, and when I asked him if he wanted me to give it to him, he said yes. So I took it and chewed it to soften it for him and gave it to him. He rubbed his teeth with it more energetically than I had ever seen him rub them before. Then he laid it down. I found him heavy on my breast, and as I looked into his face, lo, his eyes were fixed and he was saying, "No, the most Exalted Companion is of Paradise." I said, "You were given the choice and you have chosen, by Him who sent you with the truth!" And so the Messenger was taken. . . .

Al-Zuhri said, and Sa'id ibn al-Musayyib from Abu Hurayra told me: When the Messenger was dead Umar got up (in the mosque) and said: "Some of the disaffected will allege that the Messenger is dead, but by God, he is not dead: he has gone to his Lord as Moses son of Imran went and was hidden [on Sinai] from his people for forty days. By God, the Messenger will return as Moses returned and will cut off the hands and feet of men who allege that the Messenger is dead." When Abu Bakr heard what had happened he came to the door of the mosque as Umar was speaking to the people. He paid no attention but went into Aisha's room to the Apostle, who was lying covered by a mantle of Yemeni cloth. He went and uncovered his face and kissed him saying, "You are dearer than my father and mother. You have tasted the death that God had decreed; a second death will never overtake you."

Then he replaced the mantle over the Apostle's face and went out. Umar was still speaking and Abu Bakr said, "Gently, Umar, be quiet." But Umar refused and went on talking, and when Abu Bakr saw that he would not be silent, he went forward himself to the people who, when they heard his words, came to him and left Umar. Giving thanks and praise to God, he said: "O men, if anyone worships Muhammad, Muhammad is dead; if anyone worships God, God is alive, immortal." Then he recited this verse: "Muhammad is nothing but an Apostle. Apostles have passed away before him. Can it be that if he were to die or be killed you would turn back on your heels? He who turns back does no harm to God and God will reward the grateful" (Quran 3:144). By God, it was as if the people did not know that this verse had not come down until Abu Bakr recited it that day. The people took it from him and it was constantly on their tongues. Umar said, "By God, when I heard Abu Bakr recite those words I was dumbfounded so that my legs would not bear me and I fell to the ground realizing that the Messenger was indeed dead." (*Life* 1000–1013) [IBN ISHAQ 1955: 678–683].

44. The Beginning of the Muslim Era

In his Traces of the Past *the Muslim chronographer Biruni (d. 1048 C.E.) reports the traditions concerning the beginning of the reckoning of a special era for Muslims.*

The era of the Hijra [or Emigration] of the Prophet Muhammad from Mecca to Medina is based upon lunar years, in which the commencements of months are determined by the (actual) appearance of the new moon and not by calculation. It is used by the whole Muslim world. The circumstances under which this point was adopted as an epoch and not the time when the Prophet was either born, or was entrusted with his divine mission, or died, were the following. Maymun ibn Mihran relates that Umar ibn al-Khattab [Caliph, 634–644 C.E.], when people one day handed him a check payable in the month of Sha῾ban, said: "Which Sha῾ban is meant? The one in which we are or the next Sha῾ban?"

Thereupon he assembled the Companions of the Prophet and asked their advice regarding the matter of chronology, which troubled his mind. . . . Then Umar spoke to the Companions of the Prophet: "Establish a mode of dating for the intercourse of people." Now some said, "Date according to the era of the Greeks, for they date according to the era of Alexander." Others objected that this mode was too lengthy, and said, "Date according to the era of the Persians." But then it was objected that as soon as a new king arises among the Persians he abolishes the era of his predecessor. So they could not come to an agreement.

Aisha relates that Abu Musa al-Ash'ari wrote to Umar ibn al-Khattab: "You send us letters without a date." Umar had already organized the (government) registers, had established the taxes and regulations, and was in want of an era, not liking the old ones. On this occasion he assembled the Companions and took their advice. Now the most authentic date, which involves no obscurities or possible mishaps, seemed to be the date of the Hijra of the Prophet, and of his arrival at Medina on Monday, the eighth day of the month First Rabi', while the beginning of the year was a Thursday. Now he adopted this epoch and fixed thereby the dates in all his affairs. This happened in 17 of the Era of the Hijra [that is, 638 C.E.].

The reason why Umar selected this event as an epoch, and not the time of the birth of the Prophet, or the time when he was entrusted with his divine mission, is this, that regarding those two dates there was such a divergency of opinion as did not allow it to be made the basis of something which must be agreed upon universally. . . . Considering further that after the Hijra the affairs of Islam were thoroughly established, while heathenism decreased, that the Prophet was saved from the calamities prepared for him by the infidels of Mecca, and that after the Hijra his conquests followed each other in rapid succession, we come to the conclusion that the Hijra was to the Prophet what to kings is their accession and their taking possession of the whole sovereign power. (al-Biruni, *Traces of the Past* [BIRUNI 1879: 34–35]

45. Muhammad and Islam: An Early Christian Summary

The rapid Muslim conquest of the Near East made the Christians there quickly aware of the military and political aspects of the new Islamic society under which they would henceforward live. It took somewhat longer for them to come to an understanding, however imperfect, of the religious message that stood behind the conquest. The earliest to have attempted to put Islam into some kind of religious perspective was the Christian monk and theologian John of Damascus. He was well equipped to do so, since his family had already served in the Muslim administration of his native city, and John himself appears to have known Arabic and to have studied not only the Quran but also the Prophetic traditions. The result was a full-scale polemical assault on the new religion, which is taken up in Chapters 100–101 of John's On Heresies, written in 743 C.E., a little more than a century after the death of Muhammad.

There is also the still-prevailing deceptive superstition of the Ishmaelites, the forerunner of the Antichrist. It takes its origin from Ishmael, who was born to Abraham from Hagar, and that is why they also call them Hagarenes and Ishmaelites. They also call them Saracens, allegedly for having been sent away by Sarah empty; for Hagar said to the angel, "Sarah has sent me away empty." These then were the idolators, and they venerated the morning star and Aphrodite, whom notably they called *Khabar* in their own language, which means "great"; therefore until the time of (the Emperor) Heraclius they were undoubtedly idolators.

From that time a false prophet appeared among them, surnamed Mamed, who, having been casually exposed to the Old and the New Testament, and supposedly encountered an Arian monk, formed a heresy of his own. And after, by pretense, he managed to make the people think of him as a God-fearing fellow, he spread rumors that a Scripture was brought down to him from heaven. Thus, having drafted some pronouncements in his book, worthy (only) of laughter, he handed it down to them in order that they might comply with it.

He says that there exists one God, Maker of all, who was neither begotten nor has He begotten. He says that Christ is the Word of God and His Spirit, created and a servant, and that he was born without a seed from Mary, the sister of Moses and Aaron. For, he says, the Word of God and the Spirit entered Mary and she gave birth to Jesus who was a prophet and a servant of God. And that the Jews, having themselves violated the Law, wanted to crucify him and after they arrested him they crucified his shadow; but Christ himself, they say, was not crucified nor did he die; for God took him up to Himself into heaven because He loved him. And this is what he says, that when Jesus went up to the heavens, God questioned him, saying: "O Jesus, did you say that 'I am the Son of God and God'?" And Jesus, they say, answered: "Be merciful to me, Lord; You know that I did not say so, nor will I boast that I am your servant;

but men who have gone astray wrote that I made the statement, and they said lies against me and they have been in error." And God, they say, answered him: "I knew that you would not say this thing."

If this was one of the earliest Christian experiences of the Muslim religion, it must also have been the Muslims' first encounter with a sophisticated Christian refutation of their claims.

And although he (Muhammad) includes in this writing many more absurdities worthy of laughter, he insists that this was brought down to him from God. And we ask: "And which is the one who gives witness, that God has given to him the Scriptures? And which of the prophets foretold that such a prophet would arise? And because they are surprised and at a loss, (we tell them) that Moses received the Law by the side of Mount Sinai in the sight of all the people when God appeared in a cloud and fire and darkness and storm, and that all the prophets, starting from Moses and onward, foretold of the advent of Christ and that Christ is God and that the Son of God will come by taking up flesh and that he will be crucified and that he will die and that he will be asked to judge the living and the dead alike." And when, then, we ask, "How is it that your prophet did not come this way, by having others bearing witness to him . . . so that you too have an assurance?" they reply that God does whatever He pleases. "This," we say, "is what we also know; but how did the Scripture come down to your prophet, this is what we are asking?" And they answer that while he was asleep the Scripture came down upon him. . . .

Moreover, they call us "Associators" because, they say, we introduce beside God an associate to Him by saying that Christ is the Son of God and God. To whom we answer that this is what the prophets and Scripture have handed down to us; and you, as you claim, accept the prophets. If therefore we say that Christ is the Son of God, they also were wrong who taught and handed it down to us so. And some of them mention that we have added such things, by having allegorized the prophets. Others hold that the Jews, out of hatred, deceived us with writings which supposedly originated from the prophets, so that we might get lost. . . .

They also defame us as being idolators because we venerate the Cross, which they despise; and we respond to them: "How is it that you rub yourselves against a stone by your *Chabatha* [that is, the Ka'ba], and you express your adoration for the stone by kissing it?" And some of them answer that it was because Abraham had intercourse with Hagar on it; others, because he tied his camel around it when he was about to sacrifice

Isaac. And we respond to them: "Since the Scripture says that there was a wooded mountain and timber, from which Abraham cut even for the holocaust of Isaac, and that he also left the asses behind with the servants, whence, then, is your idle tale? For in that place (of the Haram) there is neither wood from a forest nor do asses pass through." And they are embarrassed. They maintain nonetheless that the stone is of Abraham. Then we respond: "Suppose that it is of Abraham, as you foolishly maintain; are you not ashamed to kiss it for the sole reason that Abraham had intercourse with a woman upon it, or because he tied his camel to it, and yet you blame us for venerating the Cross of Christ, through which the power of the demons and the deceit of the devil has been destroyed?" This, then, which they call "stone" is the head of Aphrodite, whom they used to venerate (and) whom they called Chaber, on which those who understand it exactly can see traces of engraving even to this day.

John then turns his attention to the Quran, on which he is obviously informed in some detail. Equally obviously, his choice of details—Sura 4 contains 177 verses—is dictated by polemical considerations. Moreover, the themes he chose were to have an extremely long life in the Christian argument against Islam.

This Muhammad, as has been mentioned, composed many idle tales, on each one of which he prefixed a title, like for example the discourse (called) "The Woman" (Sura 4) in which he clearly legislates that one may have four wives and, if he can, one thousand concubines, as many as he can maintain beside his four wives; and that one can divorce whomsoever he pleases, if he so wishes, and have another (wife in her place). He made this law because of the following case (Quran 33:37). Muhammad had a comrade named Zayd. This man had a beautiful wife with whom Muhammad fell in love. While they were once sitting together Muhammad said to him, "O you, God has commanded me to take your wife." And he (Zayd) replied, "You are a Messenger; do as God has told you; take my wife."

After mocking the story of a camel that turns up in a number of suras (7:77; 26:141–159; 101:14), John touches upon "The Table Spread" of Sura 5:114.

Muhammad also talks about the Discourse of the Table. He says that Christ requested from God a table, and it was given to him. Because, he says, He told him, "I have given to you and your (companions) an incorruptible table."

Also the Discourse of the Cow (Sura 2), and several other tales worthy of laughter, which, because of their number, I think I should skip.

He made a law that they and the women should be circumcised, and he commanded (them) neither to observe the Sabbath, nor to be baptized and, on the one hand, to eat what was forbidden in the Law and, on the other, to abstain from others (which the Law permits); he also forbade the drinking of wine altogether. (John of Damascus, *On Heresies* 100–101) [SAHAS 1972: 133–141]

46. Maimonides on Muhammad

We have already seen in Chapter 2 the common interpretation of the "little horn" of Daniel's apocalyptic vision as referring to Antiochus Epiphanes. That connection, however, is nowhere stated explicitly in the text—an attractive ambiguity that permitted the vision to be later construed in other, no less political ways. After the seventh century of the Christian era one commonplace interpretation of the prophecy was that it referred to the rise of Islam, as we have noted in one exegetical text. It was also understood in that fashion by Maimonides (d. 1204 C.E.), the Jewish scholar who spent all of his life under Islamic sovereignty.

This event [that is, the rise of Islam] was predicted in the divinely inspired prophecy of Daniel, according to which a person would one day appear with a religion similar to the true one, and with a book of Scriptures and oral communications, and he will arrogantly pretend that God has granted a revelation to him, and indeed that he has spoken with Him, as well as other extravagant claims. In this manner, when he was describing the rise of the Arab kingdom after the fall of the Roman Empire (in the seventh century C.E.), he referred to the appearance of the Madman (Muhammad) and his victories over the Roman, Persian and Byzantine Empires in his vision of the horn which grew and became long and strong. This is clear from a verse which can be understood by the masses as well as by the select few. Since this interpretation is borne out by the facts of history, no other meaning can be attributed to the following verse: "I considered the horns, and behold, there came among them another horn, a little one, before which three of the first horns were plucked up by the roots; and behold, in this horn were eyes like the eyes of man, and a mouth speaking great things" (Dan. 7:8).

Now consider how remarkably apt is the imagery (of this verse). Daniel says he saw a small horn that was growing. When it became longer, even remarkably longer, it cast down before it the (other) three horns and behold, in the side of the horn there were two eyes like the eyes of a man, and a mouth speaking bold words. This obviously refers to someone who will found a new religion similar to the divine Law, and make claims to a revelation of a Scripture, and to prophecy. He will, furthermore, attempt to alter and abolish the Law, as it is said, "And he will seek to change the seasons and the law" (Dan. 7:25). (Maimonides, *Letter to the Yemen*)

47. A Muslim's Appreciation of Muhammad

Both the Christian John of Damascus and the Jew Maimonides are hostile witnesses on the Prophet of Islam. The Prophet appeared quite differently in the eyes of his followers, of course, and the accents of reverence and respect of the earliest of them still echo through the pages of Ibn Ishaq's Life of the Apostle of God. *Nor did the reverence or the respect diminish over the centuries. This, for example, is how Muhammad and his work appeared in the eyes of al-Damiri, an Egyptian writer who died in 1405 C.E.*

Historians record that the first who ever undertook to be a true leader of the (Arab) people was the Prophet, upon whom be God's blessing and peace. God sent him after a long break (in the succession of Messengers) to be a mercy to mankind, and he delivered His message. He strove with true diligence in the cause of God, gave proper advice to the people, and served his Lord till death came to him. He was the most favored of all creatures, the noblest of the Messengers, the Prophet of Mercy, the leader of convinced believers, who on the Day will bear the Standard of Praise, be the general intercessor, occupy the glorious station, have the pool which many will frequent, and gather under his banner Adam and all who came after him.

He is the best of Prophets and his community is the best of communities. His Companions are, after the Prophets, the choicest of mankind, and his is the noblest of sects. He performed astonishing miracles, possessed great natural abilities, had a sound and powerful intelligence, a most distinguished genealogy, and perfect beauty. His generosity was boundless, his bravery unchallengeable, his forbearance excessive, his knowledge profitable, his actions ever honorable, his fear of God complete, his piety sublime. He was the most eloquent of men, perfect in every respect, and the furthest of all mankind from things base and vicious. Of him the poet has said:

"None like Muhammad has the Merciful ever created,
Nor such, to my thinking, will He ever again create."

Aisha, with whom may God be pleased, said: "The Prophet, upon whom be God's blessing and peace, when he was at home used to be at the service of his household, that is, he used to act as servant to them. He used to delouse his own clothes and patch them, mend his own sandals and serve himself. He used to see to the feeding of his own domestic camel, sweep the house with a broom, hobble the camel, eat with the servant and help her knead her dough, and used to carry his own purchases home from the market." Moreover, he, upon whom be God's blessing and peace, used to be continually in grief, ever occupied by anxious thought, never having any rest. . . .

It is said that his death, upon him be God's blessing and peace, took place after God had perfected our religion for us and brought to completion His favor to us, at midday on the 12th of the month of First Rabi' in the year 11 A.H. [632 C.E.], when he, upon whom be God's blessing and peace, was sixty-three years of age. Ali ibn Abi Talib took charge of washing him for burial, and he was interred in the apartment of Aisha, the Mother of the Believers, with whom may God be pleased. (Damiri, *The Book of Animals* 1.40–41) [JEFFERY 1962: 331–332]

5. "A Kingdom of Priests and a Holy Nation"

From Adam to Abraham, the Bible sketches what appears to be a history of all mankind, as viewed from the perspective of that time and that place. But when the account reaches the generation of Abraham, God pronounces a choice, or, perhaps, since the notion of exclusion is not stressed in the narrative at that point, God displays His particular favor toward Abraham and his descendants. That favor was to be shown in two ways, both highly appropriate to the small seminomadic clan constituted by Abraham and his family: they would increase in number, and they would someday come into possession of a land of their own. For his part, Abraham was bound to the circumcision of the males among his kin. What else might be required of the children of Abraham by way of reciprocation for the favor of God is not spelled out in Genesis, but over the following half-millennium or so, when the biblical account focuses almost exclusively upon Abraham's clan, those details are supplied: the Promise is succeeded by a Covenant, and the terms it imposed upon the growing number of those who called themselves "Children of Israel" were laid down in their fullest form by the Lord once Moses had led the Israelites from their bondage in Egypt.

1. Holiness and the Covenant

To put it most generally, the Children of Israel were set apart by virtue of their holiness: they will be, in God's own striking phrase, a "nation of priests."

On the third new moon after the Israelites had gone forth from the land of Egypt, on that very day, they entered the wilderness of Sinai. Having journeyed from Rephidim, they entered the wilderness of Sinai and encamped in the wilderness. Israel encamped there in front of the mountain, and Moses went up to God. The Lord called to him from the mountain, saying, "Thus shall you say to the house of Jacob and declare to the children of Israel. 'You have seen what I did to the Egyptians, how I bore you on eagles' wings and brought you to Me. Now, then, if you will obey Me faithfully and keep My Covenant, you shall be My treasured possession among all the peoples. Indeed, all the earth is Mine, but you shall be to Me a kingdom of priests and a holy nation.' These are the words that you shall speak to the children of Israel." (Exodus 19:1–6)

The Lord spoke to Moses, saying: Speak to the Israelite people and say to them:

"I am the Lord your God. You shall not copy the practices of the land of Egypt where you dwelt, or of the land of Canaan to which I am taking you; nor shall you follow their laws. My rules alone shall you observe, and faithfully follow My laws: I am the Lord your God.

"You shall keep My laws and My rules, by the pursuit of which man shall live: I am the Lord." (Leviticus 18:1–5)

Do not defile yourselves in any of those ways [described in Lev. 18:6–23], for it is by such that the nations which I am casting out before you defiled themselves. Thus the land became defiled; and I called it to account for its iniquity, and the land spewed out its inhabitants. But you, unlike them, must keep My laws and My rules, and you must not do any of those abhorrent things, neither the citizen nor the stranger who resides among you; for all these abhorrent things were done by the people who were in the land before you and the land became defiled. So let not the land spew you out for defiling it, as it spewed out the nations that came before you. All who do any of these abhorrent things—such persons shall be cut off from their people. You shall keep my charge not to engage in any of the abhorrent practices that were carried out before you, and you shall not defile yourselves through them: I am the Lord your God. (Leviticus 18:24–30)

2. God's Final Punishment of Disobedience

That these are not simply counsels or recommendations is likewise made unmistakably clear.

And if, despite this, you disobey Me and remain hostile to Me, I will act against you in wrathful hostility; I for my part will discipline you seven times for your sins. You shall eat the flesh of your sons and the flesh of your daughters. I will destroy your cult places and cut down your incense stands, and I will heap your carcasses upon your lifeless fetishes. I will spurn you. I will lay your cities in ruin and make your sanctuaries deso-

late, and I will not savor your pleasing odors. I will make the land deso-
late, so that your enemies who settle in it shall be appalled by it. And you
I will scatter among the nations and I will unsheath the sword against you.
Your land shall become a desolation and your cities a ruin. . . . As for
those of you who survive, I will cast a faintness into their hearts in the
land of their enemies. The sound of a driven leaf shall put them to flight.
Fleeing as though from the sword, they shall fall though none pursues.
With no one pursuing, they shall stumble over one another as before the
sword. You shall not be able to stand your ground before your enemies,
but you shall perish among the nations; and the land of your enemies shall
consume you.

. . . Then at last shall their obdurate heart humble itself, and they
shall atone for their iniquity. Then will I remember My Covenant with
Jacob; I will remember also My Covenant with Isaac, and also My Covenant with Abraham; and I will remember the land. . . . Even then, when
they are in the land of their enemies, I will not reject them or spurn them
so as to destroy them, annulling My Covenant with them: for I am the
Lord their God. I will remember in their favor the Covenant with the
ancients, whom I freed from the land of Egypt in the sight of their nations
to be their God: I, the Lord.

These are the laws, rules and directions that the Lord established,
through Moses on Mount Sinai, between Himself and the Israelite people.
(Leviticus 26:27–46)

3. The Chosen People

*God had settled His Covenant, with all its demands, promised rewards, and threat-
ened punishments, on the children of Abraham—Isaac in the first generation, and
then Jacob and his offspring. And despite intimations by the prophets and insistence
by the Christians of an extension to the Gentiles, there it remained, at least in Jewish
eyes. Counterclaims to the notion of a "chosen people" come up in an interesting
context in a dialogue written by Judah Halevi in 1130–1140 C.E., when Christians
were on the offensive in Spain, the author's homeland, and in possession of the holy
places in Jerusalem. The questioner is an imaginary king of Khazars who is investi-
gating the claims of various religions, and the respondent is a rabbi who speaks for
Judah Halevi himself.*

The Khazar King: . . . The perfection of his [Moses'] work was
marred by the fact that his book was written in Hebrew, which made it
unintelligible to the peoples of Sind, India and Khazar. They would,
therefore, be unable to practice all his laws until some centuries had

elapsed, or they had been prepared for it by changes of conquest or alliance, but not through the revelation of the prophet himself, or another who would stand up for him and testify to his law.

The Rabbi: Moses invited only *his* people and those of his own tongue to accept the law, while God promised that at all times there should be prophets to expound His law. This He did as long as they found favor in His sight and His presence was with them.

The Khazar King: Would it not have been better or more commensurate with divine wisdom if all mankind had been guided on the true path?

The Rabbi: Or would it not have been best for all animals to have been reasonable beings? You have apparently forgotten what we said previously concerning Adam's progeny, and how the spirit of divine prophecy rested on one person (in each generation), who was chosen from his brethren and was the essence of his father. It was he on whom this divine light was concentrated. He was the kernel, while the others were as husks which had no share in it. (All) the sons of Jacob were, however, distinguished from other people by godly qualities, which made them, so to speak, an angelic caste. . . . We do not deny that the good actions of any man, to whichever people he may belong, will be rewarded by God. But the priority belongs to people who are near God during their life, and we estimate the rank they occupy after death accordingly.

After this preliminary exploration of the concept of a chosen people and its limitations, the discussion turns in the direction of the social consequences of such a notion. Do we not have a right to expect that God's people of choice would be so signaled by their position in the world, the Khazar king asks.

The Rabbi: I see you reproaching us with our degradation and poverty, while the best of other religions boast of both (high station in this world and the next). Do they not glorify him [that is, Jesus] who said: "He who strikes you on the right cheek, turn to him the left also; and he who takes your coat, let him have your shirt as well" (Matt. 5:39–40)? He and his friends and followers, after hundreds of years of contumely, flogging and slaying, attained their well-known success, and in the very things they glorify. This is also the history of the founder of Islam [that is, Muhammad] and his friends, who eventually prevailed and became powerful. The nations boast of these, but not of those kings whose power and might are great, whose walls are strong and whose chariots are terrible. Yet our relation to God is a closer one than if we had reached greatness already on earth.

The Khazar King: This might be so, if your humility were voluntary; but it is involuntary, and if you had power you would slay.

The Rabbi: You have touched our weak spot, O King of the Khazars. If the majority of us, as you say, would learn humility toward God and His Law from our low station, Providence would not have forced us to bear it for such a long period. Only the smallest portion (of us) thinks this; the majority may expect reward, because they bear their degradation, partly from necessity, partly from their own free will. . . . If we bear our exile and degradation for God's sake, as is meet, we shall be the pride of the generation which will come with the Messiah, and accelerate the day of deliverance we hope for.

Now we do not allow anyone who embraces our religion theoretically by means of word alone to take equal rank with ourselves, but demand actual self-sacrifice, purity, knowledge, circumcision and numerous religious ceremonies. The convert must adopt our way of life entirely. . . . Those, however, who become Jews do not take equal rank with born Israelites, who are specially privileged to attain to prophecy, while the former can only achieve something by learning from them, and become pious and learned, but never prophets. (Judah Halevi, *The Khazar King*) [HALEVI 1905: 72–79]

4. A Muslim Wonders about the "Children of God"

When the Muslim essayist al-Jahiz (d. 868 C.E.), in his Refutation of the Christians, *came to the question of Jesus as Son of God, he was quickly drawn into the larger question of the divine paternity and the use made of it by the Jews in their Covenant history.*

In general, we cannot grant that God has a son, either by carnal begetting or by adoption. To concede that would be to manifest enormous ignorance, indeed, to commit blasphemy. Thus, if God is Jacob's father, then He must be Joseph's grandfather, and once we admit that He can be a father and a grandfather, even without conceding actual (physical) paternity, and introduce some complication or otherwise lessen His divine majesty and magnitude, we are then forced to concede that He is a paternal and maternal uncle; for if it is proper (as in the case of Jacob) to call God father by reason of His mercy, His affection for a person of His own choosing and His willingness to raise him, then it must be equally appropriate for someone who wishes to honor Him and acknowledge His superiority and mastery over the whole of creation to call him brother and find a companion and friend for Him. Now this is lawful only for someone who does not acknowledge God's greatness and man's insignificance compared to Him. . . .

There is another side to this question, which will show you how well based my argument is. Had God known that in the Books which He revealed to the Israelites the following words occurred: "Your father was my firstborn, and you are the children of my firstborn," he would not have been angry when they said: "We are God's children." For how could God's son's son be anything else than God's grandson? That would have been a mark of complete respect and perfect love, all the more because He Himself said in the Torah, "The Israelites are the children of My firstborn son." Thus it is clear that when the (pagan) Arabs asserted that the angels were God's daughters (Quran 16:59), God regarded this belief as a grave sin and manifested His anger against those who had said it, even though He was well aware that they did not impute them to Him as the offspring of His flesh. How then can we suppose that God declared beforehand to His creatures that Jacob was His son, like Solomon, or Ezra or Jesus? God is too great to have paternity among His attributes, and man is too contemptible to claim to have been begotten of God. (Jahiz, *Refutation of the Christians* 143–144)

5. The Restoration of Israel's Holiness after the Exile

The restoration of Israel in Judea after 538 B.C.E. required more than simply bringing back numbers of the former population. The Israelites had also to be reconstituted as a community, a complex act that involved in the first instance the revival of the worship of the God of Israel in the sanctified place atop Mount Moriah, the rebuilding of the Temple, and the restoration of the priesthoods and Levitical orders—in short, a renewal of the Covenant (see Chapter 2 above). But if renewal and restoration were one part of the program, purification, and thus inevitably separation, was another. A fastidious observance of the Sabbath commandment was one instrument to achieve this end, as we shall see, but the problem of mixed marriages, whether of the returnees or of those Israelites who had remained behind in Judea, was perhaps more complex and its solution in the end more painful. The narrative is Ezra's.

. . . The officers approached me, saying, "The people of Israel and the priests and Levites have not separated themselves from the peoples of the land whose abhorrent practices are like those of the Canaanites, the Hittites, the Perizzites, the Jebusites, the Ammonites, the Moabites, the Egyptians and the Amorites. They have taken their daughters as wives for themselves and for their sons, so that the holy seed has become inter-mingled with the peoples of the land; and it is the officers and prefects who have taken the lead in this trespass."

When I heard this, I rent my garment and robe, I tore hair out of my head and beard, and I sat desolate. Around me gathered all who were concerned with the words of the God of Israel because of the returning exiles' trespass, while I sat desolate until the evening offering. At the time of the evening offering I ended my self-affliction; still in my torn garments and robe, I got down on my knees and spread out my hands to the Lord my God. . . . "Bondsmen we are, though even in our bondage God has not forsaken us, but has disposed the king of Persia favorably toward us, to furnish us with sustenance and to raise again the House of our God, repairing its ruins and giving us a hold in Judah and Jerusalem.

"Now, what can we say in the face of this, O our God, for we have forsaken your commandments, which You gave us through Your servants the prophets when You said, 'The land which you are about to possess is a land unclean through uncleanness of the peoples of the land, through their abhorrent practices with which they, in their impurity, have filled it from one end to the other. Now, then, do not give your daughters in marriage to their sons or let their daughters marry your sons; do nothing for their well-being or their advantage, then you will be strong and enjoy the bounty of the land and bequeath it to your children forever.' " (Ezra 9:1–12)

While Ezra was praying and making confession, weeping and pros-trating himself before the House of God, a very great crowd of Israelites gathered about him, men, women and children; the people were weeping bitterly. Then Shecaniah son of Jehiel of the family of Elam spoke up and said to Ezra, "We have trespassed against God by bringing into our homes foreign women from the peoples of the land; but there is still hope for Israel despite this. Now, then, let us make a covenant with our God to expel all these women and those who have been born to them, in accor-dance with the bidding of the Lord and of all who are concerned over the commandment of our God, and let the Torah be obeyed. Take action, for the responsibility is yours and we are with you. Act with resolve!"

. . . Then a proclamation was issued in Judah and Jerusalem that all who had returned from the exile should assemble in Jerusalem, and that anyone who did not come in three days would, by a decision of the officers and elders, have his property confiscated and himself excluded from the congregation of the returning exiles.

All the men of Judah and Benjamin assembled in Jerusalem in three days; it was the ninth month, the twentieth of the month. All the people sat in the square of the House of God, trembling on account of the event and because of the rains. Then Ezra the priest got up and said to them, "You have trespassed by bringing home foreign women, thus aggravating the guilt of Israel. So now, make confession to the Lord, God of your fathers, and do His will, and separate yourselves from the peoples of the land and from the foreign women."

The entire congregation responded in a loud voice, "We must surely do just as you say. However, many people are involved, and it is the rainy season; it is not possible to remain in the open, nor is this the work of a day or two, because we have transgressed extensively in this matter. Let our officers remain on behalf of the entire congregation, and all our townspeople who have brought home foreign women shall appear before them at scheduled times, together with the elders and judges of each town, in order to avert the burning anger of our God from us on this account. . . . "

The returning exiles did so. Ezra and the men who were the chiefs of the ancestral clans—all listed by name—sequestered themselves on the first day of the tenth month to study the matter. By the first day of the first month they were done with all the men who had brought home foreign women. (Ezra 9:1–10:17)

In the Book of Nehemiah, as well, the problem of the intermingling of the Israelites with foreigners in their land is raised and addressed, at first as part of the people's formal renewal of their Covenant with God.

(We) . . . take an oath with sanctions to follow the Torah of God . . . namely: we will not give our daughters in marriage to the peoples of the land, or take their daughters for our sons. The peoples of the land who bring their wares and all sorts of foodstuffs for sale on the sabbath day— we will not buy from them on the sabbath or a holy day. We will forgo (the produce of) the seventh year, and every outstanding debt. (Nehemiah 10:30–31).

Later it is Nehemiah himself who speaks.

At that time I saw men in Judah treading winepresses on the sabbath, and others bringing heaps of grain and loading them on asses, also wine, grapes, figs, and all sorts of goods, and bringing them into Jerusalem on the sabbath. I admonished them there and then for selling provisions. Tyrians who lived there brought fish and all sorts of wares and sold them on the sabbath to the Judahites in Jerusalem. I censured the nobles of

Judah, saying to them, "What evil thing is this that you are doing, profaning the sabbath day! This is what your ancestors did, and for it God
brought all this misfortune on this city; and now you give cause for
further wrath against Israel by profaning the sabbath!"

When shadows filled the gateways of Jerusalem at the approach of
the sabbath, I gave orders that the doors be closed, and ordered them not
to be opened until after the sabbath. I stationed some of my servants at
the gates, so that no goods should enter on the sabbath. . . . I gave orders
to the Levites to purify themselves and come and guard the gates, to
preserve the sanctity of the sabbath. . . .

Also at that time, I saw that Jews had married Ashodite, Ammonite
and Moabite women; a good number of their children spoke the language
of Ashod and the language of those various peoples, and did not know
how to speak Judean. I censured them, cursed them, flogged them, tore
out their hair, and adjured them by God, saying, "You shall not give your
daughters in marriage to their sons, or take any of their daughters for
your sons or yourselves. It was just in such things that King Solomon of
Israel sinned! Among the many nations there was not a king like him, and
so well loved was he by his God that God made him king of all Israel, yet
foreign wives caused even him to sin. How, then, can we acquiesce in
your doing this great wrong, breaking faith with our God by marrying
foreign women?"

One of the sons of Joiada son of the high priest Eliashib was a
son-in-law of Sanballat the Horonite; I drove him away from me. Remember to their discredit, O God, how they polluted the priesthood, the
covenant of the priests and Levites. I purged them of every foreign element, and arranged for the priests and Levites to work each at his tasks
by shifts, and for the wood offering (to be brought) at fixed times, and for
the firstfruits. (Nehemiah 13:15–31)

6. Conversion

As related by Ezra and Nehemiah, the return of the Israelites from exile in Babylo-
nia was accompanied by an effort to restore Judaism to its older ethnic basis by
dissolving the marriages that had inevitably occurred between the Jews living abroad
and the native non-Jewish peoples who were their hosts. But not all the Jews had
returned from Babylon; nor did other Jews cease to choose or to be constrained to
a life outside the geographical boundaries of Eretz Israel. From the perspective of
the "ethnic purists," the growth of Diaspora Judaism led to the inevitable dilution
of the tribal heritage of the Covenant. But it also gave rise to an increasing interest

in Judaism on the part of the Gentiles, most notably perhaps from the Hellenes and the Hellenized, with their own new sophistication and openness to the previously scorned manners and customs of the "barbarians." The phenomenon was remarked upon by the historian Josephus, writing toward the end of the first Christian century.

There is not one city, Greek or barbarian, to which our custom of abstaining from work on the seventh day has not spread, and where the fasts and the lighting of lamps and many of our prohibitions in the matter of food are not observed. Moreover, they attempt to imitate our unanimity, our liberal charities, our devoted labor in the crafts, our endurance under persecution on behalf of our laws. (Josephus, *Against Apion* 2.38)

The Jews were not oblivious to what was happening or, as it appears, indifferent to it. Matthew has Jesus say in the course of a long diatribe against the Pharisees, "Alas for you, lawyers and Pharisees, hypocrites! You travel over sea and land to make one convert; and when you have won him, you make him twice as fit for hell as yourselves" (Matt. 24:15). Post-Exilic Judaism unmistakably encouraged conversion, for a time at least, and set out the provisions whereby the Gentile might become, by affiliation, a member of the Chosen People.

Rabbi says: Just as Israel did not enter the Covenant except through three things, through circumcision, through immersion and through the acceptance of sacrifice, so it was the same with the proselytes. (Sifre on Numbers 108)

The "acceptance of sacrifice" makes it certain that we are dealing here with a pre–70 C.E. perspective on the conditions of conversion, just as the following Talmudic text, which sets forth the actual procedure of formal conversion and yet makes no mention of sacrifice, must reflect the conditions prevailing after the destruction of the Temple.

Our rabbis taught: A proselyte who comes to convert at this time, we say to him: Why did you decide to convert? Do you know that Israel at this time is afflicted, oppressed, downtrodden, and rejected, and that tribulations are visited upon them? If he says, "I am aware, but I am unworthy," we accept him immediately, and we make known to him a few of the lighter commandments and a few of the weightier commandments, and we make known to him the penalty for transgression of gleaning (the poor man's share of the harvest), the forgotten (sheaves), the corner, and the poor man's tithe. And we make known to him the punishment for violating the commandments. . . . And just as we make known to him the punishment for violating the commandments, so also we make known to him their reward. . . . We are not too lengthy with him nor are we too detailed. If he accepts this, we circumcise him immediately. . . . Once he has recovered (from circumcision), we immerse him immediately. And two scholars stand over him and make known to him some of the lighter and some of the weightier commandments. If he is immersed validly, he is like an Israelite in all matters. (In the case of a woman) women position her in the water up to her neck, and two scholars stand outside and make known to her some of the lighter commandments and some of the weightier commandments. (BT.Yebamoth 47a–b)

7. The Pharisaic Program: Separate as Holy

Despite the Lord's avowed intention of creating all Israel as "a nation of priests," the Torah legislation given to the Israelites seems to envision a body of priests maintaining a special and high degree of purity within Israelite society. If the cited passages in Exodus and Leviticus were the ideal, then many centuries passed before it was constituted, if not a reality, then at least a possibility. The responsibility for this profound transformation at the heart of Judaism appears to have been the work of that somewhat mysterious group of men called Pharisees, the same who were so severely taken to task by Jesus. There would be no mystery to the Pharisees if we were simply to read Josephus' clear and coherent description.

The Jews, from the most ancient times, had three philosophies pertaining to their traditions, that of the Essenes, that of the Sadducees, and thirdly, that of a group called the Pharisees. . . . The Pharisees simplify their standard of living, making no concession to luxury. They follow the guidance of that which their doctrine has selected and transmitted as good, attaching the chief importance to the observance of those commandments which it has seen fit to dictate to them. They show respect and deference to their elders, nor do they rashly presume to contradict their proposals.

Though they postulate that everything is brought about by fate, still they do not deprive the human will of the pursuit of what is in man's power, since it was God's good pleasure that there should be a fusion and that the will of man with his virtue and vice should be admitted to the council chamber of fate. They believe that souls have the power to survive death and that there are rewards and punishments under the earth for those who have led lives of virtue and vice: eternal imprisonment is the lot of evil souls, while the good souls receive an easy passage to a new life. Because of these views they are, as a matter of fact, extremely influential among the townsfolk; and all prayers and sacred rites of divine worship are performed according to their exposition. This is the great tribute that the inhabitants of the cities, by practicing the highest ideals both in their way of living and in their discourse, have paid to the excellence of the Pharisees. (Josephus, *Antiquities* 18.11–13)

According to Josephus, then, the Pharisees were a party of Jews who enjoyed a great deal of popular support in the centuries immediately preceding and following the beginning of the Christian era. They were characterized not only by their theological positions, such as a belief in the afterlife, but also by their respect for and devotion to the Law, both the written Torah and the oral "traditions from the Fathers." The Gospels, as we shall see, are more polemical and disapproving of them than Josephus, who was himself, after all, one of their number. Yet the Gospels' portrait of the Pharisees is not so very different: the Pharisees are punctilious observers of the Law who seek to impose their standards of observance on the whole people.

Neither Josephus nor the Gospels explain the meaning of "Pharisaioi," a transparently foreign term transcribed in Greek. When we turn to the rabbinic sources, we do not find the same transcription; but there occurs throughout a term that easily suggests itself as the original of "Pharisees," namely, perushim, literally "the Separate" or "the Separated." We might be willing to accept this identification of "Pharisees" and the Perushim except for two chief reasons. First, in those rabbinic sources the Perushim do not appear as a cohesive party or association, as they clearly are in the Greek-language texts. Second, the rabbis do not speak very highly of them or of their opinions, which they might reasonably be expected to do of men who were their unmistakable predecessors in the exaltation and refinement of the Law. The matter is not simple, however, as we have already seen. In many texts the rabbinic program hovers over the notion of "separateness," with close verbal associations with perushim, as in these rabbinic comments on the Torah's expression "a holy people."

"Holy": that is, holy and sanctified, *separated* from the world and their abominations. (Mekilta on Exodus 19:9)

"For I am the Lord your God, you shall sanctify yourselves and be holy, for I am holy": that is, even as I am holy, so you shall be holy; even as I am *separate*, so also shall you be *separated* (perushim). (Sifra on Leviticus 11:44)

"You shall sanctify yourselves and be holy": this means the sanctification which consists in *separation* from the heathen. It is nothing other than the sanctification which consists in observing all the commandments, as it says, "You shall be holy." (Sifra on Leviticus 20:7)

"As I am holy, so you shall be (holy)": that is, as I am *separate*, so you shall be *separated* (perushim). If you are *separated* from the nations, you belong to me . . . but if you are not, then you belong to Nebuchadnezzar, king of Babylon, and his companions. (Sifra on Leviticus 20:26)

Separateness from the surrounding heathen is a commonplace prescription repeated again and again in Scripture, as we have seen. What the Pharisees brought to the advice was an attitude toward the heathen within Israel, that is, those people, Jews by birth, whose lack of strict observance rendered them unclean and so unholy, like the "publicans and sinners" with whom Jesus dined. These are the am ha-Aretz, the "commoners of the land" who appear and reappear as the target of the Perushim and of the rabbis themselves throughout the rabbinic writings.

Our rabbis taught: Who is an *am ha-Aretz*? Whoever does not recite the *Shema* morning and evening with its accompanying benedictions. So according to Rabbi Meir. The Sages say, "Whoever does not put on phylacteries." Ben Azzai says, "Whoever has not fringe upon his garment." Rabbi Jonathan ben Joseph says, "Whoever has sons and does not rear them to study Torah." Others say, "Even if he learnt Torah and Mishna and did not attend upon rabbinic scholars, he is an *am ha-Aretz*. If he learned Scripture but not Mishna, he is a boor; if he learnt neither Scripture nor Mishna, concerning him Scripture declares, 'I will sow Israel and Judah with the seed of man and the seed of cattle' (Jer. 31:27))." (BT. Sotah 22a)

8. Jesus on the Pharisees

Although Jesus may have agreed with the end, and indeed even with many of the means, he did not much approve of either the attitudes or the example of the Pharisees of his day. For some of his many criticisms of the Pharisees recorded in the Gospels, we can look particularly to Matthew.

Jesus addressed the people and his disciples in these words: "The doctors of the Law and the Pharisees sit in the chair of Moses: therefore do what they tell you; pay attention to their words. But do not follow their practice; for they say one thing and do another. They make up heavy packs and pile them on men's shoulders, but do not lift a finger to lift the load themselves. Whatever they do is done for show. They go about with broad phylacteries and with large fringe upon their robes; they like to have places of honor at feasts and the chief seats in the synagogues, to be greeted respectfully in the streets, and to be addressed as 'rabbi.' " (Matthew 23:1–7)

Alas for you, lawyers and Pharisees, hypocrites! You pay tithes (even) of mint and dill and cumin; but you have overlooked the weightier demands of the Law, justice, mercy and good faith. It is those you should have practiced, without neglecting the others. Blind guides! You strain off a gnat (from your drink), yet gulp down a camel!

Alas for you, lawyers and Pharisees, hypocrites! You clean the outside of the cup and dish, which you have filled inside by robbery and self-indulgence. Clean the inside of the cup first; then the outside will be clean also.

Alas for you, lawyers and Pharisees, hypocrites! You are like tombs covered with whitewash; they look well from the outside, but inside they are full of dead men's bones and all kinds of filth. So it is with you: outside you look like honest men, but inside you are brim-full with hypocrisy and crime. (Matthew 23:23–28)

As he passed from there, Jesus saw a man named Matthew at his seat in the customhouse, and said to him, "Follow me"; and Matthew rose and followed him. When Jesus was at table in the house, many bad characters, tax gatherers and others, were seated with him and his disciples. The Pharisees noticed this, and said to his disciples, "Why is it that your master eats with tax gatherers and sinners?" Jesus heard it and said, "It is not the healthy that need a doctor, but the sick. Go and learn what the text means, 'I require mercy not sacrifice.' I did not come to invite virtuous people but sinners." (Matthew 9:9–13)

The Pharisees had their own views on tax collectors, those unjust dealers with the Gentiles.

At first they [the Pharisees] used to say: if an associate [or member] becomes a tax collector, he is deprived of his status as an associate. Later they altered this and said: As long as he is a tax collector, he is not considered reliable; once he has withdrawn from being a tax collector, he is reliable. (Tosefta Demai 3:4)

The tax collector was in effect banned from Pharisaic society.

9. Bans and Excommunication

The Torah recognized that there were certain transgressions for which one might atone. Indeed, the whole principle of sin offerings in Israel is based on such a premise. Other acts, however, are of such gravity that, if they were performed knowingly and deliberately, had irremediable and permanent effects, ranging from the death penalty to the separation of the offender from the community. We can observe the distinction at work in this text from Numbers.

In the case of an individual who has sinned unwittingly, he shall offer a she-goat in its first year as a sin offering. The priest shall make expiation before the Lord on behalf of the person who has erred, for he sinned unwittingly, making such expiation for him that he may be forgiven. For the citizen among the Israelites and for the stranger who resides among them—you shall have one ritual for anyone who acts in error.

But the person, be he citizen or stranger, who acts defiantly reviles the Lord; that person shall be cut off from among the people. Because he has spurned the word of the Lord and violated His commandment, that person shall be cut off—he bears his guilt. (Numbers 15:27–31)

In the post-Exilic period, the following action is ascribed to Ezra in the early days of the restoration of the community in Judea.

. . . Then a proclamation was issued in Judah and Jerusalem that all who had returned from the exile should assemble in Jerusalem, and that anyone who did not come in three days would, by a decision of the officers and elders, have his property confiscated and himself excluded from the congregation of the returning exiles. (Ezra 10:7–8)

Ezra and his fellow leaders of the time, whoever exactly is meant by the latter, must have enjoyed the kind of authority that made such an exclusion both plausible and enforceable. That those conditions lasted very long may be doubted, since we hear little more of such acts of excommunication until the rise of fairly well-defined and voluntary sectarian groups like the Pharisees and the community of Qumran, who could use the weapon of exclusion to preserve their own integrity and discipline. The following bans, for example, like the ban on the tax collector cited in the Tosefta, appear to be from the pre-70 C.E. Pharisaic community.

Akabya ben Mahalaleel testified to four opinions. They answered: Akabya, retract these four opinions you have given and we will make you Ab Beth Din [that is, second officer of the Great Sanhedrin]. He said to them: Better that I be called a fool all my days than that I be made a godless man before God even for an hour; for they shall say of me, he retracted for the sake of (gaining) the office. He declared unclean the residuary hair [in a leprosy symptom], and also the yellow blood, while the Sages declare them clean. If the hair of a blemished firstling fell out and one put it in a wall niche and afterwards slaughtered the animal, he used to permit the hair to be used, while the Sages forbade it. . . . Whereupon they laid him under a ban; and he died while he was still under the ban and they stoned his coffin. (M.Eduyoth 5:6)

The same text continues:

Rabbi Judah said: God forbid that it was Akabya who was under the ban! For the gate of the Temple Court was never shut against the face of any man in Israel so wise and God-fearing as Akabya ben Mahalaleel. But whom did they put under a ban? Eleazer ben Enoch, because he cast doubt on (the teaching of the Sages concerning) the cleaning of hands. And when he died the Court sent and laid a stone on his coffin; whence we learn that if any man is put under a ban and dies while yet under the ban, his coffin must be stoned.

If the grounds in the cases of the tax collector, Akabya, and Eleazer ben Enoch all seem appropriately Pharisaic—all variations on the theme of ritual purity (though the first case has to do with contracting it and the latter two with teaching on the subject)—we do not know what form the ban had or whether it had any set term. It did not, certainly, disqualify one from being thought of as a Jew, and in the case of Akabya there is even some doubt whether he ceased being a respected teacher. After 70 C.E., however, two things occurred to alter the situation. First, the ideals of Pharisaism prevailed as the normative standard of Jewish observance. Second, with the disappearance of all other parties and sects, power was concentrated in Pharisaic hands and wielded through a rabbinic-dominated Sanhedrin, which the Romans themselves acknowledged as the chief judicial body of the Jewish nation.

After 70, then, there were juridical standards—the Pharisees'—for using the ban penalty throughout the community, and there was an authority competent and willing to use it: the Nasi, or head of the Sanhedrin. We are told of two major types of ban: the nidduy of thirty days and the herem of indefinite extension. The person banned was treated juridically like the leper: everyone had to keep a distance of six feet from him. That, at any rate, was the theory. As a matter of fact, the only cases we know of such excommunication have to do with rabbis, and the grounds were incorrect teaching on the matter of ritual purity, insulting another rabbi, or casting ridicule on the Law. Excommunication, as far as we can tell, seems to have remained primarily a weapon in an academic debate.

10. Grave Sins and Light Offenses

The text in Numbers cited above on the subject of inadvertent and presumptuous sin looked primarily at intention. Some later rabbis attempted to be more specific about the deeds themselves, though the penalty of outlawry was now notably postponed to the world to come, as in M.Sanhedrin 10:1. This may indeed have been the venue where excommunication functioned most effectively.

Basing himself on the severe verse, Numbers 15:31, Rabbi Elazar of Modin said: If a man says, "I accept all the Torah with one exception," or if he says, "All the Torah was spoken by God with the exception of one passage, which was spoken by Moses," he has despised the word of God, and is worthy to be thrust out of the world (to come). (Sifre on Numbers, Shelah 112)

Rabbi Elazar of Modin said: He who profanes the Holy Things (of the Temple), and despises the holy days, and breaks the Covenant of Abraham our father, even if he has in his hand many (fulfilled) commandments, he is worthy to be thrust out of the world (to come). (Ibid.)

What is apparently happening in these instances, though still in a somewhat haphazard and unsystematic fashion, is an attempt to define, or at least isolate, what might be considered the fundamentals of a Jewish life, not now in any sectarian fashion, like the threats against the Sadducees already cited above, or in the manner of a homily, like the search for the "great commandment." Implicit in this search is a distinction among moral acts, and we have already seen how instructions regarding proselytes recommended their being introduced to both the "weighty" and the "light" commandments. Whatever those terms might have meant in that particular context—more or less important, more difficult or easier to observe—this distinction of commandments carried an implication that bothered some of the Sages, and they reacted against it. Our first passage is in the form of a reflection on the fact that in Deuteronomy "length of days" is promised to both the one who honors his parents—where disobedience is punishable by stoning—and the one who releases a mother bird found brooding on her nest (Deut. 22:6–7).

Rabbi Abba ben Kahana said: the Scripture has made the lightest command in the Torah equal to the heaviest command; for the reward of length of days is attached to both cases (cited). Rabbi Abun said: If in a commandment (like this), which is, as it were, the payment of a debt, the reward of length of days is added, how much more should it be appended to commandments which involve loss of money or danger to one's life. (JT.Kiddushin 61b)

Rabbi Judah the Prince said: Be as heedful of a light precept as of a grave one, for you know not the reward for each. Reckon the loss incurred by fulfilling a precept against the reward secured by its observance, and the gain gotten by its transgression against the loss that such involves. Reflect upon three things and you will not come within the power of sin: Know what is above you—a seeing eye, and a hearing ear, and all your deeds written in a book. (M.Pirke Aboth 2:1)

Maimonides, in his commentary on this passage, provides some examples of the two types of precept, though with Rabbi Judah's same caveat regarding observation.

This means that one should be just as mindful of a commandment which he considers a minor one, for example the command to rejoice during the festivals, to learn the Holy Tongue [that is, Hebrew], as he is to a commandment of whose major importance we have been informed, the law of circumcision, for example, or that of "fringes" [Num. 15:37–41], or the Passover offering. . . . For as regards the positive commandments, we have never been told what reward the Lord, blessed be He, has set aside for each of them . . . and that is why we must be attentive to all of them. (Maimonides, *Commentary on Mishna Aboth* 2.11)

Not unnaturally, the early Christians were drawn into making the same distinctions in offenses against God's commandments. Here the author is the Alexandrian Origen, struggling ca. 230 C.E. with the Christian's dilemma between faith in Jesus and the deeds that in fact belie that faith.

Whoever dies in his sins, even if he says he believes in Christ, in truth he does not believe in him. Even if it is called faith, it exists without good works and such faith is dead, as we read in the letter that circulates in the name of James. Who is then the believer if not he who comes to such a state . . . without falling into those sins which are called "mortal." (Origen, *Commentary on John* 19, 23)

Those sins were called "deadly" or "mortal" by John in one of his letters included in the New Testament.

If a man sees his brother committing a sin which is not a mortal sin, he should pray to God for him, and He will grant him life, that is, when men are not guilty of mortal sin. There is such a thing as deadly sin, and I do not suggest that he should pray about that; but although all wrongdoing is sin, not all sin is deadly sin. (John, *Letter* 1.2:16–17)

Quite naturally, the rabbis issued the same kind of warning about relying too much on the distinction between "great" and "small" sins. In this instance the caution comes from the Christian Basil of Caesarea (ca. 370–379 C.E.).

How are we to deal with those who avoid the graver sins but commit the smaller ones indiscriminately? First, we should know that this distinction is not found in the New Testament. We have but one statement about all sins, when the Lord said, "Who commits a sin is the slave of sin" (John 8:34). . . . And if we are permitted to speak of a small and a great sin, it must be said that the great sin is the one which exercises dominion over us and the small one is that over which we conquer. As in an athletic contest, the stronger is the one who triumphs and the defeated is weaker than the victor, whoever he happens to be. (Basil, *Shorter Rule* 293)

The classification of sins fell into two different sets of hands in Christianity. First, since the forgiveness of sins was a formal judicial procedure, namely the sacrament of penance, as it came to be called (see below), the specific gravity of sins had to be weighed by those of the clergy delegated to sit in judgment over the sinner and assess the penalties for sin. But it was likewise a matter of concern for the moral theologian—that characteristically Christian figure born of the union of Gospel morality and Greek philosophical ethics. "Mortal sin" is still the subject, but the terms of the discussion are now derived directly from Aristotle's Ethics.

The difference between venial and mortal sin is consequent upon the difference in that lack of order which constitutes the nature of sin. For lack of order is twofold, one that destroys the principle of order and another which, though it does not destroy the principle of order, does bring about a lack of order in the things that follow that principle. Thus, in an animal's body, the frame may be so out of order that the vital principle is destroyed: this is death; while, on the other hand, there is the instance where the vital principle remains but there might be, for example, a disorder of the vital humors: and then there is sickness. Now the principle of entire moral order is the last end, which stands in the same relation to matters of action as an indemonstrable principle does to matters of speculation. Therefore, when the soul is so disordered by sin as to turn away from its last end, to wit, God, to Whom it is united by charity, there is mortal sin; but when it is disordered without turning away from God, then there is venial sin. For even as in the body, the disorder of death which results from the separation of the principle of life is irreparable according to nature, while the disorder of sickness can be repaired because the vital principle itself remains, so it is in matters of the soul. . . . Likewise, in practical matters, he who by sinning turns away from his last end, if we consider the nature of his sin, falls irreparably and is therefore said to sin mortally and to deserve eternal punishment. But when a man sins without turning away from God, by the very nature of his sin his disorder can be repaired because the principle of the order is not destroyed; and therefore he is said to sin venially because he does not sin so as to deserve to be punished eternally. (Thomas Aquinas, *Summa Theologica* I/2, ques. 72, art. 5) [AQUINAS 1945: 2:576–577]

The characterization of certain sins as grave or serious and, by implication, of others as less serious appears in the Quran in the context of forgiveness.

If you keep away from the deadly sins that have been forbidden, We will efface your faults and lead you to a place of honor. (Quran 4:31)

It is narrated on the authority of Abd al-Rahman ibn Abi Bakr that his father said: We were in the company of the Messenger of God, may peace be upon him, when he said: "Should I not inform you about the most grievous of the grave sins?" He repeated it three times, and then he said: "They are: associating anyone with God, disobedience to one's parents, false testimony or false utterance." The holy Prophet was reclining as he spoke, then he sat up, and he repeated it so many times that we wished that he should become silent. (Muslim, *Sahih* 39.158)

Ubaydallah ibn Abi Bakr said: I heard Malik ibn Anas saying that the Messenger of God, may peace be upon him, talked about the great sins, and he observed that they were associating anyone with God, killing a person, disobedience to parents. (Ibid. 39.160)

It is reported on the authority of Abu Hurayra that the Messenger of God, may peace be upon him, observed: "Avoid the seven harmful things." It was said by his hearers, "And what are they, Messenger of God?" He replied, "Associating anything with God, magic, killing someone whom God has declared inviolate without a just cause, consuming the property of an orphan, the consumption of (the fruits of) usury, turning back when the army advances, and slandering chaste women who are believers but unwary." (Ibid. 39.161)

God is indeed a stern judge, but He is also willing to requite charity with mercy and to grant forgiveness in exchange for sincere repentance.

From Abu Tha'laba . . . with whom may God be pleased, (quoting) from the Apostle of God, upon whom be God's blessing and peace, that he said: "Truly God, may He be exalted, has laid down ordinances, so neglect them not; he has set limits, so do not exceed them; He has marked certain things as forbidden, so do not commit violations with regard to them; and He has said nothing about certain things, as an act of mercy toward you, not out of forgetfulness, so do not go inquiring into these." An excellent tradition which al-Daraqutni and others have related. (Nawawi, *The Forty Traditions*, no. 29) [JEFFERY 1962: 155]

From Abu Hurayra, with whom God be pleased, from the Prophet, upon whom be God's blessing and peace, who said: "Whoever dispels from a true believer some grief pertaining to this world, God will dispel from him some grief pertaining to the Day of Resurrection. Whoever makes things easy for someone who is in difficulties, God will make things easy both in this life and the next. Whoever shields a Muslim, God will shield him in this world and the next. God is ready to aid any servant so long as the servant is ready to aid his brother. Whosoever walks a path to seek knowledge therein, God will make easy for him a path to Paradise. No community ever assembles in one of God's houses to recite God's Book and carefully study it among themselves but that tranquillity descends to them and mercy covers them, and the angels surround them, and God makes mention of them among those who are with Him. He whose work detains him will not be hastened by his noble ancestry." Muslim relates this tradition in these words. (Ibid., no. 36)

[JEFFERY 1962: 157–158]

From Anas, with whom may God be pleased, who said: I heard the Apostle of God, upon whom be God's blessing and peace, say: "God, may He be exalted, has said: 'O son of Adam, so long as you call upon Me and hope in Me, I will forgive you for all that comes from you, caring not, O son of Adam, should your sins reach the horizon of the sky. Even then, O son of Adam, if you asked My forgiveness, I should forgive you. O son of Adam, were you to come to Me with enough sins to well nigh fill the earth, and then meet Me without associating anything with Me, I should come to you with a like size of forgiveness.' " Al-Tirmidhi relates it, saying: "It is an excellent, sound tradition." (Ibid., no. 42) [JEFFERY 1962: 160]

Finally, there is an attempt by Baydawi (d. 1286 C.E.), in his commentary on the Quran, to systematize the various Prophetic traditions on the subject.

There is disagreement about the grave sins. The most natural (interpretation) is that a grave sin is one for which the Lawgiver prescribed a specific punishment or pronounced a threat of punishment. Others hold that what is meant is those (commandments) whose inviolability is clearly acknowledged. . . . Some say (further): the lack of gravity (of certain sins) is relative to the sins that are above them and the sins that are below them. The gravest sin is associating (other gods with God), and the lightest is that the soul harbors sinful thoughts. Between these two extremes lie the middle ones that are of the two kinds [that is, the graver and the lighter]. If two (such kinds) present themselves to someone and his soul is drawn toward them because he lacks self-control, and if he restrains his soul from the graver of the two, then what he does commit will be blotted out as a reward for his avoiding the graver sin. This is one of those matters which vary according to the people and situations involved; God, for example, reproved His Prophet for many thoughts which would not be reckoned a sin in another man and certainly would not lead to his punishment. (Baydawi, *Commentary*, on 4:31)

11. The Fundamental Principles of
Jewish Belief

All the rabbinic rulings and advisories on sin shared a conviction that the bond of Jewish cohesiveness was the Law and its observance. That was how the Covenant was understood at the beginning, and the understanding of the Law and its observance continued to be the chief preoccupations of those who were given or assumed responsibility for the community. Some, however, were concerned with belief or, to put it somewhat differently, with what constituted heresy. The earliest statement of a concern expressed in those terms appears to be a text of the Mishna that is addressed quite specifically to the Sadducees, since it is precisely their opinions that here exclude one from a share in the afterlife.

The following are those who do not have a portion in the world to come: the one who says there is no resurrection of the dead, the one who says that the Torah is not from heaven, and the Apiqoros [that is, the "Epicurean," someone who denies divine providence]. (M.Sanhedrin 10:1)

This statement, which responds to a specific and immediate need, does not, obviously, constitute a comprehensive statement of Jewish beliefs, no more than did the attempts at isolating the "weighty" commandments. There were such creed-like statements early in Christianity, as we shall see, prompted by profound differences within the community. But when Judaism too eventually began to produce such statements, the point of departure was not so much a need to define the community and so preserve its integrity as it was an attempt to understand the reality that lay behind what continued to be the pre-eminent good of Judaism, namely, the Law.

For some, that reality was the truths of philosophy—which were of course, the philosophers would quickly add, the truths of God Himself. Those truths could be pursued for their own sake, a course taken by very few of the Children of Abraham; or they could be converted to or reconciled with the Law, a more properly Jewish undertaking. This is what Philo attempted, and Saadya, and Maimonides. In the case of the latter thinker the effort produced not merely reflections or commentary but something that might be regarded as a Jewish creed, a systematic statement of the propositions whose acceptance is fundamental to Jewish belief. Unlike the Christian creeds, however, which, as we shall see, were formally promulgated and at times were administered by the authority of the bishop or of the Great Church as tests for orthodoxy at baptism or elsewhere, Maimonides' list of Thirteen Principles was personal and doctrinal. Despite his conviction that they might serve as such, his principles were never used as either a yardstick or a test for membership in the Jewish community.

The First Fundamental Principle is to believe in the existence of the Creator; that there is an Existent perfect in all the senses of the term "existence." He is the cause of all existence; in Him all else subsists and from Him all else derives. It cannot be that He does not exist. . . .

The Second Fundamental Principle is to believe that God is one, and the cause of all oneness. He is not like a member of a pair, nor a species with respect to a genus, nor a person divided into many discrete elements. Nor is He one in the sense that a simple body is. . . . Rather, God is one in that He is unique. . . .

The Third Fundamental Principle is to believe that He is incorporeal, that His unity is neither potentially nor actually physical; none of the attributes of matter can be predicated of Him, neither motion, nor rest, for example. . . . And whenever Scripture describes Him in corporeal terms, like walking, standing, sitting or speaking, and the like, it is speaking metaphorically. . . .

The Fourth Fundamental Principle is to believe that the One is absolutely eternal. . . .

The Fifth Fundamental Principle is that He alone is rightfully worshiped, exalted and obeyed. One must not pray to anything beneath Him in existence, neither to angels, stars, planets nor the elements, nor to anything composed of these. . . .

The Sixth Fundamental Principle is (the affirmation of) the principle of prophecy, that certain men are so favored and so perfected that they are capable of acquiring pure intellectual form. Their human intellect adheres to the Active Intellect, whither it is gloriously raised. These men are prophets; this is in what prophecy consists. . . .

The Seventh Fundamental Principle is the (fact of) prophecy of Moses our teacher. We must believe that he is the chief of all other prophets before and after him, all of whom were his inferiors. He was the chosen one of all men, superior to all, past and future, in gaining knowledge of God. . . . Moses' prophecy must be distinguished from that of all other prophets in four respects: (1) All other prophets were spoken to by God through intermediaries, only Moses immediately. (2) Prophecy came to all others in their sleep or in daytime when a trance fell on them. . . . This state is called "vision" or "insight," as in the expression "visions of God." But the Word came to Moses in broad daylight, when he stood by the two cherubs, as God had promised. . . . (3) Even if another prophet were to receive a vision of God through the mediation of an angel, his powers would fail; he would be overcome with dread and almost lose his mind, which never happened to Moses. (4) None of the other prophets could attain a vision (of God) whenever they pleased. All depended on God's will. . . . Moses our teacher, on the other hand, could say, whenever he wished, "Wait and I shall hear what the Lord commands you" (Num. 9:8). . . .

The Eighth Fundamental Principal is that the Torah came from God. We must believe that the whole Torah was given us, in its entirety, by God through Moses our teacher. When we call the Torah "God's word" we are speaking metaphorically, since we do not know exactly how it reached us, but only that it came to us through Moses, who acted like a secretary taking dictation. . . . All (its verses) came from God, and all are the Torah of God, perfect, pure, holy and true. . . . The authoritative commentary on the Torah is also the Word of God. The *sukkah* we build today, or the *lulab*, shofar, fringes, phylacteries, etc. we use, all are exact replicas of those which God showed to Moses and which Moses faithfully described for us. . . .

The Ninth Fundamental Principle is the authenticity of the Torah. that is, that this Torah was precisely transcribed from God and no one else. To the Torah, Oral and Written, nothing must be added, nor anything subtracted from it. . . .

The Tenth Fundamental Principle is that God knows all that men do and never removes His eyes from them. . . .

The Eleventh Fundamental Principle is that God rewards those who perform the Torah commandments and punishes those who transgress its admonitions. The greatest reward is the world to come; the worst punishment is extinction. . . .

The Twelfth Fundamental Principle has to do with the the age of the Messiah. We must believe that the Messiah will in fact come and not think of him as delayed. If he does delay, then wait for him without setting a time limit for his coming. One must not make scripturally based conjectures as to when he will come. . . . We must believe that the Messiah will have a higher position and greater honor than all the kings who ever lived, as all the prophets from Moses to Malachi have prophesied. . . . A corollary of this principle is the assertion that the (Messianic) king of Israel must come from the house of David and the seed of Solomon. Anyone who rejects this family contradicts God and the words of His prophets.

The Thirteenth Fundamental Principle is a belief in the resurrection of the dead. The resurrection of the dead is one of the cardinal principles established by Moses our teacher. A person who does not believe in this principle has no real religion, certainly not Judaism. Resurrection is, however, reserved for the righteous. . . . All men must die and their bodies decompose.

Maimonides concludes:

When a man believes in all these fundamental principles, and his faith is thus made clear, he is then one of that "Israel" whom we are to love, pity and treat, as God commanded, with love and fellowship. Even though a Jew might commit every possible sin, whether from lust or because he has been overcome by his lower nature, he will surely be punished for his sins but he will still possess a share in the world to come. He is one of the "sinners of Israel." If, on the other hand, a man surrenders any one of these fundamental principles, he has removed himself from the Jewish community. He is an atheist, a heretic, an unbeliever who "cuts among the plantings." We are commanded to hate him and destroy him. Of him it is said: "Shall I not hate those who hate You, O Lord?" (Ps. 139:21). (Maimonides, *Helek*: Sanhedrin 10)

In the end Maimonides' Thirteen Principles had as little effect on Judaism as the distinction between weighty and light commandments: there is no sign that any Jew was rooted out of the Jewish community or regarded as a non-Jew on the basis of a violation of what surely must be considered as fundamental beliefs, whether thirteen or more or less. On one level, the reverence for the Torah, every word and syllable of it, carried all before it; on another, a tribal community where birth and blood were the essential characteristics of membership found no commodious or convincing way of dissolving the bond of blood on the basis of either belief or behavior, no matter how unlikely or outlandish.

12. The Muslim Articles of Faith

It might be useful here to compare Maimonides' Thirteen Principles with the meditation of another, somewhat later Spanish thinker on the same subject. This one is a Muslim, however. In his Prolegomenon to History, Ibn Khaldun (d. 1406) offers his list of the articles of the Muslim faith as an illustration for the science of dialectical theology, whose primary purpose was to expand and defend such Scripture-derived articles through rational arguments. He begins, however, with Muhammad's own, far more modest list of the fundamentals of Muslim belief.

It should be known that the Lawgiver [that is, Muhammad] . . . specified particular matters he charged us to affirm with our hearts and believe in our souls, while at the same time acknowledging them with our tongues. They are the established articles of the Muslim faith. When

Muhammad was asked about his faith, he said, "(Faith is) the belief in God, His angels, His Scriptures, His Messengers, the Last Day, and the belief in predestination, whether it be good or bad" (Muslim, *Sahih* 1.29).

These (following) are articles of faith as established in the science of speculative theology. Let us describe them in summary fashion, so that the real character of speculative theology and the way it originated may become clear. We say:

It should be known that the Lawgiver (Muhammad) commanded us to believe in the Creator whom he considered the sole source of all actions. . . . He informed us that this belief means our salvation, if we have it when we die. However, he did not tell us about the real being of this worshiped Creator, because it is something too difficult for our perception and above our level. He made it our first obligation to believe that He in His essence cannot be compared with created beings. Otherwise, it would not be correct that He was their Creator since in this way there would be no distinction (between Him and them).

Then (He obliged us to believe that) He cannot be described in any way as deficient. Otherwise, he would be similar to created beings. Then, he (obliged us to believe in) His Oneness as divine being. Otherwise, the creation could not have taken place on account of mutual antagonism (between two principles). Then there are the following articles of faith:

God is knowing and powerful. In this way, all actions materialize as witnesses . . . to the perfection of the act of creation.

He has volition. Otherwise, no created thing would be differentiated from the other.

He determines the fate of each created thing. Otherwise volition would be something that comes into being.

He causes our resurrection after death. This constitutes the final touch to His concern with the first creation. If created things were destined to disappear completely, their creation would have been frivolous. They are destined for eternal existence after death.

Further articles of faith are: God sent His Messengers in order to save us from trouble on the Day of Resurrection, because that Day may mean either trouble or happiness, and we would not know that. He wanted to complete His kindness toward us by informing us about this situation and explaining to us the two possibilities and that Paradise means bliss and Hell means punishment. (Ibn Khaldun, *Muqaddima* 6.14) [IBN KHALDUN 1967: 3, 43–45]

Muslim children were taught the elements of Islam by theologians and learned them in the same catechetical fashion that was popular in Christianity. The following excerpt is from a modern example of the genre, though of a highly traditional type going back to the Middle Ages.

Q.: What is the number of the Messengers (of God)?

A.: They are many. No one knows their number save God, may He be exalted. Nevertheless it is incumbent to recognize twenty-five of them by name.

Q.: Who are these twenty-five?

A.: They are Adam, Idris, Noah, Hud, Salih, Lot, Abraham, Ishmael, Isaac, Jacob, Joseph, Shucayb, Aaron, Moses, David, Solomon, Job, Dhu al-Kifl, Jonah, Elijah, Elisha, Zachariah, John, Jesus and Muhammad. May God's blessing and peace be upon them all.

Q.: What is the Last Day, and what is meant by faith in it?

A.: The Last Day is the Day of Resurrection, and the meaning of faith in it is confident assertion of its reality as a coming event, and of all that it will comprise, such as the resurrection of created things, their giving an account (of their deeds), the weighing of their deeds, their passing over the Bridge, and the entering of some of them justly into the Fire [that is, Hell] and some of them by grace into the Garden [that is, Paradise].

Q.: What is the meaning of faith in predestination?

A.: It is that you should firmly believe and confidently affirm that God, may He be exalted, decreed both good and evil before the Creation, that all that has been and all that will be is by the predetermination of God, may He be exalted, by His decree and will. Among the Prophetic traditions (there is one) that faith in this drives away both anxiety and grief.

Q.: What is Islam?

A.: It is that you should bear witness that there is no god but the God and that you should bear witness that Muhammad is the Messenger of God; that you should perform the prayers, pay the alms tax, fast during Ramadan, and go on Pilgrimage to the House, if you are able to make the journey there.

Q.: What is the meaning of the two acts of bearing witness?

A.: The meaning of the first is that you should know, confidently affirm and acknowledge that there is no true object of worship in existence save God, may He be praised and exalted. The meaning of the second is that you should know, confidently affirm and acknowledge that

Muhammad is the Messenger of God, whom He sent to all mankind. His age at that time was forty years. He is the most excellent of created beings, be they in heaven or on earth. He, may God bless him and grant him peace, was born in Mecca, the ennobled city, which he did not leave till he had reached the age of fifty-three years, when God, may He be exalted, bade him emigrate from it to Medina, the illuminated. So he emigrated from it to Medina, where he died at the age of sixty-three.

Q.: What was his genealogy on his father's side?

A.: He was the son of Abdullah, son of Abd al-Muttalib, son of Hashim, son of Abd Manaf, son of Qusayy, son of Hakim, son of Murra, son of Ka'b, son of Lu'ay, son of Ghalib, son of Fihr, son of Malik, son of al-Nadr, son of Kinana, son of Khuzayma, son of Mudrika, son of Ilyas, son of Mudar, son of Nizar, son of Ma'add, son of Adnan.

Q.: What was his genealogy on his mother's side?

A.: He was the son of Amina, daughter of Wahb, son of Abd al-Manaf, son of Zuhra, son of Hakim, the one mentioned above in the genealogy of his father.

Q.: How many children did he have?

A.: Seven, three males and four females. In order of their birth they were al-Qasim, then Zaynab, then Ruqayya, then Fatima, then Umm Kulthum, then Abdullah, then Ibrahim. All of them were by his wife Khadija, save Ibrahim, who was by his concubine, Mary the Copt.

Q.: How many wives did he have?

A.: They were twelve: Khadija, daughter of Khuwaylid; Sawda, daughter of Zam'a; Aisha, daughter of Abu Bakr; Hafsa, daughter of Umar; Zaynab, daughter of Khuzayma; Hind, daughter of Abu Umayya; Zaynab, daughter of Jahsh; Juwayriya, daughter of al-Harith, Rayhana, daughter of Zayd; Ramla, daughter of Abu Sufyan; Safiya, daughter of Huyayy; and Maimuna, daughter of al-Harith. Some hold that Rayhana belongs to the concubines and not the wives.

Q.: How many concubines did he have?

A.: They are three: Mary the Copt, who was presented to him by the Muqawqas, ruler of Egypt; Nafisa, whom Zaynab daughter of Jahsh gave him; Zulaykha of the Qurayza. According to those who hold that Rayhana was a concubine, there would have been four. (Jurjani, *The Clear Answers*) [JEFFERY 1962: 460–462]

13. Jews and Gentiles in One Community

The Christian mission to the Gentiles violated in some profound way the Jewish sense of peoplehood. Over the centuries since Abraham, priests, prophets, and doctors of the Law had made every effort to keep the Jewish community separate from those heathen peoples about them, whether that separation was understood as not sharing in their cults, as in the earliest biblical narratives, or not marrying their women, as in Ezra and Nehemiah, or, now under the Pharisees, not failing to observe a degree of ritual purity that extended through all forms of social intercourse and ended at the table. The Christians, perhaps only some Christians at the outset, said that another consideration was more important than the Law and circumcision, namely belief in the Messiahship of Jesus, and that sharing in that belief constituted a new fellowship, a new community of Jew and Gentile, a new people.

Remember your former condition: you, Gentiles, as you were outwardly, you, the "uncircumcised" so called by those who are called "the circumcised"—but only with reference to an outward rite—you were at that time separate from Christ, strangers to the community of Israel, outside God's covenants and the promise that goes with them. Your world was a world without hope and without God. But now in union with Christ Jesus you who were once far off have been brought near through the shedding of Christ's blood. For he is himself our peace. Gentiles and Jews, he has made the two one, and in his own body of flesh and blood has broken down the enmity which stood like a dividing wall between them. For he annulled the Law with its rules and regulations, so as to create out of the two a single new humanity in himself, thereby making peace. This was his purpose, to reconcile the two in a single body to God through the cross, on which he killed the enmity.

So he came and proclaimed the good news: peace to you who were far off, and peace to those who were nearby; for through him we both have access to the Father in the one Spirit. Thus you are no longer aliens in a foreign land, but fellow citizens with God's people, members of God's household. You are built upon the foundation laid by the Apostles and the prophets, and Christ Jesus himself is the foundation stone. In him the whole building is bonded together and grows into a holy temple in the Lord. In him you too are being built with all the rest into a spiritual dwelling for God. (Paul, *To the Ephesians* 2:12–22)

Paul uses another figure.

Christ is like a single body with its many limbs and organs, which, as many as they are, make up one body. For indeed we are all brought into one body by baptism, in the one Spirit, whether we are Jews or Greeks, whether slaves or free men, and that one Spirit has poured out all of us to drink.

A body is not a single organ but many. Suppose the foot should say, "Because I am not a hand, I do not belong to the body," it does belong to the body nonetheless. Suppose the ear should say, "Because I am not an eye, I do not belong to the body," it still belongs to the body. If the body were all eye, how could it hear? If the body were all ear, how could it smell? But in fact God appointed each limb and organ to its own place in the body, as He chose. If the whole were one single organ, there would not be a body at all; in fact, however, there are many different organs and one body. . . . If one organ suffers, they all suffer together. If one organ flourishes, they all rejoice together. (Paul, *To the Corinthians* 1:12–26)

14. Citizens of Heaven in the World of Men

Sometime about 124 C.E. a pagan named Diognetus asked a Christian for some information on his sect. The anonymous author replied with this characterization, a description filled with implicit contrasts with the Jewish communities of that day.

The difference between Christians and the rest of mankind is not a matter of nationality or language or customs. Christians do not live apart in separate cities of their own, speak any special dialect or practice any eccentric way of life. The doctrine they profess is not the invention of busy human minds and brains, nor are they, like some, adherents of this or that school of human thought. They pass their lives in whatever township, Greek or foreign, each man's lot has determined; and conform to ordinary legal usage in their clothing, diet and other habits. Nevertheless the organization of their community does exhibit some features that are remarkable, and even surprising. For instance, though they are residents at home in their own country, their behavior there is more like transients; they take their full part as citizens, but they also submit to everything and anything as if they were aliens. For them, any foreign country is a motherland, and any motherland is a foreign country.

Like other men, they marry and beget children, though they do not expose their infants. Any Christian is free to share his neighbor's table, but never his marriage bed. Though destiny has placed them here in the flesh, they do not live after the flesh; their days are passed on the earth, but their citizenship is above in the heavens. They obey the prescribed laws, but in their own private lives they transcend the laws. They show love to all men, and all men persecute them. They are misunderstood and condemned, and yet by suffering death they are quickened to life. They are poor, yet making many rich; lacking all things, yet having all things in abundance. . . .

To put it briefly, the relations of Christians to the world is that of a soul to the body. As the soul is diffused through every part of the body, so are Christians through all the cities of the world. The soul too inhabits the body, while at the same time forming no part of it; and Christians inhabit the world, but they are not part of the world. . . . The flesh hates the soul and wars against her without any provocation because she is an obstacle to its own self-indulgence; and the world similarly hates the Christians without provocation because they are opposed to its pleasures. . . . The soul, shut up inside the body, nevertheless holds the body together; and though they are confined within the world as in a dungeon, it is the Christians who hold the world together. The soul, which is immortal, must dwell in a mortal tabernacle; and the Christians, as they sojourn for a while in the midst of corruptibility here, look for incorruptibility in the heavens. Finally, just as to be stinted of food and drink makes for the soul's improvement, so when Christians are every day subjected to ill treatment, they increase the more in numbers. Such is the high post of duty in which God has placed them, and it is their moral duty not to shrink from it. (*Letter to Diognetus* 5–6) [STANIFORTH 1968: 176–178]

15. Paul Reflects on the Role of the Jews in History

The overwhelming number of Christians in Paul's day would still have identified themselves in some manner as Jews. Dissociation from their heavily-laden Jewish past, which for some must have seemed like a repudiation, could not have been easy. Was the past worth nothing then? It is possible to discern the question behind Paul's answer.

I am speaking the truth as a Christian, and my own conscience, enlightened by the Holy Spirit, assures me it is no lie. In my heart there is great grief and unceasing sorrow. For I could even pray to be an outcast from Christ myself for the sake of my brothers, my natural kinfolk. They are Israelites; they were made God's sons; theirs is the splendor of the divine presence, theirs the covenants, the Law, the Temple worship, and the promises. Theirs are the patriarchs, and from them, in natural descent, sprang the Messiah. May God, supreme over all, be blessed forever! Amen.

It is impossible that the word of God should have proved false. For not all descendants of Israel are truly Israel, nor, because they are Abraham's sons, are they all his true children, but in the words of Scripture, "Through the line of Isaac your descendants shall be traced." That is to say, it is not those born in the course of nature who are children of God; it is the children born through Abraham's promise who are reckoned as Abraham's descendants. For the promise runs: "At the time fixed I will come, and Sarah shall have a son. . . ."

Brothers, my deepest desire and my prayer to God is for their [that is, the Jews'] salvation. To their zeal for God I can testify; but it is an uninformed zeal. For they ignore God's ways of righteousness, and try to set up their own, and therefore they have not submitted themselves to God's righteousness. For Christ ends the Law and brings righteousness for everyone who has faith. . . .

Scripture says, "Everyone who has faith in him will be saved from shame" (Isa. 52:7)—everyone: there is no distinction between Jew and Greek, because the same Lord is the Lord of all, and is rich enough for the need of all who invoke him. For as it says again, "everyone who invokes the name of the Lord will be saved" (Joel 2:23). How could they invoke one in whom they had no faith? And how could they have faith in one they had never heard of? . . .

What follows? What Israel sought, Israel has not achieved, but the selected few have achieved it. The rest were made blind to the truth, exactly as it stands written: "God brought upon them a numbness of spirit; he gave them blind eyes and deaf ears, and so it is still" (Isa. 29:10). . . .

I now ask, did their failure mean complete downfall? Far from it! Because they offended, salvation has come to the Gentiles, to stir Israel to emulation. But if their offense means the enrichment of the world, and if their falling-off means the enrichment of the Gentiles, how much more their coming to full strength! (Paul, *To the Romans* 10:1–12)

16. The Olive Tree That Is Israel

If this is Paul's consolation to Israel, it is not a source of boasting for the Gentiles who in increasing numbers constituted the new Israel.

But I have something to say to you Gentiles. I am a missionary to you Gentiles, and as such as I give all honor to that ministry when I try to stir emulation in the men of my own race, and to save some of them. For if their rejection has meant the reconciliation of the world, what will their acceptance mean? Nothing less than life from the dead! If the first portion of the dough is consecrated, so is the whole lump. If the root is consecrated, so are the branches. But if some of the branches are lopped off, and you, a wild olive, have been grafted in among them, and have come to share the same root and sap as the olive, do not make yourselves superior to the branches. If you do, remember that it is not you who sustain the root; the root sustains you.

You will say, "Branches were lopped off so that I might be grafted in." Very well: they were lopped off for lack of faith, and by faith you hold their place. Put away your pride and be on your guard; for if God did not spare the native branches, no more will he spare you. Observe the kindness and severity of God—severity to those who fall away, divine goodness to you, if only you remain within its scope. Otherwise you too will be cut off, whereas they, if they do not continue faithless, will be grafted in; for it is in God's power to graft them in again. For if you were cut off from your wild olive and against all nature grafted into the cultivated olive, how much more readily will they, the natural olive branches, be grafted into their native stock! (Paul, *To the Romans* 11:13–24)

17. The Old Priesthood and the New

But you are a chosen race, a royal priesthood, a dedicated nation and a people claimed by God for his own, to proclaim the triumph of him who called you out of the darkness into his own marvelous light. You are now the people of God, who were once not His people; outside His mercy once, you have now received His mercy. (Peter, *Letter* 1.2:9–10)

So Peter, Jesus' chosen Apostle, addressed the newborn community of Christians, on whom he easily bestows the proudest titles of what was already being thought of as "the old Israel." Those same Christians searched the Jewish Bible and found there ample evidence to demonstrate not merely that Jesus was the Messiah but also that his Messianic kingdom was the new Israel, wherein he served as both king and priest. And nowhere perhaps is that stated more clearly than in the passage in 2 Samuel where a "man of God" comes to the priest Eli and speaks as follows.

This is the word of the Lord: You know that I revealed Myself to your forefather (Aaron) when he and his family were in Egypt in slavery in the house of the Pharaoh. You know that I chose him from all the tribes of Israel to be My priest, to mount the steps of My altar, to burn sacrifices and to carry the ephod before Me; and that I assigned all the food offerings of the Israelites to your family. Why then do you show disrespect for My sacrifices and the offerings which I have ordained? What makes you resent them? Why do you honor your sons more than Me by letting them batten on the choicest offerings of My people Israel?

The Lord's word was: "I promise that your house and your father's house shall serve me for all time"; but now His word is: "I will have no such thing; I will honor those who honor Me, and those who despise Me shall suffer contempt. The time is coming when I shall lop off every limb of your own and of your father's family, so that no man in your house shall come to old age. If I allow any to survive to serve my altar, his eyes will grow dim and his appetite fail, his issue will be weaklings and die off. The fate of your two sons shall be a sign to you: Hophni and Phineas shall both die on the same day. I will appoint for Myself a priest who will be faithful and who will do what I have in My mind and My heart. I will establish his house to serve in perpetual succession before my anointed one. Any of your family that still live will come and bow down before him to beg a fee, a piece of silver or a loaf, and will ask for a turn of priestly duty to earn a morsel of bread." (2 Samuel 2:27–35)

Augustine dwells at length on this passage in his City of God.

We cannot say that this prophecy, in which the change of the ancient priesthood is foretold with so great plainness, was fulfilled in Samuel [as the sequel in the biblical account would seem to suggest]; for although Samuel was not of another tribe than that which had been appointed by God to serve at the altar, yet he was not of the sons of Aaron, whose offspring were set apart that the priests might be taken out of it. And thus by that transaction also the same change which should come to pass through Christ Jesus is shadowed forth, and the prophecy itself in deed, not in word, properly belonged to the Old Testament, but figuratively to the New, signifying by the fact exactly what was said by the word to Eli the priest through the prophet. For there were afterwards priests of Aaron's race, such as Zadok and Abiathar during David's reign, and others in succession, before the time came when those things which were predicted so long before about the changing of the priesthood behoved to be fulfilled by Christ. But who that now views these things with a believing eye does not see that they are fulfilled? Since indeed no Tabernacle, no Temple, no altar, no sacrifice, and therefore no priest either, has remained to the Jews, to whom it was commanded in the Law of God that he should be ordained of the seed of Aaron. This too is mentioned by the prophet (in the same text), when he says: "The Lord's word was: 'I promise that your house and your father's house shall serve me for all time'; but now His word is: 'I will have no such thing; I will honor those who honor Me, and those who despise Me shall suffer contempt.' " . . . It was of his [that is, Aaron's] lineage, therefore, he has said in this passage that it should come to pass that they would no longer be priests; which already we see fulfilled. If faith is watchful, the things are before us; they are discerned, they are grasped, and forced on the eyes of the unwilling, so that they are seen: "The time is coming," he says, "when I shall lop off every limb of your own and of your father's family, so that no man in your house shall come to old age. If I allow any to survive to serve my altar, his eyes will grow dim and his appetite fail, his issue will be weaklings and die off." Behold, the days which were foretold have already come. There is no priest in the succession of Aaron; and whoever is a man of his lineage, when he sees the sacrifices of the Christians prevailing over the whole world, but that great honor taken away from himself, his eyes and his soul melt away consumed with grief.

. . . The things which follow are said of Christ Jesus, the True Priest of the New Testament: "I will appoint for Myself a priest who will be faithful and who will do what I have in My mind and My heart. I will establish his house. . . ." The same is the eternal Jerusalem above. "To serve in perpetual succession before my anointed one" [Augustine reads "My Christ"]. (Augustine, *City of God* 17.5) [AUGUSTINE 1948: 2:377]

18. "The Remnant Shall Be Saved"

The final verse of the passage in Samuel turns Augustine to a reflection on the fate of the Jews in the new dispensation.

But what is added, "Any of your family that still live will come and bow down before him," is not said properly of the house of this Eli, but of that of Aaron, the men of which remained even to the coming of Jesus Christ, of which race there are not wanting men even to this present. . . . Therefore if it is of these, the predestined remnant, about whom another prophet has said, "The remnant shall be saved" (Isa. 10:21), wherefore the Apostle (Paul) also says, "Even so then at this time also the remnant according to the election of grace is saved"; since, then, it is easily to be understood to be of such a remnant that the present verse speaks, "any of your family that still live," assuredly he believes in Christ. Just as in the time of the Apostle (Paul) very many of that nation (that is, the Jews) believed; nor are there now wanting those (Jews), although very few, who yet believe, and in them is fulfilled what this man of God has here immediately added, "will come and bow down before him to beg a fee," to bow down before whom, if not that High Priest who is also God? For in that priesthood in the succession of Aaron men did not come to the Temple or the altar of God for the purpose of worshiping the priest. (Augustine, *City of God* 17.5) [AUGUSTINE 1948: 2:378–379]

19. The Separation of the Christians from the Jews

As appears from both the Acts of the Apostles and the letters of Paul, Christianity spread through the eastern Mediterranean chiefly through the network of syna-gogues where Jewish preachers of the Jewish Messiah Jesus had easy access at first. Converts were quickly made among the Gentile populations of those same centers, however, and tension grew between the communities of new Gentile converts and those of the Jewish followers of Jesus. A deeper, though less visible, conflict spread between the Christians and the unconvinced Jews.

One leader who had to deal with the problem in Anatolia, where there were large communities of both Jews and Jewish Christians, was Ignatius, the bishop of Antioch. In his letters he discouraged Jewish practices among Christians who were, or recently had been, themselves Jewish. He died a martyr for his belief in Jesus sometime about 107 C.E.

Never permit yourselves to be misled by the teachings and the worn-out tales of another people [that is, the Jews]. There is nothing useful that can be gotten from them. If we are still following Jewish practices, it is an admission on our part that we have failed to receive the gift of grace. Even the lives of the divinely inspired (biblical) prophets were redolent of Jesus Christ, and the reason they suffered persecution was because they were inspired by his grace so that they might convince future believers that the one sole God has revealed Himself in His Son Jesus Christ, His own Word which came forth from silence, and who in all he was and and all he did gladdened the heart of the One who sent him.

We have seen how those who once followed the ancient customs have attained new hope. They have given up keeping the Sabbath and in its place they now order their lives on the Lord's Day, the day when life first dawned on us, thanks to him and his death. That death, though some deny it, is the very mystery which made believers and enabled us to endure tribulation and so prove ourselves pupils of Jesus Christ, our teacher. How, then, is it possible that we grant him no place in our lives, when even the ancient prophets were themselves his disciples in spirit and looked forward to him as their teacher? That was indeed the very reason why he, whom they were rightly awaiting, came to visit them and raised them from the dead. (Ignatius, *To the Magnesians* 8–9)

The already cited Letter to Diognetus, *written about 124 C.E., shows no inclination to move naturally and persuasively, as Augustine did, from the biblical prophets to a belief in Christ. The author here was almost certainly a Gentile Christian. He was writing to a pagan, perhaps in reply to a request that he explain how Christians differed from Jews.*

Next I expect what you most want to hear about is our Christian unwillingness to accept the faith of the Jews. Admittedly, since they are unwilling to have any truck with the sort of (pagan) religion I have been describing, the Jews may fairly claim to be devotees of the one true God and to acknowledge Him as their sovereign. Nevertheless, insofar as they do him service with rites similar to those of the heathen, they are in error. For if the Greeks must stand convinced of absurdity by the offerings they make to senseless and dumb idols, the Jews ought to realize that it shows equal absurdity, and no true piety, to conceive of God Himself as in want of such things. The maker of heaven and earth and all therein, the supplier of our every need, could never Himself be in any need of the very things which are actually His own gifts to the self-styled givers. Indeed, so long as they believe themselves to be fulfilling their sacrificial duty to Him by means of blood and fat and burnt offerings, and fancy that they are doing Him honor by such rites, I cannot see that there is anything to choose between them and the men who lavish similar attentions on deaf and dumb idols. One party, it seems, makes its offerings to creatures who cannot partake of the gifts, and the other to One who needs none of them.

As for their scrupulousness about meats, and their superstitions about the Sabbath, and their much vaunted circumcision, and their pretentious festivals and new moon observances, all of them too nonsensical to be worth discussing, I hardly think you need instruction from me. For how can it be anything but impious to accept some of the things which God has created for our use and assert their creation to have been commendable, but to reject others as being needless and good-for-nothing? And what can there be but profanity in the slanderous charge that God

objects to a good deed being done on a sabbath day? And surely, when
they boast that a body mutilation is evidence of their inclusion among the
elect, as though it gave them some special claim to God's love, what does
this deserve but to be laughed out of court. As for the minute way in
which they scrutinize the moon and stars for the purpose of ritually
commemorating months and days, and chop up the divinely appointed
cycle of the seasons to suit their own fancies, pronouncing some to be
times for feasting and others for mourning, could anyone pretend that
this indicates true reverence and not simply a deranged intellect?

I imagine that you have heard enough now to see how right the
Christians are in repudiating the folly and delusion common to these two
cults, as well as the fussy practices of which the Jews are so proud. At
the same time, however, you must never expect to learn the inward
mystery of their own religion from merely human lips. (*Letter to Diognetus*
3–4) [STANIFORTH 1968: 175–176]

The argument of the Letter to Diognetus *is not a little disingenuous, concealing
as it does the affiliation of the Christians to the Jews and the fact that the Jews'
"fussy practices" derived from books that the Christians too regarded as divinely
inspired Scripture. The problem of affiliation could, however, be dealt with in other,
more complex ways than those that suited the innocent Diognetus. Some Christians
of his day, for example, were ready to adopt a far more radical procedure for the
separation of Christianity from Judaism, to reject not merely the Jewish Scriptures
but the very God who had revealed them and had created this world of ours. Though
there were others who took the same position, it is most closely associated with
Marcion, a native of Pontus in Anatolia who was a member of the Christian
community in Rome sometime about 160 C.E.*

Marcion of Pontus succeeded him [Cerdon] and developed his
school, advancing the most daring blasphemy against Him who is proclaimed as God by the Law and the Prophets, declaring him to be the
author of evils, a lover of war, inconstant in judgment and contrary to
Himself. But Jesus being derived from that Father who is above the God
who made the world, and coming into Judea in the times of Pontius Pilate
the governor, who was procurator of Tiberius Caesar, was manifested in
the form of a man to those who were in Judea, abolishing the Prophets
and the Law and all the works of the God who made the world, whom
he also calls "Ruler of the World."

Besides this, he mutilates the Gospel which is according to Luke,
removes all that is written respecting the generation of the Lord and sets
aside a great deal of the teaching of the Lord's discourses in which the

Lord is recorded as most clearly confessing that the Maker of this universe is his Father. . . . In like manner too he dismembered the letters of Paul, removing all that is said by the Apostle respecting that God who made the world, to the effect that He is the Father of our Lord Jesus Christ, and also those passages from the prophetic writings which the Apostle quotes in order to teach us that they announced beforehand the coming of the Lord. (Ireneus, *Against the Heresies* 1.27.1–2)

Marcion's special and principal work is the separation of the Law and the Gospel, and his disciples will not be able to deny that their supreme authority has its basis in this (separation), an authority by which they initiate and confirm themselves in this heresy. This is Marcion's "Antitheses" or contradictory propositions, which aim at committing the Gospel to be at variance with the Law in order that from the diversity of the two documents which contain them, they may argue for a diversity of gods as well. (Tertullian, *Against Marcion* 1.19)

20. The Jewish Christians

That there were Jewish believers in the Messiahship of Jesus who nonetheless wished, despite Paul, to continue their observance of the Mosaic laws and commandments is already obvious from the Acts of the Apostles. The leadership of the original community in Jerusalem continued for a while to be closely associated with the family of Jesus (see Chapter 6 below), and the bishops there, as Eusebius calculated them, were all "Hebrews," that is, practicing Jews, down to the second destruction of the city in 135 C.E., "for at that time their whole church consisted of Hebrew believers who had continued from Apostolic times down to the later siege in which the Jews, after revolting a second time from the Romans, were overwhelmed in a full-scale war." Thereafter the history of the Jewish Christians was not a happy one, as the Gentile Christians sought to separate themselves to an ever greater degree from their Jewish origins. In 150 the converted philosopher Justin was still willing to maintain communion with them; by the time in the fourth century that Eusebius wrote his Church History, *those Jewish Christians found, or had placed, themselves in a position that the rest of the Great Church regarded as purely and simply heretical.*

Trypho [a Jewish rabbi] inquired again: If a man, aware that this is so, after he has also plainly known that this (Jesus) is the Christ, and believed and obeyed him, wishes to keep these precepts (of the Mosaic Law) as well, shall he be saved?

In my opinion, Trypho, I answered, such a man will be saved, unless he strenuously does his utmost to persuade others—I mean those Gentiles who have been circumcised by Christ from their error—to keep the same Mosaic commandments that he does, saying that they will not be saved unless they keep them. For this is what you yourself did at the beginning of our discussion, when you declared that I will not be saved unless I keep them.

He answered: Why then do you say: "It is my opinion that such a man will be saved?" Are there any who maintain that such a one will not be saved?

There are, Trypho, I replied, and there are even some who are bold enough not even to join such in social converse and meals, though I do not agree with them. But if they [the Jewish Christians], out of the weakness of their mind, wish to observe such of the sayings of Moses as are now possible—which in our view were ordained because of the hardness of people's hearts—while they still place their hopes in this Christ of ours, and also keep those commandments commending the practice of righteousness and of piety—which are everlasting and in accordance with nature—and who choose to live with Christians and believers without, as I said before, persuading them either to undergo circumcision like themselves, or to keep the Sabbath, or to observe other things of the same kind—I declare that we must fully receive such and have communion with them in all respects, as being of one family and as brothers. But if, Trypho, I said, they who are of your race say they believe in this Christ of ours, and in every way compel those who are of Gentile birth and believe in this Christ to live in accordance with the Law appointed by Moses, or choose not to have communion with them that have such a life in common—these also in like manner I do not accept.

Now they that follow their advice [that is, the advice of the Jewish Christians] and live under the Law, as well as keep their profession in the Christ of God, will, I suppose, be saved. But they that once professed and recognized that this is the Christ, and then for some reason or other passed over into the life under the Law, denying that this is the Christ, and do not repent before death, cannot, I declare, in any wise be saved. (Justin, *Dialogue with Trypho* 47.1–4)

What happened to these Jewish followers of Jesus appears obscurely, and not entirely sympathetically, through the lines of Eusebius' Church History.

There were others whom the evil demon, unable to shake their devotion to the Christ of God, caught in a different trap and made their own. Ebionites they were appropriately named by the first Christians, in view of the poor and mean opinion they held about Christ. They regarded him as plain and ordinary, a man esteemed as righteous through growth of character and nothing more, the child of a normal union between a man and Mary; and they hold they must observe every detail of the (Mosaic) Law—by faith in Christ alone, and a life built upon that faith, (they maintain) they would never win salvation.

A second group went by the same name, but escaped the outrageous absurdity of the first. They did not deny that the Lord was born of a virgin and the Holy Spirit, but nevertheless shared their refusal to acknowledge his pre-existence as God the Word and Wisdom. Thus the impious doctrine of the others was their undoing as well, especially as they placed equal emphasis on the outward observance of the (Mosaic) Law. They held that the letters of the Apostle (Paul) ought to be rejected altogether, calling him a renegade from the Law; and using only the "Gospel of the Hebrews," they treated the rest with scant respect. Like the others they observed the Sabbath and the whole Jewish system; yet on the Lord's day they celebrated rites similar to our own in memory of the Savior's resurrection. (Eusebius, *Church History* 3.27)

21. The Banishment of the Christians from the Synagogue

If the presence of Jewish Christians became increasingly less comfortable within the Church, it was a source of even less comfort in the synagogues, which had been the original locus for the spread of the Christian faith. Sometime during the presidency of Gamaliel II (80–110 C.E.) a remedy of sorts was contrived in the form of a new "benediction," the twelfth, added to those that constituted the normal synagogue prayer of the Tefilla. This was the euphemistically named "blessing of the Minim," the latter some type of apostate group and possibly the Jewish Christians themselves, though these are mentioned separately by name.

For apostates let there be no hope, and the dominion of arrogance do Thou speedily root out in our days; and let the Nazarenes and the Minim perish as in a moment, let them be blotted out of the book of the living and let them not be written with the righteous. Blessed art Thou, O Lord, who humbles the arrogant.

This new "prayer," like the parallel rejection of the Christians' Scriptures, effectively prevented the Jewish followers of Jesus from participating in a central Jewish liturgy in which they were constrained to curse themselves, a fact well known to Jerome in the fourth century. He remarks that "the Jews day and night blaspheme the Savior, and, as I have often remarked, three times daily heap curses on the

Christians under the name of 'Nazarenes.' " The Christian could, of course, decline to repeat it, but his silence would equally surely betray him, as appears in the Talmud's account of the original framing of this formula.

Our Rabbis taught: Simeon the cotton merchant arranged the eighteen benedictions in order before Rabban Gamaliel [II] in Jabneh. Said Rabban Gamaliel to the Sages: Can any among you frame a benediction relating to the Minim? Samuel the Lesser arose and composed it. The following year he forgot it and he tried for two or three hours to recall it, and they did not remove him [from his post as a reader]. Why did they not remove him seeing that Rab Judah had said in the name of Rab: If a reader made a mistake in any of the other benedictions, they did not remove him, but if in the benediction of the Minim, he is removed, because we suspect him of being a Min. (BT.Berakoth 28b–29a)

22. Baptism in the Early Church

Read out of the Jewish congregations, the Christians began to constitute their own. Unlike the Jews, for whom someone born of a Jewish mother was under the Law necessarily Jewish, no one was born a Christian. Every member of the Christian community was in effect a convert, and from the beginning each was treated as the Jews treated their proselytes: they were baptized, just as Jesus had been baptized by John (Matt. 3:13–17) and just as he had commanded his disciples after his resurrection, apparently with a direct reference to the mission to the Gentiles.

The eleven disciples made their way to Galilee, to the mountain where Jesus had told them to meet him. When they saw him, they fell prostrate before him, though some were doubtful. Jesus then came up and spoke to them. He said: "Full authority in heaven and on earth has been committed to me. Go forth therefore and make all nations my disciples: baptize men everywhere in the name of the Father and the Son and the Holy Spirit, and teach them to observe all that I have commanded. And be assured that I am with you always, to the end of time." (Matthew 28:16–20)

From the Acts of the Apostles onward, the practice is attested to as a necessary preliminary to membership in the Church. Here is how the ritual is described in summary in the anonymous Teaching of the Apostles *from early in the second century.*

The way of baptizing is as follows. After completing all the preliminaries, immerse (the candidate) in running water (saying), "In the Name of the Father and of the Son and of the Holy Spirit." If no running water is available, immerse in ordinary water. This should be cold if possible, but otherwise warm water (will do). If neither is practical, then sprinkle water three times on his head (saying), "In the Name of the Father and of the Son and of the Holy Spirit." Both the baptizer and baptized should fast before the baptism, as well as any others who can do so; but the candidate himself should be instructed to observe a fast for a day or two beforehand. (*Teaching of the Apostles* 7)

By the beginning of the third century, as the numbers of would-be Christians increased, more attention was paid to those preliminaries. The following is from the Apostolic Tradition *attributed to Hippolytus (ca. 220 C.E.).*

Those who present themselves for the first time to hear the word should first be brought to the teachers at the house (of prayer) before all the people (of the congregation) arrive. They should be questioned as to why they have come forward to the faith. And their sponsors should witness for them, whether they are able to hear (the word of God). Their life and manner of living should be investigated, and whether they are slave or free.

There follow the rules for different types of candidates for baptism.

If a man is a pimp who supports whores, he should either cease or be rejected (as a candidate for baptism). If a man is a sculptor or a painter, he should be cautioned not to make idols; if he will not leave off this practice, he should be rejected. If a man teaches children worldly [that is, pagan] knowledge, it would be well if he stopped, but if he has no other livelihood, he may be forgiven. If a man is an actor or someone who produces shows in the theater . . . a charioteer likewise, or one who takes part in the games or who attends the games . . . a gladiator or a trainer of gladiators, an animal hunter or someone involved with wild animal shows . . . a priest of idols or a keeper of idols, either he must cease or else be rejected. . . . If a man has a concubine who is a slave, let her too attend the instruction, but only on condition that she has already raised her children, and if she is living with him alone. If not, she should be turned away. If a man has a (free woman) concubine, he should end (the relationship) and contract a legal marriage; if he refuses, he should be rejected.

The catechumen should be instructed for three years; but if a man is earnest and perseveres well in the matter, he may be received (earlier), because it is not the time that is being weighed but his conduct. . . . And when they are chosen who are set apart to receive baptism, then their lives should be examined, whether they are living piously as catechumens, whether they have "honored the widows," visited the sick, fulfilled every good work. If those who sponsored them can bear witness that they have done thus, then let them hear the Gospel. . . .

Those who are to be baptized should be instructed to wash and cleanse themselves on the fifth day of the week; and if any woman is menstruating, her baptism should be postponed till another day. Those who are to receive baptism should fast on Friday and Saturday. And on the Saturday the bishop should assemble all those who are to be baptized in one place, and bid them all to bow and genuflect. And laying his hand on them he shall exorcize every evil spirit to flee from them and never to return to them henceforward. And when he has finished exorcizing, let him breathe on their faces and seal their foreheads and ears and noses and then raise them up.

At the hour when the cock crows they shall first pray over the water. When they come to the water, let the water be pure and flowing. And they shall put off their clothes. And they shall baptize the little children first. And if they can answer for themselves, let them answer; but if they cannot, let their parents answer or someone else from their family. And next they shall baptize the grown men; and last the women, who shall have loosed their hair and laid aside their gold ornaments. Let no one go down to the water having any alien object with them. (Hippolytus, *The Apostolic Tradition*)

At almost the same time, Tertullian (ca. 160–222 C.E.) took up the question of who may perform this ritual of baptism.

It remains also to remind you of the correct observance of the giving and the receiving of baptism. The chief priest, who is the bishop, has the right of giving it; in the second place, the presbyters and deacons, yet not without the bishop's authority, on account of the honor of the Church, for when this has been preserved, peace is preserved. Besides these, even laymen have the right; for what is equally received can be equally given. If there are no bishops, priests, or deacons, other disciples are called. The word of the Lord ought not to be hidden away by anyone. In like manner also, baptism, which is equally God's property, can be administered by all; but how much more is the rule of reverence and modesty incumbent on laymen, since these things belong to their superiors, lest they assume to themselves the specific functions of the episcopate. Emulation of the episcopal office is the mother of schism. (Tertullian, *On Baptism* 17)

23. Faith, Sin, and Repentance

Unlike the Jews, who never lost their strong tribal affiliation and whom both their neighbors and Roman law regarded as a "nation," the Christians constituted nothing else but a community of believers. If a hasty reading of Paul suggested that only faith or disbelief in Christ qualified or disqualified one for continued membership in that society, a more Jewish emphasis on observance appears precisely where we might expect it: in the New Testament Letter of James, that Torah–observant "brother of the Lord" in Jerusalem, who in the course of his advice casts a sidelong and not entirely disinterested glance at Paul's favorite example of justification through faith, Abraham.

My brothers, what use is it for a man to say he has faith when he has nothing to show for it? Can that faith save him? Suppose a brother or a sister is in rags with not enough food for a day and one of you says, "Good luck to you, keep yourselves warm, and have plenty to eat," but does nothing to supply their bodily needs, what is the good of that? So with faith; if it does not lead to action, it is a lifeless thing. But someone may object: "Here is one who claims to have faith and another who points to his deeds." To which I reply: Prove to me that this faith you speak of is real though not accompanied by deeds, and by my deeds I will prove to you my faith. . . . Can you not see, you quibbler, that faith divorced from deeds is barren? Was it not by his action, in offering his son Isaac upon the altar, that our father Abraham was justified? Surely you can see that faith was at work in his actions, and that by these actions the integrity of his faith was fully proved. Here was the fulfillment of the words of Scripture: "Abraham put his faith in God and it was counted to him as righteousness"; and elsewhere he is called "God's friend." You see then that a man is justified by deeds and not by faith alone. (James, *Letter* 2:14–24)

If good works save, then assuredly sin kills, and for eternity. Such at least is the opinion of the author of the "Letter to the Hebrews."

When men have once been enlightened, when they have had a taste of the heavenly gift and a share in the Holy Spirit, when they have experienced the goodness of God's word and the spiritual energies of the age to come, and after all this have fallen away, it is impossible to bring them once again to repentance; for with their own hands they are crucifying the Son of God and making mock of his death. (Hebrews 6:4–6)

And if one looks at the severity of the penalties in the Mosaic Law, the same conclusion imposes itself.

If we wilfully persist in sin after receiving the knowledge of the truth, no sacrifice for sins remains: only a terrifying expectation of judgment and fierce fire which will consume God's enemies. If a man disregards the Law of Moses, he is put to death without pity on the testimony of two or three witnesses. Think how much more severe a penalty that man will deserve who has trampled under foot the Son of God, profaned the blood of the Covenant by which he was consecrated and affronted God's gracious spirit! For we know who it is who has said "Justice is mine: I will repay"; and again, "The Lord will judge His people." It is a terrible thing to fall into the hands of the Living God. (Hebrews 10: 26–31)

This severe view did not long survive. The Gospels, after all, were filled with encouragement to repentence and forgiveness, and not merely by Jesus. Forgiveness was also available to his followers, as when he said:

I tell you this: no sin, no slander is beyond forgiveness for men; but whoever slanders the Holy Spirit can never be forgiven; he is guilty of eternal sin. (Mark 3:29)

Or here, addressing Peter, or perhaps all the Apostles:

I will give you the keys of the kingdom of Heaven; what you forbid on earth shall be forbidden in heaven, and what you allow on earth will be allowed in heaven. (Matthew 16:19)

Both these passages are difficult, but the Church recognized that sins committed after Christian baptism could be forgiven. Sin was a fact of life, as Tertullion concedes:

We ourselves do not forget the distinction between sins, which was the starting point of our discussion. John has sanctioned it [in the letter cited earlier] and there are in fact some sins of daily committal to which we are all liable; for who is free from the accident of being angry unjustly and after sunset; or even of using bodily violence; or easily speaking evil; or rashly swearing; or forfeiting his promised word; or lying from bashfulness or necessity? In business, in official duties, in trade, in food, in sight, in hearing, by how great temptations are we assailed. But if there were no pardon for such simple sins as these, salvation would be unattainable by any. Of these then there will be pardon through the successful intercessor with the Father, Christ. (Tertullian, *On Shame* 19)

These are the Torah's "inadvertent sins," for which "the priest shall make expiation before the Lord for the said individual, and he shall be forgiven" (Num. 15:27–28). But like the Torah, Tertullian recognizes that there are other, graver sins, perhaps beyond the possibility of forgiveness or atonement.

. . . Wholly different from these, graver and more destructive, such as are incapable of pardon—murder, idolatry, fraud, apostasy, blasphemy, and, of course, adultery and fornication, and whatever other violation of the temple there may be. For these Christ will no more be the successful intercessor; these will not at all be committed by anyone who has been born of God, for he will cease to be the son of God if he commits them. (Tertullian, *On Shame* 19)

Tertullian did not always feel that even those grave sins were unforgiveable. In an earlier essay, "On Penance," he wrestled with the question more hopefully. Conversion and baptism, he knew, wiped the slate clean for the new Christian. But what of the possibility of a second "conversion"—the Greek word for conversion is the same as that used by the Christians for repentance—after baptism? He is not entirely easy with the possibility.

I shrink from mentioning a second, or rather a final, hope, for to treat of any further opportunity of repentance seems almost to suggest another chance to sin. Still . . . though the great gate of forgiveness has been barred and bolted at baptism, second repentance waits in the vestibule to open a postern door once more to those who knock. But once more only, for it is the second time; never again if this once fails. Surely this once is enough; it is a mercy wholly undeserved. . . . The postern is narrow and hard to pass . . . but the alternative is hell.

24. Confession and the Punishment of Sin

By Tertullian's day, then, the Church recognized, if somewhat reluctantly at times, that as far as concerned the "grave sins"—the lesser infractions seem to have required little formality for forgiveness—there existed the possibility of earning a second, postbaptismal forgiveness. This was accomplished through "penance," a word that did service for the confession of one's sins, penalties the Church attached to their forgiveness, and that forgiveness itself, the sinner's reconciliation with the Church. Tertullian continues on the subject of this second chance offered to the sinner.

The second and only remaining penitence is so critical a matter that the testing of it is correspondingly laborious; it is not enough for it to be witnessed by mere admission of guilt; it has also to be carried out in action. This action is more commonly expressed and spoken of under its Greek name, *exomologesis*, by which we confess our sin to the Lord; not indeed as if He were ignorant, but inasmuch as the process of satisfaction is set in motion by confession, and by confession penitence is produced, and by penitence God is appeased.

Thus *exomologesis* is a discipline consisting in prostration and humiliation, imposing on the offender such a demeanor as to attract mercy. With regard also to the very dress and food of the penitent, this discipline enjoins him to go about in sackcloth and ashes, to cover his body in the squalor of mourning, to cast down his spirit with grief, to exchange his self-indulgence for harsh treatment of himself; to have no acquaintance with any food or drink but the plainest, and this not for his stomach's sake but his soul's; in general, to nourish prayers with fasting, to groan, to weep and moan day and night to the Lord his God, to prostrate himself before the presbyter, and to kneel before God's dear ones; to invoke all the brethren as sponsor of his prayers for mercy. The purpose of *exomologesis* is to enhance penitence, to honor God by showing dread of the peril of His anger; by itself pronouncing judgment on the sinner to act as a surrogate for God's indignation; and by temporal affliction, I would not say to frustrate, but to cancel eternal punishment. (Tertullian, *On Penance* 9)

As Tertullian's text reveals, this ecclesiastical punishment was both severe and public. Jerome has left us a rhetorically enhanced picture of just such a case in Rome. Letter 77 was written in 399 C.E. on the occasion of the death of Fabiola, a rich Roman woman under his spiritual care. She had divorced her first husband, "a man of such unspeakable vices that even a whore or a common slave would not have put up with him," Jerome says. Her remarriage was a sin for a Christian woman or man, since, as Jerome points out with pride, "for us what is unlawful for women is equally unlawful for men, and as both sexes serve God they are bound by the same conditions." Fabiola, it appears, was not aware of the prohibtion against remarriage in such cases.

At the death of her second husband she came to herself, and at a time when widows have shaken off the yoke of slavery, live more carelessly and recklessly, frequent the baths, flit here and there across the public places and show off their harlot faces, she put on sackcloth and made a public confession of her mistake. On the eve of Easter, as all of Rome looked on, she took her place with the other penitents in the basilica where once Lateranus perished by Caesar's sword. There in the presence of the bishop and priests and a weeping populace, she exposed her disheveled hair, her wan face, her soiled hands, her dust-stained neck. . . .

This I will say: . . . Fabiola was not ashamed of the Lord on earth and He will not be ashamed of her in heaven. She exposed her wound to all, and Rome tearfully beheld the scar upon her livid body. She uncovered her limbs, bared her head and closed her mouth. Like Moses' sister Mary, she sat alone outside the camp until the priest who cast her out should call her back. She came down from her couch of luxury, she took up the millstone and ground meal, with unshod feet she passed through rivers of tears. She sat upon coals of fire and these were her helpers. She struck the face by which she had won her second husband's love, she abhorred all jewelry, she could not so much as look upon linen, she shrank from all adornment. She grieved as if she had been guilty of adultery, and she expended money on many medicines to cure one wound. (Jerome, *Letter* 77:4–5)

The rite of public penance normally began on Ash Wednesday, when the penitents presented themselves to the bishop at the cathedral door. After the penitents had been led into the church and after the bishop and the clergy had prostrated themselves and tearfully chanted the seven penitential psalms, the bishop sprinkled them with holy water, cast ashes over them, covered their heads with sackcloth, and made formal announcement of their excommunication and the penance required for their readmission to the Church. After the prescribed time, many years in some cases, reconciliation with the Church and readmission to the sacraments took place on Holy Thursday. There were in addition continuing disabilities. Readmission could occur only once in a lifetime, and those who submitted to it could not afterwards marry or, if they already were married, they could not henceforward engage in sexual relations with their spouses. Nor could they enter the army or take up the clerical life. The infamy of the condition and the severity of the penalties made confession and penance a heroic act indeed for most Christians, and there appear to have been few willing to submit to the ordeal. Many preferred to postpone the act of reconciliation to their deathbed. Others, we must think, preferred to throw themselves on the mercy of God.

The reasons are complex, but attitudes and practices began to change in the Western churches in the sixth century. It was no longer thought that repentance and reconciliation were a once-in-a-liftetime possibility, and the bishop was no longer regarded as the Church's sole instrument in effecting that reconciliation. Christians began confessing to their ordinary parish priests; these latter in turn increasingly imposed penances that were, like the confessions that preceded them and the reconciliation or absolution that followed, a private matter. By the beginning of the thirteenth century, frequent private confession was not merely possible, it was required of European Christians, as prescribed by the twenty-first canon of the Fourth Lateran Council.

Every Christian of either sex, after attaining years of discretion, shall faithfully confess all his sins to his own priest at least once a year, and shall endeavor according to his ability to fulfill the penance enjoined him, reverently receive the sacrament of the Eucharist at least at Easter, unless perchance, on the advice of his own priest, for some reasonable cause, he determines to abstain for a time from receiving it. Otherwise he shall both be withheld from entrance into the church while he lives and be deprived of Christian burial when he dies. Wherefore this salutary enactment shall be frequently published in the churches lest anyone assume a veil of excuse in the blindness of ignorance.

The entire proceeding is to be conducted with the most rigorously maintained confidentiality.

Further, he [that is, the confessor] is to give earnest heed that he does not in any way betray the sinner by word or sign or in any other way; but if he needs more prudent advice he shall seek this cautiously, without any divulging of the person, since we decree that whoever shall presume to reveal a sin made known to him in the adjudication of penance is not only to be deposed from the priestly office but also to be thrust into a strict monastery to do perpetual penance. (Acts of the Fourth Lateran Council [1215]) [MCNEILL & GAMER 1938: 413–414]

The desired spiritual, psychological, and even physical circumstances of private confession are succinctly set out in the statutes of a Paris synod of sometime about 1197 C.E.

Priests shall apply the greatest care and caution with regard to confession, namely, that they diligently search out sins, the habitual ones severally, the occasional ones only indirectly or circumstantially, still in such a way that the matter of the confession is supplied from the sins.

Priests shall select for themselves a place easy of access in the church so that they can be seen by all generally; and no one shall hear confessions in a secret place or outside the church, except in great need or sickness.

The priest shall have a humble countenance in confession, and he shall not look at the face of the confessant, especially of a woman, on account of the obligation of honor; and he shall patiently hear what she says in a spirit of mildness and to the best of his ability persuade her by various methods to make an integral confession, for otherwise he shall say it is of no value to her.

Having heard the confession, the confessor shall always ask the confessant if he is willing to refrain from every mortal sin; otherwise he shall not absolve him nor impose a penance upon him. . . .

In imposing slight penances priests shall take heed to themselves, for the nature of the penance ought to be according to the nature of the guilt and the capacity of the confessant.

In confession confessors shall take heed to themselves not to inquire the names of persons with whom the confessants have sinned, but only the circumstances and nature (of the sins), and if the confessant tells the names, the confessor shall rebuke him and shall hold this as secret as the sin of the confessant.

He shall not dare to reveal anybody's confession to any person, from anger or hatred or even from fear of death, by sign or word, generally or specifically. . . . And if he reveals it he ought to be degraded without mercy. (Synodical Constitutions of Odo of Paris [ca. 1197])

[McNEILL & GAMER 1938: 412]

6. Priests, Princes, and Overseers

1. The Governance of Israel

The Hebrews were governed as we should expect them to be, by a tribal shaykh, *and from Abraham onward that elder received directions and occasional visitations from the God who had Himself announced that He was their Lord. But after the sojourn in Egypt, their Lord intervened more frequently in the affairs of His people and often, as in the wilderness of Sinai, in a quite direct fashion. In Sinai, Moses was both a spokesman for the deity and a charismatic tribal leader, but even under those quite extraordinary conditions there are traces of other, more obscure organs of government, many of them doubtless cast back upon that generation of pioneers by later Israelite society. In Numbers, for example, Moses speaks to the Lord:*

"I cannot carry all this people by myself, for it is too much for me. If You would deal thus with me, kill me rather, I beg you, and let me see no more of my wretchedness." Then the Lord said to Moses, "Gather Me seventy of Israel's elders of whom you have experience as elders and officers of the people, and bring them to the Tent of Meeting and let them take their place with you. I will come down and speak with you there, and I will draw upon the spirit that is on you and put it upon them; they shall share the burden of the people with you, and you shall not bear it alone. . . ."

Moses went out and reported the words of the Lord to the people. He gathered seventy of the people's elders and stationed them around the Tent. Then the Lord came down in a cloud and spoke to him; He drew upon the spirit that was on him and put it upon the seventy elders. And when the spirit rested upon them, they spoke in ecstasy, but did not continue. (Numbers 11:14–25)

2. The Establishment of the Priesthood

Whether or not Moses had a prototype Sanhedrin at his side, the early Israelites almost certainly had another institution, again on the direct authority and command of the Lord. This was the body of priests, a group of men—a caste in effect—whose function, mode of life, and even dress set apart them apart from the other Israelites. The first of them was Moses' own brother Aaron. The Lord is once again speaking to Moses.

You shall bring forward your brother Aaron, with his sons, from among the Israelites, to serve me as priests: Aaron, Nadab and Abihu, Eleazar and Ithamar, the sons of Aaron. Make sacral vestments for your brother Aaron, for dignity and adornment. Next you shall instruct all who are skillful, whom I have endowed with the gift of skill, to make Aaron's vestments, for consecrating him to serve Me as priest. These are the vestments they are to make: a breastplate, an ephod, a robe, a fringed tunic, a headdress and a sash. They shall make these sacral vestments for your brother Aaron and his sons, for priestly service to Me; they, therefore, shall receive the gold, the blue, purple, and crimson yarns, and the fine linen. (Exodus 28:1–5)

You shall make the fringed tunic of fine linen. You shall make the headdress of fine linen. You shall make the sash of embroidered work. And for Aaron's sons also you shall make tunics, and make sashes for them, and make turbans for them, for dignity and adornment. Put these on your brother Aaron and on his sons as well; anoint them, and ordain them and consecrate them to serve me as priests.

You shall also make for them linen breeches to cover their nakedness; they shall extend from the hips to the thighs. They shall be worn by Aaron and his sons when they enter the Tent of Meeting or when they approach the altar to officiate in the sanctuary, so that they do not incur punishment and die. It shall be a law for all time for him and for his offspring to come. (Exodus 28:39–43)

If Aaron and his descendants were thus set apart from the other Israelites, it was for a purpose: they were to be, in effect, living paradigms of holiness.

The Lord spoke to Aaron saying: Drink no wine or other intoxicant, you or your sons with you, when you enter the Tent of Meeting, that you may not die—it is a law for all time throughout the ages. For you must distinguish between the sacred and the profane, and between the unclean and the clean; and you must teach the Israelites all the laws which the Lord has imparted to them through Moses.

The priests should perform none of the ordinary tribal functions; rather, they would be supported out of the sacrificial offerings of the people.

Moses said to Aaron and to his remaining sons Eleazar and Ithamar, "Take the meal offering from what is left over from the Lord's offerings by fire and eat it unleavened beside the altar because it is most holy. You shall eat it in the sacred precinct, inasmuch as it is your due, and that of your children, from the Lord's offerings by fire; for so I have been commanded. But the breast of the wave offering and the thigh of the heave offering you, and your sons and daughters with you, may eat in any clean place, for they have been assigned as a due to you and your children from the Israelites' sacrifices of well-being." (Leviticus 10:8–14)

Though there is clear evidence that the entire tribe of Levi was once designated as priests (see, for example, Deut. 18:1ff.), the finished version of the Israelite tradition reproduced in Exodus made a sharp and important distinction. Moses and Aaron were both of that tribe, but other members of Levi under a certain Korath rose up against the two leaders and attempted to seize control of the priestly functions (Num. 16–17). God intervened to punish the rebels, and the sequel defined a new role for the rest of the tribe of Levi.

The Lord said to Aaron: You with your sons and the ancestral house under your charge shall bear any guilt connected with the sanctuary; you and your sons alone shall bear any guilt connected with your priesthood. You shall associate with yourself your kinsmen of the tribe of Levi, your ancestral tribe, to be attached to you and to minister to you and to your sons under your charge before the Tent of the Pact. They shall discharge their duties to you and to the Tent as a whole, but they must not have any contact with the furnishings of the Shrine or with the altar, lest both they and you die. They shall be attached to you and discharge the duties of the Tent of Meeting, all the services of the Tent; but no outsider shall intrude upon you as you discharge the duties connected with the Shrine and the altar, that wrath may not again strike the Israelites.

I hereby take your fellow Levites from among the Israelites; they are assigned to you in dedication to the Lord, to do the work of the Tent of Meeting, while you and your sons are careful to perform your priestly duties in everything pertaining to the altar and to what is behind the curtain. I make your priesthood a service of dedication; any outsider who encroaches shall be put to death. (Numbers 18:1–7)

3. The Support of the Priestly Class

On this occasion, too, the support of the priestly class out of the offerings for sacrifice is further defined.

The Lord spoke further to Aaron: I hereby give you charge of My gifts, all the sacred donations of the Israelites; I grant them to you and your sons as a perquisite, a due for all time. This shall be yours from the most holy sacrifices, the offerings by fire: every such offering that they render to Me as most holy sacrifices, namely, every meal offering, every sin offering, and penalty offering of theirs, shall belong to you and your sons. You shall partake of them as most sacred donations: only males may eat them; you shall treat them as consecrated.

This too shall be yours: the heave offerings of their gifts, all the wave offerings of the Israelites, I give to you, to your sons, and to the daughters that are with you, as a due for all time; everyone of your household who is clean may eat it.

All the best of the new oil, wine and grain—the choice parts that they present to the Lord, I give to you. The first fruits of everything in their land, that they bring to the Lord, shall be yours; everyone of your household who is clean may eat them. Everything in Israel that has been proscribed in Israel shall be yours. . . .

And the Lord said to Aaron: You shall, however, have no territorial share among them or own any portion in their midst; I am your portion and your share among the Israelites.

And to the Levites I hereby give all the tithes in Israel as their share in return for the services that they perform, the services of the Tent of Meeting. Henceforth, Israelites shall not trespass on the Tent of Meeting, and thus incur guilt and die: only Levites shall perform the services of the Tent of Meeting; others would incur guilt. It is a law for all time throughout the ages. But they shall have no territorial share among the Israelites; for it is the tithes set aside by the Israelites as a gift to the Lord that I give to the Levites as their share. (Numbers 18:8–24)

4. The Purity of the Priesthood

Since the Jewish priesthood was in effect a tribal caste whose membership was determined by descent alone, special attention was given to maintaining its ethical and ethnic purity, particularly with regard to marriage.

The Lord said to Moses: Speak to the priests, the sons of Aaron, and say to them: None shall defile himself for any (dead) person among his kin, except for the relatives that are closest to him. . . . They shall not shave smooth any part of their heads, or cut the side growth of their beards, or make gashes in their flesh. They shall be holy to their God and not profane the name of their God; for they offer the Lord's offerings by fire, the food of their God, and so must be holy.

A priest shall not marry a woman degraded by harlotry, nor shall they marry one divorced from her husband. For they are holy to their God and you must treat them as holy, since they offer the food of your God. They shall be holy to you, for I the Lord who sanctify you am holy. When the daughter of a priest degrades herself through harlotry, it is her father whom she degrades; she shall be put to the fire.

The priest who is exalted among this fellows [that is, the High Priest], on whose head the anointing oil has been poured and who has been ordained to wear the vestments, shall not bare his head nor rend his vestments. He shall not go where there is any dead body; he shall not defile himself even for his father or mother. He shall not go outside the sanctuary and profane the sanctuary of his God, for upon him is the distinction of the anointing oil of his God, Mine, the Lord's. He may marry only a woman who is a virgin. A widow or a divorced woman or one who is degraded by harlotry—such he may not marry. Only a virgin of his own kin may he take to wife—that he may not profane his off-spring among his kin, for I the Lord have sanctified him.

Speak to Aaron in these words: No man among your offspring throughout the ages who has a defect shall be qualified to offer the food of his God: no man who is blind, or lame, or has a limb too short or too long; no man who has a broken leg or a broken arm; or who is a hunch-back, or a dwarf, or who has a growth in his eye, or has a boil scar or scurvy, or crushed testes. . . . He may eat the food of his God, of both the most holy as well as of the holy; but he may not enter behind the curtains or come near the altar, for he has a defect. He shall not profane those places sacred to me, for I the Lord have sanctified them. . . .

No man of Aaron's offspring who has an eruption or a discharge shall eat of the sacred donations until he is clean. If one touches anything made unclean by a corpse, or if a man has an emission of semen, or if a man touches any swarming thing by which he is made unclean or any human being by which he is made unclean—whatever his uncleanness— the person who touches such shall be unclean until evening and shall not eat of the sacred donations unless he has washed his body in water. (Leviticus 21:1–22:7)

How seriously the question of priestly descent was taken, to the point even of keeping careful genealogical records, is manifest in what occurred upon the return to Judea after the Exile.

The following were those who returned from Tel-melah, Tel-harsha, Kerub, Addan, and Immer, but could not establish their father's family nor whether by descent they belonged to Israel: the family of Delaiah, the family of Tobiah, and the family of Nekoda, six hundred and fifty-two. Also of the priests: the family of Hobaiah, the family of Hakkoz, and the family of Barzillai who had married a daughter of Barzillai of Gilead and went by his name. These searched for their names among those enrolled in the genealogies, but they could not be found: they were disqualified for the priesthood as unclean, and the governor forbade them to partake of the most sacred food until there should be a priest able to consult the Urim and the Thummim.

The prospects for those thus barred were not good: the practice of consulting the sacred lots called Urim and Thummim (see 1 Sam. 14:38–42) had long since been discontinued, with little expectation that it would soon be restored. At a later stage, and perhaps earlier as well, a claimant to the priesthood, given the proper genealogical certification, had to present himself to the High Council (Sanhedrin) to be certified on physical grounds.

The Chamber of Hewn Stone—there used the Great Sanhedrin of Israel to sit and judge the priesthood; and if in any priest a blemish was found, he clothed himself in black and veiled himself in black and deported and went his way; and he in whom no blemish was found clothed himself in white and veiled himself in white and went in and ministered with his brethren the priests. And they kept it as a festival day that no blemish had been found in the seed of Aaron the priest. And thus they used to say: "Blessed be God, blessed be He, in that no blemish has been found in the seed of Aaron! And blessed be He that chose Aaron and his sons to stand and serve before the Lord in the Holy of Holies!" (M.Middoth 5:4)

5. The Priestly Courses

There were more priests in Israel than were needed for the service at any one time, so the whole number of families who constituted the offspring of Aaron were divided into "courses" (mishmarot), twenty-four of them in all. Their members served in turn, probably from one Sabbath to the next, in the Temple. This is how the first Book of Chronicles explains the arrangement at the time of King David.

The divisions of the Aaronites were: the sons of Aaron: Nadab and Abihu, Eleazar and Ithamar. Nadab and Abihu died in the lifetime of their father, and they had no children, so Eleazar and Ithamar served as priests. David: Zadok of the sons of Eleazar and Ahimelech of the sons of Ithamar divided them into offices by their tasks. The sons of Eleazar turned out to be more numerous by male heads than the sons of Ithamar, so that they divided the sons of Eleazar into sixteen chiefs of clans, and the sons of Ithamar into eight clans. They divided them by lot, both on an equal footing, since they were all Sanctuary officers and officers of God—the sons of Eleazar and the sons of Ithamar. Shemaiah the son of Nathanel, the scribe, who was of the Levites, registered them under the eye of the king, the officers, and Zadok the priest, and Ahimelech son of Abiathar, and the chiefs of clans of the priests and Levites—one clan more taken for Eleazar for each taken of Ithamar.

The list of the heads of the twenty-four courses then follows in order. The text concludes:

According to this allocation of offices by tasks, they were to enter the House of the Lord as was laid down for them by Aaron their father, as the Lord God of Israel had commanded him. (1 Chronicles 24:1–19)

Whatever its beginnings, this arrangement continued until the destruction of the Temple. We catch a glimpse of its operation in the opening chapter of the Gospel of Luke.

In the days of Herod king of Judea, there was a priest named Zechariah, *of the division of the priesthood called after Abiah* [that is, the eighth of the twenty-four courses listed in 1 Chron. 24:7–18]. His wife was also of priestly descent; her name was Elizabeth. Both of them were upright and devout, blamelessly observing all the commandments and ordinances of the Lord. But they had no children, for Elizabeth was barren, and both were well on in years.

Once, *when it was the turn of his division and he was there to take part in the divine service, it fell to his lot, by priestly custom, to enter the sanctuary of the Lord and offer the incense*; and the whole congregation was at prayer outside. It was the hour of the incense offering.

An angel appears to Zechariah and announces to him the future birth of his son, John, the later Baptist.

Meanwhile the people were waiting for Zechariah, surprised that he was waiting so long inside. When he did come he could not speak to them, and they realized that he had a vision in the sanctuary. He stood there making signs to them, and remained dumb.

When his period of duty was completed, Zechariah returned home. After this his wife Elizabeth conceived. (Luke 1:5–24)

6. A King in Israel

We have already seen in Chapter 1 above the Israelite monarchy in its glory under David and Solomon and in less honorable circumstances under some of their successors. But the people had been warned of this institution, which the Lord had granted only reluctantly. We return to the days of Samuel, before there was a king in Israel.

When Samuel grew old, he appointed his sons judges over Israel. The name of the firstborn was Joel, and his second son's name was Abijah; they sat as judges in Beer-sheba. But his sons did not follow in his ways; they were bent on gain, they accepted bribes, and they subverted justice. All the elders of Israel assembled and came to Samuel at Ramah and they said to him, "You have grown old, and your sons do not follow in your ways. Therefore appoint a king for us, to govern us like all other nations." Samuel was displeased that they said "Give us a king to govern us." Samuel prayed to the Lord, and the Lord replied to Samuel, "Heed the demand of the people in everything they say to you. For it is not you they have rejected; it is Me they have rejected as their king. Like everything else they have done since I brought them out of Egypt to this day— forsaking Me and worshiping other gods—so they are doing to you. Heed their demand, but warn them solemnly, and tell them about the practices of any king who will rule over them."

Samuel reported all the words of the Lord to the people who were asking for a king. He said, "This will be the practice of the king who will rule you. He will take your sons and appoint them his charioteers and horsemen, and they will serve as outrunners for his chariots. He will appoint them as his chiefs of thousands and fifties; or they will have to plow his fields, reap his harvest, and make his weapons and the equipment for his chariots. He will take your daughters as perfumers, cooks and bakers. He will seize your choice fields, vineyards and olive groves, and give them to his courtiers. He will take your male and female slaves, your choice young men and your asses, and put them to work for him He will take a tenth part of your flocks and you shall become his slaves. The day will come when you will cry out because of the king whom you yourselves have chosen; and the Lord will not answer you on that day."

But the people would not listen to Samuel's warning. "No," they said. "We must have a king over us, that we may be like all the other nations. Let our king rule over us and go out at our head and fight our battles." When Samuel heard all that the people said, he reported it to the Lord. And the Lord said to Samuel, "Heed their demands and appoint a king for them." (1 Samuel 8:1–22)

7. The Courts and the Judiciary

The king was not the only ruler of Israel. There were the priests, the wardens of God's worship, and other less well-defined groups like "the Elders of Israel, all the heads of tribes who were chiefs of families in Israel" (1 Kings 8:1), who appear from time to time in the royal chronicles, though they do not seem to have had any real power. There was also a judicial machinery, as appears to lie behind these enactments in Deuteronomy.

If a case is too baffling for you to decide, be it a controversy over homicide, civil law or assault—matters of dispute in your courts—you shall promptly repair to the place which the Lord your God will have chosen, and appear before the levitical priests, or the magistrate in charge at the time, and present your problem. When they have announced to you the verdict in the case, you shall carry out the verdict which is announced to you from that place which the Lord chose, observing scrupulously all their instructions to you. You shall act in accordance to the instructions given you and the ruling handed down to you; you must not deviate from the verdict they announce to you either to the right or to the left. Should a man act presumptuously and disregard the priest charged with serving the Lord your God or the magistrate, that man shall die. Thus you will sweep out evil from Israel: all the people will hear and be afraid and not act presumptuously again. (Deuteronomy 17:8–13)

8. The Role of the Priests

The passage in Deuteronomy is strong on exhortation but less generous in explaining means and procedures, perhaps deliberately so. Solomon had put down the foundations of empire, but many years were to pass before the machinery of organization and rule grew to maturity in Jerusalem and the rest of the kingdom. Most of the process is lost to our sight, since it was not of great concern to the anonymous transmitters who stand behind the books called Kings and Chronicles. There are only

glimpses. For example, King Jehoshaphat (871–849 B.C.E.) set up a judicial ma-
chinery with a competence in matters of both religious and royal statute law, as well
as with what appears to be a police function on the part of the Levites.

He appointed judges in the land, in all the fortified towns of Judah,
in each and every town. He charged the judges: "Consider what you are
doing, for you judge not on behalf of man, but on behalf of the Lord, and
He is with you when you pass judgment. Now let the dread of the Lord
be upon you; act with care, for there is no injustice or favoritism or
bribe-taking with the Lord our God." In Jerusalem Jehoshaphat also
appointed some Levites and priests and some heads of the clans of Israelites for rendering judgments in matters of the Lord, and for disputes.
Then they returned to Jerusalem. He charged them, "This is how you
shall act, in fear of the Lord with fidelity, and with whole heart. When
a dispute comes before you from your brothers living in their towns,
whether about homicide or about ritual, you must instruct them so that
they do not incur guilt before the Lord. . . . See, Amariah the chief priest
is over you in all cases concerning the Lord, and Zebadiah son of Ishmael
is the commander of the house of Judah in all cases concerning the king;
the levitical officers are at your disposal; act with resolve and the Lord be
with the good." (2 Chronicles 19:5–11)

9. Judea after the Exile

With exile came the end of the monarchy; but once restored to Judea by Cyrus, the
Jews were confronted again with some degree of self-rule, now no longer under the
politically unacceptable institution of kingship but in some other form that would
serve the community's own needs and represent them vis-à-vis their new sovereigns,
Persian, Greek, and Roman. That form was likely an aristocratic council—what the
Greeks later called a boule *and the Romans a senate. There is no direct evidence*
from the Persian period (ca. 538–332 B.C.E.). Writing at the very beginning of the
Greeks' settlement into the land, Hecateus describes the Jewish form of self-govern-
ment, an arrangement that he casts back, perhaps with the assistance of a helpful
priestly informant, into an idealized Mosaic past.

Moses chose the men of the greatest refinement and the greatest
ability to lead the entire nation, and he appointed them priests; and he
ordered that they should have to do with the Temple and the honors and
sacrifices offered to their God. These same men he appointed to be judges
in all major disputes, and he entrusted to them the guardianship of the
laws and customs. For this reason the Jews never have a king, and authority over the people is regularly vested in whichever priest is regarded as

superior to his colleagues in wisdom and virtue. This man is called the High Priest, and it is believed that he acts as a messenger to them of God's commandments. It is he, we are told, who in their assemblies and other gatherings announces what has been decreed, and the Jews are so docile in such matters that they straightway fall to the ground and do reverence to the High Priest when he declares the commandments to them. (Hecateus, *Aegyptiaca*)

That is not the picture we are given about a century later, when the Jews' new Greek sovereign, Antiochus III, enters Jerusalem.

King Antiochus to Ptolemy, greetings. Since the Jews, beginning from the time that we entered their territory, have testified to their zeal in our regard, and since, from our arrival in their city they have received us in a magnificent manner and came out to meet us with their senate [*gerousia*, literally "Council of Elders"], have contributed generously to the upkeep of our soldiers and our elephants, and have assisted us in capturing the Egyptian garrison in the citadel, we have judged it proper that we too should respond to those good offices by restoring their city destroyed by the misfortunes of war and repopulating it by bringing back all those people dispersed from it. (Josephus, *Antiquities* 12.3.3)

10. A Hero High Priest of the Second Temple

We are given a vivid, if somewhat idealized, portrait of a High Priest presiding over the Temple ritual in Ecclesiasticus, or the Wisdom of Jesus ben Sira. Simon son of Onias, after whom the portrait was drawn, was High Priest in Jerusalem ca. 225–200 B.C.E. and was probably personally known to Ben Sira.

It was the High Priest Simon son of Onias in whose lifetime the House [that is, the Second Temple, built by Zerubbabel after the return from the Babylonian exile] was repaired, in whose days the Temple was fortified. How glorious he was, surrounded by the people, when he came from behind the Temple curtain! He was like the morning star appearing through the clouds or the moon at the full; like the sun shining on the Temple of the Most High or the light of the rainbow on the gleaming clouds. . . . When he put on his gorgeous vestments, robed himself in perfect splendor, and went up to the holy altar, he added luster to the court of the sanctuary. When the priests were handing him the portions of the sacrifice, as he stood by the altar hearth with his brothers round him like a garland, he was like a young cedar of Lebanon in the midst of a circle of palms.

All the sons of Aaron in their magnificence stood with the Lord's offering in their hands before the whole congregation of Israel. To complete the ceremonies at the altar and adorn the offering of the Most High, the Almighty, he held out his hand for the libation cup and poured out the blood of the grape, poured its fragrance at the foot of the altar to the Most High, the King of all. Then the sons of Aaron shouted and blew their trumpets of beaten silver; they sounded a mighty fanfare as a reminder before the Lord. Instantly the people as one man fell on their faces to worship the Lord their God, the Almighty, the Most High. Then the choir broke into praise, in the full sweet strains of resounding song, while the people of the Most High were making their petitions to the merciful Lord, until the liturgy of the Lord was finished and the ritual complete. Then Simon came down and raised his hands over the whole congregation of Israel, to pronounce the Lord's blessing, proud to take His name on his lips: and a second time they bowed in worship to receive the blessing from the Most High. (Ecclesiasticus 50:1–21)

11. Hasmonean Sovereignty

In 200 B.C.E., then, there was both a High Priest and a Council of Elders ruling over the Jews, though under the sovereignty of a Greek king in Antioch and whatever delegates and lieutenants he chose to send out to his province of Judea. That arrangement was not a happy one, as we have seen in Chapter 2 above, and Jewish discontent with the Seleucid lords and their policy of Hellenization led first to insurrection and then to a kind of autonomy.

The Maccabees won the effective independence of a Jewish state in Judea through the force of arms; what remained was to negotiate that effective control into recognized and juridical sovereignty, something that could be bestowed only by the Seleucid sovereigns with whom they had been at war. But in the mid-second century B.C.E. the Seleucids were even more deeply engaged in a war among themselves, and in the context of this rivalry the new Judean state appeared not so much as a rebellious vassal but as an ally to be wooed and won—first by the pretender Alexander Balas and then by his rival Demetrius—on terms acceptable to the new Maccabean leader, Jonathan.

King Alexander (Balas) to his brother Jonathan, greeting:

We have heard about you, what a valiant man you are and how fit to be our friend. Now therefore we do appoint you this day to be High Priest of your nation with the title of "King's Friend," to support our cause and to keep friendship with us.

Thus, with the blessings of Alexander Balas, Jonathan assumed the vestments of the High Priest and ruler of the Jewish state on the Feast of Tabernacles in 152 B.C.E.

When this news reached Demetrius, he was mortified. "How did we come to let Alexander forestall us," he asked, "in gaining the friendship and support of the Jews? I too will send them cordial messages and offer honors and gifts to keep them on my side." So he sent a message to the Jews to this effect:

"King Demetrius to the Jewish nation, greeting. . . . Jerusalem and all its environs, with its tithes and tolls, shall be sacred and tax-free. I also surrender authority over the citadel in Jerusalem and grant the High Priest the right to garrison it with men of his own choice. . . .

"Ptolemais and the lands belonging to it I make over to the Temple in Jerusalem, to meet the expenses proper to it. I give 15,000 silver shekels annually, charged on my own royal accounts, to be drawn from such places as may prove convenient. And the arrears of the subsidy, insofar as it has not been paid by the revenue officials, as it formerly was, shall henceforward be paid in for the needs of the Temple. In addition, the 5,000 silver shekels that used to be taken from the annual income of the Temple are also released, because they belong to the ministering priests. . . . The cost of rebuilding and repair of the Temple shall be borne by the royal revenue; also the repair of the walls of Jerusalem and its surrounding fortifications, as well as of the fortresses of Judea, shall be at the expense of the royal revenue." (1 Maccabees 10:18–45)

There was, however, even greater power within the grasp of the house of Hasmon, and it was bestowed on one of them, Simon, not by a foreign sovereign in Antioch but by the Jewish people themselves.

On the eighteenth day of the month Elul, in the year 172 [140 B.C.E.], the third year of Simon's High Priesthood, at Asaramel, in a large assembly of priests, people, rulers of the nation and elders of the land, the following facts were placed on record. . . .

The Jews and their priests confirmed Simon as their leader and High Priest in perpetuity until a true prophet should appear. He was to be their general, and to have full charge of the Temple; and in addition to this the supervision of their labor, of the country, and of the arms and fortifications was to be entrusted to him. He was to be obeyed by all; all contracts in the country were to be drawn up in his name. He was to wear the purple robe and the golden clasp.

None of the people or the priests shall have authority to abrogate any of these decrees, to oppose commands issued by Simon or to convoke any assembly in the land without his assent, to be robed in purple or to wear the gold clasp. Whosoever shall contravene these provisions or neglect any of them shall be liable to punishment. It is the unanimous decision of the people that Simon shall officiate in the ways here laid down. Simon has agreed and consented to be High Priest, General and Ethnarch of the Jews and the priests, and to be the protector of them all. (1 Maccabees 14:25–47)

This was power indeed, more than had been possessed by any previous Jewish leader, whether Moses, David, or Solomon in all his glory. From Simon down to Alexander Janneus, the Hasmonean rulers of Israel were both kings and High Priests.

12. The Pharisees

The surrender to the house of Hasmon of such enormous power, civil and religious, did not obliterate the other sources of authority and autonomy in the Jewish polity: the Gerousia and "the people" still fitfully appear throughout the Hasmonean period, though the former began to show some remarkable changes. Beginning with the reign of John Hyrcanus (134–104 B.C.E.), the Pharisees seem to have enjoyed a more important position in the affairs of state, either as opponents of the crown or, with Alexandra Salome, as its most trusted advisers. Witness Alexander Janneus' (103–76 B.C.E.) deathbed advice to his queen, Alexandra.

She should yield a certain amount of power to the Pharisees, (he said), for if they praised her in return for this sign of regard, they would dispose the nation favorably toward her. These men, he assured her, had so much influence over their fellow Jews that they could injure those whom they hated and help those with whom they were friendly; for they had the complete confidence of the masses when they spoke harshly of any person, even when they did so out of envy; and he himself, he added, had come into conflict with the (Jewish) nation because these men had been badly treated by him. . . .

(After the death of Janneus) Alexandra appointed (her son) Hyrcanus as High Priest because of his greater age but more especially because of his lack of energy; and she permitted the Pharisees to do as they liked in all matters, and also commanded the people to obey them; and whatever regulations, introduced by the Pharisees in accordance with the traditions of their fathers, had been abolished by her father-in-law (John) Hyrcanus, these she again restored. And so, while she had the title of sovereign, the Pharisees had the power. For example, they recalled exiles and freed prisoners, and in a word, in no way differed from absolute rulers. (Josephus, *Antiquities* 13.15.5–16.2)

13. Herod and the Sanhedrin

The pre-eminence of the Pharisees was no match for the ambitions or nakedly wielded power of Herod (37–4 B.C.E.). Although they continue to appear in the narrative of Josephus, it is often in the role of the ill-treated conscience of the king. The tone was set, perhaps, early in Herod's career, when he was still only the teen-aged governor of Galilee on behalf of his father, Antipater. In the course of his stormy stewardship he caught and executed an insurrectionist named Ezekias.

The chief Jews were in great fear when they saw how powerful and reckless Herod was and how much he desired to be dictator. And so they came to Hyrcanus [High Priest and, at the death of Salome, king of Judea], and now openly accused Antipater, saying, "How long will you keep quiet in the face of what is happening? Do you not see that Antipater and his sons have girded themselves with royal power, while you have only the name of king given you? . . . They are openly acknowledged to be masters. Thus Herod, his son, has killed Ezekias and many of his men in violation of our Law, which forbids us to slay a man, even an evildoer, unless he has been first condemned by the Synhedrion [that is, the Sanhedrin] to suffer this fate. He, however, has dared to do this without authority from you."

Having heard these arguments, Hyrcanus was persuaded. . . . Hyrcanus summoned Herod to stand trial for the crimes of which he was accused. Accordingly, after he had settled affairs in Galilee . . . he came with a troop sufficient for the purposes of the journey, and that he might not appear too formidable to Hyrcanus by arriving with a large body of men and yet not be entirely unarmed and unprotected; and so he went to his trial. However, Sextus, the (Roman) governor of Syria, wrote to urge Hyrcanus to acquit Herod of the charge and added threats as to what would happen if he disobeyed. The letter from Sextus gave Hyrcanus a pretext for letting Herod go without suffering any harm from the Synhedrion, for he loved him as a son. But when Herod stood in the Synhedrion with his troops, he overawed them all, and no one of those who had denounced him before his arrival dared to accuse him thereafter; instead there was silence and doubt as to what was to be done. (Josephus, *Antiquities* 14.9.2–4)

Herod later murdered most, if not all, of the Sanhedrin if we are to trust Josephus. The objects of his anger appear not to have been the Pharisees but the priests and aristocracy who shared membership in that council with the Pharisees. The Sanhedrin continued to function during Herod's reign, no longer as a powerful or important political body but simply as a religious court, where the Pharisees' views continued to prevail, which had been one of its functions from the beginning. But then, with the end of the Herodians and the Romans' assumption of direct rule in Judea, the makeup of the Sanhedrin reverted to what it had been before Herod's purge: an aristocratic body dominated by the High Priests, just as it appears on the occasion of the trial of Jesus (see Chapter 3 above).

14. The Great Sanhedrin

Our problems with understanding the Sanhedrin—how many there were (one or two or more), who they were, and what was their competence—are compounded by the fact that there are two bodies of sources that speak of it: the Greek-language testimonies, notably Philo, Josephus, and the New Testament, which often make it sound like a governing as well as a judicial body; and the rabbinic sources, which most often speak of it as a religious court, a Bet Din. In reality, it was probably both. A single body of seventy-one principals, with a mixed priestly and scholarly membership—the "chief priests, scribes, and elders" of the Gospel accounts— undoubtedly held jurisdiction over cases arising from the Mosaic Law, which was in effect the constitution of the Jewish commonwealth, and exercised as much or as little power to govern as the actual ruler—the Hasmoneans, Herodians, or Romans— chose to grant it. The third-, fourth-, and fifth-century rabbis, whose own interests were overwhelmingly legal, saw the Sanhedrin as essentially a judicial and religious body run by people like themselves, and they projected their view of the institution back into a period when its powers were wider and often considerably more secular. The Mishnaic tractate "Sanhedrin," for example, dwells chiefly on cases before the court, but it does occasionally comment more generally.

The greater Sanhedrin was made up of one and seventy (judges) and the lesser by three and twenty. Whence do we learn that the greater Sanhedrin was made up of one and seventy? It is written, "Gather to Me seventy men from the elders of Israel" (Num. 11:16, cited above), and Moses added to them makes one and seventy. (M.Sanhedrin 1:6)

The Sanhedrin was arranged like the half of a round threshing floor so that all might see one another. Before them stood the two scribes of the judges, one to the right and one to the left, and they wrote down the words of them that favored acquittal and the words of them that favored conviction. . . . Before them sat three rows of disciples of the Sages, and each knew his proper place. (Ibid. 4:3–4)

Again, the two sets of sources differ on the presidency of the Great Sanhedrin. The Greek-language testimonies, which speak of the situation before the destruction of the Temple, put the High Priest in charge; the Mishna and Talmud name the "pairs" of scholars who are the heads of the Pharisaic schools (see M.Pirke Aboth 1, cited in Chapter 5 above). The "former (or the senior of the pairs) were Presidents (Nasi), and the others were Fathers of the Court (Ab Bet Din)" (M.Hagigah 2:2).

15. Jesus Commissions the Twelve

Jesus made his public appearance in Israel when the Jewish and Roman organs of government were operating in the land side by side. He was constrained on occasion to advert to the Romans' institutions of sovereignty—their tax collectors, garrisons, and courts—but when his own community began to develop modest institutional organs, it is far more likely that they had Jewish rather than Roman prototypes.

Jesus went round all the towns and villages teaching in their synagogues, announcing the good news of the Kingdom and curing every kind of ailment and disease. The sight of the people moved him to pity; they were like sheep without a shepherd, harassed and helpless; and he said to his disciples, "The crop is heavy, but laborers are scarce; you must therefore beg the owner to send laborers to harvest his crop."

Then he called his twelve disciples to him and gave them authority to cast out unclean spirits and to cure every kind of ailment and disease. These are the names of the twelve apostles: first Simon, also called Peter, and his brother Andrew; James son of Zebedee, and his brother John; Philip and Bartholomew, Thomas and Matthew the tax gatherer; James son of Alpheus, Lebbeus [or Thaddeus]; Simon, a member of the Zealot party; and Judas Iscariot, the man who betrayed him.

These twelve Jesus sent out with the following instructions: "Do not take the road to Gentile lands, and do not enter any Samaritan town; but go rather to the lost sheep of the house of Israel. And as you go, proclaim the message: 'The Kingdom of heaven is upon you.' Heal the sick, raise the dead, cleanse lepers, cast out devils. You received without cost; give without charge." (Matthew 9:35–10:8)

And finally, in an eschatological context:

Peter said, "We have left everything to become your followers. What will there be for us?" Jesus replied, "I tell you this: in the world that is to be, when the Son of Man is seated on his throne in heavenly splendor, you my followers will have thrones of your own, where you will sit as judges over the twelve tribes of Israel." (Matthew 19:27–28)

In at least one celebrated passage (cited in Chapter 3 above) Peter is singled out in a special fashion among the followers of Jesus. The passage describes a conversation at Caesarea Philippi in which Peter, when asked by Jesus, "And you, who do you say I am?" responds, "You are the Messiah, the Son of the Living God."

Then Jesus said, "Simon, son of Jonah, you are favored indeed! You did not learn that from mortal man; it was revealed to you by my heavenly Father. And I say this to you: You are Peter, the Rock; and on this rock I will build my church (*ekklesia*), and the powers of death shall never conquer it. I will give you the keys of the Kingdom of Heaven." He then gave his disciples strict orders not to tell anyone that he was the Messiah. (Matthew 16:17–20)

16. The Bishops of Jerusalem

Whatever else Matthew's Gospel may have meant, or have been intended to mean, it was not understood by Jesus' immediate followers in Jerusalem as anointing Peter as the single head of the new Christian community. Peter is prominent in the events recorded in the Acts of the Apostles, but if there was any implied head of the church there, one is far more likely to think that it was James, "the brother of the Lord."

Then there was James, who was known as the brother of the Lord; for he too was called Joseph's son, and Joseph Christ's father, though in fact the Virgin was his betrothed, and before they came together she was found to be with child by the Holy Spirit, as the inspired Gospel narrative tells us. This James, whom the early Christians surnamed "the Righteous" because of his outstanding virtue, was the first, as the records tell us, to be elected to the episcopal throne of the Jerusalem church. Clement, in his *Outlines* Book VI puts it thus: "Peter, James and John, after the Ascension of the Savior, did not claim pre-eminence because the Savior had specially honored them, but chose James the Righteous as Bishop of Jerusalem." (Eusebius, *Church History* 2.1)

Eusebius kept close track of such matters as the episcopal succession in the various churches of the empire. This is what he has to say of the "Mother Church of all Christians," as it was called.

After the martyrdom of James [ca. 62 C.E.] and the capture of Jerusalem which instantly followed [this actually occurred in 70 C.E.], there is a firm tradition that those of the Apostles and disciples of the Lord who were still alive assembled from all parts of the empire, together with those who, humanly speaking, were kinsmen of the Lord—for most of them were still alive. Then they all discussed together whom they should choose as a fit person to succeed James, and they voted unanimously that

Symeon, son of the Clopas mentioned in the Gospel narrative (John 19:25), was a fit person to occupy the throne of the Jerusalem see. He was, so it was said, a cousin of the Lord. (Eusebius, *Church History* 3.11)

Of the dates of the bishops of Jerusalem I have failed to find any written evidence—it is known that they were very short-lived—but I have received documentary proof of this, that up to Hadrian's siege of the Jews [in 135 C.E.] there had been a series of bishops there. All are said to have been Hebrews in origin [that is, Jewish Christians], who had received the knowledge of Christ with all sincerity, with the result that those in a position to decide such matters judged them worthy of the episcopal office. For at that time their whole church consisted of Hebrew believers who had continued from Apostolic times down to the later siege in which the Jews, after revolting a second time from the Romans, were overwhelmed in a full-scale war. (Ibid. 4.5)

17. Early Christian Elders

James is never actually called "bishop" in the Acts of the Apostles. Eusebius was doubtlessly assimilating James' position to the state of affairs in his own day in the early fourth century. By then the powers and functions of a Christian "overseer" were already well defined. But that organization took some time to develop; early on, both the language and the understanding of who governed the communities of Christians were considerably looser. Indeed, "elder" (presbyteros) and "overseer" (episkopos) sometimes appear to be used interchangeably.

My intention in leaving you behind in Crete was that you should set in order what was left over, and in particular should institute elders [or presbyters] in each town. In doing so, observe the tests I prescribed: is he a man of unimpeachable character, faithful to one wife, the father of children who are believers, who are under no imputation of loose living, who are not out of control? For as God's steward the overseer (*episkopos*) must be a man of unimpeachable character. He must not be overbearing or short-tempered; he must be no drinker, no brawler, no money-grubber, but hospitable, right-minded, temperate, just, devout and self-controlled. He must adhere to the true doctrine, so that he may be well able both to move his hearers with wholesome teaching and to confuse objectors. (Paul, *To Titus* 1:5–9)

There is a popular saying, "To aspire to leadership is an honorable ambition." Our leader, therefore, or overseer, must be above reproach, faithful to one wife, sober, temperate, courteous, hospitable, and a good teacher. . . . He must be one who manages his own household well and wins obedience from his children, and a man of the highest principles. If a man does not know how to control his own family, how can he look after a congregation of God's people? He must not be a convert newly baptized, for fear the sin of conceit should bring upon him a judgment contrived by the devil. He must moreover have a good reputation with the non-Christian public, so that he may not be exposed to scandal and get caught in the devil's snare. (Paul, *To Timothy* 1.3:1–7)

18. A Distinction of Functions and Gifts

If there was some kind of formal authority even in the earliest Christian congregations, there was also both a functional and a charismatic variety.

During this period, when disciples [that is, Christians] were growing in number, there was disagreement between those who spoke Greek and those who spoke the language of the Jews. The former party complained that their widows were being overlooked in the daily distribution. So the Twelve called the whole body of disciples together and said, "It would be a grave mistake for us to neglect the word of God in order to wait at table. Therefore, friends, look out seven men of good reputation from your number, and we will appoint them to deal with these matters, while we devote ourselves to prayer and to the ministry of the Word." This proposal proved acceptable to the whole body. They elected Stephen, a man full of faith and of the Holy Spirit, Philip, Prochorus, Nicanor, Timon, Parmenas and Nicolaus of Antioch, a former convert to Judaism. These they presented to the Apostles, who prayed and laid their hands on them. (Acts of the Apostles 6:1–6)

There are varieties of gifts, but the same Spirit. There are varieties of service, but the same Lord. There are many forms of work, but all of them, in all men, are the work of the same God. In each of us the Spirit is manifested in one particular way, for some useful purpose. One man, through the Spirit, has the gift of wise speech, while another, by the power of the same Spirit, can put the deepest knowledge into words. Another, by the same Spirit, is granted faith; another, by the same Spirit, the gift of healing, and another miraculous powers; another has the gift of prophecy, and another ability to distinguish true spirit from false; yet another has the gift of ecstatic utterance of different kinds, and another the ability to interpret it. But all the gifts are the work of one and the same Spirit, distributing them separately to each individual at will.

For Christ is like a single body with its many limbs and organs, which many as they are, together make up one body. . . . Now you are Christ's body and each of you a limb or organ of it. Within our community God has appointed, in the first place apostles, in the second place prophets, thirdly teachers; then miracle workers, then those who have the gift of healing, or the ability to help others or power to guide them, or the gift of ecstatic utterance of various kinds. Are all apostles? All prophets? All teachers? Do all work miracles? Have all gifts of healing? Do all speak in tongues of ecstasy? Can all interpret them? The higher gifts are those you should aim at. (Paul, *To the Corinthians* 1.12:4–31)

19. The Christian Hierarchy

These charismatic offices eventually disappeared from the Christian community, or perhaps were simply abandoned in the wake of the growing realization that the Second Coming was not as imminent as once had been thought. In any event, the more formal authority prevailed. This is how it appeared to Clement at Rome in the last years of the first Christian century.

The Apostles have preached the Gospel to us from the Lord Jesus Christ; Jesus Christ was sent from God. Christ then is from God, and the Apostles from Christ. Both therefore came in due order from the will of God. Having therefore received his instructions and being fully assured through the Resurrection of our Lord Jesus Christ, they went forth in confidence in the word of God and with the full assurance of the Holy Spirit, preaching the Gospel that the Kingdom of God was about to come. And so, as they preached in the country and in the towns, they appointed their firstfruits, having proved them by the spirit, to be bishops [*episkopoi*: "overseers"] and deacons [*diakonoi*: "ministers"] of them that should believe. And this was no novelty, for of old it had been written concerning bishops and deacons, for the Scripture says in one place, "I will set up their bishops in righteousness and their deacons in faith" [Isa. 60:17, which says in the Greek version "princes" and "overseers" and in the Hebrew "officers" and "taskmasters"]. (Clement of Rome, *To the Corinthians* 42)

And again, from Ignatius, leader of the church at Antioch about 112 C.E.:

Since you are subject to the bishop as to Jesus Christ, you appear to me to live not in the manner of men, but according to Jesus Christ, who died for us in order that by believing in his death you yourselves may escape death. It is necessary then that you do as you do, that without the bishop you should do nothing and that you should also be subject to the presbyters, as to the Apostles of Jesus Christ, our Hope. . . . It is right too that the deacons, being ministers of the mysteries of Jesus Christ, should in every respect be well pleasing to all. For they are not the ministers of meat and drink but servants of the Church of God. It is necessary, then, that they guard themselves from all grounds of accusation as they would from fire.

In like manner, let all reverence the deacons as Jesus Christ, as also the bishop, who is a type of the Father, and the presbyters, who are the Sanhedrin of God and the assembly of the Apostles. Apart from these there is no Church. (Ignatius, *To the Trallians* 2–3)

Avoid divisions as the beginning of evils. All of you follow the bishop as Jesus Christ followed the Father, and follow the presbyters as the Apostles, and respect the deacons as you do the commandment of God. And let no man do anything concerning the church without the bishop. Let that be considered a valid Eucharist over which the bishop presides, or one to whom he commits it. Wherever the bishop appears, there let the people be, just as, wherever Christ Jesus is, there the Catholic Church is. It is not permitted either to baptize or hold a love feast apart from the bishop. But whatever he may approve, that is well pleasing to God, that everything you do may be sound and valid. (Ignatius, *To the Smyrneans* 8)

20. The Apostolic Succession of the Episcopate

By the fourth century, the Christian Church could boast that it was One, Holy, Catholic, and Apostolic. Among those claims, it was probably that of being Apostolic that constituted its own strongest sense of authenticity and validity. It was a trait remarked upon and cherished very early in the history of the community. Here it appears about 175 C.E. in the work of Hegesippus, as cited by Eusebius.

The Church of Corinth remained in the right doctrine down to the episcopate of Primus at Corinth. I spoke with him on my journey to Rome, and we took comfort together in the right doctrine. After arriving in Rome, I made a succession down to Anicetus, whose deacon was Eleutherus. To Anicetus succeeded Soter, who was followed by Eleutherus. In every succession and in every city things are ordered according to the preaching of the Law, the Prophets and the Lord. (Hegesippus, cited by Eusebius, *Church History* 4.22)

Come now, you who wish to indulge a better curiosity, if you would apply it to the business of your salvation, run over the Apostolic churches, in which the very thrones of the Apostles are still pre-eminent in their places, in which their own authentic writings are still read, uttering the voice and representing the law of each of them severally. Achaea is very near you, in which you find Corinth. Since you are not far from Macedonia, you have Philippi and the Thessalonians. Since you are able to cross to Asia, you get Ephesus. Since, moreover, you are close upon Italy, you have Rome, from which there comes even into our own hands the very authority of the Apostles themselves. How happy is that church, on which the Apostles poured forth all their teaching along with their blood! Where Peter endured a suffering like his Lord's; where Paul wins a crown in a death like John's; where the Apostle John was first plunged unhurt into boiling oil, and thence was sent to his island exile [that is, to Patmos]. See what she learned, what taught; what fellowship she had even with our churches in Africa. (Tertullian, *A Ruling against Heretics* 36)

The tracing of this same succession is the very first objective in Eusebius' writing of his monumental Church History *sometime about 312 C.E., as the author explains in its opening lines.*

Since it is my purpose to hand down a written account of the successions of the holy Apostles as well as of the times extending from our Savior to ourselves; the number and the nature of the events which are said to have been treated in church history; the number of those who were her illustrious guides and leaders in especially prominent dioceses; the number of those who in each generation by word of mouth or by writings served as ambassadors of the word of God; the names, the number and the times of those who out of a desire for innovation launched into an extremity of error and proclaimed themselves the introducers of knowledge falsely so called. (Eusebius, *Church History* 1.1)

That the point of the inquiry is not simply a historian's antiquarian curiosity but something essential to the Church's claim to authenticity is clear at almost every point that the "Apostolic Succession" is cited, as here by Ireneus.

Those who wish to discern the truth may observe the apostolic tradition made manifest in every church throughout the world. We can enumerate those who were appointed bishops in the churches by the Apostles, and their successors down to our own day, who never taught, and never knew such absurdities as these (heretical) men produce. For if the Apostles had known hidden mysteries which they taught the perfect in private and in secret, they would surely have committed them to those to whom they entrusted the churches. For they wished these men to be perfect and unblamable whom they left as their successors and to whom they handed over their own office and authority. . . . We point to the apostolic tradition and the faith that is preached to men, which has come down to us through the succession of bishops; the tradition and creed of the greatest, the most ancient church, which was founded and set up at Rome by the two most glorious apostles, Peter and Paul. For with this church, because of its position of leadership and authority, must needs agree every church, that is, the faithful everywhere, since in her the apostolic tradition has always been preserved by the faithful from all parts. (Ireneus, *Against the Heresies* 3.3:1)

Therefore we ought to obey only those presbyters who are in the Church, who trace their succession from the Apostles, as we have shown; who with their succession to the episcopate have received the sure gift of the truth according to the pleasure of the Father. The rest, who stand aloof from the primitive succession, and assemble in any place whatever, we must regard with suspicion, either as heretics and evil-minded; or as schismatics, puffed-up and complacent; or again as hypocrites, acting thus for the sake of gain and vainglory. All these have fallen from the truth. (Ibid. 4.26:2)

21. The Consecration of Bishops, Priests, and Deacons

We have two very early testimonies on the choice and consecration of the bishops who were becoming the paramount rulers of the Church and the true source of all authoritative teaching.

Chose for yourselves bishops and deacons worthy of the Lord, men who are gentle and not covetous, true men and approved; for they also serve you in the service of the prophets and teachers. Therefore do not despise them, for these are they that are honored of you with the prophets and teachers. (*Teaching of the Apostles*)

We turn to the subject of the tradition which is proper for the churches, in order that those who have been rightly instructed may hold fast to that tradition, which has continued until now; and, once they fully understand it from our exposition, they may stand the more firmly in it. . . .

Let the bishop be ordained who is in all respects without fault and who has been chosen by all the people. And when he has been proposed and found acceptable to all, the people should assemble on the Lord's day together with the presbyters and such bishops as may attend, and the choice should be generally approved. Let the bishops lay hands on him (who has been chosen) while the presbyters stand by in silence. And all shall keep silence, praying in their hearts for the descent of the Spirit.

After this, one of the bishops present, at the request of all, should lay his hand on him who is ordained bishop and pray as follows: ". . . Father, who knows the hearts of all, grant to this Your servant whom You have chosen for the episcopate to feed Your holy flock and serve as Your High Priest, that he may minister blamelessly by night and day, that he may unceasingly behold and propitiate Your countenance and offer to You the gifts of Your holy Church. And that by the high priestly Spirit he may have the authority to forgive sins according to Your command, to assign lots according to Your bidding, to loose every bond according to the authority You gave to the Apostles, and that he may praise You in meekness and purity of heart, offering to You a sweet-smelling savor through Your Child Jesus Christ our Lord, through whom to You be glory, might and praise, to the Father and to the Son with the Holy Spirit now and ever and world without end. Amen." . . .

And when a presbyter is ordained the bishop shall lay his hand upon his head, and the presbyters shall also touch him. And he shall pray over him according to the aforementioned form which we gave previously in the case of the bishop, praying and saying, ". . . Look upon this Your servant and impart to him the spirit of grace and counsel, that he may share in the presbyterate and govern Your people with a pure heart. As You looked upon the people of Your choice and commanded Moses to choose presbyters whom You filled with the spirit which You had granted to Your minister, so now, O Lord, grant that there may be preserved among us unceasingly the Spirit of Your grace, and make us worthy that in faith we may minister to You, praising you in singleness of heart through Your Child Jesus Christ our Lord, through whom to You be glory, might and praise, to the Father and to the Son with the Holy Spirit now and ever and world without end. Amen."

And when a deacon is to be appointed, he should be chosen according to what has been said before, the bishop alone laying hands upon him in the same manner. Nevertheless, we order that the bishop alone shall lay on hands at the ordination of a deacon for this reason: that he is not ordained for a priesthood, but for the service of a bishop, that he may do only the things commanded by him. For he is not appointed to be the fellow counselor of the whole clergy but to take charge of property and to report to the bishop whenever necessary. He does not receive the Spirit which is common to all the presbyterate, in which the presbyters share, but rather that which is entrusted to him under the bishop's authority. Nor is he appointed to receive the Spirit of greatness which the presbyters share, but to give attention and to be worthy of the bishop's trust and to be diligent about what is fitting. . . .

But in the appointment of a presbyter, the other presbyters also lay their hands upon him because of the similar Spirit which is common to all the clergy. For the presbyter has authority only to receive, but not to grant, holy orders. Wherefore he does not ordain a man to orders, but by laying on hands at the ordination of (another) presbyter he only blesses while the bishop ordains. (Hippolytus of Rome, *The Apostolic Tradition* 1–9)

22. The Regulation of Church Orders

In addition to publishing a statement of faith to serve as a yardstick for orthodox belief, the first ecumenical council of the Great Church, held at Nicea in Anatolia in 325 C.E., issued various disciplinary decrees or canons regulating the Church orders. Its example was followed by most subsequent synods, that at Antioch in 341, for example.

Nicea, Canon 4: It is most proper that a bishop should be constituted by all the bishops of the province; but if this is difficult on account of some urgent necessity or by the length of the journey, that at all events three (bishops) should meet together at the same place, the absentees giving their suffrages and consent in writing, and then the ordination be performed. The confirming, however, of what is done in each province belongs to its Metropolitan [that is, the presiding bishop of its metropolis].

Antioch, Canon 4: If any bishop is deposed by a synod, or any presbyter or deacon who has been deposed by his bishop, shall presume to perform any function of the ministry, whether it is a bishop acting as a bishop, and the same holds true of a presbyter or a deacon, he shall no longer have any prospect of restoration by another synod nor any opportunity of stating his case; but whoever communicates with him shall be cast out of the Church, and particularly if they have presumed to communicate with any of the persons aforementioned with full knowledge of the sentence that had been pronounced against them.

Another recurrent problem was the movement of the clergy from one jurisdiction to another:

Nicea, Canon 15: On account of the great disturbance and discords that occur, it is decreed that the custom prevailing in certain places contrary to the canon must wholly be done away with; so that neither bishop, presbyter nor deacon shall pass from city to city. But if anyone, after this decree of the holy and great synod, shall attempt any such thing or continue in such a course, his proceedings shall be utterly void, and he shall be restored to the church for which he was ordained bishop or presbyter.

Nicea, Canon 16: Neither presbyters, deacons, nor any others enrolled among the clergy, who, not having the fear of God before their eyes, nor regarding the ecclesiastical canon, shall recklessly remove from their own church, ought by any means to be received by another church; but every constraint should be applied to restore them to their own dioceses; and if they will not go, they must be excommunicated. And if one shall dare to carry off someone in secret and ordain him on his own, though he belongs to another, and this without the consent of the bishop on whose clergy list he was enrolled and then seceded, let the ordination be void.

23. The Episcopal Hierarchy

The same councils, as well as those held at Constantinople in 381 and Chalcedon in 451 C.E., likewise touched upon another delicate question, that of an episcopal hierarchy. It might be argued, as it was, that all bishops were equal; but as Cyprian had already suggested and Nicea acknowledged, some bishoprics were more equal than others.

Nicea (325 C.E.), Canon 6: Let the ancient customs hold good which are in Egypt and Libya and the Pentapolis, according to which the Bishop of Alexandria has authority over all these places. For this is also customary to the Bishop of Rome. In like manner in Antioch and in the other provinces, the privileges are to be preserved to the churches. But this is clearly to be understood, that if any one be made a bishop without the consent of the Metropolitan, the Great Synod declares that he shall not be a bishop. If, however, two or three bishops (of a province) shall from private contention oppose the common choice of all the others, it being a reasonable one and made according to the ecclesiastical canons, let the choice of the majority prevail.

What custom and the ancient tradition could grant, political reality could take away, often in the space of the same sentence.

Nicea (325 C.E.), Canon 7: Since custom and ancient tradition have prevailed that the bishop of Aelia [that is, Jerusalem] should be honored, let him, saving the dignity appropriate to the (provincial) metropolis [that is, Caesarea], have the next place of honor.

Caesarea Maritima was the metropolis or provincial capital of Palestina Prima, where Jerusalem was located as well. Neither custom nor ancient tradition could at this point override that political fact. It took a powerful and aggressive bishop of Jerusalem, Juvenal, to move his see past Caesarea and onto equal footing with the patriarchal sees of Alexandria and Antioch.

The ecclesiastical province would conform, as the next canon makes clear, with the territorial and jurisdictional lines of Roman imperial organization.

Antioch (341 C.E.), Canon 9: It behooves the bishops in each province to acknowledge the bishop who presides in the metropolis and who has to take thought of the entire province, because all men of business come together from every quarter to the metropolis. Wherefore it is decreed that he have precedence in rank (over the other bishops of the province) and that the other bishops do nothing extraordinary without him, according to the ancient canon which prevailed from the time of our fathers, or such things only as pertain to their own particular dioceses and the districts subject to them. For each bishop has jurisdiction over his own diocese, both to manage it with piety, which is incumbent on everyone, and to make provision for the whole district which is dependent upon his city; to ordain presbyters and deacons; and to settle everything with judgment. But let him not undertake anything further without the bishop of the metropolis; neither the latter without the consent of the others.

Constantinople (381 C.E.), Canon 2: The bishops are not to go beyond their dioceses to churches lying outside their bounds, nor bring confusion on churches; but let the bishop of Alexandria, according to the canons, alone administer the affairs of Egypt; and let the bishops of the East administer the East alone, the privileges of the church in Antioch, which are mentioned in the canons of Nicea, being preserved; and let the bishops of the Asian diocese administer the Asian affairs only; and the Pontic bishops only Pontic matters; and the Thracian bishops only Thracian matters. And let the bishops not go beyond their dioceses for ordination or any other ecclesiastical ministrations, unless they are invited. And the aforesaid canon concerning dioceses being observed, it is evident that the synod of each province will administer the affairs of that particular province, as decreed at Nicea. But the churches of God in pagan nations must be governed according to the custom which has prevailed from the time of the Fathers.

What was true on the provincial level proved equally true on the imperial level. Under Constantine the capital of the Roman Empire had been moved from Rome to his new city of Constantinople, the former Byzantium, on the Bosphorus. This political move soon had its effect on the hierarchical organization of the Christian Church.

Constantinople, Canon 3: The bishop of Constantinople, however, shall have the prerogative of honor after the bishop of Rome, because Constantinople is New Rome.

Canon 28 of Chalcedon goes much further in an administrative sense. The bishops of Asia, Pontus, and Thrace, who were being restrained from tampering at Constantinople in 381, now found themselves under the jurisdiction of the imperial Patriarch of the New Rome.

Chalcedon, Canon 28: Following in all things the decisions of the holy Fathers, and acknowledging the canon, which has just been read, of the one hundred and fifty bishops [assembled in Constantinople in 381], beloved by God, we also do enact and decree the same thing concerning the privileges of the most holy Church of Constantinople or New Rome. For the Fathers rightly granted privileges to the throne of the Old Rome, because it was the royal city, and the one hundred and fifty most religious bishops, moved by the same considerations, gave equal privileges to the most holy throne of the New Rome, judging with good reason that the city which is honored with the sovereignty and the Senate, and always enjoys equal privileges with old imperial Rome, should in ecclesiastical matters also be magnified as she [Rome] is, and rank next after her; so that in the dioceses of Pontus, Asia and Thrace the metropolitans and such bishops also of the dioceses aforesaid as are among the barbarians, should be ordained only by the aforesaid most holy throne of the most holy Church of Constantinople; every metropolitan of the aforesaid dioceses, together with the bishops of his province, may ordain bishops of the province, as has been declared by the divine canons, but the metropolitans of the dioceses, as has been said above, shall be ordained by the archbishop of Constantinople, after the proper elections have been held according to custom and have been reported to him.

24. "The Greatest Church": The Issue of Roman Primacy

The decrees of the Council of Chalcedon in 451 brought the churches of Rome and Constantinople into direct conflict on the issue of the principal and primary bishopric of the Church. The New Rome was manifestly growing at the expense of the Old. Rome protested the expansionist claims of Canon 28 of Chalcedon, but to no great avail. The realities of shifting political power and of deepening cultural differences were drawing East and West into separate spheres and, in the end, separate ecclesiastical jurisdictions.

But there was a matter of principle involved as well: that between an episcopal oligarchical Church and a papal monarchical one. A quasi-monarchical papacy had solid historical claims for many of the early Fathers, whether that pre-eminence was understood as one of honor, as the councils seemed to define it, or whether it rested on Rome as the final court of appeal in ecclesiastical disputes. Sometime about 175 C.E. Ireneus, bishop of Lyons, wrote his Against the Heresies and invoked the principle of the teaching of the Apostles as the main criterion of truth in the Church. That teaching was transmitted by the Apostles to their successors, the bishops of the various Christian congregations. The authority of these men rested, then, on the validity of their succession from the Apostles. Ireneus assures his readers that Christians can trace that uninterrupted succession in any or all of the churches. But this would be an impractical notion, and so he takes another course.

But since it would be very long in a book like this to count up the successions in all the churches, we confound all those who, whether through self-pleasing or vainglory, or through blindness and evil opinion, gather together otherwise than they ought by pointing out the traditions derived from the Apostles of the greatest, most ancient and universally known church, one founded and established by the two most glorious Apostles Peter and Paul, and also the faith declared to men which through the succession of bishops comes down to our times. For with this church, on account of its more powerful leadership, every church, that is, the faithful, who are from everywhere, must needs agree, since in it that tradition which is from the Apostles has always been preserved by those who are from everywhere.

The blessed Apostles having founded and established the Church (at Rome), entrusted the office of the episcopate to Linus. Paul speaks of this Linus in his Letters to Timothy. Anacletus succeeded him, and after Anacletus in the third place from the Apostles, Clement received the episcopate. He had seen and conversed with the blessed Apostles, and their teaching was still sounding in his ears and their tradition was still before his eyes. Nor was he alone in this, for many who had been taught by the Apostles still survived. In the times of Clement a serious dissension having arisen among the brethren in Corinth, the Church of Rome sent a suitable letter to the Corinthians, reconciling them in peace, renewing their faith and proclaiming the teaching lately received from the Apostles. . . .

Evaristus succeeded Clement, and Alexander Evaristus. Then Sixtus, the sixth from the Apostles, was appointed. After him Telesphorus, who suffered martyrdom gloriously, and then Hyginus; after him Pius, and after Pius Anicetus, and now, in the twelfth place from the Apostles, Eleutherus [174–189 C.E.] holds the office of bishop. In the same order and succession the tradition and the preaching of the truth which is from the Apostles have continued down to us. (Ireneus, *Against the Heresies* 3.3.2–3)

This same Ireneus, however, admonished the bishop of Rome not to disrupt the unity of the Church by excommunicating the churches of Asia on the matter of the observance of Easter.

25. Tradition and Authority

The practices and beliefs of any given Christian congregation could be validated by showing that they were in conformity with the teaching of the Apostles, a case that was rendered infinitely simpler if it could be demonstrated that the church in question was an Apostolic foundation and that its succession of bishops went back in an unbroken line to one of the Apostles. By the second century the Apostolic tradition was confronted not so much by a challenge in principle as by the presence of other manifestations of authority—a number of bishops acting collegially, for example, or the fact that some churches, and so their bishops, enjoyed a somewhat more intimate connection with the Apostolic tradition than did others.

The conflict implicit in this unfolding of ecclesiastical authority found its sharpest manifestation in a question that had puzzled Christians from the beginning: their relationship with Judaism. The Jews, on their side, dissolved that affiliation rather abruptly by effectively excluding Christians from the synagogue (see Chapter 5 above); for the Christians, however, the separation could never be quite complete—the proofs of the Messiahship of Jesus had no other ground than the Bible. But there remained to be settled other matters of connection with Judaism: their relationship to the Law, for example; certain questions of cult, such as the observance of the Sabbath; and, in the last decade of the second century, the divisive question of the date of Easter. Jesus had died on the eve of Passover and had risen on the day after that feast. The Resurrection, then, would seem to be tied directly to the fourteenth of Nisan in the Jewish calendar.

At this time a question of no small importance arose. For the parishes of all Asia, being from an older tradition, held that the fourteenth day of the moon [that is, of the lunar month], since this was the day on which the Jews were commanded to sacrifice the (Passover) lamb, should be observed as the feast of the Savior's Passover, and that it was necessary, therefore, to end their fast on that day, whatever the day of the week on which it should happen to fall. It was not, however, the custom of the churches elsewhere to end it at this time, but they observed the practice, which from Apostolic tradition had prevailed to the present time, of ending the fast on no other day than that of the Resurrection of the Savior. Synods and assemblies of bishops were held on this account, and all with one consent, by means of letters addressed to all, drew up an ecclesiastical decree that the mystery of the Resurrection of the Lord from the dead should be celebrated on no other day than on the Lord's Day [that is, Sunday], and that we should observe the close of the Paschal fast on that day only. There is still extant a writing of those who were then assembled in Palestine, over whom Theophilus, bishop of the parish [that is, the diocese] of Caesarea, and Narcissus, bishop of Jerusalem, presided; also another of those who were assembled in Rome, on account of the same question, which bears the name of Victor. (Eusebius, *Church History* 5.23)

The bishops of Asia, the chief proponents of the fourteenth of Nisan as the day ending the Passover fast, were not convinced by this assertion of collegial episcopal authority. They were not likely to raise the Jewish precedent, however; rather, they referred to what they regarded as the true Apostolic tradition. Whatever others might do, they had venerable Christian examples on their side.

But the bishops of Asia, led by Polycrates, decided to hold fast to the customs handed down to them. He himself, in a letter addressed to Victor and the church of Rome, set forth the tradition which had come down to him as follows: "We observe the exact day, neither adding nor taking anything away. For in Asia great lights have fallen asleep, which shall rise again on the day of the Lord's coming, when he shall come with glory from heaven and shall seek out all the saints. Of these were Philip, one of the twelve Apostles, who fell asleep at Hierapolis . . . and, moreover, John, who reclined on the Lord's bosom, and being a priest wore the sacerdotal miter, who was both a witness and a teacher; he fell asleep at Ephesus; and further, Polycarp in Smyrna, both a bishop and a martyr. . . . All these observed the fourteenth day of the Passover, according to the Gospel, deviating in no respect, but following the rule of faith. And

I, Polycrates, do the same, the least of you all, according to the tradition of my relatives, some of whom I have closely followed. For seven of my relatives were bishops, and I am the eighth. And my relatives always observed the day when the people put away the leaven. I, therefore, am not affrighted by terrifying words. For those greater than I have said, 'We ought to obey God rather than men.' "

Polycrates, it will be noted, ignored the church in Jerusalem and others that had ruled against him. He seemed to appeal the ruling, or at least chose to present his case, to the bishop of Rome, the presiding bishop at one of the adjudicating synods. And it was from the bishop of Rome that he received his reply.

Thereupon Victor, who was over the church of Rome, immediately attempted to cut off from the common unity the parishes of Asia, with the churches that agreed with them, as being heterodox. And he published letters declaring that all the brethren there were wholly excommunicated. But this did not please all the bishops, and they besought him to consider the things of peace, of neighborly unity and love. Words of theirs are still extant, rather sharply rebuking Victor. (Eusebius, *Church History* 5.24)

One such letter came from Ireneus, bishop of Lyons in the last quarter of the second century, whose views on the validity of Apostolic tradition have already been quoted. Here he underlines some of the dangers of understanding it too monolithically.

The controversy is not merely concerning the day [Ireneus wrote] but also concerning the very manner of the fast. For some think they should fast one day, and others two, yet others more. . . . And this variety of observance has not originated in our times but long before, in the days of our ancestors. It is likely that they did not hold to strict accuracy, and thus was formed a custom for their posterity, according to their own simplicity and their peculiar method. Yet all of these lived more or less in peace, and we also live in peace with one another, and the disagreement in regard to the fast confirms the agreement in faith. . . . Among those were elders before Soter, who presided over the church (of Rome) which you (Victor) now rule. We mean Anicetus, and Pius, and Hyginus, and Telesphorus, and Sixtus. They neither observed it [that is, the fast of the fourteenth of Nisan], nor did they permit others after them to do so. And yet, though they did not observe it themselves, they were nonetheless at peace with those who came to them from the parishes in which it was observed. . . . But none was ever cast out on account of this practice, but the elders before you, who did not observe it, nevertheless sent the eucharist to those parishes who did observe it. (Cited by Eusebius, *Church History* 5.24)

Ireneus' conciliatory view prevailed on this occasion, but the sense of hierarchy was as deeply felt in some churches as the need of unity. Such was the view of Cyprian, the bishop of Carthage in 251 C.E. For him, "the episcopal power was one and undivided"; but the source and type of that unity of both Church and episcopate rested in Peter and the See of Rome, as the sixteenth chapter of Matthew bears unmistakable witness.

The Lord says to Peter, "I say to you, you are Peter and upon this rock I will build my Church, and the gates of hell shall not overcome it. I will give to you the keys of the kingdom of heaven. And what you shall bind upon earth shall be bound also in heaven, and what you shall loose upon earth shall be loosed also in heaven" (Matt. 16:18–19). It is on one man that he builds the Church, and though he assigns a like power to all the Apostles, after his resurrection, saying, "As the Father sent me, I am also sending you. . . . Receive you the Holy Spirit. If you forgive any man his sins, they will be forgiven him; if you retain any man's, they shall be retained" (John 20:21–23). Yet, in order that that unity might be unmistakable, he established by his own authority a source for that oneness having its origin in one man alone. No doubt the other Apostles were all that Peter was, endowed with equal dignity and power. But the beginning comes from him alone, to show that the Church of Christ is unique. (Cyprian, *On the Unity of the Church* 4)

26. Leo, Bishop of Rome

The strongest case for Roman primacy was of course made by the bishops of Rome themselves, and by none more strongly than by Leo, called the Great, who held that see from 440 to 461 C.E. and was one of the moving forces behind the Council of Chalcedon. Early in his tenure, in 444 C.E., Leo put forth the jurisdictional claims of the See of Rome in a letter written to the bishop of Thessalonica.

Those of the brethren who have been summoned to a synod should attend and not deny themselves to the holy congregation. . . . If, however, any more important questions should arise, of a type that cannot be settled there under your presidency, my brother, then send your report and consult us, so that we may respond under the revelation of the Lord, by whose mercy alone we can accomplish anything, because he has breathed favorably upon us. And this so that we might by our decision vindicate our right of recognition in accordance with long-standing tradition and the respect that is due to the Apostolic See. Just as we wish you to exercise your authority in our place, so also we reserve to ourselves issues which cannot be decided on the spot and persons who have appealed to us. (Leo, *Letter* 6 to Anastasius)

Somewhat later, to the same Anastasius of Thessalonica on the principle of hierarchy in the Church:

And from this model [of the differences in rank and order of the Apostles] has arisen a similar distinction among bishops, and by an important ordinance it has been provided that everyone should not claim everything for himself, but that there should be in each province one whose opinion should have priority among the brethren; and again, that those whose appointments are in the greater cities should undertake fuller responsibility, and that through them the care of the universal Church should converge toward Peter's one seat, and nothing anywhere should be separated from its head. (Leo, *Letter* 14 to Anastasius)

The following is from one of Leo's sermons.

From Christ's overruling and eternal providence we have received also the support of the Apostle's aid, which assuredly still operates; and the strength of the foundation, on which the whole lofty building of the Church is reared, is not weakened by the temple that rests upon it. For the solidity of that faith which was praised in the chief of the Apostles is perpetual; and as there survives what Peter believed in Christ, so there also survives what Christ instituted in Peter. For when, as has been read in the Gospel lesson (of the day), the Lord had asked the disciples whom they believed him to be, amid the various opinions that were held, the blessed Peter replied, saying, "You are the Christ. . . ."

The dispensation of the truth therefore abides, and the blessed Peter, persevering in the strength of the rock which he has received, has not abandoned the helm of the Church which he undertook. For he was ordained before the rest in such a way that since he was called the rock, since he is pronounced the foundation, since he is constituted the door-keeper of the kingdom of heaven, since he is set up as the judge to bind and to loose, whose judgments shall retain their validity in heaven, from all these mystical titles we might know the nature of his association with Christ. And even today he more fully and effectually performs what is entrusted to him, and carries out every part of his duty and charge in Christ and with Christ, through whom he has been glorified.

And so if anything is rightly done or rightly decreed by us [that is, Peter's successor], if anything is obtained from the mercy of God by daily supplications, it is his work and merits whose power lives on in his See and whose authority excels. For this, dearly beloved, that confession (of Peter) gained, that confession which, inspired in the Apostle's heart by God the Father, transcends all the uncertainties of human opinions, and was endowed with the firmness of rock, which no assaults could shake. For throughout the Church Peter daily says, "You are the Christ, the Son of the Living God," and every tongue that confesses the Lord is inspired by the teaching authority [*magisterium*] of that voice. (Leo, *Sermon* 3)

Leo's words are homiletic and inspirational, as befits a sermon. The hard edge of polemic emerges more clearly on the issue of the claims of Constantinople and the purport of Canon 28 of Chalcedon. The first text is a letter written by Leo to Emperor Marcian in 452, immediately after the council.

Let the city of Constantinople have, as we desire, its glory, and may it, under the protection of God's right hand, long enjoy the rule of your Clemency. Yet the basis of things secular is one thing and the basis of things divine is another; and there can be no sure building except on the rock that the Lord laid as a foundation. He that covets what is not his due, loses what is his own. Let it be enough for the aforesaid Anatolius [bishop of Constantinople, 449–458 C.E.] that by the aid of your Piety and that with my favorable assent he has obtained the bishopric of so great a city. Let him not disdain a royal city, which he cannot, however, make into an Apostolic See; and let him on no account hope to be able to rise by injury to others. For the privileges of the churches, as determined by the canons of the holy Fathers and fixed by the decrees of the Synod of Nicea, cannot be overthrown by an unscrupulous act, nor disturbed by an innovation. And in the faithful execution of this task by the aid of Christ, it is necessary that I show an unflinching devotion; for it is a charge entrusted to me, and more, it tends to condemnation if the rules sanctioned by the Fathers and laid down under the guidance of God's Spirit at the Synod of Nicea for the government of the whole Church are violated with my connivance—which God forbid—and if the wishes of a single man have more weight with me than the common word of the Lord's entire house. (Leo, *To Marcian* 3)

27. Bishop of Rome, Absolute Primate or First among Equals?

In a letter to Anatolius written in the same year of 452, Leo undertakes to defend the rights of other primatial bishoprics.

Your purpose is in no way whatever supported by the written assent of certain bishops, given, as you allege, sixty years ago [that is, at the Council of Constantinople in 381], and never brought to the knowledge of the Apostolic See (of Rome) by your predecessors; under this present scheme, which from its outset was tottering and has already collapsed, you now wish to place too late and useless props. . . . Metropolitan bishops ought not be defrauded of privileges based on antiquity. The See of Alexandria may not lose any of that dignity which it merited through St. Mark, the evangelist and disciple of the blessed Peter. . . . The Church of Antioch too, in which, at the preaching of the blessed Apostle Peter, the Christian name first was used, must continue in the position assigned to it by the Fathers, and being set in the third place [by Canon 6 of Nicea], must never be lowered therefrom. For the see is one thing and those who preside in it are something different; and an individual's great honor is his own integrity. (Leo, *Letter* 106 to Anatolius)

Leo's vindication of the rights of the other great sees of Constantinople, Alexandria, and Antioch corresponds to the Eastern view of how the highest ecclesiastical authority was distributed in the Church. It is restated here, though with a slightly different nuance, by the monk Theodore of Studium (d. 826), one of the most prominent churchmen of his generation in Constantinople.

It is not the affairs of the world of which we speak: the right to judge them belongs to the emperor and the civil tribunal. Here it is rather a question of divine and heavenly judgments, and these are reserved alone to whom the word of God was addressed: "Whatsoever you shall bind upon earth, will be bound in Heaven, and whatsoever you loose upon earth shall be loosed in Heaven" (Matt. 16:19).

We are at the heart of the matter. This celebrated saying remained the primary proof-text of the Christian Church's spiritual powers and, indeed, of their consequences in the affairs of the secular realm. Theodore continues:

And who are the men to whom this command was given? The Apostles and their successors. And who are their successors? In the first place, whoever occupies the throne of Rome; second, the one who sits on the throne of Constantinople; and after them are those of Alexandria, Antioch and Jerusalem. That is the fivefold authority in the Church. It is to them that all decisions belong in matters of divine dogma. The Emperor and the secular authority have the duty to assist them and to confirm what they have decided. (Theodore of Studium, *Letters*)

It should be recalled, however, that between the time of Leo's letters and that of Theodore, three of those five great patriarchal sees—those of Alexandria, Antioch,

*and Jerusalem—had fallen under the political sovereignty of Islam, a fact that gave
a decidedly theoretical air to the notion of "fivefold authority." There were, in fact,
but two effective claimants to primacy: the bishop of Rome and the bishop of
Constantinople.*

28. Roman Primacy

*The occasion for the Pope to assert a far broader claim to absolute primacy in the
Great Church arose in a critical form with the appointment of a certain Photius, an
immensely learned man but a layman, to the Patriarchate of Constantinople, the
highest ecclesiastical post of Eastern Christendom He replaced the monk Ignatius,
who had been pressured to resign. The party of Ignatius then appealed to the bishop
of Rome. The case grew more complex, but at its heart was the issue of the primacy
of the Roman see. Pope and emperor exchanged letters. In his response to Emperor
Michael III in 865 C.E., Pope Nicholas I states the Roman case.*

. . . The privileges of the Roman church of Christ, confirmed from
the mouth of the Blessed Peter, laid down in the church itself, acknowledged even from the earliest days, celebrated by the holy ecumenical
councils, and consistently reverenced by all churches, may be diminished
in no manner whatsoever, nor altered, since no mortal should dare to
move the foundation which God has laid down, and what He has established remains strong and unshaken. . . .

These privileges of this holy church, which were given by Christ and
not granted by councils, privileges which are both widely known and
highly regarded, which are to us so much an honor as a burden, even
though we have come to this honor not through any merits of our own
but by command of the grace of God mediated through and in the Blessed
Peter, it is these privileges, we say, which oblige us to be solicitous of all
the churches of God. For the company of the Blessed Apostle Paul was
added to that of the Blessed Peter . . . and these two, like two great
heavenly luminaries, placed by the divine ordination in the Roman
church, have marvelously lit up the the whole world by the splendor of
their brightness. . . .

These things, then, constrain me to come to the assistance of the
Patriarch Ignatius as a brother who has been deposed by no rule or
ecclesiastical order. . . . These divinely inspired privileges have thus ordained that, since Photius, while Ignatius was still alive, improperly came
to the Lord's sheepfold, overthrew the shepherd and dispersed our sheep,
he must vacate the position he has usurped and leave the communion of
the Christian community. And since we think that nothing would be

more discreet, mild or useful to either Ignatius or Photius than that each should come to an investigation to be renewed in Rome, we desire this greatly and we admonish for your own good that you assent. (Nicholas I, *Letter to the Emperor Michael III*)

There was a considerable range of Eastern reactions to this and other Papal asser-
tions on the subject of the Roman primacy. Many were willing to concede some form
of primacy—of protocol or honor, for example. It was the monarchical principle
that was unacceptable. This is one Eastern bishop's careful reading of the problem,
expressed during a Greco-Latin debate on the subject in Constantinople in 1136 C.E.

I neither deny nor reject the primacy of the Roman Church. . . . We read in the ancient accounts that there were in fact three Patriarchal Sees closely linked in brotherhood, those of Rome, Alexandria and Antioch, and among them it was Rome, the highest see in the empire, which was granted the primacy. For this reason Rome has been called the first see: it is to her that appeal must be made in doubtful ecclesiastical cases, and it is to her judgment that all matters that cannot be settled according to the normal rules must be submitted. . . .

That is what we discover, my dear brothers, written in the ancient historical documents. But the Roman Church to which we do not deny the primacy among her sisters, and whom we recognize as holding the highest place in any general council, the first place of honor, that Church has separated herself from the rest by her pretensions. She has appropriated to herself the monarchy which is not contained in her office and which has split the eastern and western bishops and the churches since the partition of the empire. (Nicetas of Nicomedia, *Discourse*)

One result of this schism over the Roman "monarchy," Nicetas claimed, was that
what were once regarded as ecumenical councils were no longer universal in either
their representation or their binding power.

When, as a result of these circumstances, she [that is, the Roman Church] assembles a council of the Western bishops without allowing us (in the East) to participate in it, it is perfectly appropriate that her own (Western) bishops should accept the council's decrees and observe them with the veneration that is due to them . . . but as for us (in the East), though we do not disagree with the Roman Church in the matter of the Catholic faith, how can we be expected to accept those decisions which were taken without our advice and of which we know nothing, since we were not present at the council at the time? If the Roman Pontiff, seated upon his lofty throne of glory, wishes to fulminate against us and fire off his orders from the height of his sublime dignity, if he wishes to sit in judgment on our churches with a total disregard of our advice but only in accordance with his own will, as he does seem to wish, what brotherhood and what fatherhood can we discern in such a manner of acting? Who could ever accept such a situation? In such circumstances we could not be called, nor would we really any longer be, sons of the Church but slaves. (Ibid.)

What neither reason nor discussion could accomplish, the political fears of the Eastern Empire did: on two occasions Eastern and Western Christendom came together as one Church, at Lyons in 1274 and at Florence in 1439. The terms were Western, and one of them was the question of Roman primacy. This is the Eastern emperor Michael VIII saying what was required of him in 1274.

The Holy Roman Church likewise possesses the highest and most complete primacy and authority over the universal catholic church, it sincerely and with all humility acknowledges that it has received that primacy, together with the fullness of its power, from the Lord himself in the person of the Blessed Peter, chief or head of the Apostles, whose successor the Roman Pontiff is. And since his chief responsibility is the defense of the truth of the Faith, so it is his judgment that shall prevail in matters of defining that Faith. Anyone who is accused can appeal to his authority in matters pertaining to the tribunals of the Church, and in all that concerns ecclesiastical jurisdiction, there is to be recourse to his judgment. All the churches are subject to his jurisdiction, and the prelates owe obedience and reverence to him. The fullness of his power is such that it invites all the other churches to partake of his solicitude. This same Roman Church has honored many of the churches by bestowing various privileges, and especially the Patriarchal churches. But its prerogative power is always reserved to itself except in general councils or on various other occasions. (Acts of the Council of Lyons [1274])

29. Moscow, the Third Rome

The issue of Roman primacy had been moved forward on the agenda by the transfer of the capital of the Roman Empire from Rome to Constantinople. If Rome's argument was based on the primacy of Peter among the Apostles, Constantinople's rested to some extent on the fact that after 330 C.E. it was the seat of the empire, the New Rome. Whatever the force or validity of that latter argument, it had an unforeseen sequel. When in 1453 Constantinople fell to the Muslim Turks, there was no formal transfer of power to a new Christian capital. But there were those who had no doubts where the mantle descended.

The Church of old Rome fell because of its heresy; the gates of the second Rome, Constantinople, were hewn down by the axes of the infidel Turks; but the Church of Moscow, the Church of the new Rome, shines brighter than the sun in the whole universe. You are the one universal sovereign of all the Christian people, you should hold the reins in awe of God; fear Him who has committed them to you. Two Romes are fallen, but the third stands fast; a fourth there cannot be. The Christian kingdom shall not be given to another. (Philotheus of Pskov)   [Cited by ZERNOV 1945: 51]

7. The Church and the State/ The Church as the State

1. God and Caesar

The growth of the institutional Church from assemblies with presiding presbyters to more formal communities governed by episcopal "overseers" with ever-increasing administrative and doctrinal authority took place beyond the care or even the notice of the secular powers of the Roman Empire. Roman administrators were chiefly concerned with good order and took little note of the internal disputes of their sometimes notorious and sometimes obscure sectarians, except when they offended against that order.

The Jews were both notorious and, as we have seen, at times offensive to Roman order. The Christians, once distinguished from the Jews, began to enjoy a notoriety of their own. In the second and third centuries the Church and its leaders had to face an increasingly hostile secular authority; then, in the fourth century, somewhat to its own surprise, the Church found within its communion the emperor himself, first as an ally and then as a competitor.

The Christians, even the first generation of them, were not entirely oblivious of the various magistrates—municipal, provincial, and imperial—who ruled them. Jesus himself had been posed the question of political authority. In the highly charged political atmosphere of first-century Palestine the wonder is not that he should have been confronted with the issue of Roman-Jewish relations that exercised so many of his contemporaries but rather how infrequently it arises in the Gospels. The Synoptics record one such confrontation and Jesus' reply.

Then the Pharisees went away and agreed on a plan to trap him in his own words. Some of their followers were sent to him in company with men of Herod's party. They said, "Master, you are an honest man, we know; you teach in all honesty the way of life that God requires, truckling to no man, whoever he may be. Give us your ruling on this: are we or are we not permitted to pay taxes to the Roman Emperor?" Jesus was aware of their malicious intention and said to them, "Why are you trying to catch me out? Show me the money in which the tax is paid." They handed him a silver piece. Jesus asked, "Whose head is this and whose inscription?" "Caesar's," they replied. He said to them, "Then pay Caesar what is due to Caesar, and pay God what is due to God." This answer took them by surprise and they went away and left him alone. (Matthew 22:15–22)

Outside of Palestine the distinction drawn by Jesus was not so urgent perhaps. Paul, at any rate, saw no snare when in his letter to the Romans he addressed the issue of secular authority in more general terms.

Every person must submit to the supreme authorities. There is no authority but by act of God, and the existing authorities are instituted by Him; consequently anyone who rebels against authority is resisting a divine institution, and those who so resist have themselves to thank for the punishment they will receive. For government, a terror to crime, has no terrors for good behavior. You wish to have no fear of the authorities? Then continue to do right and you will have their approval, for they are God's agents working for your good. But if you are doing wrong, then you will have cause to fear them; it is not for nothing that they hold the power of the sword, for they are God's agents of punishment, for retribution on the offender. That is why you are obliged to submit. It is an obligation imposed not merely by fear of retribution but by conscience. That is also why you pay taxes. The authorities are in God's service, and to these duties they devote their energies. (Paul, *To the Romans* 13:1–6)

Much the same sentiment is echoed by Peter in one of his letters.

Submit yourselves to every human institution for the sake of the Lord, whether to the sovereign as supreme, or to the governor as his deputy for the punishment of criminals and the commendation of those who do right. For it is the will of God that by your good conduct you should put ignorance and stupidity to silence. Live as free men; not however, as though your freedom were there to provide a screen from wrongdoing, but as slaves in God's service. Give due honor to everyone: love to the brotherhood, reverence to God, honor to the sovereign. (Peter, *First Letter* 2:13–17)

2. The Last Great Persecution

The power of the sovereign may not have appeared quite so innocuous to either Peter or Paul, both of whom perished, the tradition relates, in a recklessly offhanded persecution instigated by Nero against the Christians in Rome. Toward the end of the first century such episodic persecutions became better focused, and by the second they were systematic. Churches and property were confiscated, the clergy arrested, and ordinary Christians put to death for public refusal to sacrifice to the emperor. The last great outburst occurred in 303 C.E. under Emperor Diocletian and is graphically described by Eusebius in his Church History.

It was in the nineteenth year of the reign of Diocletian, in the month of Dystus, called March by the Romans, when the feast of the Savior's passion was near at hand, the imperial edicts were published everywhere commanding that the churches be leveled to the ground, the Scriptures be destroyed by fire, and that all holding places of honor be branded with infamy; and that household servants, if they persisted in their profession of Christianity, be deprived of their freedom.

Such was the original edict against us. But not long after other decrees were issued, commanding that all the leaders of the churches everywhere should be thrown into prison and afterward compelled by any means to offer sacrifice. (Eusebius, *Church History* 8.2)

That is what happened at Nicomedia at the beginning of the persecution. But not long after, as persons in the region called Melitene and others throughout Syria attempted to usurp the government, an imperial edict commanded that leaders of the churches everywhere be thrown into prison and chains. What was seen after this defies description. Large numbers were imprisoned everywhere, and all the prisons, which had been set up for murderers and grave robbers, were filled instead with bishops, presbyters and deacons, readers and exorcists, so that there was no longer any room in them for condemned criminals. And as other decrees followed the first, directing that those in prison, if they offered sacrifice, should be set free from prison, but that those who refused should be harassed and tortured, how could any one again number the great host of martyrs in every province (of the Empire), and especially those in Africa and Mauritania and Thebais and Egypt? (Ibid. 8.6)

3. An Edict of Toleration,
311 C.E.

The Emperor Caesar Galerius Valerius, Maximianus, Invictus Augustus, Pontifex Maximus, Germanicus Maximus, Egyptiacus Maximus . . . ; (and) the Emperor Caesar Flavius Valerius, Constantinus Pius Felix Invictus Augustus, Pontifex Maximus . . . ; and the Emperor Caesar Val-

erius Licinianus Licinius Pius Felix Invictus Augustus Pontifex Maximus
. . . to the people of their several provinces, greeting.

Among the other steps that we are taking for the advantage and
benefit of the nation, we have desired hitherto that every deficiency
should be made good, in accordance with the established law and public
order of Rome; and we made provision for this—that the Christians who
had abandoned the convictions of their forefathers should return to
sound ideas. For through some perverse reasoning such arrogance and
folly had seized and possessed them that they refused to follow the path
trodden by earlier generations (and perhaps blazed long ago by their
own ancestors), and made their own laws to suit their own ideas and
individual tastes and observed these, and held various meetings at various
places.

Consequently, when we issued an order to the effect that they were
to go back to the practices established by the ancients, many of them
found themselves in great danger, and many were proceeded against and
punished with death in many forms. Many of them indeed persisted in the
same folly, and we saw that they were neither paying to the gods in
heaven the worship that is their due nor giving any honor to the god of
the Christians. So in view of our benevolence and the established custom
by which we invariably grant pardon to all men, we have thought proper
in this matter also to extend our clemency most gladly, so that the Christians may again exist and rebuild the houses in which they used to meet,
on condition that they do nothing contrary to public order. (Eusebius,
Church History 8.17)

Two years later the co-emperors Constantine and Licinius—Galerius had died
shortly after the original edict—issued this instruction from Milan.

When I, Constantine Augustus, and I, Licinius Augustus, had hap-
pily met together at Milan, and considered everything that concerns the
welfare and security of the state, we thought that, among other things
which seemed likely to be of general profit to men, we ought first to order
the conditions of the reverence paid to the Deity by granting to the
Christians and to all others full permission to follow whatever form of
worship each of them chooses. In that way whatever Deity there is in
heaven may be benevolent and propitious to us and to all subject to our
authority. Therefore we deemed it right, with the benefit of sound counsel and right reason, to lay down this law, that we in no way deny the legal
right to any man devoted either to the observance or to that worship
which he personally feels best suited to himself, to the end that the

Supreme Deity, whose worship we freely follow, may continue to grant us His accustomed favor and goodwill. . . .

Further, as regards the Christians, we have thought fit to ordain this as well, that if anyone has bought, either from our exchequer or from others, the places in which they were formerly accustomed to congregate . . . that the same be restored to the Christians, without delay or dispute, and without payment or the demand for such. Those who have obtained such places as gifts should likewise restore them to the said Christians without delay. (Lactantius, *On the Death of the Persecutors* 48)

The Christian Church was at last free to pursue its own course—and to discover that it had a new and highly complex relationship with that "Caesar" so effortlessly separated by Jesus three centuries before.

4. The Conversion of Constantine,
312 C.E.

Whether those decrees of toleration were motivated by liberal piety, by simple pragmatism, or by an uncanny reading of the future, and however welcome they were to the Christians, they could scarcely have foretold the course taken by one of those emperors who issued the instruction at Milan only the year before.

The anniversary of Maxentius' accession, the twenty-seventh of October, was near, and his (own first) five years of rule were drawing to a close. Constantine [who was camped opposite Maxentius' forces at the Milvian Bridge near Rome] was directed in a dream to mark the heavenly sign of God on the shields of his soldiers and then to begin the battle. He did as he was ordered, and with the cross-shaped letter X, with its top bent over, he marked Christ on the shields. (Lactantius, *On the Deaths of the Persecutors* 44.3–6)

Accordingly, he [Constantine] prayed to his father's god in heaven, beseeching him and imploring him to tell him who he was and to stretch out his right hand to help him in his present difficulties (with Maxentius). And while he was praying thus fervently, a truly incredible sign appeared to him from heaven, the account of which might have been difficult to believe had it been related by any other person. But since the victorious emperor himself long afterwards described it to the writer of this account, when he was honored with his acquaintance and company, and confirmed his statement with an oath, who could hesitate in accepting the story as true, especially since the testimony that followed has established its truth?

He [Constantine] said that about noon, when the day was already beginning to wane, he saw with his own eyes the victory signal of a cross of light in the heavens, above the sun, and the legend, "Conquer by this," attached to it. At this sight he himself was struck with amazement, and his whole army as well, which was accompanying him on expedition and witnessed the miracle.

He said, further, that he had his own doubts about the meaning of this portent. And while he was pondering and thinking about its meaning, night overtook him; then the Christ of God appeared to him in his sleep and commanded him to make a likeness of the sign which he had seen in the heavens, and to use it as a protection in all engagements with his enemies. (Eusebius, *Life of Constantine* 1.28–29)

5. Christianity as the State Church of the Roman Empire

The results of Constantine's conversion to the Christian faith were quick in coming: benefits and exemptions for the clergy began to be written into Roman law (see below), new churches were endowed out of state funds, and in Palestine in particular Constantine interested himself in the monumental enshrinement of the places associated with the life and death of Jesus. It was Constantine who convened the first ecumenical council of the bishops of the Great Church at Nicea in 325 C.E., and he also presided over its deliberations.

These were only beginnings. Later in that same century other emperors intervened even more directly in the affairs of the Church. The following is an imperial edict, dated 27 February 380 and issued in the names of the co-emperors Gratian and Valentinian II in the West and Theodosius in the East. It undertakes to define, in the formal context of Roman law, the official teaching of the Catholic Church and, in effect, to constitute it the imperial church of the Roman Empire.

It is our will that all the peoples whom the government of our Clemency rules shall follow the religion which a pious belief from Peter to the present declares that the holy Peter delivered to the Romans, and which it is evident that the pontiff Damasus (bishop of Rome) and Peter, bishop of Alexandria, a man of Apostolic sanctity, follow; that is, according to the Apostolic discipline and evangelical teaching we believe in the deity of the Father and the Son and the Holy Spirit of equal majesty, in a Holy Trinity. *Those who follow this law we command shall be comprised under the name of Catholic Christians*; but others, indeed, we require, since they are insane and raving, to bear the infamy of heretical teaching; their gatherings shall not receive the name of churches; they are to be smitten first

with the divine punishment, and after with the vengeance of our indignation, which has the divine approval. (Theodosian Code 16.1.2)

*On the occasion of another ecumenical council, held in the imperial capital of
Constantinople in 381 C.E., the assembled bishops made a final report to Emperor
Theodosius that reveals in its unstated but obvious premises the importance and
prestige of the Roman emperor in the affairs of what had become the state church.*

We begin our letter to your Piety with thanks to God, who has
established the empire of your Piety for the common peace of the
churches and for the support of the True Faith. And after rendering due
thanks to God, as is our duty, we lay before your Piety the things which
have been done in the Holy Synod.

When, then, we had assembled in Constantinople, in accordance
with the letter from your Piety, we first of all renewed our unity of heart
with each other, and then we pronounced some concise definitions, rati-
fying the faith of the Fathers at Nicea and anathematizing the heresies
which have sprung up contrary to that faith. Besides this we also framed
certain canons for the better ordering of the churches, all of which we
have appended to this letter. We therefore beseech your Piety that the
decree of the synod may be ratified, to the end that, as you have honored
the Church by your letter of convocation, so you should set your seal to
the conclusion of what has been decreed. (Council of Constantinople,
Address to Theodosius)

6. The Roman State and the Catholic Church in the Fourth Century

*The course of imperial favor, and of a hardening of attitudes toward other forms of
religion, can be clearly charted in the series of enactments dealing with the Christian
Church that began to appear in Roman law in the fourth century. These start with
a modest decree concerning what was still in 321 C.E. called the "Day of the Sun."*

3 July 321 C.E.: Just as it appears to Us most unseemly that the Day
of the Sun which is celebrated on account of its own veneration should
be occupied with legal altercations and with noxious controversies of the
litigation of contending parties, so it is pleasant and fitting that those acts
which are especially desired shall be accomplished on that day. Therefore
all men have the right to emancipate and to manumit on this festive day,
and the legal formalities thereof are not forbidden. Given on 3 July at
Cagliari in the second consulate of Crispus and Constantine Caesars.
(Theodosian Code 16.2.8)

The Church was also given corporate status, with the obviously beneficial effect that it could thereafter inherit.

3 July 321 C.E.: Every person shall have the liberty to leave at his death any property that he wishes to the most holy and venerable council of the Catholic Church. Wills (to that effect) shall not become void. There is nothing which is more due to men than that the expression of their last will, after which they can no longer will anything, shall be free, and the power of choice, which does not return again, shall be unhampered. (Ibid. 16.2.4)

Paganism was repressed in a number of imperial decrees.

341 C.E.: Superstition shall cease; the madness of sacrifices shall be abolished. For if any man in violation of the law of the sainted Emperor, Our father, and in violation of the command of our clemency, should dare to perform sacrifices, he shall suffer the infliction of a suitable punishment and the effect of an immediate sentence. (Ibid. 16.10.2)

8 November 392 C.E.: Hereafter no one of whatever race or dignity, whether placed in office or discharged therefrom with honor, powerful by birth or humble in condition or fortune, shall in any place or in any city sacrifice an innocent victim to a senseless image, venerate with fire the household deity by a more private offering, and burn lights, place incense or hang up garlands.

If anyone undertakes by way of sacrifice to slay a victim, or to consult the smoking entrails, let him be guilty of lese majesty, receive the appropriate sentence, having been accused by a lawful indictment. . . . If anyone, by placing incense, venerates either images made by mortal labor, or those which are enduring, or if anyone in ridiculous fashion forthwith venerates what he has represented, either by a tree encircled by garlands, or an altar of cut turfs . . . let him be guilty of sacrilege and punished by loss of house or property in which he worshiped according to the heathen superstition. For all places which shall smoke of incense, if they shall be proved to belong to those who burn incense, shall be confiscated. (Ibid. 16.10.12)

399 C.E.: Whatever privileges were conceded by the ancient laws to the priests, ministers, prefects, hierophants of sacred things, or by whatever name they may be designated, are abolished henceforth, and let them not think that they are protected by a granted privilege when their religious confession is known to have been condemned by the law. (Ibid. 16.10.14)

399 C.E.: If there are temples in the fields [that is, outside the cities], let them be destroyed without crowd and tumult. For when these have been thrown down and carried away, the support of superstition will be consumed. (Ibid. 16.10.16)

There was some concern, however, for the magnificent urban temples that by then constituted monuments to local pride or the historical landmarks of an already vanished antiquity.

399 C.E.: We prohibit (pagan) sacrifices, and yet we wish that the ornaments of public works be preserved. And to prevent those who overthrow them from flattering themselves that they do it with some authority, if they allege that they possess some rescript or cite some law, let these documents be taken from their hands and referred to Our knowledge. (Ibid. 16.10.15)

As for the pagans themselves:

416 C.E.: Those who are polluted by the error or crime of pagan rites are not to be admitted to the army or to receive the distinction and honor of administrator or judge. (Ibid. 16.10.21)

And finally:

423 C.E.: Although the pagans that remain ought to be subjected to capital punishment if at any time they are detected in the abominable sacrifices to demons, let exile and confiscation of goods be their punishment. (Ibid. 16.10.23)

Christian clerics, on the other hand, were granted generous privileges and exemptions.

319 C.E.: Those who in divine worship perform the services or religion, that is, those who are called clergy, are altogether exempt from public obligations, so that they may not be called away from their sacred duty by the sacrilegious malice of certain persons. (Ibid. 16.2.2)

Such exemptions did not apply to the heretics and schismatics who might lay claim to being Christians.

326 C.E.: Privileges which have been bestowed in consideration of religion ought to be of advantage only to those who observe the Catholic law. It is our will that the heathen and schismatics be not only without privileges but bound by, and subject to, various political burdens. (Ibid. 16.5.1)

26 May 353 C.E.: In order that organizations in the service of the churches may be filled with a great multitude of people, tax exemption

shall be granted to clerics and their acolytes, and they shall be protected from the exaction of compulsory public services of a menial nature. They shall by no means be subject to the tax payments of tradesmen, since it is manifest that the profits which they collect from stalls and workshops will benefit the poor. We decree also that their men who engage in trade shall be exempt from all tax payments. Likewise, the exaction of services for the maintenance of the supplementary post wagons shall cease. This indulgence We grant to their wives, children and servants, to males and females equally, for We command that they also shall continue exempt from tax assessments. (Ibid. 16.2.10)

They were likewise removed in many instances from the jurisdiction of Roman law.

7 October 355 C.E.: By a law of Our Clemency We prohibit bishops from being accused in the courts, lest there should be an unrestrained opportunity for fanatical spirits to accuse them, while the accusers assume they will obtain impunity by the kindness of the bishops. Therefore, if any person should lodge any complaint, such complaint must unquestionably be examined before other bishops, in order that an opportune and suitable hearing may be arranged for the investigation of all pertinent matters. (Ibid. 16.2.12)

Finally, the Roman state began to surrender some of its own authority to the chief executives of the Christian Church. The empire's effective control of its own provincial cities was in notable decline by the sixth century, and the once prosperous urban aristocracies appeared near collapse. The only real government left in those cities was the Church's, and this law of 530 C.E. officially confirms that the Christian bishop was in effect the chief magistrate in many cities.

With respect to the yearly affairs of cities, whether they concern the ordinary revenues of the city, either from funds derived from the property of the city, or from legacies and private gifts, or given or received from other sources, whether for public works, or for provisions, or for aqueducts, or the maintenance of baths or ports, or the construction of walls or towers, or the repairing of bridges and roads, or for trials in which the city may be engaged in reference to public or private interests, we decree as follows: The very pious bishop and three men of good reputation, in every respect the first men of the city, shall meet and each year not only examine the work done, but take care that those who conduct them or have been conducting them, shall manage them with exactness, shall render their accounts, and show by the production of public records that they have duly performed their engagements in the administration of the sums appropriated for provisions, or baths, or for the expenses involved in the maintenance of roads, aqueducts, or any other work. (Code of Justinian 1.4.26)

The "overseer" had become in fact an overseer!

7. The Roman State and the Jews

The newly Christianized empire also paid new attention to Jews.

18 October 315 C.E.: It is our will that the Jews and their elders and patriarchs shall be informed that if, after the issuance of this law, any of them should dare to attempt to assail with stones or with any other kind of madness—a thing which We have learned is now being done—any person who has fled their wild animal sect and has resorted to the worship of God, such assailant shall be immediately delivered to the flames and burned, with all his accomplices. Moreover, if any person from the people should betake himself to their nefarious sect and should join their assemblies, he shall sustain with them deserved punishments. (Theodosian Code 16.8.1)

If the Jews were compelled to show restraint in what were for them dangerously changing circumstances, the new order of things did not mean an end to the longstanding privileges and exemptions accorded them by Roman law. Those now stood as a shield between the Jews and some of the more fanatic Christians.

November 330 C.E.: If any person with complete devotion should dedicate themselves to the synagogues of the Jews as patriarchs and priests and should live in the aforementioned sect and preside over the administration of their law, they shall continue to be exempt from all compulsory public services that are incumbent on persons, as well as those due to the municipalities. Likewise, such persons who are now perchance decurions [that is, members of municipal councils] shall not be assigned to any duties as official escorts, since such men shall not be compelled for any reason to depart from those places in which they are. Moreover, such persons who are not decurions shall enjoy perpetual exemption from the decurionate. (Ibid. 16.8.2)

29 September 393 C.E.: It is sufficiently established that the sect of the Jews is forbidden by no law. Hence We are gravely disturbed that their assemblies have been forbidden in certain places. Your Sublime Magnitude will, therefore, after receiving this order, restrain with proper severity the excesses of those people who, in the name of the Christian religion, presume to commit certain unlawful acts and attempt to destroy and despoil the synagogues. (Ibid. 16.8.9)

398 C.E.: Jews living in Rome, according to the common right, in those cases which do not pertain to their superstition, their court, laws and rights, must attend the (ordinary) courts of justice, and are to bring and defend legal actions according to the Roman laws; hereafter let them be under our laws. If, however, any, by an agreement similar to that for the appointment of arbitrators, decide that the litigation is to be before the Jews or their patriarchs by the consent of both parties and in business of a purely civil character, they are not forbidden by public law to choose their own courts of justice; and let the provincial judges execute their decisions as if the arbitrators had been assigned to them [that is, the Jews] by the decree of a judge. (Ibid. 2.1.10)

6 July 412 C.E.: If it should appear that any places are frequented by conventicles of Jews and are called by the name of synagogue, no one shall dare to violate or to occupy or to retain such places, since all persons must retain their own property in undisturbed right, without any claim of religion or worship.

Moreover, since indeed ancient custom and practice have preserved for the aforesaid Jewish people the consecrated day of the Sabbath, We also decree that it shall be forbidden that any man of the aforesaid faith be constrained by any summons on that day, under the pretext of public or private business, since all the remaining time appears sufficient to satisfy the public laws, and since it is most worthy of the moderation of Our time that the privileges granted should not be violated, although sufficient provision appears to have been made with reference to the aforesaid matter by general constitutions of earlier Emperors. (Ibid. 16.8.20)

8. The City of God and the City of Man

This comfortable political relationship between the Roman state and the Christian Church, though occasionally embarrassing to one side or the other, continued to flourish in the eastern provinces of the Roman Empire. But in the European and African provinces, the Latin-speaking part of the empire, the connection was an increasingly troubling one by the fifth century. The Roman state had come to its term, it was clear, under the attacks of barbarians, and the Church's close association with this other, perishing institution raised questions in the minds of some. Would the collapse of one signal the collapse of the other?

In 426 C.E. Augustine, the learned bishop of Hippo in what is today Algeria, took up the task of distinguishing, and so separating, the two—the dying earthly "City of Man" that was Rome and the celestial "City of God" where all Christians held their true citizenship, as the Letter to Diognetus had already suggested.

Augustine accomplished this through a dense meditation on the twin threads of Roman and biblical history. Though in one sense the true heavenly city is the afterlife, the community of saints in the bosom of God, at least one strand of human society, the Israelites, had joined and pursued together the twin aims of justice on earth and beatitude hereafter through the giving of God's Law. But at some point the two became dissociated, and the earthly city of the Israelite kingdom—and its successor states of the Greeks and then the Romans—were no more than worldly kingdoms, subject to the usual laws of sin and corruption, of prosperity followed by collapse and destruction. The heavenly city, still in its earthly passage toward eternity, is thus constrained to find its latter-day abode in human societies that do not share its goal and purposes.

The earthly city, which does not live by faith, seeks an earthly peace, and the end it proposes, in the well-ordered concord of civic obedience and rule, is the combination of men's wills to attain the things that are helpful to this life. The heavenly city, or rather that part of it that sojourns on earth and lives by faith, makes use of this peace only because it must, until the mortal condition which necessitates it shall pass away. Consequently, so long as it lives like a captive and a stranger in the earthly city, though it has already received the promise of redemption and the gift of the spirit as the earnest of it, it makes no scruple to obey the laws of the earthly city, whereby the things necessary for the maintenance of this mortal life are administered: and thus, as this life is common to both cities, so there is harmony between them in regard to what belongs to it. But as the earthly city has had some philosophers whose doctrine is condemned by the divine teaching, and who, being deceived either by their own conjectures or by demons, supposed that many gods must be invited to take an interest in human affairs and assigned to each a separate function and a separate department ... and as the celestial city on the other hand, knew that one god only was to be worshiped, and to Him alone was due that service which the Greeks call *latreia* and which can be given only to a god, it has come to pass that the two cities could not have common laws of religion, and the heavenly city has been compelled in this manner to dissent, and to become obnoxious to those who think differently, and to stand the brunt of their anger and hatred and persecutions, except insofar as the minds of their enemies have been alarmed by the multitude of Christians and quelled by the manifest protection of God accorded to them.

This heavenly city, then, while it sojourns on earth, calls its citizens out of all nations and gathers together a society of pilgrims of all languages, not scrupling about diversities in the manners, laws and institutions whereby earthly peace is secured and maintained, so long only as no hindrance to the worship of the one supreme and true God is thus introduced. Even the heavenly city, therefore, while in its state of pilgrimage, avails itself of peace on earth, and so far as it can without injuring faith and godliness, desires and maintains a common agreement among men regarding the acquisition of the necessaries of life, and makes this earthly peace bear upon the peace of heaven; for this alone can be truly called and esteemed the peace of reasonable creatures, consisting as it does in the perfectly ordered and harmonious enjoyment of God and of one another in God. (Augustine, *City of God* 19.17) [AUGUSTINE 1948: 2:493–494]

9. "There Are Two Powers"

Augustine's philosophical approach to the dissociation of the Roman City of Man from the Christians' City of God looked to history. The bishop of Rome, who claimed a primacy of ecclesiastical jurisdiction, had to deal with a closer political reality: his relationship with another primate, the emperor in Constantinople. In 494 C.E. the imperial incumbent was Anastasius, and in that year Pope Gelasius wrote to him in an effort to set the emperor straight on the matter of authority.

I implore your Piety not to judge a sense of duty to the divine truth as a form of arrogance. I trust that it will not have to be said of a Roman Emperor that he resented the truth being told him. There are indeed, most august Emperor, two powers by which this world is chiefly ruled: the sacred authority of the Popes and the royal power. Of the two the priestly power is much the more important because it must give an account of the kings of men themselves before the divine tribunal. For you know, our most clement son, that though you have the first place in dignity over the human race, yet you must submit yourself faithfully to those who have the charge of divine things and look to them for the means of your salvation. You know that you should, when it concerns the reception and reverent administration of the sacraments, be obedient to the Church's authority rather than seek to control it. So too in such matters you ought to depend on the Church's judgment instead of seeking to bend it to your own will.

For if, in matters that deal with the administration of public discipline, the bishops of the Church, since they are well aware that the Empire has been conferred on you, are themselves obedient to your laws, so that in purely material matters they ought not to voice contrary opinions, with what willingness, I ask you, should you obey those to whom is assigned the administration of the divine mysteries? So just as there is great danger for the Popes in not saying what is necessary in matters of the divine honor, so there is great danger for those who are obstinate in resistance—which God forbid should happen—at the very time they should be obedient. And if the hearts of the faithful ought to be submitted to all priests in general, who rightly administer holy things, how much more ought assent be given to him who presides over the See which the Supreme Godhead Himself desired to be pre-eminent over all priests, and which the pious judgment of the whole Church has honored ever since? (Gelasius, *Letter to Anastasius*)

10. The Imperial View

The issue of the two spheres of authority, the spiritual and the temporal, argued with such economic finesse by Gelasius, could hardly be gainsaid by any Christian. But even granting the argument, with or without the corollary of Papal primacy, there were other considerations and other equally persuasive responsibilities. These are set forth by Emperor Justinian, who was not unsympathetic to Papal claims, in a letter not just to the bishop of Rome but to all his Roman subjects. The imperial decree, which had the force of law, is dated 17 April 535 C.E.. It begins with a respectful echo of Gelasius' own argument.

The greatest of the gifts which God in His heavenly mercy has given to men are the priesthood and the imperial authority. The former ministers to divine matters and the latter presides and watches over human affairs; both proceed from one and the same source, and together they are adornments of human life. And so nothing is so close to the hearts of emperors as the moral well-being of the priesthood, since it is the priests who have the task of perpetual prayer to God on behalf of the emperors themselves. For if the priesthood is entirely free from vice and filled with faith in God, and if the imperial authority sets in order the commonwealth committed to its charge in justice and efficiency, there will come about an ideal harmony providing whatever is useful for the human race. We therefore have the greatest anxiety for the true doctrines of God and for the moral well-being of the priesthood by which, if it is preserved, we believe that the greatest gifts will be given to us by God and we shall preserve undisturbed those things which we have and moreover gain the benefits which we presently do not possess. But all things are done rightly and efficiently if a beginning is made which is fitting and agreeable to God. We believe that this will come about if there is due care for the observance of the holy canons, which the justly praised Apostles and venerated eyewitnesses and servants of the word of God handed down and which the Fathers preserved and interpreted. (Justinian, *Novella* 6)

11. The Keys of the Kingdom

On 15 March 1081 Pope Gregory VII sent a latter to Hermann, bishop of Metz, on the subject of the Pope's power over the secular authority, in this instance Emperor Henry. The letter's title in the papal archives is "Against those who stupidly maintain that the Emperor cannot be excommunicated by the Roman Pontiff," and that appears to be an adequate summary of both its tone and its contents. None of the themes are new, perhaps, but they are marshaled with marvelous force, ease, and confidence.

It seems hardly necessary for us to comply with your request, namely, that we lend some assistance with a letter of ours and fortify you against the madness of those who keep repeating with perverse mouth that the Holy and Apostolic See has no authority to excommunicate Henry—a man who despises Christian law, destroys the churches and the Empire, sponsors and sustains heretics—and to absolve any from the oaths of fealty sworn to him. Indeed this enterprise seems to us hardly necessary because of the many and perfectly clear proofs that are available in Holy Scripture. . . . To say only a few words out of many, who does not know the words of our Lord and Savior Jesus Christ, who says in the Gospel, "You are Peter and upon this rock I will build my Church, and the gates of hell shall not prevail against it; and I will give you the keys of the kingdom of heaven; and whatsoever you shall bind upon earth will be bound also in heaven; and whatsoever you shall loose upon earth shall be loosed also in heaven"? Are kings excepted here? Are they not among the sheep that the Son of God committed to St. Peter? Who, I ask, can consider himself as exempted from this universal power of binding and loosing conferred on St. Peter, except perhaps some unfortunate who, because he is unwilling to bear the yoke of the Lord, subjects himself to the burden of the devil and refuses to be among Christ's sheep? For such a one it will be a small addition indeed to his wretched freedom if he shakes off from his proud neck the power divinely granted to St. Peter; the more anyone, out of pride, refuses to bear it, the more heavily it shall press upon him and he shall carry it to his damnation at the Judgment.

The Holy Fathers, supporting and serving the Holy Roman Church with great veneration, called her the Universal Mother in the Councils and by other such titles in their writings and acts. In doing this they supported and served this institution of the divine will, this pledge of a dispensation to the Church, this privilege handed on from the beginning to St. Peter, chief of the Apostles, and confirmed to him by a heavenly decree. And in assenting to the proofs of all this and by including them in the confirmation of the faith and in the doctrine of the holy religion, they also accepted her judgments; by their assent in this regard, they also agreed, with one spirit and one voice as it were, that all major affairs and important matters, as well as jurisdiction over all the churches, ought to be referred to her as mother and head; that from her there is no appeal; and that no one should or could retract or repudiate her judgments. . . .

But to return to the point, ought not an authority which has been established by laymen, perhaps even by those who had no knowledge of God, be subjected to an authority which the Providence of Almighty God established for His own honor and which He gave, in His mercy, to the world? For His Son, just as he is believed to be God and man, is also held to be the High Priest, the head of all priests, who sits at the right hand of the Father and is always interceding for us; and he despised a secular kingship, with which the children of this world are so puffed up, and entered freely into the priesthood of the Cross. Who is not aware that kings and princes are sprung from those who, unmindful of God, urged on in fact by the devil, the prince of the world, and by pride, plunder, treachery, murders and by almost every crime, have striven with blind greed, cupidity and intolerable presumption to hold dominion over their equals, that is to say, over men? . . . Who can doubt that the priests of Christ are to be accounted fathers and judges of kings and princes and of all the faithful? Is it not recognized as a form of wretched madness if a son tries to gain ascendancy over his father, or a pupil over his teacher; or to subdue to his own domination, by unlawful pressure, someone to whom, it is believed, has been entrusted not only the earthly but the heavenly power of binding and loosing?

The Emperor Constantine the Great, lord of all the kings and princes throughout almost the entire world, clearly knew this fact . . . when, sitting in the Council of Nicea as the inferior of all the bishops, he did not presume to pass any verdict or judgment upon them; but going so far as to call them gods, he decreed that they were not to be subject to his judgment, but rather that he himself would depend on their opinion.

And finally, on the intrinsic grace of the office:

Therefore all Christians who wish to reign with Christ should be warned not to try to rule with ambition for temporal power. . . . If those who fear God are forced with great misgivings to ascend the Apostolic throne, in which those properly ordained are made better by the merits of blessed Peter the Apostle, with how much more misgiving and apprehension should the throne of the kingdom be approached, in which even the good and the humble—as is made plain in the cases of Saul and David—are made worse! For what we have said previously about the Apostolic See is contained in the following words found in the decrees of Symmachus the Pope—and we know it well enough from our own experience—"He [that is, the blessed Peter] transmitted to his successors an everlasting gift of merits together with an inheritance of innocence"; and shortly after that he states, "Who may doubt that he is holy whom the loftiness of so great a dignity [as the bishopric of Rome] elevates? In this dignity, if virtues won by his own merits are not present, those suffice which are supplied by his predecessor. For he (St. Peter) either raises eminent men to his exalted office or else enlightens those who are so exalted." (Gregory VII, *To Hermann of Metz*)

12. The Two Swords

The debate went on between the bishop of Rome and the waxing and waning monarchs of Europe, its terms dictated by the personalities on each side and by the extent of the political power each wielded. One of its most explosive fusillades was heard in 1302, when Pope Boniface VIII promulgated his bull called, from its opening words in Latin, Unam sanctam. *It was provoked by his struggle with Philip the Fair of France, but its claims and its echoes far transcended that contest.*

The image of the two swords, which derives from a brief and enigmatic incident just before the arrest of Jesus in Gethsemane, had been invoked in an earlier debate between Church and State to distinguish and above all to separate into two distinct and autonomous spheres the temporal and spiritual powers contested between king and Pope. In Unam sanctam, *however, Pope Boniface VIII firmly grasps both swords in his own pontifical hands.*

We are taught by the words of the Gospel that in this Church and in its power there are two swords, a spiritual, to wit, and a temporal. For when the Apostles said, "Behold, here are two swords" (Luke 22:38)— that refers to the Church since it is the Apostles who are speaking—the Lord does not reply that it was too many, but enough. And he who denies that the temporal sword is in the power of Peter has wrongly understood the word of the Lord when he says (to Peter), "Put up again your sword in its place" (John 18:10–11). It follows then that both (swords) are in the power of the Church, namely, the spiritual and the material swords; the one indeed to be wielded for the Church, the other by the Church; the former by the priest, the latter by the hand of kings and knights, but at the will and sufferance of the priest. For it is necessary that one sword should be under another and that the temporal authority should be subjected to the spiritual. . . . But it is necessary that we affirm all the more clearly that the spiritual power exceeds any earthly power in dignity and nobility, just as spiritual things excel temporal ones. This we can clearly see with our own eyes from the giving of tithes, from the acts of benediction and sanctification, from the recognition of this power and from the exercise of government over these same things. For with the truth as witness, the spiritual power has also to establish the earthly power and judge it, if it is not good. So is verified the prophecy of the prophet Jeremiah concerning the Church and the power of the Church, "Behold, I have set you this day over the nations and over the kingdoms. . . ."

If, then, the earthly power errs, it should be judged by the spiritual power; if the lesser spiritual power errs, it should be judged by the higher competent spiritual power; but if the supreme spiritual power errs, it can be judged only by God, not by man; to which the Apostle (Paul) bears witness: "The spiritual man judges all things; and he himself is judged by no man" (1 Cor. 2:15). It is for this reason that this authority, although given to man and exercised by man, is not human, but rather divine, being given to Peter from God's mouth and founded for him and his successors on the rock by him whom he confessed, when the Lord said to the same Peter, "Whatsoever you shall bind. . . ." Whoever therefore resists this power thus ordained by God, resists the ordination of God. . . . *Consequently we declare, state, define and pronounce that it is altogether necessary to salvation for every human creature to be subject to the Roman Pontiff.* (Boniface VIII, *Unam sanctam*)

13. The Great Schism

Rome's claims to primacy early prevailed over all the other bishoprics in the Latin-speaking European and African provinces of Church and empire. Its Petrine claim, its prestige as an imperial seat, and its lack of serious competition for authority in what were once prosperous Roman provinces but were rapidly becoming Gothic, German and Frankish principalities—all these advantages gave a powerful preeminence to the bishop who held the See of Rome and was called "the Pope." But the eastern provinces of that same empire suffered no similar decline. They had, moreover, episcopal sees of great antiquity and prestige. Alexandria and Antioch had long been great cities in their own right, and after Constantine their company was

joined by Constantinople, whose rise through the episcopal hierarchy we have al-
ready seen. From the beginning, Rome had taken ill to what it saw as episcopal
presumption and had protested it, though to no great avail.

The papally inspired formulas of the ecumenical council of Chalcedon in 451
drove a fatal doctrinal wedge between Constantinople, which accepted the formulas,
and its eastern sister sees, which did not. The case was rendered moot, perhaps, when
in the 630s Muslim armies swept over the provinces of Syria and Egypt and detached
them from at least the immediate jurisdiction of Constantinople. Rome and Con-
stantinople were left to pursue their rivalry alone, and they soon found a new venue:
the recently converted barbarian tribes in the Balkans, particularly the Bulgarians,
whom both great sees struggled to wrestle into their fold.

As time passed, the theological issues between the Greek East and the Latin
West multiplied. But in fact, only two mattered, one theoretical and one practical:
whether the Roman see had a de jure absolute primacy within the Church; and
where, de facto, the jurisdictional line between them was to be drawn. They broke
and restored relations a number of times. The first great rupture took place in 866,
when Patriarch Photius of Constantinople wrote an encyclical letter to his fellow
prelates of the East.

. . . Now the barbarian tribe of the Bulgarians, who were hostile and
inimical to Christ, has been converted to a surprising degree of meekness
and knowledge of God. Beyond all expectation they have in a body embraced the faith of Christ, departing from the worship of devils and of
their ancestral gods, and rejecting the error of pagan superstition.

But what a wicked and malignant design, what an ungodly state of
affairs! The previous report of good news has been turned into dejection,
delight and joy have been changed into sadness and tears. That people had
not embraced the true religion of Christians for even two years, when
certain impious and ominous men, or whatever name a Christian might
call them, emerged from the darkness, darkness I say because they came
from the West. . . . They have villainously devised to lead them away
from the true and pure doctrine and from an unblemished Christian faith
and in this way destroy them.

The first unlawful practice they have set up is fasting on Saturday.
Such slight regard for the traditional teaching usually leads to the complete abandonment of the entire doctrine. They separated the first week
of Lent from the rest and allowed them [that is, the Bulgarians] milk,
cheese and other gluttonous practices during this time. From here they
made the road of transgressions wider and wider and removed the people
more and more from the straight and royal road. They taught them to
despise the priest living in lawful matrimony, and by rejecting matrimony

spread the seed of Manicheism, while they themselves practiced adultery. They did not shrink from reconfirming those who had been anointed by priests with the chrism, and presenting themselves as bishops, they declared the confirmation administered by priests as useless and invalid. . . .

They have not only introduced the committing of such outrages, but now the crown of all evils is sprung up. Besides these offenses that have already been mentioned, they have attempted to adulterate the sacred and holy creed, which had been approved by all the ecumenical synods and has invincible strength, with spurious arguments, interpolated words, and rash exaggerations. They are preaching a novel doctrine: that the Holy Spirit proceeds not from the Father alone, but from the Son as well. . . .

These new forerunners of apostasy, these servants of the anti-Christ, who have deserved death a thousand times, . . . these deceivers and enemies of God, we have by the resolution of the Holy Synod sentenced, or rather declared, that by previous resolutions of synods and by Apostolic laws, they are already condemned, and are made manifest to all. People are so constituted by nature that they are more restrained by present and visible punishments than by previously afflicted ones. Thus because these men persist in their manifold errors, we consider them banished by public proclamation from the company of Christians. (Photius, *Encyclical Letter*)

The response was quick. In the following year Pope Nicholas I wrote a letter to the bishops of the Western empire in which he cast the dispute into a far broader context.

Assuredly among the difficulties which cause us great concern are those, especially disturbing to us, which the Greek emperors Michael and Basil and their subjects inflict on us, and truly on the whole West. Inflamed with hate and envy against us, as we will specify later, they attempt to accuse us of heresy. With hatred indeed, for we not only disapproved but even condemned by deposition and anathematization the advancement attained by Photius, a neophyte, usurper and adulterer of the Church of Constantinople. The ejection from this church of Ignatius [the deposed patriarch of Constantinople], our brother and co-minister, perpetrated by his own subjects and the imperial power, did not receive our approval. And with envy because they learned that Michael, king of the Bulgarians, and his people received the faith of Christ and now desired St. Peter's See to provide teachers and instructors for them.

Instead they wish eagerly to lead the Bulgarians from obedience to the blessed Peter and to subject them shrewdly to their own authority under the pretext of the Christian religion. They preach such things about the Roman Church, which is without spot or wrinkle or anything of the kind, that those ignorant of the faith who hear these things avoid us, shy away, and almost desert us as criminals spotted with the filth of various heresies. . . .

They strive particularly to find fault with our church and generally with every church that speaks Latin, because we fast on Saturdays and profess that the Holy Spirit proceeds from the Father and the Son, whereas they confess that He proceeds merely from the Father. Besides this, they claim that we detest marriage, since we do not allow priests to marry. They blame us because we prohibit priests from anointing the foreheads of the baptized with chrism, which chrism they falsely accuse us of making from fresh water.

They try to blame us because we do not fast, according to our custom, from meat during the eight weeks before Easter, and from cheese and eggs during the seven weeks before the Pasch. They also lie, as their other writings show, when they say that we bless and offer a lamb on the altar, after the Jewish custom, together with the Lord's Body on the feast of Passover. They are certainly pleased with fault-finding! They complain that our priests do not refuse to shave their beards and that we ordain a deacon not yet raised to the priesthood to the episcopacy. They complain even though they appointed as their patriarch a layman, hastily become a monk and tonsured, and then, as they realized, advance him at a leap, without any fear and through the imperial power and favor, directly to the episcopacy. Yet what is more insulting is that they tried to demand a testimony of faith from our messengers, if they wished to be received by them, something which is against every rule and custom. In it [that is, in the required profession of faith] these doctrines of ours and those holding them are anathematized. They even impudently demanded a canonical letter from them, to give to the one they call their "Ecumenical Patriarch." . . .

With what great malice and foolishness those aforementioned Greek leaders and their henchmen are armed against us, because we did not consent to their evil ravings, is clearly revealed. The charges with which they try to stain us are either false or against what has been guarded in the Roman Church, indeed in the whole West, from the earliest times without any contradiction. When great doctors of the Church began to emerge among them, none of them was critical of those practices. Only those among them [that is, the Greeks] who burned not with a just zeal but driven by an evil zeal seek to tear to pieces the traditions of the Church. (Nicholas, *Encyclical Letter*)

A far more grievous schism—one that has never been truly healed—occurred between the Eastern and Western Churches in 1054, when Michael Cerularius was Patriarch and Leo IX Pope. The latter sent a Papal envoy to Constantinople to effect a political alliance between himself and the then emperor, Constantine IX. The envoy, Cardinal Humbert of Silvia Candia, immediately ran afoul of the Patriarch, who opposed the alliance. Humbert himself describes the sequel.

While Michael Cerularius avoided meeting and holding discussions with the (Papal) envoys, and persevered in his folly, those same envoys, defeated by his obstinacy, entered the Church of Hagia Sophia on the Sabbath, July 16, and at about the third hour [that is, about 9 A.M.], when the clergy is customarily preparing for the liturgy, placed the text of an excommunication upon the High Altar under the eyes of the attendant clergy and people. Quickly departing from that place, they also shook the dust from their feet to witness to them, crying out the phrase of the Gospel: May God see and judge.

So the deed was done. This is in part the bill of particulars on the excommunication.

The Holy Roman, First and Apostolic See, to which as the head belongs the special care of all the churches, for the sake of peace and profit of the Church has deigned to make us its messengers to this city (of Constantinople), so that, as our written instructions direct, we might come over and see whether in fact the outcry continues which continuously rises from that city to the Roman See's ears. . . . In what pertains to the pillars of empire and its honored wise citizens, the city is most Christian and orthodox. As to Michael, however, miscalled the Patriarch, and the supporters of his folly, they daily sow abundant tares of heresy in its midst. Whereas like Simoniacs they sell God's gifts and like Valesians they castrate their serfs and not only promote them into the clergy and even to the episcopate; like Arians they rebaptize those baptized, and especially Latins, in the name of the Holy Trinity; like Donatists they declare that, except for the Greek Church, the Church of Christ and true communion and baptism have vanished from the whole world; like the Nicolaites they allow and maintain carnal marriage for ministers of the sacred altar [that is, priests]; like the Severians they call the law of Moses accursed; like the enemies of the Holy Spirit or enemies of God they remove from the Creed the procession of the Holy Spirit from the Son; like the Manicheans, among other things they declare anything fermented alive; like the Nazarenes they hold to Jewish norms of ritual purity to such an extent that they forbid infants who die before the eighth day from their birth [when a Jewish infant would normally be circumcised] to be baptized and forbid women in menstruation or endangered in childbirth to take communion, or, if they are pagans, to be baptized; and being people who cultivate the hair of the head and beard, they do not receive in communion those who cut their hair and shave their beards in accordance with the teachings of the Roman Church.

This Michael, though he had been admonished by the letter of our lord Pope Leo for these errors and many other acts, has contemptuously refused to come to his senses. . . . We thus subscribe to the anathema which our most reverend Pope pronounced alike on Michael Cerularius and his followers, unless they regained their senses, as follows:

"Let Michael the neophyte, miscalled Patriarch, who put on the garb of the monk out of fear alone, and who is now also defamed for most wicked crimes, and with him Leo the archdeacon, called bishop of Ochrida . . . and all their followers in the aforementioned errors and audacities, be *Anathema Maranatha* (1 Cor. 16:22) . . . with all heretics, indeed, with the devil and his angels, unless perchance they recover their sense. Amen. Amen. Amen." (Humbert of Silvia Candia, *Memorandum*)

14. The Caliphate

Islam had no caesar, no ruler inherited from an earlier and different political tradition, as Christianity had. It had no law but its own and no ruler but a Muslim one, called in the years following the death of Muhammad in 632 C.E., the Caliph. The word first appears in the Quran, in a passage already cited in Chapter 1 in connection with the fall of the angels.

Remember, when the Lord said to the angels: "I have to place a deputy on the earth." They said: "Will you place one there who would create disorder and shed blood, while we intone Your litanies and sanctify Your name?" And God said: "I know what you do not know." (Quran 2:30)

This dialogue between God and the angels refers to God's creation of Adam. But the Arabic word used in 2:30 and here translated as "deputy" or "viceroy" is khalifa—in English, "Caliph"—the same word employed by the early Muslims to designate Muhammad's successor as the head of the Islamic community. The same word appears again in the Quran, in connection with the king and prophet David, and there presents an even more apposite context for the later Islamic office.

And We said to him: O David, We have made you a trustee (*khalifa*) on the earth, so judge between men equitably and do not follow your lust lest it should lead you astray from the way of God. (Quran 38:26)

There was no question of another prophet after Muhammad. Neither in his Life nor in the other traditions attributed to him is there anything to suggest that Muhammad appointed a member of the community as his political "viceroy." But a "successor" or Caliph there was, and not without controversy—not about the office but about who should hold it. The historian Tabari (d. 923 C.E.) gives an account of events in Medina immediately after the death of the Prophet.

Hisham ibn Muhammad told me on the authority of Abu Mikhnaf, who said: Abdullah ibn Abd al-Rahman ibn Abi Umra, the Helper [that is, a Medinese convert], told me:

"When the Prophet of God, may God bless him and save him, died, the (Medinese) Helpers assembled on the porch of the Banu Saʿida and said, 'Let us confer this authority, after Muhammad, upon him be peace, on Saʿd ibn Ubayda.' Saʿd , who was ill, was brought to them, and when they assembled Saʿd said to his son or one of his nephews, 'I cannot, because of my sickness, speak so that all the people can hear my words. Therefore, hear what I say and then repeat it to them so that they may hear it.' Then he spoke and the man memorized his words and raised his voice so that the others could hear.

"He said, after praising God and lauding Him, 'O company of Helpers! You have precedence in religion and merit in Islam which no other Arab tribe has. Muhammad, upon him be peace, stayed for more than ten years (in Medina) amid his people, summoning them to worship the Merciful One and to abandon false gods and idols. But among his own people (in Mecca) only a few men believed in him, and they were not able to protect the Prophet of God or glorify his religion nor to defend themselves against the injustice which beset them. God therefore conferred merit on you and brought honor to you and singled you out for grace. . . . And when God caused him to die, he was content with you and delighted with you. Therefore keep this authority for yourselves alone, for it is yours against all others.'

"They all replied to him, 'Your judgment is sound and your words are true. We shall not depart from what you say and we shall confer this authority on you. You satisfy us and you will satisfy the right believer.' Then they discussed it among themselves and some of them said: 'What if the (Meccan) Emigrants of the Quraysh refuse and say, "We are the Emigrants and the first Companions of the Prophet of God, we are his clan and his friends. Why therefore do you dispute the succession of his authority with us?" ' Some of them said, 'If so, we should reply to them, "A commander from us and a commander from you (then). And we shall never be content with less than that." ' Sa'd ibn Ubayda, when he heard this, said, 'This is the beginning of weakness.'

"News of this reached Umar, and he went to the house of the Prophet, may God bless and save him. He sent to Abu Bakr, who was in the Prophet's house with Ali ibn Abi Talib, upon him be peace, preparing the body of the Prophet, may God bless and save him, for burial. He sent asking Abu Bakr to come to him, and Abu Bakr sent a message in reply saying that he was busy. Then Umar sent saying that something had happened which made his presence necessary, and he went to him and said, 'Have you not heard that the Helpers have gathered in the porch of the Banu Sa'ida? They wish to confer this authority on Sa'd ibn Ubayda, and the best they say is "a commander from among us and a commander from among the Quraysh." ' They made haste toward them, and they met Abu Ubayda ibn Jarrah. The three of them went on together and they met Asim ibn Adi and Uwaym ibn Sa'ida, who both said to them: 'Go back, for what you want will not happen.' They said, 'We will not go back,' and they came to the meeting.

"Umar ibn al-Khattab said: We came to the meeting, and I had prepared a speech which I wished to make to them. We reached them, and I was about to begin my speech when Abu Bakr said to me, 'Gently! Let me speak first and then afterwards say whatever you wish.' He spoke. Umar said, 'He said all I wanted to say and more.'

"Abdullah ibn Abd al-Rahman said: Abu Bakr began. He praised and lauded God and then he said, 'God sent Muhammad as a Prophet to His creatures and as a witness to His community that they might worship God and God alone. . . . It was a tremendous thing for the Arabs to abandon the religion of their fathers. God distinguished the first Emigrants of his people by allowing them to recognize the truth and believe in him and console him and suffer with him from the harsh persecution of his people when they gave them the lie and all were against them and reviled them. . . . They were the first in the land who worshiped God and who believed in God and the Prophet. They were his friends and his clan and the best entitled of all men to this authority after him. Only a wrong-doer would dispute this with them. And as for you, O company of Helpers, no one can deny your merit in the faith or your great precedence in Islam. . . . (But) we are the commanders and you the viziers. We shall not act contrary to your advice and we shall not decide things without you.' . . .

"Abu Bakr said, 'Here is Umar and here is Abu Ubayda. Swear allegiance to whichever of them you choose.' The two of them said, 'No, by God, we shall not accept this authority above you, for you are the worthiest of the Emigrants and the second of the two who were in the cave (Quran 19:40) and the deputy (*khalifa*) of the Prophet of God in prayer, and prayer is the noblest part of the religion of the Muslims. Who would then be fit to take precedence of you or to accept this authority above you? Stretch out your hand so that we may swear allegiance to you.'

"And when they went forward to swear allegiance to him [Abu Bakr], Bashir ibn Saʿd went ahead of them and swore allegiance to him . . . and when the (Medinese) tribe of Aws saw what Bashir ibn Saʿd had done . . . they came to him and swore allegiance to him. . . ."

Hisham said on the authority of Abu Mikhnaf: Abdullah ibn Abd al-Rahman said: People came from every side to swear allegiance to Abu Bakr. (Tabari, *Annals* 1.1837–1844) [LEWIS 1974: 1:3–5]

15. After Abu Bakr

Abu Bakr served as Caliph for two scant years (632–634 C.E.). Although his successor, Umar ibn al-Khattab, held the Caliphate longer (634–644 C.E.), the process of succession still remained uncertain, as illustrated by this tradition attributed to Umar himself.

It has been narrated on the authority of Abdullah ibn Umar who said: I was present when my father was (fatally) wounded (by an assassin). People praised him and said: May God give you a noble recompense! He said: I am hopeful as well as fearful. People said: Appoint someone as your successor. He said: Should I carry the burden of conducting your affairs in my death as well as my life? I wish I could acquit myself (before God) in a way that there is neither anything to my credit nor anything to my discredit. If I should appoint my successor, I would because someone better than I did [that is, Abu Bakr, who appointed Umar]. If I would leave you alone (without a successor), I would do so because one better than I, the Messenger of God, may peace be upon him, did so. Abdullah says: When he mentioned the Messenger of God, may peace be upon him, I realized that he would not appoint anyone as Caliph. (Muslim, *Sahih* 18.755)

But one small problem at least was solved.

I heard from Ahmad ibn Abd al-Samad al-Ansari, who heard from Umm Amr bint Husayn, the Kufan woman, on the authority of her father, who said: When Umar was appointed Caliph [in 634 C.E.], they said to him, "O Deputy of the Deputy of the Prophet of God!" And Umar, may God be pleased with him, said, "This is a thing that will grow longer. When another Caliph comes, they will say 'O Deputy of the Deputy of the Deputy of the Prophet of God.' You are the Faithful and I am your Commander." So he was called Commander of the Faithful. . . .

I heard from Ibn Humayd, who heard from Yahya ibn Wadih, who heard from Abu Hamza, on the authority of Jabir, who said: A man said to Umar ibn al-Khattab, "O Deputy of God!" Umar said, "May God turn you from such a thing!" (Tabari, *Annals* 1.2748) [LEWIS 1974: 1:17]

16. Caliph and Imam

Thus the Muslim community seemed to have taken its first successful steps toward establishing a non-Prophetic ruler, the "Caliph" or "Successor of the Prophet." If the Quran itself gave little or no guidance on this new office in Islam, there were soon circulating Prophetic traditions on the nature and qualifications for the office of Caliph, or the Imam, "he who stands before," as he is more frequently called in theoretical discussions. Ibn Khaldun explains the difference between the two terms.

The Caliphate substitutes for the Lawgiver [that is Muhammad] in as much as it serves, like him, to preserve the religion and to exercise political leadership of the world. The institution is called "the Caliphate" or "the Imamate." The person in charge is called "Caliph" or "Imam." . . .

The name "Imam" is derived from the comparison with the leader of prayer [also called an imam] since he is followed and taken as a model like the prayer-leader. Therefore the institution is called "the Great Imamate." The name "Caliph" is given to the leader because he "represents" the Prophet in Islam. One uses "Caliph" alone or "Caliph of the Messenger of God." There is some difference of opinion on the use of "Caliph of God." Some consider the expression permissible as derived from the general "caliphate" of all the descendants of Adam . . . [based on the Quranic verses cited above]. But in general it is not considered permissible to use the expression since the Quranic verses quoted has no (specific) reference to it.

Ibn Khaldun then reflects briefly on the circumstances under which the office arose.

The position of Imam is a necessary one. The consensus of the men around Muhammad and the men of the second generation shows that the Imamate is necessary according to the religious law. At the death of the Prophet the men around him proceeded to render the oath of allegiance to Abu Bakr and to entrust him with the supervision of their affairs. And so it was with all subsequent periods. In no period were the people left in a state of anarchy. This was so by general consensus, which proves that the position of Imam is a necessary one. (Ibn Khaldun, *Muqaddima* 3.24) [IBN KHALDUN 1967: 1:388–389]

17. Prophetic Traditions on the Caliphate

Consensus on the Caliphate was transmitted, among other ways, through traditions from the Prophet and his Companions. Many of them are frankly redolent of a day when there already was a Caliph—one, it appears, whose authority was being challenged.

Bukhari and Muslim, from Abu Hurayra: The Messenger of God, may God's blessings and peace be upon him, said: "Whoever obeys me obeys God, and whoever disobeys me disobeys God. Whoever obeys the Commander (of the Faithful) obeys me, and who disobeys him disobeys me. The Imam is simply a shield behind whom the fighting takes place, from which one seeks protection. So when he orders fear of God and is just, he shall receive his reward, but if he holds otherwise, it will bring guilt upon him."

Muslim, from Umm al-Husayn: The Messenger, may God bless him and peace be upon him, said: "Even if a mutilated slave is made your Commander, and he leads you in accord with the Book of God, hear him and obey." (Baghawi, *Mishkat al-Masabih*, 17.1.1)

In other traditions, however, the emphasis and the implications for political obedience are quite different.

Bukhari and Muslim from Ibn Abbas: The Messenger of God, may God's blessing and peace be upon him, said: "If anyone sees something hateful in his Commander, let him be patient, for no one separates from the collectivity by so much as a handspan without dying the death of paganism."

Muslim from Awf ibn Malik al-Ashjaʿi, from the Messenger of God, on whom be the blessing of God and peace: "Your best Imams are those you love, who love you, whom you bless and who bless you. The worst are those you hate, who hate you, whom you curse and who curse you."

We said: "Messenger of God, should we not depose them when that happens?" but he said, "No, not so long as they keep the ritual prayers with you; not so long as they keep the prayers. When anyone has a ruler placed over him who is seen doing something which is rebellion against God, he must disapprove of that rebellion, but never withdraw his hand from obedience." (Ibid.)

We cannot be certain exactly when those traditions were put into circulation, but we do know there were serious challenges to both the current Caliph and the office of the Caliphate itself in the wake of the conspiratorial murder of Uthman in 656 C.E. and the accession of the fourth Caliph, Ali ibn Abi Talib. Ali was an early convert to Islam. He was, moreover, a cousin of the Prophet, the husband of his daughter Fatima, and the father of two of the Prophet's favorite grandchildren, Hasan and Husayn. Whatever his advantages, Ali appeared to many to be ambivalent about punishing the assassins of Uthman, the scion of one of the great pre-Islamic houses of Mecca. His hesitation gave his enemies in various camps—Muhammad's wife Aisha and Uthman's relative Mu'awiya prominent among them—an opportunity to drive Ali first out of Medina and then into a kind of Caliphate-in-exile in Iraq, where he had to fight to hold his office. Ali was himself assassinated in 661 C.E. by a schismatic. Over the succeeding years there grew up a body of the "partisans of Ali" (shi'at Ali) who attempted to vindicate not only his claims to the office of Imam but also those of his descendants.

18. The Ruler, Chosen by the People or Designated by God?

With the rise of the Shi'ite movement—never quite politically powerful enough to seize the rulership in Islam but potent enough in its propaganda and ideology to threaten it—the rest of the "Sunni" community, so called because they supported "tradition [sunna] and the commonality," were forced to re-examine and defend their own positions on the nature of sovereignty in Islam. Here one of them, the essayist al-Jahiz (d. 886 C.E.), easily converts necessity into a virtue.

. . . If we were to be asked, which is better for the community, to choose its own leader or guide, or for the Prophet to have chosen him for us? Had the Prophet chosen him, that would of course have been preferable to the community's own choice, but since he did not, it is well for it that he left the choice in its own hands. . . . Had God laid down the procedure for the nomination of the Imam in a detailed formula with its own precise directions and clear signs, that would indeed have been a blessing, for we know that everything done by God is better. But since He did not make specific provision (for the office), it is preferable for us to have been left in our present situation. How can anyone oblige or constrain God to establish an Imam according to a formula simply because in your view such a solution would be more advantageous and less troublesome, and better calculated to avoid error and problems? (Jahiz, *The Uthmanis* 278–279)

This was the view of most historians, the Shi ᶜ*ites of course excepted. At least one Prophetic tradition took no chances and put the choice of a successor directly in the Prophet's mouth.*

Aisha told that during his illness God's Messenger said to her: "Call me Abu Bakr your father, and your brother, so that I may write a document, for I fear that someone may desire to succeed me and that one may say 'It is I,' whereas God and the believers will have no one but Abu Bakr." Muslim transmitted this tradition. (Baghawi, *Mishkat al-Masabih* 26.30.1)

And again, with even more extended foresight:

Jabir reported God's Messenger as saying, "Last night a good man had a vision in which Abu Bakr seemed to be joined to God's Messenger, Umar to Abu Bakr, and Uthman to Umar." Jabir said: When we got up and left God's Messenger we said that the good man was God's Messenger and that their being joined together meant that they were the rulers over the matter with which God had sent His Prophet. (Ibid. 26.34.3)

We return to Jahiz.

There are three different ways of establishing an Imam. The first way is as I have described [that is, following the overthrow of a usurper], or, second, under the kind of circumstances in which the Muslims put into power Uthman ibn Affan [Caliph, 644–656 C.E.], after Umar [Caliph, 634–644 C.E.] had designated (a council of) six person of comparable worth and they in turn had elected one of their number. . . . A third possibility is the situation that prevailed when the community made Abu Bakr Caliph [632–634 C.E.]; the circumstances were different from those of Uthman's election, since the Prophet had not appointed a council as Umar did. . . . In Abu Bakr's case the community did not compare the respective merits of the Emigrants or announce the reasons for the superiority of the person elected; they were, after all, Muslims who had known each other intimately for twenty-three years . . . and so Abu Bakr's merits were immediately obvious to them; on the Prophet's death they had no need to form an opinion, since they already knew. (Jahiz, *The Uthmanis* 270)

The developed Shi͑ite view on this obviously crucial matter of the selection of the Imam or Caliph of the Muslim community is presented in the theological handbook called The Eleventh Chapter, *written by the Shi͑ite scholar al-Hilli (d. 1326 C.E.), with a commentary by another later author of the same name. The thesis is set out in the section devoted generally to the Imamate. In the passage immediately preceding our selection, Hilli had demonstrated that the Imam had of necessity to be immune to sin.*

The Third Proposition: It is necessary that the Imam should be designated for the Imamate since immunity to sin is a matter of the heart which is discerned by no one save God Most High. Thus the designation must be made by one who knows that the Imam has the immunity to sin necessary for the office, or else some miracle must be worked through him to prove his truthfulness.

[Commentary:] This refers to the method of appointing the Imam. Agreement had been reached that in appointing the Imam the designation can be made by God and His Prophet, or by a previous Imam in an independent way [that is, without the consent of the people]. The disagreement concerns only whether or not the Imam's appointment can be effected in any way other than by designation. Our fellow Imamites (Shi͑ites) deny that absolutely, and hold that there is no way except by designation. For, as we have explained, immunity to sin is a necessary condition of the Imamate, and immunity to sin is a hidden matter, and no one is informed of it except God. In such circumstances, then, no one knows in whom it might be found unless He who knows the unseen makes it known. And that occurs in two ways: first, by making it known to someone else immune to sin, such as the Prophet, and then this latter tells us of the Imam's immunity to sin, and of his appointment; and second, by the appearance of miracles worked through his [the Imam presumptive's] power to prove his truthfulness in claiming the Imamate.

The Sunnis, on the other hand, say that whenever the community acknowledges anyone as its chief, and is convinced of his ability for the Imamate, and his power increases in the regions of Islam, he becomes the Imam. . . . But the truth is contrary to this for two reasons: first, the Imamate is a "Caliphate" [or "succession"] from God and His Messenger and so it cannot be acquired except by the word of them both; and second, the establishment of the Imamate by acknowledging someone as chief and by the latter's claim to the office would result in conflict because of the probability that each faction would acknowledge a different Imam. (Hilli, *The Eleventh Chapter* 186–188)

19. Ali, the First Imam

If, on the Shi'ite view, the Imam must be "designated" rather than simply "acknowledged," that condition must have occurred in the case of the very first of them, Ali ibn Abi Talib. The Fifth Proposition of Hilli's work takes up that much-disputed question.

The Fifth Proposition: The Imam after the Messenger of God is Ali ibn Abi Talib: First, because of his designation, which has been handed down in a number of distinct lines of Prophetic traditions; and second, because he is the best of his generation, by the word of the Most High . . . ; and third, because it is necessary for the Imam to be immune from sin, and there is no one among those who claim the office who is so immune except Ali, as all agree; and fourth, because he was the most knowledgeable (about Islam), since the Companions consulted him about their problems . . . ; and fifth, because he is more ascetic than any one else, so that he divorced the world three times.

The first point is critical here, since the Shi'ite proposition of the Prophet's designation of Ali was confronted with the undeniable historical reality that the Muslim community was in fact ruled by three other men—Abu Bakr, Umar, and Uthman—before its choice fell upon Ali. This is how Hilli's commentator deals with that difficulty.

[Commentary:] . . . There are differing opinions regarding the appointment of the Imam. Some claim that after the Messenger of God the Imam was Abbas ibn Abd al-Muttalib because he was his heir. And most Muslims affirm that he was Abu Bakr because the people chose him. And the Shi'ites maintain that he was Ali ibn Abi Talib because of the designation which came down directly from God and His Messenger to him, and that is the truth. And the author [that is, Hilli] has proved Ali's right in several ways: first, that unbroken tradition of the very words of the Prophet which the Shi'ites quote regarding the right of Ali, and from which certitude can be elicited, namely, "Greet him as the chief of the believers" and "You are the successor after me," and other words which prove what we intended, to wit, that he is the Imam. (Hilli, *The Eleventh Chapter* 191–192)

To view the Shi'ite claims from the Sunni side of the Islamic community, we can turn to the popular theological manual by the Sunni scholar al-Nasafi (d. 1114 C.E.).

The objection may be raised that it is related of the Prophet, upon whom be God's blessing and peace, that he once said to Ali, with whom may God be pleased: "You are to me the same as Aaron was to Moses—on both of whom be blessings and peace—save that there will be no prophet after me." Now as the deputyship of Aaron admitted no possibility of substitution, so (the Shi'ites claim) is the case here (between Muhammad and Ali).

The Sunni response is not to deny that the Prophet made the statement but to invoke the circumstances under which it was pronounced.

The reply is that the Prophet's honoring him was not in the way you [that is, the Shi'ites] take it, for (it is common knowledge that) the Prophet, upon whom be God's blessing and peace, appointed Ali as his deputy over Medina while he went out on one of his raids, and as a result the evilly-disposed said: "Look, the Prophet has turned his back upon him and confined him to the house." This grieved Ali, so the Prophet said to him: "You are to me the same as Aaron was to Moses." Another indication (that their interpretation is false) is the fact that Aaron died before Moses, so it would only be sound if he had said: "You are to me the same as Joshua son of Nun," for he was the real successor to Moses.

This was one of the contentions of the moderate Shi'a who looked upon Ali as the designated, and so the only legitimate successor to Muhammad. Others, however, would have put Ali above or beside Muhammad in the ranks of the Messengers.

One group of the Rafidites [that is, one of the radical Shi'ite sects] teaches that the revelations (brought by Gabriel) were meant for Ali, with whom may God be pleased, but that Gabriel, on whom be peace, made a mistake. Another group of them teaches that Ali was associated with Muhammad in the prophetic office. All these are disbelievers for they disavow both the text of the Quran and the consensus of the community, for God has said: "Muhammad is God's Messenger" (Quran 48:29). Some of them teach that Ali was more learned than the Apostle of God and is in the position (with regard to him) that al-Khidr held to Moses [that is, the mysterious figure who serves Moses as mentor in Quran 18:66–83]. The answer to this is that saying of the Prophet which shows such knowledge as Ali had was from the teaching of the Prophet (who said): "I am the city of learning and Ali is its gate."

Another indication (of the unsoundness of their teaching) is the fact that Ali was a Saint but the Apostle of God was a Prophet, and a Prophet ranks higher than a Saint. As for al-Khidr, on whom be peace, he had direct knowledge (of things divine) for God said: ". . . whom We taught knowledge such as We have" (Quran 18:66). He means there inspired knowledge, but even so Moses was superior to him since he had a body of religious Law and a Book, and he who has a religious Law and a Book is superior. A case in point is that of David and Solomon, where David is superior.

Another group of them teaches that there never is a time when there is no Prophet on earth, and that this prophetic office came by inheritance to Ali, with whom may God be pleased, and his progeny, so that anyone who does not regard obedience to him (and his progeny) as an incumbent duty is in unbelief. The truly orthodox people [that is, the Sunnis] teach that there is no Prophet after our Prophet, for this is proved by God's words "and seal of the Prophets" (Quran 33:40). It is related on the authority of Abu Yusuf that the Prophet said: "If a pretender to prophecy comes forward laying claim to the prophetic office, should anyone demand from him proof (of his mission), he [the one who requested proof] would thereby show himself to be in unbelief, for he would have disavowed the text of Scripture." The same is true of anyone who has doubts about him, for one demands a proof in order to make clear what is true from what is false, but if anyone lays claim to the prophetic office after Muhammad, upon whom be blessing and peace, his claim cannot be other than false. (Nasafi, *The Sea of Discourse on Theology*)

[JEFFERY 1962: 445–446]

20. The Pool of Khum

*A more detailed version of how the Shi*ʿ*ites explained the events surrounding the designation of Ali as Imam is provided by al-Majlisi (d. 1700 C.E.). Although he comes late in the tradition, he reproduces a standard Shi*ʿ*ite contextual exegesis of the Quranic passage in question.*

When the ceremonies of the (farewell) pilgrimage were completed, the Prophet, attended by Ali and the Muslims, left Mecca for Medina. On reaching the Pool of Khum he halted, although that place had never before been a stopping place for caravans, because it had neither water nor pasturage. The reason for encampment in such a place (on this occasion) was that illustrious verses of the Quran came powerfully upon him, enjoining him to establish Ali as his successor. He had previously received communications to the same effect, but not expressly appointing the time for Ali's inauguration, which, therefore, he had deferred lest opposition be excited and some forsake the faith. This was the message from the Most High in Sura 5:67:

"O Messenger, publish what has been sent down to you from your Lord, for if you do not, then you have not delivered His message. God will protect you from men; surely God guides not unbelieving people."

Being thus peremptorily commanded to appoint Ali his successor, and threatened with penalty if he delayed when God had become his surety, the Prophet therefore halted in this unusual place, and the Muslims dismounted around him. As the day was very hot, he ordered them to take shelter under some thorn trees. Having ordered all the camel saddles to be piled up for a pulpit or rostrum, he commanded his herald to summon the people around him. When all the people were assembled he mounted the pulpit of saddles, and calling to him the Commander of the Believers [that is, Ali], he placed him on his right side. Muhammad now rendered thanksgiving to God, and then made an eloquent address to the people, in which he foretold his own death, and said: "I have been called to the gate of God, and the time is near when I shall depart to God, be concealed from you, and bid farewell to this vain world. I leave among you the Book of God, to which if you adhere, you will never go astray. And I leave with you the members of my family, who cannot be separated from the Book of God until both join me at the fountain of al-Kawthar."

He then demanded, "Am I not dearer to you than your own lives?" and was answered by the people in the affirmative. He then took the hands of Ali and raised them so high that the white (of his shirt) appeared and said, "Whoever receives me as his master (or ally), then to him Ali is the same. O Lord, befriend every friend of Ali, and be the enemy of all his enemies; help those who aid him and abandon all who desert him."

It was now nearly noon, and the hottest part of the day. The Prophet and the Muslims made the noon prayer, after which he went to his tent, beside which he ordered a tent pitched for the Commander of the Believers. When Ali was rested Muhammad commanded the Muslims to wait upon Ali, congratulate him on his accession to the Imamate, and salute him as the Commander. All this was done by both men and women, none appearing more joyful at the inauguration of Ali than did Umar. (Majlisi, *The Life of Hearts* 334)

21. "Catholic" and "Partisan" in the Muslim Community

The first part of the "creed" of Ibn Hanbal (d. 855 C.E.) concerns matters of doctrine and ritual; then the author turns his attention to a question reflected in

the traditions and arguments just cited. By Ibn Hanbal's day, these had already rent
the Muslim community with a schism more divisive than any doctrinal heresy: Who
was the legitimate head of that community, the actual Caliph or an ideal Imam?
The issue began, as we have noted, with a view of history: Who constituted the true
leadership of the body of Muslims after the death of the Prophet? Ibn Hanbal
undertakes to give the "catholic" (sunni), as opposed to the "partisan" (shi'i),
view of that history.

The best of this community (of Muslims), after its Prophet, is Abu
Bakr the Just, then Umar ibn al-Khattab, then Uthman ibn Affan [that is,
the first three Caliphs]. We give the preference of these three (over Ali)
just as the Companions of the Prophet gave preference; they did not
differ about it. Then after these three come the five Electors chosen by
Umar as he lay dying: Ali ibn abi Talib, Zubayr, Talha, Abd al-Rahman ibn
Awf, and Sa'd ibn abi Waqqas. All of them were suited for the Caliphate,
and each of them was an Imam [that is, a prayer-leader of the commu-
nity]. On this we go according to the Prophetic tradition (transmitted)
from Umar's son: "When the Messenger of God was living—God bless
him and give him peace—and his Companions were still spared, we used
to number first Abu Bakr, then Umar, then Uthman and then keep silent." (Ahmad ibn Hanbal, *Creed*) [WILLIAMS 1971: 30]

When it comes to an actual ruler, Ibn Hanbal strongly prefers the acceptance of
validly constituted authority in the name of the unity of the community, no matter
how personally unacceptable that ruler might be. To set at ease the conscience of
the scrupulous believer, Ibn Hanbal assures him that religious obligations performed
in the company or under the leadership of such rulers are valid and complete.

And hearing and obeying the Imams and the Commanders of the
Faithful (is necessary)—that is, whoever receives the Caliphate, whether
he is pious or profligate, whether the people agreed on him or were
pleased with him, or whether he attacked them with the sword until he
became Caliph and was called "Commander of the Faithful." Going on a
holy war is equally efficacious with a pious or a dissolute commander
down to the Day of Resurrection; one does not abandon him. Division of
the spoils of war and applying the punishments prescribed by the Law
belongs to the Imams: it is not for anyone to criticize them or contend
with them. Handing over the alms money to them for distribution (is
permissible) and efficacious: whoever pays them has fulfilled his obligation (to almsgiving) whether the Imam was pious or dissolute. The collec-
tive prayer led by the Imam and those he delegates is valid and complete,
both prostrations, and whoever repeats them later is an innovator, aban-

doning "the tradition" and opposed to it. There is no virtue in his Friday prayer at all, if he does not believe in praying with the Imams, whoever they are, good or bad; the "tradition" is to pray two prostrations with them and consider the matter finished. On that let there be no doubts in your bosom.

Thus, in the eyes of Ibn Hanbal, who prized above all the unity of the Muslim community, secession from that community by rejecting its duly constituted leader is the most grievous sin of all.

Whoever secedes from the Imam of the Muslims—when the people have agreed on him and acknowledged his Caliphate for any reason, either satisfaction with him or conquest, for example, that rebel has broken the unity of the Muslims and opposed the tradition coming from God's Messenger, God's blessing and peace be upon him. If the seceder dies, he dies as ignorant carrion. It is not lawful for anyone to fight against the authority or secede from it, and whoever does so is an innovator, outside "the tradition" and "the way. (Ahmad ibn Hanbal, *Creed*)

[WILLIAMS 1971: 31–32]

22. A Juridical Portrait of the Sunni Caliph

Two centuries after Ibn Hanbal, the Sunnis' understanding of the Caliphate was essentially complete, and the lawyer Mawardi (d. 1058 C.E.) was able to lay out the duties of the office and the qualifications of its tenants with all the clarity typical of a closed issue. It was closed in another sense as well: Mawardi was writing at almost precisely the point when the office of Caliph had lost most of its real powers.

God, whose power be glorified, has instituted a chief of the community as a successor to Prophethood and to protect the community and assume the guidance of its affairs. Thus the Imamate is a principle on which stand the bases of the religious community and by which the general welfare is regulated, so that the common good is assured by it. Hence rules pertaining to the Imamate take precedence over any other rules of government. . . . The Imamate is placed on earth to succeed the Prophet in the duties of defending Religion and governing the World, and it is a religious obligation to give allegiance to that person who performs those duties. . . .

Thus the obligatory nature of the Imamate is established, and it is an obligation performed for all by a few, like fighting in a Holy War, or the study of the religious sciences, and if no one is exercising it, then there emerge two groups from the people: the first being those who should choose an Imam from the community, and the second those who are fitted to be the Imam, of whom one will be invested with the Imamate. As for those of the community who do not belong to either of those two categories, there is no crime or sin if they do not choose an Imam. As to those two categories of people, each of them must possess the necessary qualifications. Those relating to the electors are three:

1. Justice in all its characteristics.

2. Knowledge sufficient to recognize who is worthy to be Imam by virtue of the necessary qualifications.

3. Judgment and wisdom to conclude by choosing the best person, who will best and most knowledgeably direct the general welfare.

As for those persons fitted for the Imamate, the conditions related to them are seven:

1. Justice in all its characteristics.

2. Knowledge requisite for independent judgment about revealed and legal matters.

3. Soundness of the senses in hearing, sight and speech, in a degree to accord with their normal functioning.

4. Soundness of the members from any defect that would prevent freedom of movement and agility.

5. Judgment conducive to the governing of subjects and administering matters of general welfare.

6. Courage and bravery to protect Muslim territory and wage the Holy War against the enemy.

7. Pedigree: he must be of the tribe of the Quraysh, since there has come down an explicit statement on this, and the consensus has agreed. There is no need of taking account of Dirar ibn Amr, who stood alone when he declared that anyone could be eligible. The Prophet said: "The Quraysh have precedence, so do not go before them," and there is no pretext for any disagreement, when we have this clear statement delivered to us, and no word that one can raise against it.

There is some further discussion of the manner of electing an Imam/Caliph, but as a matter of fact the Caliphate had been an inherited office within two families, the Umayyads and the Abbasids, uninterruptedly from 661 C.E. to the time of Mawardi's writing. He briefly averts to this situation and approves.

If the Imamate has been conferred through the designation by the previous Imam of his successor, the consensus is that this is lawful because Abu Bakr designated Umar and Umar designated the electors of his successors. (Mawardi, *The Ordinances of Government*) [WILLIAMS 1971: 84–86].

23. The Shiʿite Succession

For the Sunni, community the partisans par excellence were the Shiʿites, those "followers of Ali." It was not their partisanship for Ali, a revered figure for all Muslims, that made them suspect in Sunni eyes; rather, they rejected the consensus, as the Sunni philosopher and historian Ibn Khaldun (d. 1406 C.E.) explains in his Prolegomenon to History.

Ali is the one whom Muhammad appointed (as head of the community). The Shiʿites transmit texts (of Prophetic traditions) in support of this belief, which they interpret so as to suit their tenets. The authorities on the Prophetic tradition and the transmitters of the religious law do not know these texts. Most of them are supposititious, or some of their transmitters are suspect, or their true interpretation is very different from the wicked interpretation that the Shiʿa give them. (Ibn Khaldun, *Muqaddima* 3.25) [IBN KHALDUN 1967: 1:403]

Although the Shiʿites agreed on the general principle of the Imamate—that it was, for example, a spiritual office that passed by designation from Ali through the line of his descendants—they eventually fell into schismatic disputes on who precisely was the designated heir. By the fourteenth century, Ibn Khaldun could look back and trace an elaborately sectarian Shiʿite heresiography. The first issue to divide them was the matter of the Caliphs who preceded Ali. Were they usurpers or simply inferior?

Some Shiʿa hold the opinion that those texts [that is, the texts supporting Ali's claim to the Imamate] prove both the personal appointment of Ali and the fact that the Imamate is transmitted from him to his successors. They [that is, this group of Shiʿites] are the Imamites. They renounce the two shaykhs (Abu Bakr and Umar) because they did not give precedence to Ali and did not render an oath of allegiance to him, as required by the texts quoted. The Imamites do not take the Imamates of Abu Bakr and Umar seriously. But we do not want to bother with transmitting the slanderous things said about Abu Bakr and Umar by Imamite extremists. They are objectionable in our opinion and (should be) in theirs.

Other Shiʿites say that these proofs require the appointment of Ali not in person but insofar as his qualities are concerned. They say that people commit an error when they do not give the qualities their proper place. They are the Zaydi (Shiʿa). They do not renounce the two shaykhs Abu Bakr and Umar. They do take their Imamates seriously, but they say that Ali was superior to them. They permit an inferior person to be the Imam, even though a superior person may be alive at the same time.

Then there is the far more divisive question of the legitimate succession among Ali's descendants. Here too the Imamite and the Zaydi Shiʿa differ.

The Shiʿa differ in opinion concerning the succession to the Caliphate after Ali. Some have it passed on through the descendants of Fatima [one of Ali's wives and the daughter of Muhammad] in succession, through testamentary designation. . . . They are called Imamites, with reference to their statement that knowledge of the Imam and the fact of his being appointed are an article of faith. That is their fundamental tenet.

Others consider the descendants of Fatima the (proper) successors to the Imamate, but through the selection of an Imam from among the Shiʿa. The conditions governing the selection of that Imam are that he have knowledge, be ascetic, generous and brave, and that he go out to make propaganda for his Imamate. They who believe this are Zaydis, so named after the founder of the sect, Zayd son of Ali son of Husayn, the grandson of Muhammad. He [Zayd; d. 740 C.E.] had a dispute with his brother Muhammad al-Baqir [d. 731 C.E.] concerning the condition that the Imam had to come out openly. Al-Baqir charged him with implying that, in the way Zayd looked at it, their father Ali Zayn al-Abidin [d. ca. 712 C.E.] would not be an Imam because he had not come out openly and had made no preparation to do so. . . . When the Imamites discussed the question of Imamates of the two shaykhs Abu Bakr and Umar with Zayd, and noticed that he admitted their Imamates, they disavowed him and did not make him one of the Imams. On account of this they are called "Rafidites" or "Disavowers." . . .

There are also Shiʿa sects that are called "Extremists." They transgress the bounds of reason and the faith of Islam when they speak of the divinity of the Imams. They either assume that the Imam is a human being with divine qualities, or they assume that he is God in human incarnation. This is a dogma of incarnation that agrees with the Christian tenets regarding Jesus. . . . Some Shiʿa extremists say that the perfection of the Imam is possessed by nobody else. When he dies his spirit passes over to another Imam, so that this perfection may be in him. This is the doctrine of metempsychosis. (Ibn Khaldun, *Muqaddima* 3.26)

[IBN KHALDUN 1967: 1:404–405]

24. Awaiting the Hidden Imam

*Ibn Khaldun continues with his exposition of Shi*ism.*

Some Shi'a extremists stop (*waqafa*) with one of the Imams and do not continue (the succession). They stop with the Imam whom they consider to have been appointed last. They who believe this are the Waqifites. Some of them say that the Imam is alive and did not die.

This general typology of "Waqifite" Shi'ites brings Ibn Khaldun to an important feature of developed Shi'ism, the doctrine of the "Hidden Imam."

The extremist Imamites, in particular the Twelvers, hold a similar opinion. They think that the twelfth of their Imams, Muhammad ibn al-Hasan al-Askari, to whom they give the epithet of "The Mahdi," entered the cellar of their house in al-Hilla and was "removed" [or "concealed"] when he was imprisoned there with his mother. He has remained there "removed" [since sometime after 874 C.E.]. He will come forth at the end of time and will fill the world with justice. The Twelver Shi'a refer in this connection to the Prophetic tradition found in the collection of al-Tirmidhi regarding the Mahdi.

That tradition reads:

The world will not be destroyed until the Arabs are ruled by a man from my family, whose name shall tally with my name.

The text of Ibn Khaldun continues.

The Twelver Shi'ites are still expecting him to this day. Therefore they call him "the Expected One." Each night after the evening prayer they bring a mount and stand at the entrance to the cellar [where the Mahdi was "removed"]. They call his name and ask him to come forth openly. They do so until the stars are out. Then they disperse and postpone the matter to the following night. They have continued the custom to this time. (Ibn Khaldun, *Muqaddima* 3.26) [IBN KHALDUN 1967: 1:406–408]

If we return to the beginning of the process, we can understand somewhat better what gave rise to belief in the hidden Imam, which became normative among the great majority of Shi'ites.

The Shi'ites were the party of both hope and despair in the Islamic community: a hope that the Prophet's message would establish God's justice on earth, and despair that the community as presently constituted could achieve that goal. "As presently constituted" meant governance by the illegitimate Caliphs rather than the Imams, the divinely designated, divinely inspired, and divinely guided descendants of Ali. Those Imams had little ground for hope in the ninth century. As we shall soon

see, there had been a major schism in the Shi *a over the succession to the Imamate*
among the sons of Ja *far al-Sadiq (d. 765 C.E.), and even the main body of the*
movement, those moderates called "Imamites" who supported the line from Ja *far's*
son Musa al-Kazim (d. 800 C.E.), must have grown despondent when the eleventh
in that succession, Hasan al-Askari, died in 874 C.E. apparently without issue. A
number of views were put forward as a result, among them that there was indeed
an infant son but that he had been kept in concealment because of the danger and
difficulty of the times. The Shi *ite authority al-Nawbakhti, writing at the begin-*
ning of the tenth century, describes what came to be the majority opinion among
Shi *ites.*

We have conformed to the past tradition and have affirmed the
Imamate of al-Askari and accept that he is dead. We concede that he had
a successor, who is his own son and the Imam after him until he appears
and proclaims his authority, as his ancestors had done before him. God
allowed this to happen because the authority belongs to Him and He can
do all that He wills and He can command as He wishes concerning his
[that is, the Imam's] appearance and his concealment. It is just as the
Commander of the Faithful (Ali) said: "O God, you will not leave the
earth devoid of a Proof of Your own for mankind, be they manifest and
well known, or hidden and protected, lest Your Proof and Your signs are
annulled."

This then is what we have been commanded to do and we have
received reliable reports on this subject from the past Imams. It is im-
proper for the slaves of God to discuss divine affairs and pass judgment
without having knowledge and to seek out what has been concealed from
them. It is also unlawful to mention his [that is, the concealed Imam's]
name or ask his whereabouts until such times as God decides. This is so
because if he, peace be upon him, is protected, fearful and in concealment, it is by God's protection. It is not up to us to seek for reasons for
what God does. . . . The reason is that if what is concealed were revealed
and made known to us, then his and our blood would be shed. Therefore,
on this concealment, and the silence about it, depends the safety and
preservation of our lives. (Nawbakhti, *The Sects of the Shi* *a* 92)

[SACHEDINA 1981: 50]

Nawbakhti wrote when there was some expectation that the Imam might indeed
emerge from concealment in some ordinary political sense and assert his claim. But
as time passed without an appearance, and at the end of a normal life span, when
the hidden Imam could no longer be thought to be alive in any purely human sense,
some adjustment in thinking had to be made. What it was is apparent in al-Mufid
(d. 1022 C.E.), another Shi *ite authority, writing a century after Nawbakhti.*

When al-Askari died, his adherents were divided into fourteen factions, as reported by al-Nawbakhti, may God be pleased with him. The majority among them affirm the Imamate of his son, al-Qa'im al-Muntazar [The Awaited Redresser of Wrongs, a Messianic title]. They assert his birth and attest his (formal) designation by his father. They believe that he was someone named after the Prophet and that he is the Mahdi of the People. They believe that he will have two forms of concealment, one longer than the other. The first concealment will be the shorter, and during it the Imam will have deputies and mediators. They relate on the authority of some of their leaders that al-Askari had made him [that is, his son and successor] known to them and shown them his person. . . . They believe that the Master of the Command is living and has not died, nor will he die, even if he remains for a thousand years, until he fills the world with equity and justice, as it is now filled with tyranny and injustice; and that at the time of his reappearance he will be young and strong in (the frame of) a man of some thirty years. They proof this with reference to his miracles and take these as some proofs and signs (of his existence). (al-Mufid, *Ten Chapters on the Concealment*) [SACHEDINA 1981: 58]

In the developed form of this tradition, the young son of al-Askari went into concealment, perhaps at his father's death in 874 C.E., perhaps even earlier. During that interval the community—that is, the faithful Shi᷎ite remnant—was under the charge of four agents, as the theologian Nu᷎mani (d. 970 C.E.) explains.

As to the first concealment, it is that occultation in which there were the mediators between the Imam and the people, carrying out (the orders of the Imam), having been designated by him, and living among the people. These are eminent persons and leaders from whose hands have emanated cures derived from the knowledge and recondite wisdom which they possessed, and the answers to all the questions which were put to them about the problems and difficulties (of religion). This is the Short Concealment, the days of which have come to an end and whose time has gone by. (Nu᷎mani, *The Book of the Concealment* 91)
[SACHEDINA 1981: 85–86]

The last of the four of these agents died in 941 C.E. Then there began the Complete Concealment, which will end only with the eschatological appearance, or better, the reappearance of the Mahdi Imam. Until that occurs, the direction of the community rests, as it came to be understood, in the hands of the Shi᷎ite jurists.

The return of the Mahdi Imam must once have been a vivid expectation among the Shi᷎ites. But as occurred among the Jews regarding the Messiah and among the Christians on the Second Coming of Christ, so too the Shi᷎ites relaxed the immedi-

acy of the event into the indefinite future, as is summed up in the tradition attrib-
uted to the fifth Imam, Muhammad al-Baqir (d. 732 C.E.). He was asked about a
saying of Ali that the Shi'ites' time of trial would last seventy years. His response
both explains the delay and counsels, as so many had before and after, that "no man
can know the day or the hour."

God Most High had set a time to seventy years. But when (Ali's son) Husayn was killed [at Karbala in 680 C.E.], God's wrath on the inhabitants of the earth became more severe and that period was postponed up to a hundred and forty years. We had informed you about this, but you revealed the secret. Now God has delayed (the appearance of the Mahdi) for a further period for which He has neither fixed a time nor has He informed us about it, since "God blots and establishes whatsoever He will; and with Him is the essence of the Book." (Tusi, *The Book of the Conceal-ment* 263) [SACHEDINA 1981: 152–153]

Despite the advice not to be concerned with such matters, the unanimous Shi'ite
tradition knows at least the day and the month of the return of the Hidden Imam:
the Mahdi will return on the anniversary of Husayn's martyrdom on the tenth day
of the month of Muharram.

Ibn Khaldun ended his account with a passing reference to the ritual of
awaiting, at al-Hilla in Iraq, the return of the Hidden Imam to the very house from
which he had originally gone into "occultation." We have an eyewitness report of
the same ceremony from the traveler Ibn Battuta, written ca. 1355 C.E.

Near the principal bazaar of [al-Hilla] there is a mosque, over the door of which a silk curtain is suspended. They call this "the Sanctuary of the Master of the Age." It is one of their customs that every evening a hundred of the townsmen come out, carrying arms and with drawn swords in their hands, and go to the governor of the city after the afternoon prayer; they receive from him a horse or mule, saddled and bridled, and [with this they go in procession] beating drums and playing fifes and trumpets in front of this animal . . . and so they come to the Sanctuary of the Master of the Age. Then they stand at the door and say, "In the name of God, O Master of the Age, in the name of God come forth! Corruption is abroad and tyranny is rife! This is the hour for thy advent, that by thee God may divide the True from the False." They continue to call in this way, sounding the trumpets and drums and fifes, until the hour of the sunset prayer. For they assert that Muhammad ibn al-Hasan al-Askari entered this mosque and disappeared from sight in it, and that he will emerge from it since he is, in their view, the "Expected Imam." (Ibn Battuta, *Travels*) [IBN BATTUTA 1959–1962: 2:325]

25. "Twelvers" and "Seveners" among the Shiʿites

There were many branches of Shiʿites, as Ibn Khaldun describes in detail, but the two most important of them, in terms of the numbers of adherents they could command and the political power they could from time to time wield, were the Imamites called "Twelvers"—the term came to be almost synonymous with "Ima- mite"—and a group called either Ismaʿilis or "Seveners." Ibn Khaldun explains.

The Imamites consider the following as successors to the Imamate after Ali [d. 661 C.E.] . . . by designation as heirs: Ali's son Hasan [d. 669 C.E.], that latter's brother Husayn [d. 680 C.E.], Husayn's son Ali Zayn al-Abidin [d. 712 C.E.], the latter's son Muhammad al-Baqir [d. 731 C.E.], and his son Jaʿfar al-Sadiq [d. 765 C.E.]. From there on they split into two sects. One of them considers Jaʿfar's son Ismaʿil [d. 760 C.E.] as Jaʿfar's successor to the Imamate. They recognize Ismaʿil as their Imam and they are called Ismaʿilis. The other group considers Jaʿfar's other son, Musa al-Kazim [d. 799 C.E.], as Jaʿfar's successor in the Imamate. They are the Twelvers because they stop the succession with the twelfth Imam [that is, Muhammad al-Mahdi, mentioned above]. They saw that he remains "removed" until the end of time.

That the Shiʿite "designation" was an indelible one and signaled, like the Chris- tians' laying on of episcopal hands, the transmission of an irrevocable spiritual gift is clear from what follows.

The Ismaʿilis say that the Imam Ismaʿil became Imam because his father Jaʿfar designated him to be his successor. Ismaʿil died before his father, but according to the Ismaʿilis the fact that he was designated by his father as his successor means that the Imamate should continue among *his* successors. . . . As they say, Ismaʿil's successor as Imam was his son Muhammad the Concealed One. He is the first of the Hidden Imams. According to the Ismaʿilis, an Imam who has no power goes into hiding. His missionaries remain in the open, however, in order to estab- lish proof (of the Hidden Imam's existence) among mankind.

The Ismaʿili Imam did not recede into some remote metaphysical outback. Sometime about 900 C.E. a certain Ubaydallah appeared in North Africa and convinced enough people that he was the great-grandson of Muhammad "the Concealed One" to carry him to power and his successors to rule over Muslim North Africa and Egypt under the dynastic name of Fatimid. Ibn Khaldun wryly concludes:

The Ismaʿilis are called such with reference to their recognition of the Imamate of Ismaʿil. They are also called "Esotericists" (*batiniyya*) with reference to their speaking about the *batin*, that is, the hidden, Imam. They are also called "heretics" because of the heretical character of their beliefs. (Ibn Khaldun, *Muqaddima* 3.25) [IBN KHALDUN 1967: 1:412–413]

26. The Powers of the Caliph-Imam

As the guardian and transmitter of the Apostolic tradition, the Christian bishop had enormous spiritual powers over his community, and the bishops of Rome claimed that in their case those same powers extended over the entire flock of Christ. But no Christian "overseer" ever possessed the plenitude of what Ibn Khaldun called "the royal power" and "the religious power," which he attributed to the office of the Caliph. Indeed, one has to return to Hasmonean monarchs like Jonathan or Simon to find a parallel authority. And it is in fact no parallel at all, since the Hasmoneans possessed their powers by reason of their simultaneous tenure of two offices, that of king and High Priest, while the Muslim Caliph's flowed from a single investiture. As Ibn Khaldun explains, the Caliph held both of the "two swords" in his single hand.

It has become clear that to be Caliph in reality means acting as a substitute for the Lawgiver [Muhammad] with regard to the preservation of the religion and the political leadership of the world. The Lawgiver was concerned with both things, with religion in his capacity as the person commanded to transmit the duties imposed by the religious laws to the people and to cause them to act in accordance with them, and with worldly political leadership in his capacity as the person in charge of the (public) interests of human civilization. (Ibn Khaldun, *Muqaddima* 3.29) [IBN KHALDUN 1967: 1:448]

We can observe the early Caliphs acting in exactly this fashion. In his brief tenure (632–634 C.E.), Abu Bakr bade his fellow Muslims take up arms against those who sought to withdraw from the community at the death of the Prophet. Immediately after him, Umar (634–644 C.E.) began to set in place many of the long-term institutions of the young Islamic state.

Abu Ja'far said: Umar was the first to fix and write the date (according to the Muslim era), according to what al-Harith told me, having heard it from Ibn Sa'd, on the authority of Muhammad ibn Umar in the year 16 (A.H.) in the month of First Rabi' (March 637 C.E.). And I have already mentioned the reason for writing this and how the affair was. Umar, may God be pleased with him, was the first to date letters and seal them with clay. And he was the first to gather people before a prayer-leader to pray special prayers with them at night in the month of Ramadan, and he wrote concerning this to the provinces and commanded them to do likewise.

The most far-reaching of Umar's measures was his exercise of the "royal power" and his establishment of the first instruments of state to regulate the affairs of a rapidly expanding Islamic empire. Tabari, who is our source here, continues.

I heard from al-Harith, who heard from Ibn Saʿd, who heard from Muhammad ibn Umar, who heard from Aʿidh ibn Yahya, on the authority of Abuʾl-Huwayrith, on the authority of Jubayr ibn al-Huwayrith ibn Nuqayd, that Umar ibn al-Khattab, may God be pleased with him, consulted the Muslims concerning the drawing up of registers, and Ali ibn Abi Talib said to him, "Share out every year whatever property has accumulated to you and do not retail anything." Uthman ibn Affan said, "I see much property, which suffices for all the people and which cannot be counted until you distinguish between those who have taken (from it) and those who have not. I do not like things to be in disorder." Al-Walid ibn Hisham ibn al-Mughira said to him, "O Commander of the Faithful, I have been to Syria and have seen their kings, and they drew up a register and formed a legion. You should draw up a register and form a legion."

In question here was a list of pensioners, a register or divan *of those to whom the spoils of the new Islamic conquests would be distributed in order. Those spoils were now considerable, which explains the controversy about precedence that followed.*

Umar adopted his advice and called Aqil ibn Abi Talib and Makhrama ibn Nawfal and Jubayr ibn Mutʾim, who were genealogists of the tribe of Quraysh, and he said to them, "Write (a list) of people according to their ranks!" And they wrote, beginning with the Banu Hashim [that is, Muhammad's family], then following them with Abu Bakr and his kind and then Umar and his kind, that is, following the order of the Caliphate. When Umar looked at it he said, "I wish to God it were as you have written, but begin with the kin of the Prophet of God, may God bless and save him, then continue in order of nearness until you put Umar where God has put him."

I heard from al-Harith, who heard from Ibn Saʿd, who heard from Muhammad ibn Umar, who heard from Usama ibn Zayd ibn Aslam, on the authority of his father, on the authority of his grandfather, who said: I saw Umar ibn al-Khattab, may God be pleased with him, when the writing was shown to him, with the Banu Taym after the Banu Hashim and the Banu Adi after the Banu Taym. And I heard him say, put Umar in his proper place. . . . And the Banu Adi [that is, Umar's kin] came to Umar and said, "You are the deputy of the Prophet of God!" And he answered, "Surely (I am) the deputy of Abu Bakr and Abu Bakr was the deputy of the Prophet of God." And they said, "Why do you not put yourself where these people [that is, the genealogists] have put you?" And Umar said, "Well done, O Banu Adi! Do you want to eat off my back? Do you want me to sacrifice my honor to you? No, by God, not until your turn comes, even though the register close with you and you be written last among the people. I have two masters [Muhammad and Abu Bakr] who followed a certain path, and if I forsake them I shall be forsaken. Whatever of plenty we have attained in this world, whatever reward for our deeds we hope from God in the next world, is from Muhammad alone. He is our nobility, and his kin are the noblest of the Arabs, and then the rest, in order of their nearness to him. Indeed, the Arabs are ennobled with the Prophet of God, and perhaps some of them have many ancestors in common with him. As for us, it is clear that our stems coincide, and right back to Adam there are few ancestors that we do not have in common. But despite that, by God, if the non-Arabs come with deeds, and we come without them, they shall be nearer to Muhammad than we on the Day of Judgment. Let no man look to his ancestry but let him do God's work, and if any man's deeds fall short, his pedigree will not help him." (Tabari, *Annals* 1.2750–2752) [LEWIS 1974: 1:18–20]

27. The Delegation of the Royal Power: The Sultanate

*The "royal" or secular powers of the Caliph do not directly concern us here, and they were in any event "delegated" to other, more powerful figures in Islamic history——ministers who rose to dominate a Caliph or generals who simply cowed him. These de facto rulers of the Islamic commonwealth were generally known as "Sultans" and were even more generally former Turkish generals to whom the Caliphs owed the safety of their own houses and the protection of the "Abode of Islam." The Caliph could only hope that the Sultans who lorded it over his narrow base of operations around Baghdad might be Sunni and sympathetic and capable of controlling their troops, as they often in fact were. It fell then to the Islamic lawyers to convert this rather naked usurpation of power into a form of "delegation" and make theory of a necessity, as did Ibn Jama*ᶜ*a (d. 1335 C.E.).*

The Imam of the Muslims has the right to delegate authority over any region, country, area or province to whoever is able to hold general authority there, because necessity demands it—not least in a far country. . . . If it is to be a general delegation of power, such as is customary for sultans and kings in our own time, it is lawful for the delegate then to appoint judges and governors and rule the armies, with full disposition of the wealth from all quarters, but not to have anything to do with a region over which he is not delegated, because his is a particular government. The same qualifications apply to the delegate ruler when the Imam selects him that would apply to his own office, except that of Qurayshi descent, because he is standing in the Imam's place.

If a king attains power by usurpation and force in a (Muslim) country, then the Caliph should delegate the affairs of that place to him, in order to call him to obedience and avoid a split with him, lest there be disunity and the staff of the community be broken. In this way usurpation becomes legitimate government, issuing effective orders. (Ibn Jama'a, *Statutes*) [WILLIAMS 1971: 91–92].

Ibn Khaldun, who knew well enough how to speak like a lawyer, here chooses to write like a historian.

When royal authority is firmly established in one particular family and tribe supporting the dynasty, and when that family claims all royal authority for itself and keeps the rest of the family away from it, and when the children of that family succeed to the royal authority in turn, by appointment, then it often happens that their wazirs [that is, their ministers] and entourage gain power over the throne. This occurs most often when a little child or a weak member of the family is appointed successor by his father and made ruler by his creatures and servants. It becomes clear that he is unable to fulfill the functions of ruler. Therefore they are fulfilled by his guardian, one of his father's wazirs, someone from his entourage, one of his clients, or a member of his tribe. That person gives the impression that he is guarding the power of the (child ruler) for him. Eventually it becomes clear that he exercises the control, and he uses the fact as a tool to achieve royal authority. He keeps the child away from his people. He accustoms him to the pleasures of his life of luxury and gives him every opportunity to indulge in them. He causes him to forget to look at government affairs. Eventually he gains full control over him. He accustoms the child ruler to believe that the ruler's share in royal authority consists merely in sitting on the throne, shaking hands, being addressed as "Sire" and sitting with the women in the seclusion of the harem. All exercise of actual executive power, and the personal handling and supervision of matters that concern the ruler, such as inspection of the army, finances, and defense of the border regions, are believed to belong to the wazir. He defers to him in all these things. Eventually, the wazir definitely adopts the coloring of the leader, of the man in control.

The royal authority comes to be his. He reserves it for his family and his children after him. (Ibn Khaldun, *Muqaddima* 3.19)

[IBN KHALDUN 1967: 1:377–378]

28. The Religious Powers of the Caliph

To return to the religious powers of this primary political authority in Islam, they are described in brief by Ibn Khaldun.

It should be known that all the religious functions of the religious law, such as (leadership of) prayer, the office of judge, the office of mufti, the Holy War, and market supervision fall under the "Great Imamate," which is the Caliphate. The Caliphate is a kind of great mainspring and comprehensive basis, and all these functions are branches of it and fall under it because of the wide scope of the Caliphate, its active interest in all conditions of the Muslim community, both religious and worldly, and its general power to execute the religious laws relative to both (religious and worldly affairs). (Ibn Khaldun, *Muqaddima* 3.29) [IBN KHALDUN 1967: 1:449]

What Ibn Khaldun saw as powers, the lawyer Ibn Jama'a (d. 1335 C.E.) saw as the Caliph's duties, though both men were writing in an age when the holders of that office had little capacity for either exercising their powers or effectively fulfilling their duties.

As for the ten duties of the ruler to the subjects, the first is to protect the Muslim heritage and defend it, whether in every region, if he is Caliph, or in his own country if he is delegated over it, and to struggle against idolators and put down rebels.

The second is to guard the religion in its principles and beliefs, and put down innovation and heretics and encourage the religious sciences and the study of the Law, venerate learning and religious scholars and raise places from which the light of Islam may shine. . . .

The third is to uphold the rites of Islam, such as the obligation of prayer and the congregational prayers and the call to prayer and performance of it, and the sermons and leadership of the prayers, and the matter of the fast and the feasts, and keeping the calendar, and the pilgrimage; and part of the last is facilitating the pilgrimage from all the districts, and keeping the roads clear and giving people security on the way and appointing people to look after them.

The fourth is to make the final decisions on court cases and sentences, by appointing governors and judges, so as to reduce contentiousness. . . .

The fifth is to wage the Holy War himself and with his armies at least once a year. . . .

The sixth is to apply the punishments imposed by the Law, and make no distinction when doing so between the powerful and the weak. . . .

The seventh is to collect the alms tax and the tribute from those who are to pay it [that is, the People of the Book] and the booty and the land tax, and to use it as the Law stipulates. . . .

The eighth is to supervise pious and family foundations, keep bridges and roads in good repair and make smooth the ways of welfare.

The ninth is to supervise the division and distribution of booty. . . .

The tenth is justice in the ruler in all his affairs. (Ibn Jamaʿa, *Statutes*) [WILLIAMS 1971: 93–94]

The Caliph, it is clear, was the executor of the religious law and, unlike Muhammad, whose "successor" he was, neither the maker of new laws nor the interpreter of the old. The earliest Caliphs may have exercised some of those religious functions in fact. They certainly led prayers when their personal security permitted it, conducted military campaigns, and acted as judges for the community. But others in that rapidly expanding empire quickly took over in the Caliph's stead: ministers, bureaucrats, and specialists, like the "mufti" on Ibn Khaldun's list—literally "one capable of pronouncing a fatwa,*" that is, a legal opinion, which, if it was not binding, certainly constituted a legal precedent.*

29. The Islamic Judge

The mufti was a legal scholar, someone trained in the increasingly complex legal system of Islamic society. That training took place in one of the numerous colleges of law that arose in Islam from the eleventh and twelfth centuries onward, and most Muslim intellectuals passed through them over the following centuries. These Islamic lawyers constituted an important class in Muslim society, and at least part of their influence derived from the fact that by and large they kept themselves at a distance from the government. They were supported by their own endowments and so could defend or oppose the ruler as circumstances and issues dictated. But a few of them at least were co-opted into government service as judges to administer the Law of Islam as duly constituted delegates of the Caliph.

Nobody may be appointed to the office of judge who does not comply fully with the conditions required to make his appointment valid and his decisions effective.

This is once again al-Mawardi, the constitutional lawyer who died in 1058 C.E.

The first condition is that he must be a man. This condition consists of two qualities, puberty and masculinity. As for the child below puberty, he cannot be held accountable, nor can his utterances have any effect against himself; how much less so against others. As for women, they are unsuited to positions of authority, although judicial verdicts may be based upon what they say. Abu Hanifa said that a woman can act as a judge on matters on which it would be lawful for her to testify, but she may not act as a judge on which it would not be lawful for her to testify. Ibn Jarir al-Tabari, giving a divergent view, allows a woman to act as a judge in all cases, but no account should be taken of an opinion which is refuted by both the consensus of the community and the word of God. "Men have authority over women because of what God has conferred on one in preference to the other" (Quran 4:38), meaning by this, intelligence and discernment. He does not, therefore, permit women to hold authority over men. (Mawardi, *Statutes of Governance* 61–63) [LEWIS 1974: 2:41–42]

Mawardi goes on to rehearse the other qualifications for an Islamic justice: intelligence, freedom, membership in the Islamic faith, rectitude, soundness of sight and hearing, and finally, command of the Islamic Law in both its general principles and its specific applications.

30. The Market Inspector

In any community under Islam the presence of the state was signaled by the judge, the delegate of the religious power, and by the gendarmerie, the delegate of the "royal" power of the distant ruler. But there was a third official as well: the market inspector. The somewhat unexpected presence of this public prosecutor, guardian of public morality, and consumer advocate armed with a religious mandate sounds like a faint echo of Islam's all-inclusive command to its authorities to "summon to good and reject what is disapproved" (Quran 32:17). How the office worked is explained by the Spaniard Ibn Abdun (d. 1100 C.E.).

The judge must not appoint a market inspector without informing the prince of it, so that the judge will have a proof if he later wishes to remove him or keep him. . . . The office of the market inspector is closely akin to that of the judge and thus the occupant should only be a model person. He is the spokesman of the judge, his chamberlain, assistant and successor, and if the judge is prevented, the market inspector may give judgment in his place in what pertains to him and is within his competence. He receives a salary from the public treasury, for he takes care of many matters for the judge which in principle belong to the judge's office, thus sparing the latter fatigue and tiring scenes, and being tried by vulgar and low people, and insolent and ignorant persons from among the artisans and laborers.

The Islamic judge tried cases; the market inspector enforced the law, and his jurisdiction was wide indeed. Inspectors regulated the market, of course, both in regard to fair prices and even in the arrangement of shops and produce. But they could act elsewhere as well, in mosques, for example.

One [that is, the market inspector] must not allow any beggar to beg inside the mosque on Friday; whoever does shall be given corporal chastisement. The mosque servants and muezzins shall be told to prevent it. Also no beggar is allowed to beg at the entrance of the mosque in a loud voice once the prayer-leader of the Friday prayers has gone to the pulpit to preach. The market inspector must not allow any beast of burden to stand near the entrance, for it may make droppings or urine which destroy the ritual purity of the people coming in.

The mosques are the houses of God, places of recollection and worship, and known for purity. They are not for payments of debts, or arguments, or any of the acts of this world, for they are for the acts of the next world. Thus boys should not be taught in them, because they are careless about impurities on their feet and clothing. If it is absolutely necessary, they can be taught in the galleries (of the courtyard). Boys should not be disciplined with more than five blows with the cane for the big ones and three blows for the small ones, with severity proportionate to their ability to bear it.

The inspectors could also intervene in various professions. A number of Ibn Abdun's personal asides are drawn from his own somewhat severe morality.

Schoolmasters must be prevented from attending dinners and funerals and acting as witnesses (for a fee), except on days when they are free, for they are salaried people. They should not increase the numbers of their students: they are forbidden to do it, yet I may say that they will never observe it, for one does not voluntarily rise to serve the community, especially in the matter of teaching school. Also they never teach anything as they should. Most schoolteachers are ignorant of the art of teaching: to know the Quran is one thing and to teach it another.

Moneychangers must be prevented from usury. No currency shall be circulated except that of the land, for differing currencies lead to inflation, higher prices and unstable conditions.

Barbers must not be alone in their shops with a woman, but only in the marketplace, where they may be observed.

Prostitutes shall be forbidden to uncover their faces outside the public houses, to confuse honest women with their adornments, and shall be forbidden to reveal their secrets to married women or come to wedding parties, even if their husbands permit it. Dancing girls shall also be ordered not to uncover their heads (in public).

Pleasure-boys should be expelled from the city and chastised whenever one of them is found (in it). They should not be allowed to circulate among Muslims or participate in festivities, for they are fornicators cursed by God and all men.

And finally, in the matter of the People of the Book living inside the Abode of Islam:

A Muslim may not massage a Jew or a Christian or empty their garbage or clean their latrines, for Jews or Christians are fitter for such work. Also a Muslim may not look after the riding animal of a Jew or a Christian.

Muslim women must be forbidden to enter the infamous churches, for the priests are profligates, adulterers and sodomites. The Frankish [that is, Christian] women too should be forbidden to go in the church except on days of offices or feasts, because they go to eat and drink and fornicate with the priests, and there is not one of the priests who does not have two of them or more to sleep with him. . . . The priests should be ordered to marry, as is done in the eastern lands; if they wanted to, they could do it. . . .

Jews must not butcher an animal for Muslims, and the Jews should be ordered to set aside butcher shops for themselves.

No tax farmer or police agent or Jew or Christian should be allowed to dress like an important person, or as a jurist, or a virtuous person; rather they should be known and avoided. . . . A distinctive badge should be given them by which they may be known, to disgrace them.

No books of learning should be sold to a Jew or a Christian, unless it treats of their own law, for they translate the books and then attribute them to their own people and their bishops, although they are of Muslim authorship. It would be best to allow no Jewish or Christian doctor to treat any Muslim, for they do not have true friendships with Muslims and should treat people of their own community. Since they do not have sincere friendship for Muslims, how shall one trust them with his life? (Ibn Abdun, *On the Implementation of the Law* 59–61) [WILLIAMS 1971: 156–161]

Short Titles

ABOTH RABBI NATHAN 1955. *The Fathers According to Rabbi Nathan.* Translated by Judah Goldin. New Haven: Yale University Press.

ALEXANDER 1984. P. S. Alexander, *Textual Sources for the Study of Judaism.* New York: Barnes and Noble.

ANAWATI & GARDET 1961. G. C. Anawati and Louis Gardet, *Mystique musulmane.* Paris: Librairie philosophique J. Vrin.

AQUINAS 1945. *Basic Writings of Thomas Aquinas.* Edited and annotated by Anton Pegis. 2 vols. New York: Random House.

ARBERRY 1950. A. J. Arberry, *Sufism: An Account of the Mystics of Islam.* London: George Allen & Unwin, Ltd., 1950; rpt. New York: Harper & Row, 1970.

ARBERRY 1964. A. J. Arberry, *Aspects of Islamic Civilization, as Depicted in the Original Texts.* London: George Allen & Unwin, Ltd., 1964; pbk. Ann Arbor: University of Michigan Press, 1976.

ARNOLD 1928. T. Arnold, *Painting in Islam.* Oxford: Oxford University Press, 1928; rpt. New York: Dover Books, 1965.

ASHʿARI 1953. Richard J. McCarthy, S.J., *The Theology of al-Ashʿari.* Beirut: Imprimerie Catholique.

ATTAR 1966. *Muslim Saints and Mystics: Episodes from the Tadhkirat al-Awliya ("Memorials of the Saints") by Farid al-Din Attar.* Translated by A. J. Arberry. Chicago: University of Chicago Press.

ATTAR 1984. Farid ud-Din Attar, *The Conference of the Birds.* Translated by Afkham Darbandi and Dick Davis. Harmondsworth: Penguin.

AUGUSTINE 1947. *Writings of Saint Augustine,* vol. 4: *Christian Instruction.* Translated by J. J. Gavigan. New York: Cima Publishing Company.

AUGUSTINE 1948. *Basic Writings of Saint Augustine.* Edited by Whitney J. Oates. 2 vols. New York: Random House.

AVERROES 1954. *Averroes' Tahafut al-Tahafut (The Incoherence of the Incoherence).* Translated by Simon van den Bergh. 2 vols. London: Luzac & Company.

AVERROES 1961. *Averroes on the Harmony of Religion and Philosophy.* Translated by G. F. Hourani. London: Luzac & Company.

AVICENNA 1951. A. J. Arberry, *Avicenna on Theology.* London: John Murray.

AYOUB 1984. M. Ayoub, *The Qurʾan and Its Interpreters.* Vol. 1. Albany: State University of New York Press.

BAYNES 1955. N. H. Baynes, "Idolatry and the Early Church." In N. H. Baynes, *Byzantine Studies and Other Essays,* pp. 116–143. London: Athlone Press.

BIRUNI 1879. Al-Biruni, *The Chronology of Ancient Nations. . . .* Translated and edited by C. E. Sachau. London: 1879; rpt. Frankfurt: Minerva, 1969.

BOKSER 1981. Ben Zion Bokser, *The Jewish Mystical Tradition*. New York: Pilgrim Press.

BURTON 1977. John Burton, *The Collection of the Qur'an*, Cambridge: Cambridge University Press.

(PSEUDO)-DIONYSIUS 1987. *Pseudo-Dionysius: The Complete Works*. Translated by Colm Luibheid with Paul Rorem. New York: Paulist Press.

FARABI 1961. Al-Farabi, *Fusul al-Madani: Aphorisms of the Statesman*. Edited and translated by D. M. Dunlop. Cambridge: Cambridge University Press.

GHAZALI 1953. W. Montgomery Watt, *The Faith and Practice of al-Ghazali*. London: George Allen & Unwin, Ltd.

GUILLAUME 1924. Alfred Guillaume, *The Traditions of Islam: An Introduction to the Study of the Hadith Literature*. Oxford: Clarendon Press, 1924; rpt. Lahore: Universal Books, 1977.

HALEVI 1905. Judah Halevi, *The Kuzari: An Argument for the Faith of Israel*. Translated by H. Hirschfeld. 1905; rpt. New York: Schocken Books, 1964.

HALPERIN 1984. D. J. Halperin, "A New Edition of the Hekhalot Literature." *Journal of the American Oriental Society* 104 (1984), 543–552.

HAUSHERR 1927. I. Hausherr, *Le méthode d'oraison hésychaste*. Rome: Orientalia Christiana.

HUJWIRI 1911. *The "Kashf al-Mahjub," the Oldest Persian Treatise on Sufism by al-Hujwiri*. Translated by Reynold A. Nicholson. London: Luzac & Company, 1911; rpt. London: Luzac, 1959.

IBN AL-ARABI 1980. Ibn al-Arabi, *The Bezels of Wisdom*. Translated and edited by R.W.J. Austin. New York: Paulist Press.

IBN BATTUTA 1959–1962. *The Travels of Ibn Battuta, A.D. 1325–1354*. Translated and edited by H.A.R. Gibb. 2 vols. Cambridge: Cambridge University Press.

IBN ISHAQ 1955. *The Life of Muhammad: A Translation of Ishaq's Sirat Rasul Allah*. Translated and edited by A. Guillaume. London: Oxford University Press.

IBN KHALDUN 1967. Ibn Khaldun, *The Muqaddimah: An Introduction to History*. Translated by Franz Rosenthal. 3 vols. 2nd corrected ed. Princeton: Princeton University Press.

IBN QUDAMA 1950. H. Laoust, *Le Précis de droit d'Ibn Qudama*. Beirut: Institut Français de Damas.

JEFFERY 1962. A. Jeffery, *A Reader on Islam: Passages from Standard Arabic Writings Illustrative of the Beliefs and Practices of Muslims*. 's-Gravenhage: Mouton and Company.

JOHN CLIMACUS 1982. John Climacus, *The Ladder of Divine Ascent*. Translated by Colm Luibheid and Norman Russell. New York: Paulist Press.

JUNAYD 1962. Ali Hassan Abdel-Kader, *The Life, Personality and Writings of al-Junayd*. London: Luzac & Company.

JUWAYNI 1968. M. Allard, *Textes apolégetiques de Juwaini*. Beirut: Dar al-Machreq.

LANE 1836. Edward Lane, *Manners and Customs of the Modern Egyptians* (1836). 5th ed. rpt. New York: Dover Publications.

LAURENT 1873. J.C.M. Laurent, *Peregrinatores Medii Aevi Quattuor*. 2nd ed. Leipzig: J. C. Hinrichs.

LE GOFF 1984. Jacques Le Goff, *The Birth of Purgatory*. Chicago: University of Chicago Press.

LERNER & MAHDI 1972. R. Lerner and M. Mahdi (eds.), *Medieval Political Philosophy: A Sourcebook*. Glencoe, Ill.: Free Press, 1963; pbk. Ithaca: Cornell University Press, 1972.

LEWIS 1974. Bernard Lewis, *Islam from the Prophet Muhammad to the Capture of Constantinople*. 2 vols. New York: Harper & Row.

LEWIS 1976. Bernard Lewis, "On That Day: A Jewish Apocalyptic Poem on the Arab Conquests." In *Mélanges d'Islamologie ... de Armand Abel*, pp. 197–200. Leiden: E. J. Brill, 1974. Reprinted in Bernard Lewis, *Studies in Classical and Ottoman Islam (7th–16th Centuries)*. London: Variorum Reprints, 1976.

MCNEILL & GAMER 1938. J. T. McNeill and H. M. Gamer, *Medieval Handbooks of Penance*. New York: Columbia University Press.

MAIMONIDES 1963. Moses Maimonides, *The Guide of the Perplexed*. Translated and edited by Shlomo Pines. Chicago: University of Chicago Press.

MAIMONIDES 1965. *The Code of Maimonides: Book XIV*. New Haven: Yale University Press.

MAIMONIDES 1968. *The Commentary to Mishneh Aboth*. Translated by Arthur David. New York: Bloch Publishing Company.

MANGO 1972. Cyril Mango, *The Art of the Byzantine Empire, 312–1453: Sources and Documents*. Englewood Cliffs, N.J.: Prentice-Hall.

MASSIGNON 1968. Louis Massignon, *Essai sur les origines du lexique technique de la mystique musulmane*. Paris: J. Vrin.

MASSIGNON 1982. Louis Massignon, *The Passion of al-Hallaj: Mystic and Martyr of Islam*. Translated by Herbert Mason. 4 vols. Princeton: Princeton University Press.

MIDRASH RABBAH 1977. *The Midrash Rabbah*. Translated by H. Freedman et al. 5 vols. London, Jerusalem, New York: Soncino Press.

NACHMANIDES 1971. Ramban (Nachmanides), *Commentary on the Torah: Genesis*. Translated by C. B. Chavel. New York: Shilo Publishing House.

NEMOY 1952. *Karaite Anthology: Excerpts from the Early Literature*. Translated by Leon Nemoy. New Haven: Yale University Press.

NICHOLSON 1921. Reynald A. Nicholson, *Studies in Islamic Mysticism*. Cambridge: Cambridge University Press.

PALAMAS 1983. Gregory Palamas, *The Triads*. Edited by John Meyendorff; translation by Nicholas Gendle. New York: Paulist Press.

PESIKTA RABBATI 1968. *Pesikta Rabbati*. Translated by William G. Braude. 2 vols. New Haven and London: Yale University Press.

PETER LOMBARD 1917. E. F. Rogers, "Peter Lombard and the Sacramental System." Ph.D. diss., Columbia University.

PHILO 1945. Philo, *Selections*. Edited and translated by H. Lewy. In *Three Jewish Philosophers*. Philadelphia: Jewish Publication Society, 1945; rpt. New York: Meridian Books, 1960.

PHILO 1981. Philo of Alexandria, *The Contemplative Life, The Giants, and Selections*. Translated by David Winston. New York: Paulist Press.

PINES 1971. S. Pines, *An Arabic Version of the Testimonium Flavianum and Its Implications*. Jerusalem: Israel Academy of Sciences and Humanities.

RAHMAN 1958. F. Rahman, *Prophecy in Islam: Philosophy and Orthodoxy*. London: George Allen & Unwin, Ltd.

RUMI 1925–1940. Jalal al-Din Rumi, *Mathnawi*. Edited, translated, and annotated by R. A. Nicholson. 8 vols. London: Luzac & Company.

SAADYA 1945. Saadya Gaon, *Book of Doctrines and Beliefs*. Abridged translation by A. Altman. In *Three Jewish Philosophers*. Philadelphia: Jewish Publication Society, 1945; rpt. New York: Meridian Books, 1960.

SAADYA 1948. Saadya Gaon, *The Book of Beliefs and Opinions*. Translated by S. Rosenblatt. New Haven: Yale University Press.

SACHEDINA 1981. A. Sachedina, *Islamic Messianism: The Idea of the Mahdi in Twelver Shiʿism*. Albany: State University of New York Press.

SAHAS 1972. D. J. Sahas, *John of Damascus on Islam: The "Heresy of the Ishmaelites."* Leiden: E. J. Brill.

SCHAEFER 1982. P. Schaefer, *Synopse zur Hekhalot-Literatur*. Tübingen: J.C.B. Mohr.

SHAFIʿI 1961. *Islamic Jurisprudence: Shafiʿi's Risala*. Translated by Majid Khadduri. Baltimore: Johns Hopkins University Press.

SMITH 1931. Margaret Smith, *Studies in Early Mysticism in the Near and Middle East*. London: Sheldon Press, 1931; rpt. Amsterdam: Philo Press, 1973.

SMITH 1950. Margaret Smith, *Readings in the Mystics of Islam*. London: Luzac & Company.

SOKOLOW 1981. M. Sokolow, "The Denial of Muslim Sovereignty over Eretz-Israel in Two 10th Century Karaite Bible Commentaries." In J. Hacker (ed.), *Shalem*, 3: 309–318. Jerusalem: Yad Izhak Ben-Zvi Institute.

STANIFORTH 1968. *Early Christian Writings: The Apostolic Fathers*. Translated by Maxwell Staniforth. Harmondsworth: Penguin.

SYMEON NEOTHEOLOGUS 1980. *Symeon the New Theologian: The Discourses*. Translated by C. J. Catanzaro. New York: Paulist Press.

TRIMINGHAM 1971. J. Spencer Trimingham, *The Sufi Orders in Islam*. London: Oxford University Press.

TWERSKY 1980. I. Twersky, *Introduction to the Code of Maimonides (Mishneh Torah)*. New Haven and London: Yale University Press.

VAN BERCHEM 1922. Max Van Berchem, *Corpus inscriptionum arabicarum. Syrie du Sud*, vol. 2: *Jerusalem, "Ville."* Cairo: Institut français d'archéologie orientale.

VERMES 1968. Geza Vermes, *The Dead Sea Scrolls in English*. Harmondsworth: Penguin

WENSINCK 1932. A. J. Wensinck, *The Muslim Creed: Its Genesis and Historical Development*. Cambridge: Cambridge University Press.

WILLIAMS 1971. J. A. Williams, *Themes of Islamic Civilization*. Berkeley: University of California Press.

WRIGHT 1848. T. Wright, *Early Travels in Palestine*. London: H. G. Bohn.

ZENKOVSKY 1963. Serge A. Zenkovsky, *Mediaeval Russia's Epics, Chronicles and Tales*. New York: E. P. Dutton.

ZERNOV 1945. N. Zernov, *The Russians and Their Church*. London and New York: Macmillan.

Index